# ADAPTIVE LEARNING
# AND THE HUMAN CONDITION

Jeffrey C. Levy

*Seton Hall University*

Routledge
Taylor & Francis Group

LONDON AND NEW YORK

First published 2013 by Pearson Education, Inc.

Published 2016 by Routledge
2 Park Square, Milton Park, Abingdon, Oxon OX14 4RN
711 Third Avenue, New York, NY 10017, USA

*Routledge is an imprint of the Taylor & Francis Group, an informa business*

Cover Image: © NNI QIN/iStock
Cover Designer: Suzanne Behnke

Credits and acknowledgments borrowed from other sources and reproduced, with permission, in this textbook appear on the appropriate page within text and on page 261.

ISBN: 9780205205479 (hbk)

**Library of Congress Cataloging-in-Publication Data**
Levy, Jeffrey C.
   Adaptive learning and the human condition / Jeffrey C. Levy.
      p.  cm.
   Includes bibliographical references and index.
   ISBN-13: 978-0-205-20547-9
   ISBN-10: 0-205-20547-X
   1.  Learning, Psychology of.   I.  Title.
   BF318.L48 2013
   153.1'526—dc23
                                        2012023577

*To my mother, Hilda, who first taught me to love learning*

*To my wife, Fran, for lovingly enriching my human condition*

# CONTENTS

# PREFACE

The systematic study of adaptive learning has a long and storied history dating back to the beginning of the 20th century. At that time, Ivan Pavlov and Edward Thorndike introduced the two major experimental paradigms of classical and instrumental conditioning that have since defined this research area and stood the test of time. In the 1930s, B. F. Skinner made significant contributions to the study of instrumental conditioning. The methods and technical vocabularies he and Pavlov developed still serve as the basis of organizing the content covered in chapters and textbooks of learning.

Historically, there have been two major categories of learning textbooks: those emphasizing theories, exemplified by Hilgard and Bauer's *Theories of Learning* (1975), and those emphasizing principles, exemplified by Kimble's revision of Hilgard and Marquis's *Conditioning and Learning* (1961). The present book is in the tradition of the latter and similar in coverage to recent texts in learning and behavior (e.g., Domjan, 2009; Mazur, 2006; Powell, Symbaluk, & Macdonald, 2009; Schwartz, Wasserman, & Robbins, 2002).

Similar to other learning textbooks, *Adaptive Learning and the Human Condition* emphasizes the experimental research literatures related to classical and instrumental conditioning. Defining learning as an adaptive process through which individuals acquire the ability to predict and control the environment enables the student to appreciate why these two research paradigms, and only these two, are addressed. Adaptation requires acquiring the ability to predict, and when possible, control environmental events. Pavlov studied animals under circumstances that made it possible to predict, but not control, events. Thorndike and Skinner studied animals under circumstances in which their behavior reliably impacted (i.e., controlled) the environment. Observational learning and language are treated as indirect processes for acquiring the same abilities. This enables students to appreciate the relevance of the animal learning literature to human beings as well as the ubiquity and importance of learning principles in our everyday lives.

The first and last chapters of *Adaptive Learning and the Human Condition* begin with the same sentence. A recurring message of this book is that learning principles constitute very powerful explanations for human behavior and help us understand the way we live and why we, more than any other animal, dominate this planet. The two most fundamental ways in which this book differs from other learning textbooks are reflected in the title and this sentence. Learning is defined as an adaptive process that when combined with the human capacities for speech and creation of tools has enabled us to transform the world and thus the human condition. In addition to the usual extension of learning principles to clinical applications, they are related to such nontraditional topics as parenting, moral development, schooling, the effects of technology, and human self-actualization.

## THE "BIG MAP"

A textbook, like a course, may be described as a long journey (Levy, 1991). When writing a textbook or teaching a course, it is essential to be an effective guide and to provide useful maps. Before starting, it is often helpful to look at the "big map" portraying the entire length of the journey. This provides a sense of the scope, as well as an appreciation for where separate trips fit within the overall travel plan. Here and there we may find it necessary and/or enjoyable to take a short side trip. I hope you enjoy the ride!

The textbook (journey) is divided into four major sections (trips): Introduction to the Science of Adaptive Learning (Chapters 1–2), Predictive Learning (Chapters 3–5), Control Learning (Chapters 6–9), and The Human Condition (Chapters 10–14).

Chapter 1 considers how the assumptions, strengths, and limitations of the scientific method apply to the discipline of psychology. The goals and methods of the early schools are described as we examine how current approaches to the discipline evolved. Psychology studies how hereditary (nature) and environmental (nurture) variables affect the thoughts, feelings, and actions of individuals. Learning is seen as a ubiquitous process throughout the animal kingdom, whereby individuals change as the result of experience. It is adaptive, enabling individuals to predict and control their circumstances. The traditional classical and instrumental (or operant) conditioning paradigms, introduced by Pavlov, Thorndike, and Skinner, relate to these two components of adaptation. Classical conditioning procedures study individuals under conditions that enable them to predict, but not control, their environment. Instrumental conditioning procedures study individuals under conditions that enable them to affect the environment. Observational learning and symbolic communication (i.e., language) are treated as indirect procedures for acquiring the ability to predict and control.

The title of the book implies that a science of adaptive learning can result in principles helpful to understanding and influencing the human condition. Chapter 2 addresses the needs of a science to determine cause and effect (internal validity) under naturalistic conditions (external validity). Issues concerning the implementation of these strategies to the study of psychology are considered. The strengths of large-$N$ and small-$N$ experimental designs in addressing internal validity concerns are described. Issues related to the extension of findings obtained with other animals studied in specialized apparatuses to the human condition are considered.

Chapters 3 through 5 consider the scientific research findings related to predictive learning. Basic principles, phenomena, theoretical issues, and applications are reviewed. Chapters 6 through 8 cover the same topics for control learning. Chapter 9 describes issues related to the maintenance of learned behavior. Alternatives to punishment as a procedure to reduce problematic behaviors are considered. A unifying schema for adaptive learning is presented, consisting of the ability to predict and control the occurrence or nonoccurrence of appetitive and aversive events. In subsequent chapters, this schema is used to describe and explain the changing human condition and to generate solutions to individual and social problems.

Chapter 10 describes how adaptive learning principles may be applied to understand human personality and culture. Chapter 11 extends adaptive learning principles to concept learning, problem solving, and tool making. The abilities to learn, communicate symbolically, and use the precision grip have enabled humans to create transformational technologies. Chapter 12 describes how reading and writing enable the permanent recording of human advancement, further accelerating the transformational process. In Chapter 13, Maslow's hierarchy of human needs is used to compare the human conditions for contemporary Stone Age hunter/gatherers and technology-enhanced cultures. Chapter 14 addresses the implications of a science of adaptive learning to issues of freedom and determinism. Self-control strategies are described as alternatives to relying upon willpower to achieve personal goals and to self-actualize.

The topic of learning poses many challenges for a textbook author. The material is difficult to "chunk" into meaningful units telling a story. One must define what constitutes "the forest and the trees" in selecting articles to cite from the extensive classic and current research literature. The title of the book implies the strategies used to address each of these challenges.

The four book sections constitute the major chunks:

1. The study of learning is placed within the context of the scientific revolution originating around the time of Galileo; learning is defined as an adaptive process through which individuals acquire the ability to predict and control the environment.
2. Predictive learning (classical conditioning) methods, principles, theoretical issues, and applications are treated in depth.
3. Control learning (instrumental conditioning) methods, principles, theoretical issues, and applications are treated in depth.
4. Adaptive learning principles are applied to the understanding of the human condition.

Throughout the book, research is selected from the voluminous nonhuman literature with an eye toward application to understanding and addressing human concerns. Often, the lives of members of a Stone Age nomadic tribe (the Nukak) are contrasted with those of humans in technologically enhanced societies so that the student can appreciate the remarkable transformation that has taken place over the eons, centuries, and even within their lifetimes. Toward the end of the book, the principles are applied to help us understand the accelerating transformation of our planet and the human condition. In the final chapter, the student is asked to consider the implications and applications of learning principles to governing their own lives. The topics of freedom and self-control are considered in both theoretical and practical terms.

## LITTLE MAPS AND STUDENT LEARNING AIDS

I have tried to write *Adaptive Learning and the Human Condition* in a clear, engaging style for the undergraduate student. A few learning aids have been integrated into the text in order to help students acquire an often unfamiliar and technical vocabulary and to understand the material in a more cohesive and integrative way than is assessed through objective examination questions (i.e., multiple choice and true-false).

The four major sections constitute the big map, charting the entire journey. Chapter outlines at the beginning constitute small maps, providing the detail necessary to consider and negotiate current journeys. Even though summaries occur at the end of chapters, it would be an effective strategy to read them and consider how they relate to the outlines before actually beginning the content. The summaries are partially written in a cumulative manner. Rereading them after completing the chapters should enable the student to integrate the current material with that covered previously as the story line progresses.

Key terms are highlighted and defined in the margins near where they first appear as well as in a comprehensive glossary at the end of the book. Students often believe that studying simply consists of reading and rereading the material. I encourage a more active approach in which students ask themselves and try to answer questions requiring mastery of the factual and conceptual material. I try to assist them in becoming objective and accurate assessors of their own learning. Comprehensive essay questions are provided at the end of major sections. I suggest that students assess their mastery of the material by either standing in front of a mirror and stating the answers out loud or writing them down. The questions are difficult, and it is unlikely that the student will be able to adequately answer them by attempting to memorize the material. A thorough understanding of the rationale and details regarding the procedures, findings, and implications of the research literature is required.

I have attempted to present the material in a sufficiently interesting way so that the student recognizes its relevance and importance and becomes willing to dedicate the time and effort required to achieve a high level of mastery. From the time I was an undergraduate and fell in love with psychology, I have believed and hoped that application of the scientific method to the study of behavior could help us frame human existential issues as testable questions and develop effective technologies to address individual and social concerns. By writing this book, I have attempted to share this belief and hope with others.

# ACKNOWLEDGMENTS

My interest in learning principles dates back to my memorable experience in Edward Gavurin's undergraduate course at Hunter College, City University of New York. This interest was nurtured in the stimulating and inspirational classes and office conversations held during my graduate studies with Jeffrey Landau and Coleman Paul at Adelphi University.

My Seton Hall departmental colleague Michael Vigorito provided valuable feedback on sections of this book and was enormously helpful in the creation of many of the graphs and tables. I owe thanks to Provost Gabriel Esteban and Vice Provost Larry Robinson for making me an offer I couldn't refuse and granting me a sabbatical year to work on the book. In addition to providing her usual encouragement and support as my wife and soul mate, Fran added muse and editor to her lengthy job description. This book is dedicated to Fran and my mother, Hilda Levy, who first taught me to love learning.

Finally, I would like to thank all those at Pearson who made the editing and production process so constructive, efficient, and enjoyable.

I would also like to extend my thanks to the following individuals who reviewed my manuscript and provided many thoughtful and helpful comments and suggestions: David Rentler—University of the Rockies, Margherita Rossi—Broome Community College, Jeffrey Lamoureux—Boston College, Yosh Kawahara—San Diego Mesa College, Xiongyi Liu—Cleveland State University, Robert Boughner—Rogers State University, W. David Stahlman—UCLA, Kimberly Hall-Chambers—Cleveland State University, James Crosby—Sam Houston State University, Jonathan Kahane—Springfield College, and Peter Spiegel—California State University, San Bernardino.

*Jeffrey C. Levy*
*South Orange, New Jersey*

# ABOUT THE AUTHOR

Jeffrey C. Levy's professional career at Seton Hall University may be divided into three stages, BC, DC, and AC (before, during, and after his 24-year term as chair of the Department of Psychology). Frequently recognized for teaching excellence, he received the Deans Advisory Council's Outstanding Teacher Award for the College of Arts & Sciences and the Sears-Roebuck Award for College Teaching and Campus Leadership, and he was twice nominated by Seton Hall for National CASE Professor of the Year recognition. Trained as an experimental psychologist with interests in behavior modification, Levy regularly taught the undergraduate Learning course with and without a related animal laboratory and a graduate course in Behavior Modification. A sabbatical opportunity subsequent to his service as chair enabled him to dedicate a year to elaborating upon this teaching experience and drafting *Adaptive Learning and the Human Condition*.

# PART I   A SCIENCE OF ADAPTIVE LEARNING

## Chapter *1*

# Science, Psychology, and Adaptive Learning

## THE HUMAN CONDITION

A recurring message of this text is that learning principles constitute powerful explanations for human behavior and help us understand the way we live and why we, more than any other animal, dominate this planet. Hardin's classic cartoon is perceptive as well as funny. The human being shares many basic needs and drives with the rest of the animal kingdom and must adapt to its environment in order to survive individually and as a species. Yet we seem more "self-conscious" than even our closest DNA relatives as we ponder the meaning and significance of our existence.

In the not too distant future, it is likely that communication will occur with the remaining few cultures not yet significantly impacted by current technologies. This could cause us to forget that the biological **natural selection** process, which continues albeit slowly, evolved over millions of years in an environment that has been significantly altered by human beings. Remove the clothes from Hardin's person and place him/her in the Amazonian rain forest (see Figure 1.1) or Australian desert and it becomes startlingly clear how similar our existence becomes to that of other animals. If you or I had been born under such conditions, we would be so different from the way we are and vice versa for the Colombian or Australian young adult.

**FIGURE 1.1**   A Nukak child in the Colombian rain forest.

I hope that consideration of such a prospect enables you to appreciate the importance of the **adaptive learning** process in determining who we become as individuals and cultures. Our first topic is the advantages of the scientific method as a strategy for understanding nature, including human nature and the learning process.

## EXPLANATION AND EMPIRICISM

From our beginnings on this planet, humans have been attempting to understand nature and explain what they observe. What do we mean by an understanding or explanation of nature and how do we arrive at explanations? Explanation usually means a statement of cause and effect. Initially, we must rely upon our personal interactions with the environment, that is, **direct learning**, to determine cause and effect. Eventually, we are able to observe or communicate with others, a means of **indirect learning**.

It has been suggested that the most significant accomplishment of the previous millennium was the transition from relying upon personal experience or authority figures to relying upon **empirical** testing to understand nature (Powers, 1999). Thus, legend has it that Galileo climbed to the top of the leaning tower of Pisa to drop rocks in pairs to determine the effect of the weight of objects on how quickly they fall. Familiar experiences with very light objects (e.g., paper or feathers) could lead us to believe that heavier objects fall faster than lighter ones. However, simple tests, such as with a dime and quarter, lead to the correct conclusion reached by Galileo that the weight does not matter. It is not coincidental that reliance upon empirical testing has resulted in the tremendous strides in physics, chemistry, and biology that led to many of the technological advances we take for granted in our modern world (e.g., electricity, plastics, and inoculations against diseases). The left side of Figure 1.2 depicts what Manhattan Island looked like in 1609, before it was settled by immigrants from Europe; the right side shows what it looked like in 2009

**Adaptive Learning**
Acquiring the ability to predict and control the environment.

**Direct Learning**
A change in behavior resulting from personal interaction with the environment.

**Indirect Learning**
A change in behavior resulting from observation of others or symbolic communication (i.e., language).

**Empirical**
Observable and measurable.

**FIGURE 1.2**   A computer-generated picture of how the left side of Manhattan Island appeared in 1609 in comparison to how the right side appeared in 2009.   (Sanderson & Boyer, 2009)

(Sanderson & Boyer, 2009). Within a span of 400 years, the island was transformed from the hilly forest it had been for hundreds of thousands of years to a modern metropolis. These spectacular feats of engineering and construction would never have been possible without the systematic application of the scientific method. Clearly, we must appreciate this powerful methodology if we are to understand our contemporary human condition.

## THE SCIENTIFIC METHOD

Not everything that can be counted counts, and not everything that counts can be counted.

(Cameron, 1963)

Might a contemporary scientist be interested in determining the number of angels that could fit on the head of a pin? When I ask this question, students frequently chuckle, some seeming uncomfortable. When I ask, might a contemporary scientist be interested in determining the number of influenza viruses that could fit on the head of a pin, students usually respond "yes," immediately recognizing the difference between the questions. Given the limitations of human senses and currently existing technologies, we are unable to observe the presence of angels and therefore to count them. However, thanks to the existence of electron microscopes, we could theoretically count influenza viruses. The fact that electron microscopes did not exist until 1931 does not mean that influenza viruses did not exist or that they were not important prior to then. The **scientific method** is limited to questions that can be tested through empirical observation. Only then does the possibility for replication of results exist, a requirement for scientific advancement. If the limitations of being observable, testable, and replicable are met, we know of no more reliable, powerful strategy for determining cause and effect in nature. Next, we review the early history of psychology, considering the implications and challenges of applying the scientific method to the subject matter.

**Scientific Method**

A reliable, powerful strategy for determining cause and effect in nature when the limitations of observability, testability, and replicability are met.

■ Describe the strengths and limitations of the scientific method in determining cause and effect in nature.

## EARLY HISTORY OF PSYCHOLOGY

Wilhelm Wundt is given credit for founding the discipline of psychology at the German University of Leipzig in 1879. It is there and then that the first laboratory exclusively dedicated to psychological phenomena was established. Prior to then, research that would be considered psychological in nature was conducted in physics and neurology laboratories. Examples would include Fechner's (1860) psychophysics research investigating just noticeable differences on sensory dimensions and Helmholtz's studies of vision conducted in the 1850s and 1860s (translated into English in 1924).

Wundt (1873, 1896) defined psychology as the scientific study of conscious experience or, as some prefer, the study of the mind. The chemist Dmitri Mendeleev, who formulated the periodic chart of elements, influenced his thinking. Wundt believed that the goal of psychology should be to determine the fundamental elements of conscious experience, a sort of "mental chemistry." His research suggested that the basic elements were images, sensations, and affective states (i.e., emotions) and that these had the attributes of quality (i.e. qualitative as opposed to quantitative differences), intensity, and duration. Wundt relied upon **introspection** (i.e., looking inward) as the exclusive methodology. He believed that with extensive training, individuals could be taught to make objective judgments regarding the attributes of what they were covertly (i.e., privately) experiencing. Thus, a subject might be seated at a desk and asked to describe the intensity and duration of her/his images, sensations, and emotional experiences.

Inevitably, other scientists interested in psychology reacted to different aspects of Wundt's original approach to the discipline. In 1890, Harvard's William James published his classic textbook *The Principles of Psychology*, laying out much of the content and organization of introductory psychology textbooks since. Edward Titchener, a student of Wundt's who established a laboratory at Cornell University, made distinctions between Wundt's and James's approaches to psychology, labeling the former as **structuralism** and the latter as **functionalism** (Titchener, 1898, 1899). The University of Chicago's James Angell (1903, 1907) responded with the functionalist perspective on the same distinction. Influenced by Charles Darwin's (1859) contributions regarding natural selection, Titchener and Angell suggested that Wundt's original goal of analyzing conscious experience did not adequately emphasize the adaptive role played by the mind in survival. The major functionalists, in addition to James and Angell, included John Dewey and Harvey Carr of the University of Chicago. They argued for broadening the goals of psychology and proposed expanding the methodology beyond introspection to include active **experimentation** in which the effects of different variables could be investigated.

In 1910, Max Wertheimer, a recent doctorate in psychology, was studying the perceptual experience of apparent movement, later labeled as the **phi phenomenon**. He had purchased a toy stroboscope that subjectively produced the impression of continuity from appropriately timed presentations of still photos (similar to the projection of filmed still images in a movie theater) and was searching for subjects to investigate the effect. A friend provided laboratory facilities at the Frankfurt Psychological Institute and introduced him to Kurt Koffka and Wolfgang Kohler, two outstanding postdoctoral students to serve as subjects and colleagues (Kendler, 1987). This collaboration resulted in the formation of the distinct psychological perspective called **Gestalt psychology** (Kohler, 1929). The German word *gestalt* is usually translated as "organized whole" and the catchphrase "the whole is greater than the sum of its parts" succinctly summarizes the major message of this approach. Gestalt psychologists disagreed with structuralists' goal of analyzing conscious experience. The phi phenomenon was used to exemplify this message. Analyzing the phenomenon into distinct presentations of single photos was inappropriate. They argued that to do so misrepresented and actually destroyed the very essence of what we perceive. The work of describing conscious experience had to be done at the level of complete organized units. For example, to describe a desk in terms of the intensity and duration of visual and/or tactile sensations fails to capture the meaningful pattern that forms the basis of our perceptual experience.

**Introspection**

A methodology in which individuals are asked to describe their conscious experience.

**Structuralism**

Wundt's initial approach to psychology having the goal of analyzing conscious experience.

**Functionalism**

An early school of psychology interested in how conscious experience enabled individual adaptation to environmental demands.

**Experimentation**

A research method in which an independent variable is manipulated in order to determine an effect on a specific dependent variable.

**Phi Phenomenon**

The perceptual experience of apparent movement studied by Gestalt psychologists. For example, individual lights going on and off in sequence are perceived as a single light in motion.

**Gestalt Psychology**

An early school of psychology rejecting structuralism's goal of analyzing conscious experience and arguing that conscious experience consists of organized meaningful units. Its perspective is summarized by the statement "the whole is greater than the sum of its parts."

It has been quipped that sciences advance when one scientist stands on the shoulders of another and psychology advances when one psychologist stomps on the head of another. The originator of this comment could have had John Watson in mind. Watson was trained as a functionalist at the University of Chicago and upon graduation accepted an excellent position at Johns Hopkins, where he remained for 12 years. Publication of his *Psychological Review* article "Psychology as the Behaviorist Views It" (Watson, 1913) resulted in no less than a permanent transformation of the discipline. Unlike the functionalists and Gestalt psychologists, Watson considered Wundt's approach to have been a false start. His manifesto called for a change in the definition, goals, and methods of psychology. Watson reasoned that if psychology were to be considered a natural science, the subject matter had to meet the three criteria of being observable, testable, and replicable. Because conscious experience could not be independently verified by any means, testable questions could not be formulated and results could not be replicated. Limiting the subject matter to observable behavior and defining the discipline as the science of behavior with the goal of prediction and control enabled application of the scientific method to the subject matter. Watson's **behaviorism** was particularly critical of introspection as a method of inquiry. Not only was introspection inherently subjective, making independently verifiable replication of results impossible, it was a reactive procedure that unnecessarily limited the discipline's subject matter. A **reactive procedure** is one in which the observational procedure affects the results. Watson argued that the act of introspection necessarily altered one's conscious experience. That is, whatever reliable findings were obtained would apply only under circumstances in which an individual is engaged in introspection, which is not ordinarily the case. Because only reliable verbal human beings could serve as subjects, it was impossible to study abnormal populations, children, or other animals as subjects.

**Behaviorism**

An early school of psychology reacting to structuralism and advocating psychology as a natural science with the goal of predicting and controlling observable behavior.

**Reactive Procedure**

One in which observing a phenomenon influences the results. For example, watching someone perform could affect how the observer does.

## PSYCHOLOGY TODAY

Each of the major early schools contributed significantly to the way psychology is currently practiced. Working backward, behaviorism recognized that our scientific observations are limited to behavior that can be measured (Skinner, 1990). Then, just as in other sciences, psychology's subject matter expanded with the development of new instruments. Astronomy benefited from the invention of the telescope, biology from the microscope, and psychology from such innovations as the IQ test, personality tests, the reaction timer, galvanic skin response (GSR), electroencephalograph (EEG), magnetic response imaging (MRI), computerized recording of behavior, and so on.

The field of psychology has profited from the wisdom of the Gestalt psychologists as well. Indeed, a hard lesson was learned with the realization that many conclusions about human memory based on the study of nonsense syllables (e.g., GUX) did not apply to meaningful words and sentences. For example, recent evidence has demonstrated that the individual letters in words are processed simultaneously rather than sequentially (Adelman, Marquis, & Sabatos-DeVito, 2010).

The title of this book implies that functionalism continues to exert an influence. Indeed, evolutionary psychology has emerged recently as a significant perspective unifying such distinct content areas as physiological psychology, learning, and social psychology (Confer, Easton, Fleischman, Goetz, Lewis, & Buss, 2010).

By virtue of being first, Wilhelm Wundt was able to define, state the goals, and develop the methodology of psychology. This advantage had a cost because it provided others the opportunity to make suggestions and offer criticisms, not always in a collegial manner. Still, the most important components of structuralism have been incorporated within current practice. The fact that Introduction to Psychology textbooks universally include chapters on perception, cognition, and motivation (and as we shall see, learning) demonstrates continued interest in conscious experience. These topics however must be studied in an inferential manner based upon behavioral observations. Introspection continues as a methodology for acquiring data in the form of self-report, with the inherent limitations of such data being recognized and studied in their own right. Wherever possible, confirmatory measures other than self-report are frequently obtained. For example, in studies designed to reduce cigarette smoking, subjects are often required to provide carbon dioxide measures in addition to cigarette per day self-reports.

---

- Describe Wundt's initial structuralist definition, goals, and methods for the science of psychology along with the reactions of the functionalist, Gestalt, and behavioral schools. Show how our contemporary approach to psychology reflects the contributions of the early schools.

---

## SCIENTIFIC EXPLANATION IN PSYCHOLOGY

As mentioned previously, scientific *explanation* usually means a statement of cause and effect. Scientists refer to potential causes as **independent variables** and the related effects as **dependent variables**. Different sciences are defined by the dependent variables of interest. That is, physics studies the effects of different independent variables on matter and energy. Biology studies the effects of different independent variables on life processes. Given what was previously stated about the current approach to psychology, what does psychology study?

(Answer: The effects of different independent variables on individual behavior.)

All sciences assume that nature is lawful and that if you study nature systematically, the underlying laws can become known. This assumption is referred to as **determinism** and is not considered controversial today with respect to physics, chemistry, and biology. We look to these disciplines to provide answers about how nature works and to benefit from technological advances resulting from scientific understanding. Those who believe we possess freedom of the will, however, consider the assumption of determinism with regard to human behavior very controversial. The concept of freedom within a deterministic science of psychology is addressed in the final chapter. For now, the controversy can be reduced or eliminated by pointing out that the logical opposite of determinism is not freedom of the will, but nondeterminism. That is, the logical opposite of the assumption that nature is lawful is that nature is not lawful. Everyone, including those believing

**Scientific Explanation**
A statement of cause and effect involving specification of the relationship between separately observable independent and dependent variables.

**Independent Variable**
The potential causal variable manipulated in an experiment.

**Dependent Variable**
The variable potentially affected by the independent variable in an experiment. In psychology, the dependent variable is always a type of behavior.

**Determinism**
The assumption by all sciences that nature is lawful and may be understood through systematic study.

strongly in freedom of the will, acts as though behavior is lawful. We (usually) stop at red lights and proceed when they turn green. We (usually) take turns listening and speaking. We (usually) show up for class on time, and so on. None of this would be true if we did not expect others to act in a similarly predictable manner. Predictability, implying lawfulness, can be true only within a deterministic system.

Let us now ask what would be considered a lawful **psychological explanation** of human behavior. We start with a couple of scenarios. Imagine that you are in a classroom and a person of your age enters, walks over to a wall, and starts banging his/her head against it. Then, this person takes a seat and starts talking out loud, apparently to no one. Someone from the university counseling center enters the room and states "he/she is doing that because he/she is schizophrenic." Another person of your age enters the classroom, clearly congested and coughing. Someone from the university health services enters and states "she/he is congested because she/he has influenza."

These two scenarios appear very similar. An individual's behaviors or physical symptoms are explained by reference to an underlying condition or illness. However, the first example constitutes an example of a **pseudo-explanation** (e.g., a false one), whereas the second example could fulfill the requirements of an adequate explanation. Why is that? Both explanations involve terms that are difficult to pronounce and spell. What makes influenza a "better" explanation than schizophrenia?

Remember, by explanation we mean a statement of cause and effect. This requires a separate observable potential cause (independent variable) and effect (dependent variable). In the case of influenza, a specific bacteria or virus can be detected through the appropriate tests. The term *influenza* does not simply stand for a syndrome of symptoms. It stands for the relationship between a specific "germ" and a specific syndrome. It is possible to test and replicate the relationship between this specific germ and specific symptoms. This is not the case with the term *schizophrenia,* which is defined exclusively on the effect (dependent variable) side (DSM 4R, 2000). It is circular to explain a phenomenon with the name for the phenomenon. Why does the person behave that way? Because he/she is schizophrenic. How do you know he/she is schizophrenic? Because he/she behaves that way.

Pseudo-explanations can be extremely problematic in psychology. For example, it is known that the frequency of students' getting out of their seats can be increased through the attention of their teacher (Allen & Harris, 1966). If you were informed your child gets out of her/his seat frequently because she/he is hyperactive, you might not search for an alternate explanation. Even worse is the potential for the development of a **self-fulfilling prophecy**. That is, by virtue of being labeled hyperactive, she/he might be treated differently by others, resulting in the problem behaviors increasing in frequency. One of the most valuable lessons you can learn is when you understand a phenomenon (in psychology or otherwise) and when you do not. Be vigilant for pseudo-explanations. Always look for testable relationships between observable independent and dependent variables.

**Psychological Explanation**

Description of how hereditary (nature) and experiential (nurture) variables affect behavior.

**Pseudo-Explanation**

Use of a descriptive label for a behavior as its explanation (e.g., saying someone hits another person because he/she is aggressive). Explanation requires specification of an independent variable (cause).

**Self-Fulfilling Prophecy**

When the belief about a natural phenomenon influences the result in the described direction. For example, being told that a child is "difficult" might influence how the child is treated resulting in the continuation/intensification of the problem behavior.

> ■ Describe what is meant by a pseudo-explanation in psychology and give an example. What are the dangers of believing pseudo-explanations?

## WHERE DOES PSYCHOLOGY LOOK FOR EXPLANATIONS?

Many psychologists and psychiatrists are searching for the cause(s) of schizophrenia. Where do they look? Based on the influenza example, one possibility is a germ. If this were to be the case, schizophrenia would be considered a medical (psychiatric) condition. Psychologists look to nature (heredity) and nurture (the environment) for causes. Their assumption is that our genes determine our total potential for development that is then realized through exposure to appropriate environmental events. A high school valedictorian provided a metaphor by thanking his parents, friends, and teachers for helping him prepare for life. He thanked his parents for providing water, his friends for their sunshine, and his teachers for producing so much fertilizer!

You are no doubt familiar with so-called **nature-nurture controversies**. Some suggest that with respect to intelligence, heredity is more important than the environment or vice versa. Technical journals reference heritability ratios as indications of the extent to which intelligence or some other behavior results from hereditary influences. This is another controversy that is best reframed, as we did with questions regarding freedom of the will. Let us combine some of the elements of the novels *Jurassic Park* (Crichton, 1990) and *Tarzan of the Apes* (Burroughs, 1914) to show how.

> **Nature-Nurture Controversies**
>
> Debates regarding the importance of genetic as opposed to experiential factors with respect to various behaviors.

Someone is exploring the site where Marie Curie or Albert Einstein died and discovers a mosquito frozen in amber. Sure enough, it is determined that this mosquito stung the scientist while alive and it is possible to extract the DNA and clone it. A healthy, lively infant results and is given to a loving pair of gorillas to raise. Obviously, the known genetic potential will never be realized in this impoverished environment (by current technologically advanced standards). The reverse is also true. We could provide a wonderful, loving pair of human parents with a chimpanzee to raise (chimpanzees share 98% of their DNA with humans). This, in fact, was done with the famous chimp Washoe, the hero of a wonderful book *Next of Kin* (Fouts, 1997). This book will make you laugh and make you cry, and you will never think of chimpanzees in the same way. Still, by human standards, Washoe does not attain many of the complex abilities that the great majority of us do as adults.

It appears misleading to argue that heredity or environment is more important with respect to the development of complex human behavior. The genetic potential must be present or the complex behavior cannot occur. Even if the potential is there, without exposure to the appropriate environmental circumstances, it will not be realized. Psychology then is accurately described as the study of how genetic and environmental variables interact to influence internal processes (thoughts and feelings) as well as overt behavior in individual animals. Psychological explanations consist of descriptions of the relationships between hereditary and experiential independent variables and behavior.

---

■ Describe how it is often misleading to ask whether nature (heredity) or nurture (experience) is more important to understanding complex human behavior. Describe what constitutes an adequate psychological explanation.

### Human Genetic Potential

**Human Homunculus**

(little person) A visual representation of the amount of "brain space" allotted to different parts of the body.

A convenient way of considering our genetic potential is to examine the so-called **human homunculus** (little person). This is a representation of the amount of "brain space" in the cortex allotted to different parts of our body (Figure 1.3). A disproportionate amount of the motor cortex is allocated to our face, lips, tongue, larynx (voice box), and hands (particularly the thumb). The ability to manipulate our facial muscles, tongue, and larynx enables us to emit an enormous variety of vocalizations. Initial attempts to teach chimps to speak (Hayes & Hayes, 1952) were unsuccessful, primarily because of limitations in the use of these body parts. Our ability to manipulate our fingers and thumbs to form the **precision grip** enables us to grasp and hold objects of different sizes and shapes. Millions of years of evolution resulted in an animal with the genetic potential to speak and create tools (Pollard, 2009). As described in Chapter 11, this potential took a very long time to emerge. However, once realized, this combination of abilities resulted in an animal that dominated and changed our planet. Evolutionary biologist Jared Diamond wrote a wonderful Pulitzer Prize–winning book tracing the history of the human being leading up to and after the last ice age, approximately 13,000 years ago. He describes how features of the climate and environment impacted the course of development of humans on the different continents and why some cultures eventually dominated others. The revealing title of his book is *Guns, Germs, and Steel* (Diamond, 2005). Thus, an alternative title of this textbook could be *Thumbs, Tongues, and Cortex*. Theodosius Dobzhansky (1960), the noted Russian genetic biologist, stated

**Precision Grip**

The ability to move our fingers and opposable thumbs in order to grasp and manipulate objects of different sizes and shapes. This ability enabled humans to create and use tools.

> Mutation, sexual recombination and natural selection led to the emergence of Homo sapiens. The creatures that preceded him had already developed the rudiments of tool-using, tool making and cultural transmission. But the next evolutionary step was so great as to constitute a difference in kind from those

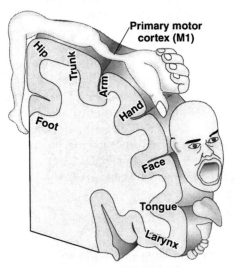

**FIGURE 1.3**   The human homunculus for the motor cortex.

before it. There now appeared an organism whose mastery of technology and of symbolic communication enabled it to create a supraorganic culture. Other organisms adapt to their environments by changing their genes in accordance with the demands of the surroundings. Man and man alone can also adapt by changing his environments to fit his genes. His genes enable him to invent new tools, to alter his opinions, his aims and his conduct, to acquire new knowledge and new wisdom.

## The Importance of Learning

One powerful experiential explanation for much of our behavior is learning. Before defining learning, we need to emphasize how important the process is in realizing our genetic potential. It is not an overstatement to suggest that all our knowledge, skills, and attitudes are learned. In fact, one would be hard pressed to come up with an example of any complex (i.e., not a simple reflex) human adult behavior that is not learned.

Also, parenting, teaching, and all psychological (as distinct from psychiatric) treatments depend upon the learning process. Procedures as diverse as psychodynamic, humanistic-existential, and cognitive-behavioral approaches to psychotherapy all involve providing a specific experience with the goal of attaining a specific behavioral change. The experiences may be as diverse as speaking about early family relationships or manipulating rewards and punishments. The therapeutic goals could be modifying interpretations of inkblots or increasing initiation of conversations with one's spouse. Much of the controversy concerning different types of psychotherapy could be diffused if they are understood as simply representing different learning experiences having different objectives.

> ▪ Describe the importance of learning as an explanation for human behavior.

## DEFINITIONS OF LEARNING

### Operational

The theme of this text involves combining and slightly modifying a couple of existing definitions of learning. The traditional definition is presented along with another that has not attained the same degree of popularity but complements it in a constructive way. Practically all textbooks provide an operational definition of learning. **Operational definitions** describe the procedures used to measure the particular term. For example, "intelligence" is often measured by the score on a paper-and-pencil test. The **operational definition of learning** describes how one objectively determines whether or not a behavioral observation is an example of the process. All sciences rely upon operational definitions in order to establish a degree of consistency in the use of terminology.

The most common operational definitions are variations on the one provided in Kimble's revision of Hilgard and Marquis's *Conditioning and Learning* (1961, p. 6).

**Operational Definition**

Describes the procedures used to measure the particular term; for example, "intelligence" is defined by the score on a paper-and-pencil test.

**Learning (Operational Definition)**

A relatively permanent change in behavior potential resulting from experience.

**Maturation**

A change in behavior resulting from aging.

**Latent Learning**

Learning is not necessarily reflected in overt behavior. Performance may be influenced by motivational and other factors as well as learning.

According to Kimble, "Learning is a relatively permanent change in behavior potentiality which occurs as a result of practice." Let us parse this definition. First, it should be noted that learning is inferred, not directly observed. Only when we see a change in behavior resulting from appropriate experience do we conclude that learning has taken place. Other possible causes of behavior change include **maturation**, which is nonexperiential, and fatigue or drugs that do not produce relatively permanent changes. Kimble includes the word *potentiality* to emphasize that even if learning has occurred, a corresponding behavior change is not guaranteed. Evidence for this conclusion is provided in Tolman and Honzik's (1930) classic demonstration of **latent learning** (i.e., learning not necessarily reflected in behavior).

The research cited in this textbook is almost all experimental. Tolman and Honzik studied three groups of rats placed in a 14-unit T-maze (Figure 1.4). Figure 1.5 is the first of many graphs portraying experimental research results. Carefully studying each graph may help you understand the research. As indicated in the operational definition of learning, experience will be manipulated and behavior observed. The graph's legend describes the experiences provided the three groups (i.e., the independent variable). One group of rats was placed in the start box and removed from the maze after reaching the end. The second group received a food reward at the end and was permitted to eat prior to being removed. The third group did not receive food at the end of the maze until the 11th day. The dependent variable (number of errors) was recorded on the *y*-axis for 17 days.

Before considering the third group, let us see how the results for the first two enable us to conclude that learning has occurred in the second group. These two groups

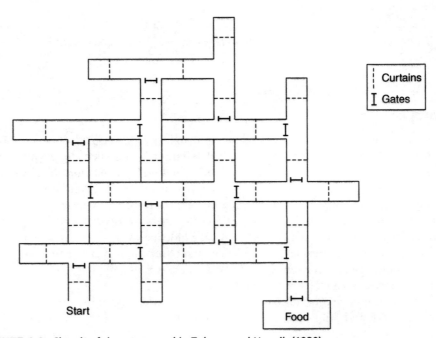

**FIGURE 1.4**   Sketch of the maze used in Tolman and Honzik (1930).

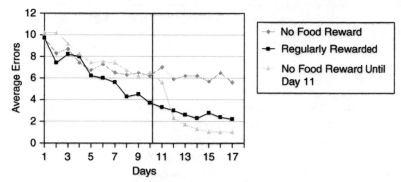

**FIGURE 1.5** Tolman and Honzik's (1930) latent learning experiment. Wrong turns in the maze (errors) hardly declined for the No Food Reward condition in comparison to the Regularly Rewarded condition, indicating that the group receiving food at the end was learning the maze. The dramatic decline in errors for the condition No Food Reward Until Day 11 indicates that the rats must have also been learning the maze on previous trials.

might be described as a **control group** and an **experimental group**. The groups are treated the same with one exception, the experimental group receives food at the end. Therefore, if the results differ, we are able to conclude that it must be this experience that made the difference. Examination of the results for the No Food Reward group reveals that the dependent variable, average errors (i.e., wrong turns in the maze), changed only slightly over the course of the experiment. However, the Regularly Rewarded group demonstrated a consistent decline in the number of errors, exactly what one would expect if learning were taking place. It would not be possible to conclude that the experience made a difference in this group without the control condition. One could argue that something else was responsible for the decline (e.g., a change in the weather, maturation).

> **Control Group**
>
> An experimental condition either not exposed to or exposed to a different level of an independent variable than the experimental group.

> **Experimental Group**
>
> A research condition exposed to an independent variable.

We have seen how it is possible to conclude that the Regularly Rewarded group learned the maze based upon a comparison of its results with the No Food Reward group. A related, seemingly logical conclusion would be that the No Food Reward group failed to learn the maze. Tolman and Honzik's third group was like the No Food Reward group for the first 10 days and like the Regularly Rewarded group for the remaining days. This third group enabled us to test whether or not the absence of food resulted in the absence of learning. It is important to understand the rationale for this condition. If this group had not learned anything about the maze on the first 10 days, the number of errors would be expected to gradually decline from day 12 on. However, if it had been learning the maze, a more dramatic decline in errors would be expected. This is indeed what occurred, leading to the conclusion that the rats in the third group had learned the maze despite the fact that it was not evident in their behavior (latent learning). Learning is but one of several factors affecting how an individual behaves. Tolman and Honzik's results imply that incentive motivation (food, in this instance) was necessary in order for the animals to display what they had learned. Thus, we see the need to include the word *potentiality* in the operational definition of learning. During the first 10 trials, the rats clearly acquired the potential to negotiate the maze.

■ State the operational definition of psychology, describing why each of the terms is
included.

**Scientific Schema**

A format for research articles
consisting of an introduction
placing the study within the
context of prior research; a
methods sections providing
sufficient detail to replicate
the procedures used in the
study; reporting of results
and statistical analyses; and
discussion of the conclusions,
implications, and limitations
of the research.

Tolman and Honzik (1930) is the first of several studies to be described
in depth. One of the objectives of this text is to encourage the development of
a **scientific schema**. All sciences use similar formats in research articles. They
generally consist of introductions placing the study within the context of prior
research; method sections providing sufficient detail to replicate the procedures;
reporting of results and statistical analyses; and discussion of the conclusions,
implications, and limitations of the research. In order to assess whether you
understand Tolman and Honzik (or any other research study), ask yourself the
following: What was the question being addressed by the investigator(s)? How
did the procedures enable the question to be addressed? What were the results and
conclusions regarding the question?

■ Describe the procedures, rationale, results, and implications of Tolman and
Honzik's study demonstrating latent learning, indicating that one cannot conclude
the absence of learning from the absence of performance.

**Structural/Functional
Definition of Learning**

Defining learning as involving
the acquisition of stimulus
and response expectancies
resulting in adaptive
responding. The definition
is structural in the sense that
expectancies are considered
the elements of conscious
experience forming the basis
of learning. It is functional in
that it describes the purpose
of learning as adaptive
responding.

**Stimulus Expectancies**

Anticipating events based
upon patterns of stimuli in
the environment (i.e., event-
event learning). For example,
"If this happens, then that
happens."

## Structural/Functional

In contrast to the traditional operational definition of learning, Tarpy (1982)
introduced what might be described as a **structural/functional definition**. It is
structural in the sense that expectancies are considered the elements of conscious
experience forming the basis of learning. It is functional in that it describes the
purpose of learning as adaptive responding. According to Tarpy, "learning is the
acquisition of expectancies, based upon patterns of stimulus inputs and response
feedback, which allow an animal to behave in an adaptive fashion" (p. 10). Tarpy
distinguishes between two types of expectancies: stimulus expectancies based
upon patterns of stimuli in the environment and response expectancies based upon
the effects of an individual's behavior on the environment (i.e., consequences
of behavior). **Stimulus expectancies** may be described as event-event learning
(i.e., if this happens then that happens). **Response expectancies** are examples of
response-event learning (i.e., if this behavior occurs then that happens). Tarpy
(1982) states,

In short, the fundamental task for any organism, in terms of learning is to
be able to predict changes in its environment, to anticipate the future....
To deny that learning involves the acquisition of expectancies would be to
fail to grasp the fundamental truth about the learning process: that it has
evolved to help animals deal with uncertainties, to allow them to perform
more adaptively in a changing world, to permit them to exert some order
over a complex and changeable environment. (pp. 8, 11)

Although Tarpy's definition has not resulted in wide-scale modification or supplementation of the traditional operational definition, it has much to recommend it. It connects the study of learning to the traditional goals of the science of psychology: to analyze and determine the adaptive nature of conscious experience.

Tarpy's structural/functional definition has an additional significant benefit. Students reading a textbook on learning or the learning chapter of an Introduction to Psychology text often notice that the term *learning*, which they associate with human beings, is hardly discussed. Most of the content is dedicated to classical and instrumental conditioning based on research with other animals. Tarpy's definition suggests why this is the case. The type of learning being considered is adaptive learning, a fundamental process characteristic of much of the animal kingdom. Classical conditioning is a research paradigm enabling the study of event-event learning whereby response-event learning is not possible. For example, as a result of stimulus patterns, Pavlov's dogs could eventually anticipate that the tone would be followed by meat powder. However, they were not able to affect the occurrence of either the tone or the meat powder. In comparison, Skinner's rats, based upon the feedback of receiving food after pressing a bar, were able to undergo response-event learning and affect food availability.

> ▪ State Tarpy's structural/functional definition of learning showing how it relates to classical and instrumental conditioning.

## Adaptive

One might question why classical and instrumental conditioning are the only two processes generally considered. This brings us to the definition of learning used for the remainder of this book: *Learning is an adaptive process whereby individuals acquire the ability to predict and control the environment.* Adaptation consists of predicting and controlling events. **Classical conditioning** procedures investigate learning how to predict when control is not possible. **Instrumental conditioning** procedures investigate learning when control is possible (i.e., from the rat's perspective, it is controlling the delivery of food). The advantage to describing learning in terms of predicting and controlling is that these are the two components of adaptation. This makes clear why only classical and instrumental conditioning processes are discussed. To add an updated version of the operational definition to the one proposed here, Domjan (2005b, p. 7) has offered "Learning is a relatively enduring change in the potential to engage in a particular behavior resulting from experience with environmental events specifically related to that behavior."

## DIRECT AND INDIRECT LEARNING

Many chapters and books on learning include a discussion of observational learning as though it were another type of learning in addition to classical and instrumental conditioning. Observational learning will be treated differently here by using the previously

**Response Expectancies**

Anticipating the effects of one's behavior on the environment (i.e., response-event learning). For example, "If I do this, then that happens."

**Classical Conditioning**

A research paradigm studying predictive (event-event) learning where control (response-event) learning is not possible. For example, Pavlov's dogs could anticipate food but not control when it occurred.

**Instrumental Conditioning**

A research paradigm studying the effect of consequences (response-event learning) when control is possible. For example, Skinner's rats could influence the delivery of food by pressing a bar.

mentioned distinction between direct and indirect learning. The conditioning processes involve an individual's direct interaction with environmental events. In contrast, observational learning is indirect in the sense that someone (or something) else is interacting with the environment. An example of indirect classical conditioning might involve one chimpanzee (the observer) witnessing another (the model) being shocked after a tone. After a few trials, the model screams upon presentation of the tone. When the observer is placed in the same situation and hears the tone, it is likely that it too will scream despite never having experienced the shock. An example of indirect instrumental conditioning might involve one chimpanzee witnessing another in a Skinner box press a bar and receive food. If placed in the box, it is likely that the observer chimp will immediately press the bar.

**Language**

A consensually agreed-upon collection of arbitrary symbols representing objects, movements, properties, and relationships. Language enables humans to learn indirectly, resulting in similar adaptive responding as occurs after direct experience.

Another indirect form of learning that is critical to human adaptation is the symbolic use of language. **Language** is a consensually agreed-upon collection of arbitrary symbols representing objects, movements, properties, relationships, and so on. Through language, humans can provide the same information as through observational means, thereby resulting in similar behaviors. For example, I can tell you that lightning predicts thunder, or that pressing any key will turn off the screen saver. Olsson and Phelps (2004) provide an excellent study examining the neuroscience underlying the direct, observational, and linguistic learning of a fear of faces. Human subjects were either exposed to a shock (direct learning) in the presence of a picture of a face, observed another person's emotional reaction to the face (indirect observational) or were told that the picture of the face would be followed by shock (indirect symbolic). The three groups subsequently demonstrated similar fear reactions (as assessed through skin conductance response) to the picture of the face. It may therefore be concluded that the three types of experiences represent three paths to the same adaptive learning (see also Kirsch, Lynn, Vigorito, & Miller, 2004). In later chapters, we will examine the research literature addressing the methods, theoretical issues, and applications of adaptive learning principles. We will observe how these principles enable us to understand and transform the human condition. In preparation, in the next chapter, we consider the challenges posed by the scientific study of the learning process.

> ■ Distinguish between and give examples of direct and indirect adaptive learning.

## Summary

Some human beings are still living Stone Age existences on our planet. What we mean by the human condition can change dramatically from place to place and from time to time. Within the past 400 years, humans have transformed the planet earth from its natural state, and many of us are now adapting to a human-constructed environment. The transition from relying upon personal experience and authority figures to the use of the scientific method to understand nature is responsible for this transformation. Science requires that its subject matter be observable and measurable. Although psychology was originally defined as the study of conscious experience (a.k.a. the study of the mind), eventually it became apparent that advancement as a science required behavioral observation. Explanation within a science usually consists of cause-and-effect relationships. Psychology studies the effect of genetic (nature) and environmental (nurture) variables on the behavior of individuals.

Learning, defined as experientially caused changes in behavior, is a powerful explanation for why we behave as we do and how we have transformed the human condition. It is appropriate and helpful to describe learning as an adaptive process through which individuals acquire the ability to predict and control their environment.

Learning can occur directly, through personal experience, or indirectly, through observation of others or symbolic means (language).

## References

Adelman, J. S., Marquis, S. J., & Sabatos-DeVito, M. G. (2010). Letters in words are read simultaneously, not in left-to-right sequence. *Psychological Science, 21*, 1799–1801.

Allen, K. E., & Harris, F. R. (1966). Elimination of a child's excessive scratching by training the mother in reinforcement procedures. *Behaviour Research and Therapy, 4*, 79–84.

Angell, J. R. (1903). The relation of structural and functional psychology to philosophy. *Philosophical Review, 12*, 243–271.

Angell, J. R. (1907). The province of functional psychology. *Psychological Review, 14*, 61–91.

Burroughs, E. R. (1914). *Tarzan of the Apes.* New York: A. L. Burt Company.

Cameron, W. B. (1963). *Informal sociology: A casual introduction to sociological thinking.* New York: Random House.

Confer, J. C., Easton, J. A., Fleischman, C. D., Goetz, D. M., Lewis, C. P., & Buss, D. M. (2010). Evolutionary psychology: Controversies, questions, prospects, and limitations. *American Psychologist, 65*, 110–126.

Crichton, M. (1990). *Jurassic Park.* New York: Alfred A. Knopf.

Darwin, C. (1859). *On the origin of species by means of natural selection.* London: Murray.

Diamond, J. (2005). *Guns, germs, and steel.* New York: W. W. Norton & Company.

Dobzhansky, T. (1960). The present evolution of man. *Scientific American, 203*, 206–217.

Domjan, M. (2005). *The essentials of conditioning and learning* (3rd ed.). Belmont, CA: Wadsworth.

Fechner, G. (1860/1966). *Elements of psychophysics* (H. Adler, Trans.). Leipzig: Briet Kopf & Hartel. New York: Holt, Rinehart & Winston.

Fouts, R. (1997). *Next of kin.* New York: Avon Books.

Hayes, K. J., & Hayes, C. (1951). The intellectual development of a home-raised chimpanzee. *Proceedings of the American Philosophical Society, 95*, 105–109.

Helmholtz, H. V. (1924). *Physiological optics* (J. P. Southall, Trans. from the 3rd German edition). Washington, DC: Optical Society of America.

Hilgard, E. R., & Marquis, D. G. (1940). *Conditioning and learning.* New York: Appleton-Century-Crofts.

Kendler, H. H. (1987). *Historical foundations of modern psychology.* Pacific Grove, CA: Brooks/Cole.

Kimble, G. A. (1961). *Hilgard and Marquis' conditioning and learning* (2nd ed.). New York: Appleton-Century-Crofts.

Kirsch, I., Lynn, S. J., Vigorito, M., & Miller, R. R. (2004). The role of cognition in classical and operant conditioning. *Journal of Clinical Psychology, 60*, 369–392.

Kohler, W. (1929). *Gestalt psychology.* New York: Liveright Publishing Corporation.

Olsson, A., & Phelps, E. (2004). Learned fear of "unseen" faces after Pavlovian, observational, and instructed fear. *Psychological Science, 15*, 822–828.

Pollard, K. S. (2009, April 20). What makes us human? *Scientific American, 300*, 44–49.

Powers, R. (1999, April 18). Best idea: Eyes wide open. *New York Times Magazine*, http://www.nytimes.com/1999/04/18/magazine/best-idea-eyes-wide-open.html?pagewanted=all&src=pm

Sanderson, E. W., & Boyer, M. (2009). *Mannahatta: A natural history of New York City.* New York: Abrams.

Skinner, B. F. (1990). Can psychology be a science of mind? *American Psychologist, 45*, 1206–1210.

Tarpy, R. M. (1982). *Principles of animal learning and motivation.* Glenville, IL: Scott Foresman and Company.

Titchener, E. B. (1898). The postulates of a structural psychology. *Philosophical Review, 7*, 449–465.

Tolman, E. C., & Honzik, C. H. (1930). Introduction and removal of reward, and maze performance in rats. *University of California Publications in Psychology, 4*, 257–275.

Watson, J. B. (1913). Psychology as the behaviorist views it. *Psychological Review, 20*, 158–177.

Wundt, W. M. (1873). *Principles of physiological psychology.* Leipzig: Engelmann.

Wundt, W. M. (1896). *Lectures on human and animal psychology.* New York: Macmillan.

# *Chapter 2*

# Adaptive Learning Research Methods

## INTERNAL AND EXTERNAL VALIDITY

Two assumptions underlie the title of this book. The first is that application of the scientific method has enabled us to develop laws (principles) of adaptive learning. The second assumption is that these principles apply to human beings under realistic everyday conditions. The first of these assumptions relates to the research issue known as internal validity and the second to the issue known as external validity. **Internal validity** is the ability to draw cause–effect conclusions from research findings. **External validity** is the ability to apply cause–effect conclusions under naturalistic conditions.

**Internal Validity**

The ability to draw cause-and-effect conclusions from research findings.

**External Validity**

The ability to apply cause-and-effect conclusions under naturalistic conditions.

It is almost universal on college campuses that the laboratory sciences occupy separate facilities from the humanities. Laboratories provide isolation from many of the extraneous variables that might influence research results. They typically include extensive electrical and plumbing requirements beyond those of "chalk-and-talk" classrooms. For example, if one were interested in replicating Galileo's observations on the effect of weight on the rate at which an object falls, it would be advantageous to perform the observations inside where the wind would not play a role. Laboratories also permit greater control of the independent variable and precision in the measurement of the dependent variable. Today, we could create perfect spheres that differ only in weight and measure the time taken to fall any distance in millionths of a second. Despite the differences between the laboratory and external environments, we would expect the findings to continue to apply. In fact, this would constitute an empirical question that could be tested using the scientific method. Any time the findings did not apply would suggest further research to determine the cause(s). For example, fans could be used to systematically study wind effects.

> ▪ Describe how the issues of internal and external validity relate to the discipline of psychology.

## NONEXPERIMENTAL RESEARCH METHODS

**Experimentation** that allows the researcher to manipulate the independent variable is the most reliable and powerful method for determining cause and effect. However, it is not always possible to conduct experiments in psychology (or other sciences, for that matter). A researcher cannot always manipulate a variable. For example, a subject cannot be made male or female or a particular age. We can only select subjects already possessing the desired attributes. We do not have the power to manipulate geographic or climatic variables to see the extent to which they influence behavior. Many variables cannot be manipulated for ethical reasons. For example, we cannot systematically punish children severely to see if that is an effective technique for eliminating undesirable behavior. Indeed, some have even questioned studying the effect of punishment on the dangerously self-destructive acts of autistic children (Bettelheim, 1985).

**Experimentation**
A research method in which an independent variable is manipulated in order to determine an effect on a specific dependent variable.

The discipline of psychology frequently applies nonexperimental designs when experimental procedures are logistically impossible, prohibitive in cost, or unethical. However, even when relationships between variables are compelling, that is, a substantial statistical **correlation** exists, it is still not possible to conclude cause and effect. A hidden third variable often underlies the correlation. For example, it is likely that a high correlation exists between the number of books in one's home and success in school. That does not mean that simply providing books to an individual will improve school performance. It is likely that the number of books in one's home is indicative of a number of economic and attitudinal advantages.

**Correlation**
A measure of the degree of relationship between two variables. For example, one could ask subjects how much coffee they drink and how many hours they sleep. There is no manipulation of an independent variable and subjects are not randomly assigned to conditions.

> ▪ Describe why one is unable to conclude cause and effect from nonexperimental research.

## EXPERIMENTAL RESEARCH METHODS

The research literature on adaptive learning is essentially experimental in nature. This means that internal validity is not a concern. We can be confident of the causes of any demonstrated learning effects. External validity is another matter. We will delay consideration of external validity until after discussion of the major experimental methods used to study adaptive learning.

## Studies Comparing Groups

**Sample Size**

The total number of subjects in a research study.

**Random Assignment**

A procedure whereby an individual subject is equally likely to be exposed to any of the experimental conditions.

**Group Design**

An experimental method in which subjects are randomly assigned to conditions and the results are analyzed statistically (e.g., *t* test, analysis of variance).

**Parametric Study**

An experimental procedure in which different values of an independent variable are presented. For example, one could present different magnitudes of a reward or present it after different delays.

**Confounding Variables**

Noncontrolled variables in an experiment that could impact the dependent variable. For example, wind could affect the time it takes for objects to fall.

Group studies conforming to major statistical designs (e.g., *t* tests, analysis of variance) are the most popular experimental procedures used to study adaptive learning. Small-*N* (i.e., small number of subjects) designs are also popular and have their distinct advantages. The rationale underlying group studies needs to be reviewed first before we discuss specific examples. As mentioned earlier, even animals of the same species (especially humans) differ from one another. The logic of group studies is that with sufficient **sample sizes** (i.e., the number of subjects in each group), **random assignment** to conditions (groups) should result in comparable averages for all subject characteristics. That is, if 200 people were randomly assigned to two conditions, we would expect each condition to start out with approximately the same gender, racial, and ethnicity composition, to be of the same average age and intelligence, and so on. Therefore, if after manipulation of an independent variable, the groups differ sufficiently, it would be possible to conclude that the variable rather than a subject characteristic caused the difference. The previously described study by Tolman and Honzik (1930) is an example of a **group design**. The same number of rats was randomly assigned to three conditions and the average number of errors compared over the course of the study. Given the differences in performance among the three groups, it was possible to conclude that the independent variable, the manner in which food was delivered, was responsible for the results.

The great majority of research studies cited in this text are group designs. The operational definition of learning requires demonstration of a behavior change resulting from experience. It is only necessary to include two groups to demonstrate adaptive learning, one receiving a type of experience (often referred to as the experimental group) and the other not receiving the experience (often referred to as the control group). If the groups differ, it would be concluded that the experience made the difference (i.e., learning had occurred). Once a learning effect has been demonstrated, subsequent research is often conducted to obtain additional information. Control groups receiving different types of experiences may be included. The nature of the control groups will determine the possible conclusions one may reach. Different components of the experience might be left out to determine what the essential component(s) is (are). For example, let us say that the success of a procedure consisting of learning to relax while imagining climbing up a ladder step by step to reduce a fear of height is indicated by the ability to climb a real ladder. Separate groups could then be taught to relax or to imagine climbing the ladder to see if both components of the procedure are necessary to receive the full benefit. **Parametric studies**, in which the independent variable is manipulated along a dimension, are often conducted to determine how the magnitude of a variable affects adaptive learning. For example, subjects might be asked to imagine climbing a three-rung ladder, six-rung ladder, nine-rung ladder, and so on.

■ Describe and give an example of a group design applied to the study of learning showing how it is possible to control for potential **confounding variables** and conclude cause and effect.

## Small-*N* Designs

**ESTABLISHING THE BASELINE**   A researcher is often interested in a small number of subjects (perhaps only one). One might suspect that it is impossible to conduct a controlled experiment with such a limited sample. That is not the case. Rather than manipulating levels of the independent variable across groups of subjects, **small-*N* designs** involve manipulation on each subject. Small-*N* designs require establishing **baselines** of performance prior to introducing the experimental intervention (see Figure 2.1). Fine-tuning of baseline performance is a critical step and can require many sessions. It is usually necessary to establish consistency of responding (as in the top graph) or responding trending in the direction opposite the expected intervention effect (as in the bottom graph). Although small-*N* designs require far fewer subjects (thus the name), they can involve similar (or greater) investments of research time because of the number of observations made during the different phases.

 Although the results may seem compelling, one cannot conclude cause and effect by simply following a baseline condition with an intervention (an AB design, see Figure 2.2). For example, let us say we were monitoring the number

> **Small-*N* Design**
> An experimental design involving systematic manipulation of an independent variable and ongoing measurement of the dependent variable.

> **Baseline**
> The first phase of a small-*N* design in which performance is assessed prior to the manipulation of an independent variable.

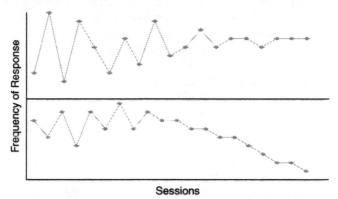

**FIGURE 2.1**   Fine-tuning the baseline. Consistent responding or responding in the opposite direction of an anticipated intervention effect constitutes a useful baseline.

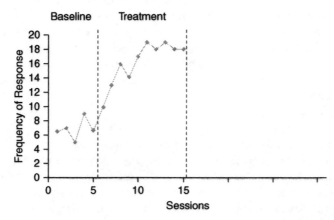

**FIGURE 2.2**   AB design.

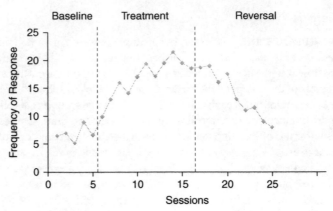

**FIGURE 2.3**   ABA reversal design.

of pages a child was reading before going to bed at night. First, we would try to establish consistency by putting the child to bed at the same time, keeping the length of reading sessions constant, and so on. After the number of pages read each night stabilized, we might introduce our planned intervention, perhaps giving "stars" for every three pages completed. Even if the number of pages read started to increase dramatically, it would not at this time be possible to conclude the stars made the difference. Although perhaps unlikely, it is logically possible to suggest that something else coincidentally occurred at the time the stars were introduced. Perhaps the book(s) became more interesting, or the weather changed, or the child started drinking orange juice.

**Reversal Design (ABA)**

A small-*N* design in which a baseline phase is followed by an intervention and then a return to the baseline procedures.

**Behavioral Trapping**

A phenomenon whereby naturally existing reinforcers are sufficient to maintain a behavior. For example, even after a child no longer receives stars for reading, the child continues to read just for the pleasure.

**REVERSAL DESIGNS**   **Reversal designs** (sometimes referred to as ABA, see Figure 2.3) are powerful and popular small-*N* adaptive learning procedures. In our example, once the intervention results stabilized or continued to increase for several sessions, we could discontinue providing stars. If the number of pages completed then decreased, it would be possible to conclude it was the stars that made the difference. It strains the limits of credulity to suggest that a second coincidence having the opposite effect occurred at precisely this time.

Although reversal procedures are the mainstay of small-*N* designs, there are unusual circumstances when reversals do not occur or when reversing the procedures would be unethical. For example, it is conceivable that after being given stars, the child discovered the intrinsic rewards provided by reading. In that instance, discontinuing the stars would have no effect. The intrinsic rewards would be sufficient to maintain the behavior, a phenomenon known as **behavioral trapping** (see Figure 2.4).

You might think that it is just the result one would hope for. That may be true as one who cares about the child. However, if you are a researcher attempting to establish cause and effect, you are back to square one.

One might also question the ethics of changing a procedure that was successful in increasing a child's reading. This concern would be more apparent in research resulting in the child's increasing a healthy behavior (e.g., wearing a seat belt) or decreasing a dangerous behavior (e.g., head banging). Clearly, in these instances, despite the requirements of science, reversal procedures should not be implemented.

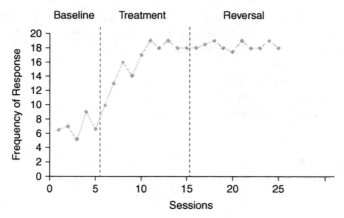

**FIGURE 2.4**   Behavioral Trapping. Naturally occurring consequences maintain the changes resulting from intervention.

**MULTIPLE BASELINE DESIGNS**   For the unusual circumstances when reversals do not occur or when reversing the procedures would be unethical, variations of **multiple baseline designs** have been developed (see Figure 2.5). Such designs consist of replications of AB designs across subjects, situations, or behaviors. For example, Juan, Dick, and Mary might be given stars for reading. Stable baselines would be established for each child and the treatment would be introduced at different times for the three children. Instead of working with three children, a similar procedure could be implemented at home at bedtime, at home with the

**Multiple
Baseline Design**

A small-*N* design consisting of a baseline followed by an intervention phase repeated at different times across different subjects, situations, or behaviors.

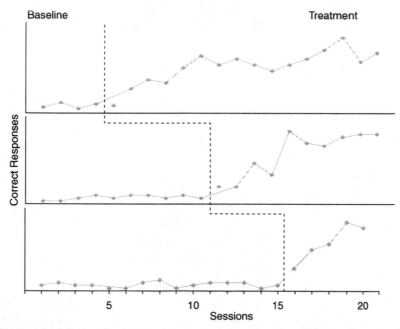

**FIGURE 2.5**   Multiple Baseline Design. Treatment is introduced at different times for different subjects, settings, or behaviors.

baby sitter, and at school. A third option would be to provide stars for reading, writing, and doing math problems. In all three instances, if improvement occurred during the intervention phase for all three children, situations, or behaviors, it would be concluded that the stars were responsible.

This concludes our discussion of the major experimental methods used to study adaptive learning. If you are a psychology major you will be exposed to other, more complicated procedures in undergraduate and graduate research methods courses.

---

■ Describe and give examples of reversal and multiple-baseline small-*N* experimental approaches to the study of learning showing how both strategies control for potential confounding variables and enable one to conclude cause and effect.

---

## ADAPTIVE LEARNING RESEARCH METHODS AND EXTERNAL VALIDITY

This textbook assumes that our current understanding of adaptive learning informs us about the human condition. This is true despite the fact that the experimental literature is based almost exclusively on research conducted on other animals in apparatuses developed for the laboratory. Recall Hardin's cartoon and the picture of the Nukak child in Chapter 1. These were included at the very beginning to make the point that humans share many characteristics and needs with other animals as we all do our best to adapt to our environmental circumstances. None of us had a choice about where or when we were born, or about the conditions under which we would have to survive and, hopefully, thrive. We all need to adapt to the circumstances we are given. Much of the animal kingdom and all humans are able to rely upon the learning process to assist in this venture we call life.

### Nonhumans as Subjects

The operational definition of adaptive learning dictates the minimal requirements of an appropriate subject. We need not only a subject capable of learning to predict or control an event, but also able to demonstrate that it has learned. That is, the researcher must be able to observe a change in behavior resulting from an appropriate experience. The subject requires the ability to experience (sense) the environment and act upon it (behave). Predictive learning (classical conditioning) and control learning (instrumental conditioning) have been demonstrated in very simple animals (Kimble, 1961 pp. 49, 72). Therefore, the amount or complexity of the brain space portrayed in the human homunculus is not necessary for adaptive learning. Does this mean that such simple animals can be used to study processes applicable to the human being? This is actually an empirical question. One could demonstrate a lawful relationship in a simple animal (e.g., an earthworm) and test whether the same relationship could be replicated with human subjects.

This issue is similar to the doubts expressed by many at the beginning of the 20th century that vivisection of other animals could tell us anything about human biology or inform surgical technique. In fact, many of the advances in our understanding of human physiology and surgical technique occurring since then would have been impossible if such research had not been conducted. As we shall see, there is much compelling evidence that the same is true with respect to adaptive learning.

Besides being relatively inexpensive to obtain and house, other animals do not raise the same internal validity issues intrinsic to human subjects. That is, they are closer to the perfect spheres we could use to replicate Galileo's findings with rocks. As we saw in Chapter 1, we explain differences in behavior as resulting from the interaction between hereditary and environmental variables. Laboratory animals can be purchased from the same litter, thereby having the same genes. They can even be bred for specific characteristics, making them ideal for specialized research projects. Naturally, being obtained soon after birth and being housed under restricted conditions, they do not have the extensive cultural and other experiential histories of humans. But they are extremely reliable subjects. They do not require phone reminders the previous night in order to show up for a study.

The American Psychological Association has very strict ethical guidelines for the care and use of animal subjects in research. The U.S. government requires that an Institutional Animal Care and Use Committee be responsible for ensuring that all requirements regarding feeding, access to water, climate control, and access to veterinary care are met. Mazur (2006, p. 13) has quipped, "It is unfortunate that there are no similar federal regulations guaranteeing adequate food, a warm place to live, and health care for the human members of our society."

The choice of a species for a research subject is often a matter of convenience, expense, and tradition regarding a particular topic area. Laboratory rats are frequently favored for these reasons and also because so much is known about their characteristics based upon their research use in other disciplines (e.g., biology). The choice of subject is sometimes dictated by species characteristics related to a particular area of interest. For example, rabbits have an extra eyelid (nictitating membrane) that facilitates attachment of an electrode, thereby making them especially suitable subjects for predictive eyelid conditioning. Pigeons have exceptional eyesight in comparison to rats and are therefore favored as subjects involving adaptation to visual stimuli.

**EXPERIMENTAL APPARATUS**    The choice of experimental apparatus often hinges on the same issues as the choice of subject: convenience, expense, and tradition. Again, the operational definition of learning dictates the only requirement. The apparatus must permit observation of a response indicative of either predictive or control learning. Ivan Pavlov and Edward Thorndike, the pioneers of the study of predictive and control learning, each studied animals in a specialized apparatus. These will be used as examples, with more current apparatuses described in the subsequent chapters reviewing the research findings. It will be seen that considerable improvement has occurred in measuring predictive and control learning since their seminal research.

Pavlov made a small incision in the dog's cheek and implanted a tube permitting saliva to be directly collected in a graduated test tube. The amount of saliva could then be accurately measured and recorded as depicted in Figure 2.6. As will be described in Chapter 3, predictive learning may be inferred when salivation occurred to a previously neutral stimulus as the result of appropriate experience.

Thorndike created mazes and puzzle boxes for use with a variety of species, including fishes, cats, dogs, and chimpanzees (Imada & Imada, 1983). Figure 2.7 provides a sketch of a cat in a puzzle box that could be rigged up in a variety of ways.

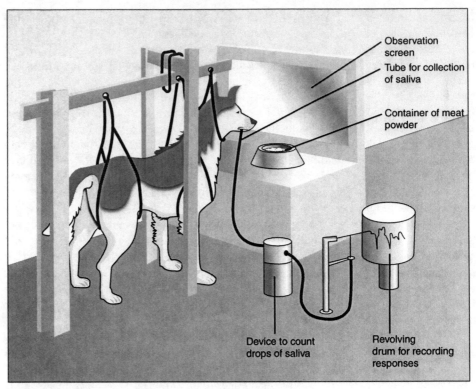

**FIGURE 2.6** Pavlov's apparatus.

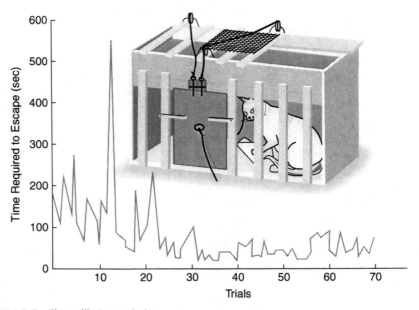

**FIGURE 2.7** Thorndike's puzzle box.

A sequence of responses was required in order to open the door leading to visible food (e.g., pulling a string, pressing a latch). A reduction in the amount of time taken to open the door indicated that control learning had occurred.

These apparatuses are considerably different from the natural environments of the species being investigated. It is an empirical question as to whether research findings obtained under these controlled conditions apply elsewhere for these species, let alone tell us anything about the human condition. As we review the empirical findings of the research literature regarding adaptive learning, we must constantly remind ourselves of this question.

All sciences must address both internal and external validity. This is especially challenging in psychology. We do not have the equivalent of perfect spheres as subjects of investigation. Rats, pigeons, chimpanzees, or people often differ from one another in significant ways. The behaviors we study may be complex and difficult to measure. The subjects and laboratory environments we use to obtain control over possible confounding variables are typically quite different from the subjects or conditions of real interest. Psychologists are left with two difficult strategies to simultaneously address internal and external validity. They can try to capture the essence of the natural environment and re-create it under more controlled laboratory conditions. The other strategy is to attempt to introduce precise manipulation of the independent variable and measurement of the dependent variable in the natural environment.

> ▪ Describe how the study of other animals as subjects in specialized apparatuses relates to the issues of internal and external validity.

In the previous chapter, we described Tolman and Honzik's (1930) latent learning study. The results support two important behavioral principles: Performance may be significantly enhanced by providing a reward, as indicated by comparison of the Regularly Rewarded and No Food Reward conditions, and the absence of performance does not necessarily reflect the inability to perform, as indicated by the comparison between the No Food Reward and No Reward Until Day 11 conditions. It is necessary to demonstrate that these principles apply to humans under naturalistic conditions. Edlund (1972) found that low-IQ Head Start children improved their scores when provided with candy for correct responses, a finding consistent with the first principle. Clingman and Fowler (1975) first failed to obtain the same result with a sample of above-average IQ children. They followed this study with one in which they evaluated the effectiveness of candy rewards on children with below-average, average, and above-average IQs. A substantial improvement was obtained only with the below-average subjects. This was interpreted as being consistent with the second principle. In this instance, one cannot conclude the absence of aptitude from a low-IQ test score. Although many students may follow the directions to perform to the best of their ability, others may require extrinsic reinforcement to do so. In this example, we see how replication of a study of maze learning in rats with IQ test performance in humans addresses the issue of external validity. The findings clearly have important implications with respect to the interpretation of IQ test scores, as well as applications with regard to the remediation of motivational deficits in schoolchildren.

In subsequent chapters, we examine the experimental research findings serving as the basis for our understanding of principles of adaptive learning. In addition to separate chapters describing applications of predictive and control learning principles, many examples are cited of the important implications and applications of these principles to the human condition.

## Summary

Psychology, as a science, attempts to discover cause-and-effect relationships that apply under naturalistic conditions. Experimentation involves manipulating an independent variable in order to determine the influence on a dependent variable. The study of adaptive learning involves systematically manipulating types of experience in order to determine how this influences the behavior of individuals. Group and small-$N$ experimental procedures have been developed for this purpose.

In order to address internal validity concerns, less complex animals whose genetics and experiences can be more controlled than humans' are often used as subjects. Adaptive learning is often studied in a specialized apparatus permitting systematic manipulation of the independent variable and precise measurement of the dependent variable. The study of other animals in specialized apparatuses usually necessitates addressing the issue of external validity through replication with humans under naturalistic conditions. It is sometimes possible to simultaneously address internal and external validity by simulating the natural environment in the laboratory or introducing precision and control into the natural environment.

## References

Bettelheim, B. (1985, November). Punishment versus discipline. *Atlantic Magazine*, http://www.theatlantic.com/magazine/archive/1985/11/punishment-versus-discipline/4097/

Clingman, J., & Fowler, R. (1975). The effects of contingent and noncontingent reinforcement on the I.Q. scores of children of above-average intelligence. *Journal of Applied Behavior Analysis, 8*, 90.

Edlund, C. (1972). The effect on the test behavior of children, as reflected in the I.Q. scores, when reinforced after each correct response. *Journal of Applied Behavior Analysis, 5*, 317–320.

Imada, H., & Imada, S. (1983). Thorndike's (1898) puzzle-box experiments revisited. *Kwansei Gakuin University Annual Studies, 32*, 167–184.

Kimble, G. A. (1961). *Hilgard and Marquis' conditioning and learning* (2nd ed.). New York: Appleton-Century-Crofts.

Mazur, J. E. (2006). *Learning and behavior* (6th ed.). Upper Saddle River, NJ: Pearson/Prentice Hall.

Tolman, E. C., & Honzik, C. H. (1930). Introduction and removal of reward, and maze performance in rats. *University of California Publications in Psychology, 4*, 257–275.

**PART II**   PREDICTIVE LEARNING

*Chapter 3*

# Predictive Learning: Basic Principles and Phenomena

M any authors of learning textbooks treat basic principles, theoretical issues, and applications within the same chapter when discussing classical and instrumental conditioning (i.e., predictive and control learning). In order to provide a linear thematic flow and more comprehensive treatment of applied issues, the following organizational structure is used: Chapters 3 and 6 cover the basic principles and phenomena of predictive and control learning, respectively. Chapters 4 and 7 describe how different variables influence predictive and control learning in addition to major theoretical issues relating to those processes. Chapters 5 and 8 show how our understanding of predictive and control learning applies to the human condition and helps us address important concerns. Later chapters build upon these basic principles as we extend them to increasingly complex behaviors and issues.

Students frequently indicate that the Chapter 3 material is the most difficult in the course. There is a sudden transition to less familiar terminology, more complex research, and more technical and theoretical concepts. You may wish to slow down your reading to ensure complete understanding of the principles, methods, findings, and conclusions.

## **Classical Conditioning**

Procedures developed by Pavlov to study learning when a stimulus event may be predicted but not controlled. In the original procedure, meat powder (the US) was presented after a tone (an initially neutral stimulus that becomes a CS) resulting in salivation (CR) to the tone.

## **Neutral Stimulus (Novel Stimulus)**

A stimulus that does not initially elicit any behavior related to a potential CS. For example, Pavlov's tone was a neutral stimulus until it acquired the capacity to elicit salivation (a CR).

## **Unconditioned Response (UR)**

A response elicited by a stimulus (US) as the result of heredity (e.g., food reflexively elicits salivation, a puff of air elicits an eye blink, etc.). See also reflexive behavior.

## PAVLOV'S CLASSICAL CONDITIONING PARADIGM

One cannot overstate the significance of the contributions Ivan Pavlov made to the study of predictive learning. These contributions include the development of apparatus (see Chapter 2), methods, a technical vocabulary, and numerous important research findings. Pavlov introduced a level of rigor and precision of measurement of both the independent and dependent variables in animal learning that did not exist at the time.

In 1904, Pavlov, a physiologist, was awarded the Nobel Prize in Medicine for his research investigating the digestive process in dogs. He became fascinated by an observation he and his laboratory assistants made while conducting this research. One of the digestive processes they studied was salivation. Saliva contains enzymes that initiate the process of breaking down what one eats into basic nutrients required to fuel and repair the body. The subjects frequently started salivating before being placed in the experimental apparatus. Pavlov described this salivation as a "psychic secretion" because it was not being directly elicited by food but appeared based upon mental anticipation. He considered the phenomenon so important that within a few years he abandoned his research program in digestion and dedicated the rest of his professional career to systematically studying its details.

This is a wonderful example of what has been described as serendipity, or accidental discovery in science. Dogs have been domesticated for thousands of years. A countless number of people probably observed dogs appearing to predict (i.e., anticipate or expect) food. Pavlov, however, recognized the significance of the observation as an example of a fundamental learning process. We often think of science as requiring new observations. Pavlov's "discovery" of the **classical conditioning** process is an example of how this is not necessarily the case. One of the characteristics of an exceptional scientist is to recognize the significance of commonly occurring observations. We now review the methodology and

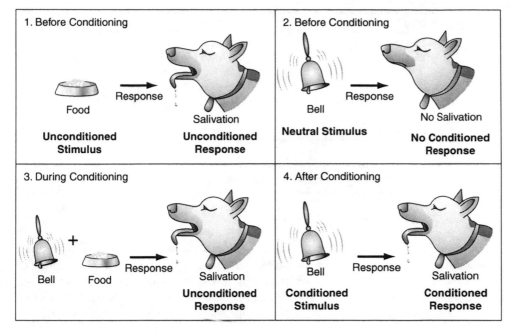

**FIGURE 3.1** Pavlov's procedures.

terminology Pavlov developed for studying predictive learning. He adapted an experimental apparatus designed for one scientific field of inquiry (the physiology of digestion) to an entirely different field (adaptive learning).

Animals inherit the tendency to make simple responses (i.e., reflexes) to specific types of stimulation. For example, infants will center a nipple placed in the corner of their mouths (rooting) and then suck upon it. This combination of reflexes clearly has the survival value of increasing the likelihood of successful nursing. Pavlov's salivation research was based on the reflexive eliciting of salivation by food (e.g., meat powder). This research was adapted to the study of predictive learning by including a **neutral stimulus**, one that did not initially elicit any behavior related to food. Pavlov demonstrated that if a neutral stimulus preceded a biologically significant stimulus on several occasions, a new response to the previously neutral stimulus would occur. Figure 3.1 uses the most popular translation of Pavlov's (who wrote in Russian) terminology. The reflexive behavior was referred to as the **unconditioned response (UR)**. Some believe the term *unconditional response* is the more accurate translation, but the former remains far more popular. The stimulus that reflexively elicited this response was referred to as the **unconditioned stimulus (US)**. By virtue of being paired in a predictive relationship (panel 3), the novel stimulus acquires the capacity to elicit a food-related response (also salivation in this instance). Once acquired, this capacity (panel 4) is referred to as the **conditioned stimulus (CS)** and the response as the **conditioned response (CR)**. The following list of USs and their corresponding URs was excerpted from Kimble (1961):

**Unconditioned Stimulus (US)**

A stimulus that elicits a response (UR) as the result of heredity (e.g., food reflexively elicits salivation, a puff of air elicits an eyeblink).

**Conditioned Stimulus (CS)**

A novel stimulus that acquires the capacity to elicit a response (the CR) as the result of occurring prior to another stimulus (the US).

**Conditioned Response (CR)**

The learned response to a previously neutral stimulus (eventually a CS) resulting from its being presented immediately prior to another stimulus (the US).

| Stimuli | Responses |
|---|---|
| • Dry food, acid | • Salivation |
| • Electric shock | • Change in skin resistance (GSR); foot or paw withdrawl |
| • Air puff | • Eyelid reflex |
| • Lithium chloride injection, X-irradiation | • Novel food aversion |
| • Insulin injection | • Change in blood sugar |

■ Describe Pavlov's original classical conditioning procedures and terminology.

## MEASUREMENT PROCEDURES

The following list contains the major procedures used to demonstrate and measure predictive learning. Some are considered direct in that they measure some characteristic of the conditioned response. The conditioned suppression procedure indirectly measures the strength of classical conditioning through observation of a change in instrumental conditioning. We will describe each of these, indicating the underlying rationale for the procedure.

- Direct Procedures
  - Anticipation
  - Blank trials
  - Sign tracking

- Indirect Procedure
  - Conditioned suppression

### Anticipation

Mentalistic terms such as *anticipation* and *expectancy* (Tolman, 1932) have been used to describe classical conditioning almost from the beginning and continue to be controversial (Kirsch, Lynn, Vigorito, & Miller, 2004). Many teachers of learning courses wish to discourage students from **anthropomorphizing** (i.e., attributing human thought processes to other animals). People often describe their pets' behaviors as reflecting thoughts and feelings (e.g., Fido *expects* me to feed him when he *feels* hungry). Although in the technical psychology literature, terms such as *anticipation*, *expectancy*, and *hunger* are operationally defined by the procedures used to measure them, one must be careful in their usage in other contexts. In this text, mentalistic terms (often placed in italics) are sometimes used to help clarify the material. The focus of this text is the application of adaptive learning principles to understanding the human condition, thus anthropomorphizing is less of an issue. Still, it is important to remember that even with humans, terms such as *anticipate*, *expect*, or *hunger* are inferences based upon behavioral observations. That is, people as well as other animals often act as though they think and feel.

Eyelid conditioning is a commonly used classical conditioning procedure with human subjects. As shown in Figure 3.2, electrodes are attached to the eyelid permitting precise graphing of movement.

**Anthropomorphizing**

Attributing human thought processes to other animals.

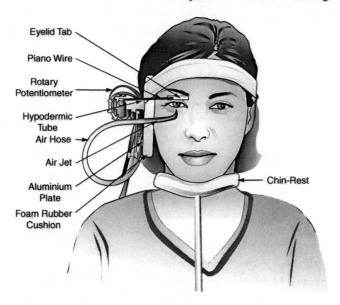

**FIGURE 3.2**    Human eyelid conditioning apparatus.

An early procedure used to demonstrate eyelid conditioning is known as the **anticipation method**. Figure 3.3 includes time lines for portraying the relationship between stimulus events and responding. Onset of a stimulus (i.e., the light or air puff) is indicated by a line going down, whereas onset of the response (eyeblink) is indicated by the line going up. Panel 1 shows a slight orienting response after the light goes on followed by a reflexive eyeblink (i.e., UR). In panel 2, we see a blink initiated prior to presentation of the US, apparently in anticipation, providing the rationale for the name of the procedure. In the final two panels, we observe the formation of one integrated response in which it is not possible to determine where the CR ends and the UR begins.

**Anticipation Method**

A procedure demonstrating classical conditioning by presenting a CS and observing whether the CR occurs prior to presentation of the US.

## Blank Trials

A blank trial presents the CS without the US. The rationale for the **blank trial procedure** is that if a response occurs in the absence of the US, it cannot be a UR and must be a CR. The most popular measure of acquisition of the response is the percentage of trials on which it occurs. However, it is also possible to measure the magnitude of the CR (e.g., amount of salivation) or, as with the anticipation procedure, the amount of time between presentation of a CS and occurrence of a CR.

**Blank Trials Procedure**

A procedure demonstrating classical conditioning by the CR occurring on test trials on which the CS is presented without the US.

## Sign Tracking

Instrumental conditioning (control learning) is often studied with animals making very simple responses. For example, a rat may be taught to press a bar or a pigeon may be taught to press a key. Rather than waiting for a response to occur at random, a procedure called *shaping* is often employed to speed things up. For example, a rat is first given

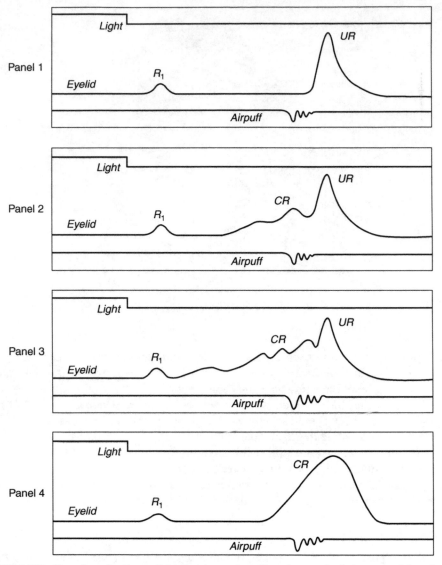

**FIGURE 3.3**  Time lines for the anticipation procedure. Data from a single human subject showing development of a conditioned eyelid response.   (Adapted from Hilgard & Marquis, 1940)

**Autoshaping
(Sign Tracking)**

Animals will track stimuli
that have been paired with
appetitive substances. For
examples, pigeons will peck
a key that has been followed
in time by food.

food for moving toward the bar and then for getting closer, centering the bar in front of it, lifting its paw, and so on. A similar procedure was traditionally used with teaching a pigeon to peck a key. Then, in 1968, Brown and Jenkins observed that if the key was lit and followed by presentation of food, the pigeon would peck the key as though it were food. This procedure became known as **autoshaping**. When it was demonstrated with other species and responses, the more generic term **sign tracking** came into use. In nature, many species are especially sensitive to stimuli (signs) associated with food. It is not uncommon for them to seek out and manipulate such stimuli. Sign tracking is now considered an example of classical conditioning and has resulted in recognition of increased generality of the process.

Moving toward the key and pecking it are not inherited (i.e., reflexive) behaviors. For many years, in large part because of the influence of Pavlov, classical conditioning had been thought to be restricted to reflexive behaviors.

This concludes our discussion of the direct procedures used to demonstrate classical conditioning. They are considered direct because each of them measures some aspect of the conditioned response. In the case of the anticipation method, its latency—that is, the amount of time from the onset of the CS—is observed. The response is considered an anticipatory CR when it occurs prior to presentation of the US. In the blank trials procedure, one usually calculates the percentage of blank trials on which a response occurs as a measure of the strength of conditioning (learning). One can also measure the magnitude of the response, as Pavlov did when he assessed the quantity of saliva on each trial. The sign-tracking procedure infers learning from the fact that a response occurs to an arbitrary stimulus (e.g., a lit key).

**Conditioned Suppression**
This procedure determines the strength of a conditioned stimulus predictive of shock from the extent to which the stimulus disrupts ongoing instrumental behavior.

> ▪ Describe the rationale for the anticipation, blank trials, and sign-tracking procedures used to directly demonstrate and measure classical conditioning.

## Conditioned Suppression

When animals sense danger, they usually become distracted from what they are doing and may freeze. This fact underlies the indirect **conditioned suppression procedure**, also known as the **conditioned emotional response, or CER, procedure** (Estes, 1944; Estes & Skinner, 1941). This procedure determines the strength of a conditioned stimulus predictive of shock from the extent to which the stimulus disrupts ongoing instrumental behavior. For example, refer to Figure 3.4. The CS and US time lines go up when turned on and down when turned off.

**Suppression (CER) Ratio**
An indirect procedure used to measure the strength of classical conditioning. The formula for suppression (CER) ratios divides the number of responses occurring when a CS is present by the number of responses occurring when it is present and absent.

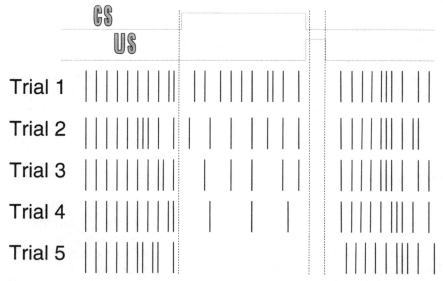

**FIGURE 3.4**  Conditioned suppression of operant responding. The vertical tick marks indicate individual bar presses.

Here we see a CS (e.g., a tone) turned on after a period of time (e.g., 1 minute) for an additional minute followed by a US (shock) for 10 seconds. Following the shock is another 1-minute interval without a tone or shock. The animal has previously been taught to press a bar for food. Each bar press is represented by a vertical tick mark in the diagram. For simplicity's sake, there are always 10 tick marks in the minutes before and after the tone/shock pairing. As we proceed from trial 1 to trial 5, we see a reduction in the number of responses occurring during the time the tone is on. Because the animal cannot predict that the tone will be followed by shock on the first trial, the number of responses remains the same at 10. However, we see reductions to 7, 5, 3, and 0 on trials 2 through 5.

The strength of the suppressive effect of the tone may be computed as a ratio of the number of responses occurring when the tone is present divided by itself plus the number of responses occurring when it is absent. This may be expressed as the following formula:

$$\text{Ratio} = \frac{\text{responses during CS interval}}{\text{responses during pre-CS interval} + \text{responses during CS interval}}$$

When we plug the numbers from our example into the equation, we obtain **suppression ratios** of .5 (10 divided by 10 + 10), .41 (7 divided by 10 + 7), .33 (5 divided by 10 + 5), .23 (3 divided by 10 + 3), and 0 (0 divided by 10 + 0). Suppression ratios range in value from .5, indicating no suppression at all, to 0, indicating total suppression. That is, on trial 1, the animal continued pressing the bar for food at the same rate during the tone, whereas on trial 5, the animal did not press the bar at all when the tone was on.

> ▪ Describe how the conditioned emotional response procedure is used to indirectly demonstrate and measure classical conditioning.

This ends our discussion of the methods used to measure predictive learning. We have seen how, consistent with the operational definition of learning, it is possible to create experimental conditions enabling the inference of a change in behavior resulting from experience. We will now review how these methods have enabled the demonstration of several basic predictive learning phenomena. This will lay the groundwork for consideration of how different variables influence classical conditioning, theoretical issues, and applications of predictive learning in the following two chapters.

## BASIC PREDICTIVE LEARNING PHENOMENA

In Chapter 1, we discussed the assumption of determinism as it applied to the discipline of psychology. If predictive learning is a lawful process, controlled empirical investigation has the potential to establish reliable cause–effect relationships. We will see that this is the case as we review several basic classical conditioning phenomena. Many of these phenomena were discovered and named by Pavlov himself, starting with the acquisition process.

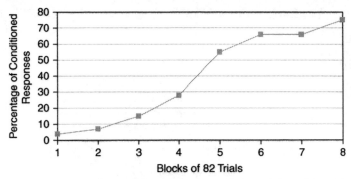

**FIGURE 3.5**   Acquisition curve for eyelid conditioning.   (Adapted from Schneiderman, Fuentes, & Gormezano, 1962)

## Acquisition

**Acquisition** refers to a procedure or process whereby one stimulus is presented in a predictive relationship with another stimulus. Predictive learning (classical conditioning) is inferred from the occurrence of a new response to the first stimulus. Keeping in mind that mentalistic terms are inferences based upon behavioral observations, it is as though the individual learns to predict *if this happens, then that happens.*

In Figure 3.5, we see a predictive acquisition **learning curve** for eyelid conditioning in rabbits. A blank trials procedure revealed slow, relatively steady increases in responding taking place over 650 trials.

## Extinction

**Extinction** refers to a procedure or process whereby a previously established predictive stimulus is no longer followed by the second stimulus. This typically results in a weakening in the strength of the prior learned response. It is as though the individual learns that *what used to happen doesn't happen anymore.* Extinction is commonly misused as a term describing only the result of the procedure or process. That is, it is often used like the term *schizophrenia*, which is defined exclusively on the dependent variable (symptom) side. Extinction is actually more like influenza, in that it is a true explanation standing for the relationship between a specific independent variable (the procedure) and the dependent variable (the change in behavior).

In Figure 3.6, we see an extinction curve for the salivation response obtained by Pavlov (1927). The amount of saliva decreased from 1 cubic centimeter to nothing over the course of only eight presentations of a tone without food.

## Spontaneous Recovery

**Spontaneous recovery** refers to an increase in the strength of the prior learned response after an extended time period between extinction trials. The individual acts as though *perhaps what used to happen still does.*

Figure 3.7 portrays Pavlov's demonstration of the phenomenon of spontaneous recovery. Note that the time between trials was 3 minutes until the last trial

**Acquisition (of a Conditioned Response)**

A procedure or process whereby one stimulus (the CS) is presented in a predictive relationship with another stimulus (the US). Eventually the subject will acquire a response (CR) to the CS in anticipation of the US.

**Learning Curve**

A graph showing a change in performance as the result of experience plotted on the *y*-axis and time or trials plotted on the *x*-axis.

**Extinction**

A procedure in which a previously established predictive stimulus (CS) is no longer followed by the second stimulus (US). This usually results in a reduction in strength of the CR.

**Spontaneous Recovery**

An increase in the strength of a prior learned response after an extended time period lapses between extinction trials.

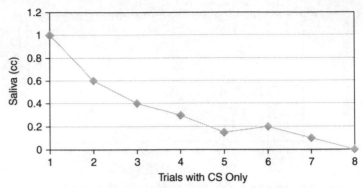

**FIGURE 3.6**   Extinction of a conditioned response.   (Adapted from Pavlov, 1927)

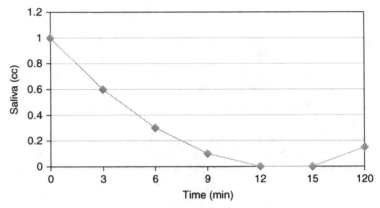

**FIGURE 3.7**   Spontaneous recovery of an extinguished response.   (Adapted from Pavlov, 1927)

that occurred 1 hour and 45 minutes later. Although no salivation was evident on the prior two trials, the dog salivated after the extended delay (i.e., the response seemed to spontaneously recover).

**External Inhibition**

If during acquisition, a novel stimulus is presented simultaneously with the CS on an individual trial, a decrease in the strength of the CR occurs on that trial.

**Disinhibition**

If during extinction, a novel stimulus is presented simultaneously with a previously established CS, the likelihood of the CR is increased on that trial.

## External Inhibition and Disinhibition

**External inhibition** refers to a phenomenon that can occur on an individual trial during acquisition. If on that trial, a novel stimulus is presented simultaneously with the conditioned stimulus, there is a decrease in the strength of the conditioned response. For example, if a tone is repeatedly paired with food, the amount of salivation to the tone will increase over trials. If on an individual trial, a tone and light were presented simultaneously, less salivation would occur on that trial. It appears to be an instance of distraction during acquisition with the individual regressing to an earlier stage of the process. **Disinhibition** is similar but occurs only during extinction. Here, a novel stimulus presented simultaneously with the previously established conditioned stimulus results in an increased likelihood of the learned response on an individual trial. For example, if the tone was no longer repeatedly followed by the food and on an individual trial, the tone and light were presented simultaneously, more salivation would occur on that trial. Regressing in this instance brings the animal back to an earlier stage of extinction when the conditioned response was stronger.

## Renewal

If extinction is conducted in one environment, it will not necessarily carry over to another environment. Mark Bouton (Bouton, 1984, 2004; Bouton & King, 1983) named this phenomenon the **renewal effect** and studied it extensively. In one study (see Figure 3.8), three groups of rats underwent a fear conditioning procedure in which a CS was followed by shock in a Skinner box (context A). Suppression ratios indicated the extent to which bar pressing for food was decreased when the CS was presented. One group underwent extinction in the same Skinner box, a second group underwent extinction in a different Skinner box (context B), and a third group did not initially undergo extinction. A subsequent extinction test phase was conducted in context A for all three groups.

> **Renewal Effect**
>
> The finding that a behavior extinguished in one context is likely to occur if the CS is presented in a different context.

As shown in the extinction phase in Figure 3.8, the course of extinction was not affected when it was conducted in a different Skinner box. The results for the context A and context B conditions were almost identical (i.e., the two lines practically overlapped). Remember, suppression ratios vary between 0 and .5 with lower values indicating greater suppression (i.e., stronger conditioning). Therefore, the suppression ratio values increase from near 0 to close to .5 as the extinction session progresses (i.e., the rate of bar pressing that had been totally suppressed in the presence of the CS increases throughout the extinction session). All three conditions underwent a test phase in which additional extinction trials were conducted in the original Skinner box (context A). As one would expect, the third group that did not undergo prior extinction trials gradually demonstrated less suppression. Its results were similar to those of the other two groups at the beginning of their extinction sessions. Despite the fact that the earlier extinction patterns for the two groups undergoing extinction in different apparatuses were almost identical, they were very different in the test phase. The group continuing in context A remained on track to .5 (decreasing suppression). The group switched back from context B to context A reverted to responding as it had prior

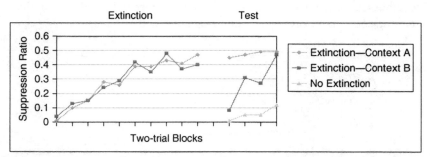

**FIGURE 3.8**  The renewal effect. After bar pressing was suppressed, one group underwent extinction in the same Skinner box (Extinction—Context A), and another group underwent extinction in a different Skinner box (Extinction—Context B). Extinction curves for both groups were similar. However, when subsequent extinction trials were conducted in context A, the second group demonstrated renewal, reverting to responding.   (Adapted from Bouten & King, 1983)

**Stimulus Generalization**

When a previously acquired learned response occurs in the presence of stimuli other than the original one, the likelihood being a function of the degree of similarity. For example, if food has been paired with a 1000 Hz tone, salivation will occur most to 1000 Hz, less to 900 Hz and 1100 Hz, and so on.

**Stimulus Discrimination**

Occurs during acquisition when one stimulus (the CS+, e.g., a light) is predictive of a second stimulus (US, e.g., food), but a different stimulus (CS–, e.g., a tone) is never followed by the US. A CR (e.g., salivation) will occur to the CS+ (light) and not to the CS– (tone).

**Higher-Order Conditioning**

A procedure or process whereby a previously neutral stimulus (CS 2, e.g., a light) is presented in a predictive relationship with a second, previously established CS 1 (e.g., a tone that had already been paired with a US of shock). This usually results in a CR occurring to CS 2 (the light) despite never having been paired with the shock.

to extinction (i.e., demonstrated renewal). You may wish to consider the important practical (e.g., treatment) implications of the renewal effect as well as other extinction-related phenomena discussed. The nature of the extinction process will be considered in the Theoretical Issues section in the following chapter.

## Stimulus Generalization and Discrimination

Just imagine if you had to learn to make the same response over and over again to each new situation. Fortunately, this is often not necessary. **Stimulus generalization** refers to the fact that a previously acquired response will occur in the presence of stimuli other than the original one, the likelihood being a function of the degree of similarity. In Figure 3.9, we see that a response learned to a 1200 Hz frequency tone occurs to other stimuli, the percentage of times depending upon the frequency of sound. It is as though the individual predicts *what happens after one event will happen after similar events.*

The fact that generalization occurs significantly increases the efficiency of individual learning experiences. However, there are usually limits on the appropriateness of making the same response in different situations. For example, new fathers often beam the first time they hear their infant say "dada." They are less thrilled when they hear their child call the mailman "dada!" It is usually necessary to conduct additional teaching so that the child says "dada" only in the presence of the father. **Stimulus discrimination** occurs when one stimulus (the S+, e.g., a tone or the father) is predictive of a second stimulus (e.g., food or the word *dada*), but a different stimulus (the S–, e.g., a light or the mailman) is never followed by that second stimulus. The individual eventually responds to the S+ (tone or father) and not to the S– (light or mailman) as though learning *if this happens then that happens, but if this other thing happens then that does not happen.*

## Higher-Order Conditioning and Sensory Preconditioning

**Higher-order conditioning** is a procedure or process whereby a previously neutral stimulus is presented in a predictive relationship with a second, previously established, predictive stimulus. Learning is inferred from the occurrence of a new response in the presence of this previously neutral stimulus.

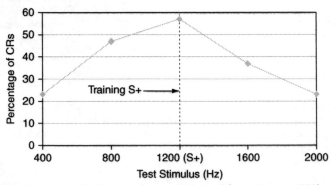

**FIGURE 3.9**   Stimulus generalization gradient.   (Adapted from Moore, 1972)

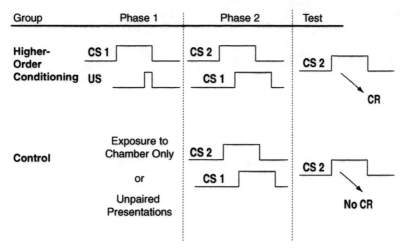

**FIGURE 3.10**  Higher-order conditioning.

Figure 3.10 diagrams a two-group design used to demonstrate higher-order conditioning. During phase 1, one group undergoes acquisition in which a stimulus (CS 1, e.g., a light) is presented in a predictive relationship with a US (e.g., shock). A control condition does not receive predictive training. This group either is exposed to the conditioning apparatus or receives unpaired presentations of CS 1 and the US (light and shock). In phase 2, a second stimulus (CS 2, e.g., a tone) precedes the original CS 1 (light), becoming a higher-order predictive stimulus for the first group (predicting the CS 1 that predicted the US). The control condition receives the pairing of the same two stimuli (tone followed by light). Learning is inferred if CS 2 (the tone) elicits a CR in the first group but not the second group. It is important to note that this occurs even though CS 2 (the tone) is never directly paired with the US (shock).

In Chapter 5, we will see that classical conditioning procedures may be used to establish word meaning (cf, Staats & Staats, 1957; Staats, Staats, & Heard, 1961). In Chapter 7, we will review the problems inherent in the use of punishment to influence human behavior. Higher-order conditioning can be used to establish language as the means of discouraging undesirable acts. Let us say a parent says "No!" before slapping a child on the wrist as the child starts to stick a finger in an electric outlet. The slap should cause the child to withdraw her/his hand. On a later occasion, the parent says "Hot, no!" as the child reaches for a pot on the stove. The initial pairing with a slap on the wrist would result in the word *no* being sufficient to cause the child to withdraw her/his hand before touching the stove. Saying "Hot, no!" could transfer the withdrawal response to the word *hot*. Here we see the power of classical conditioning principles in helping us understand language acquisition, including the use of words to establish meaning. We also see the power of language as a means of protecting a child from the "school of hard knocks" (and shocks, and burns, etc.!). We elaborate on the role of classical conditioning in language acquisition and other applications in Chapter 5.

**Sensory preconditioning** is similar to higher-order conditioning except the phases are reversed (see Figure 3.11). For clarity's sake, the notation and sequence from the higher-order conditioning example (CS 1 being a light and CS 2

**Sensory Preconditioning**

A procedure or process whereby one neutral stimulus (CS 2, e.g., a light) is presented in a predictive relationship with a second neutral stimulus (CS 1, e.g., a tone). When CS 1 is followed by a US (e.g., shock), this usually results in CRs to CS 2 as well as CS 1 even though CS 2 was never followed by shock.

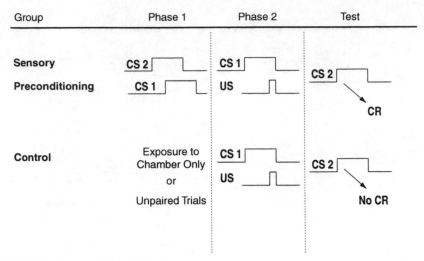

**FIGURE 3.11** Sensory preconditioning.

being a tone with the tone preceding the light) are repeated. In this case, one neutral stimulus is presented in a predictive relationship with a second neutral stimulus in the first phase. The second neutral stimulus (light) is then established as a CS by pairing it with a US (shock). Learning is inferred to the first neutral stimulus (tone) if it elicits a CR when tested.

Carrying over the previous applied example to sensory preconditioning would first involve pairing the words *hot* (CS 2 in the diagram) and *no* (CS 1) before *no* is later followed by a slap (US) on the wrist in phase 2. One might not expect this procedure to be effective, because the words *no* and *hot* have no significance in the first phase. In higher-order conditioning, the word *no* was paired with the slap in phase 1 before being used in the place of the US in phase 2. This possibility is very similar to the one tested in Tolman and Honzik's (1930) previously described latent learning study. You may recall the findings of that study indicated that maze learning (an example of control learning) was taking place despite the fact that rats were not receiving food at the end of the maze. Learning was demonstrated, however, only when food was provided as an incentive for performance. Similarly, it is necessary to pair the word *no* with a slap in the second phase of the sensory preconditioning procedure so that the person will make an obvious response (withdrawal) upon testing with the word *hot*. An important implication of these findings is that adaptive learning (either predictive or control) can and does occur in the absence of a biologically significant stimulus. Stimuli such as food and shock are required procedurally in order to produce responses from which it may be inferred that learning has taken place.

---

■ Define and give examples of the following classical conditioning phenomena: acquisition, extinction, spontaneous recovery, external inhibition, disinhibition, renewal, stimulus generalization, discrimination, higher-order conditioning, and sensory preconditioning.

## Excitatory and Inhibitory Learning

Pavlov made a distinction between **excitatory learning** and **inhibitory learning**. He believed that it was not only important to predict when one event would be followed by another, but also when one event would not be followed by another. For example, it is adaptive not only to know that lightning is followed by thunder, but also that thunder is unlikely when the sky is blue. This may be studied in the laboratory by using a discrimination training procedure (see Figure 3.12). The subjects experience two types of trials presented randomly. One stimulus (CS 1, e.g., a light) is followed by a US (shock), whereas a second stimulus (CS 2, e.g., a tone) is not. With this procedure, the light would become excitatory, predicting the occurrence of the shock. The tone would become inhibitory, predicting the absence of the shock.

It is possible to establish one component of a **compound stimulus** as excitatory and a second component as inhibitory (see Figure 3.13). Again, subjects receive two types of trials randomly. When CS 1 (the light) is presented alone, it is followed by the US, whereas when it is presented in compound (i.e., simultaneously) with CS 2 (the tone), it is not followed by shock. This procedure would also result in the light becoming excitatory (i.e., predictive of the occurrence of the shock) and the tone becoming inhibitory (i.e., predictive of the US not occurring).

Demonstrating inhibitory learning often poses methodological problems in comparison to demonstrating excitatory learning. If an animal expects an event to occur, it typically responds in a predictable manner (e.g., salivating in anticipation of food). However, animals do not necessarily respond at all if not anticipating anything to happen. A very powerful law of nature, the law of least effort, often applies.

**THE SUMMATION PROCEDURE**   Another example of Pavlov's ingenuity as a scientist is his development of the summation procedure, also known as the **compound stimulus procedure**, for the indirect demonstration of inhibitory learning (see Figure 3.15). A presumed inhibitory stimulus is presented in compound (i.e., simultaneously) with a known excitatory stimulus. If on test trials, the strength of the response is lower to this compound than to the excitatory stimulus alone, it may be concluded that the presumed stimulus is indeed inhibitory. Essentially, Pavlov established a "mixed signal," with one element of the compound predictive

### Excitatory Learning

Learning that one event will be followed by another. For example, lightning is followed by thunder.

### Inhibitory Learning

Learning that one event will not be followed by another. For example, sunshine is not followed by thunder.

### Compound Stimulus

Two or more stimuli overlapping in time (e.g., a light and tone going on and off together).

### Summation (Compound Stimulus) Procedure

A procedure used to measure inhibitory learning by demonstrating that responding to a compound stimulus including a presumed inhibitory element is different from responding to the other element by itself. For example, if a light is presumed to be inhibitory, it could be combined with a tone that had previously been paired with shock. If the conditioned response to the light/tone compound was less than to the tone alone, one could conclude the light is inhibitory.

**FIGURE 3.12**  Discrimination training with single element stimuli.

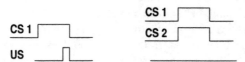

**FIGURE 3.13**  Discrimination training with single element and compound stimuli.

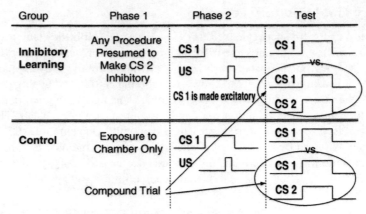

**FIGURE 3.14** The summation test for inhibitory learning.

of the occurrence of an event and the other element predictive of its absence. If animals behaved differently to the mixed signal, the inference was made that the second component was meaningful.

Research conducted by Reberg and Black (1969) represents an excellent example of the summation procedure. In the first phase, an inhibitory group is provided discrimination training in which on random trials a tone is paired with shock or a light is presented by itself. The control group receives the tone followed by shock but does not experience the light. If the light became inhibitory for the first group, less suppression should have occurred to the compound stimulus during the test trials than to the excitatory stimulus; this should not have been the case for the control group. This combination of results occurred, thereby demonstrating inhibitory learning.

> **Retardation-of-Acquisition Procedure**
>
> A procedure used to measure inhibitory learning by demonstrating that the acquisition process is slowed down for a potential CS.

**THE RETARDATION-OF-ACQUISITION PROCEDURE**    A second indirect procedure for demonstrating inhibitory learning is referred to as the **retardation-of-acquisition procedure**. After a procedure is implemented to make a stimulus inhibitory, excitatory conditioning is conducted with the same stimulus. If the acquisition process is slower (i.e., retarded) for this group in comparison to a control condition, the inference is that the stimulus had indeed been made inhibitory (see Figure 3.15).

## Latent Extinction

> **Latent Extinction (CS Pre-Exposure)**
>
> A phenomenon whereby prior exposure to a neutral stimulus slows down the process of the stimulus becoming a CS when followed by a US.

Lubow (1965) used the retardation procedure to demonstrate the phenomenon of **latent extinction**, also known as the **CS pre-exposure effect**. Three groups of sheep received either no, 10, or 20 exposures to a light before it was paired with shock over 4 days. As shown in Figure 3.16, the pace of acquisition was slowed (i.e., retarded) as a direct function of the number of prior exposures to the light without shock. It was possible for Tolman and Honzik (1930) to infer that rats learned the maze in the absence of food by introducing food at a later time and demonstrating a sudden change in behavior. In the same way, Lubow was able to conclude that the sheep learned that the light was not predictive by later making it predictive and demonstrating that this took more time, thus the term *latent extinction*.

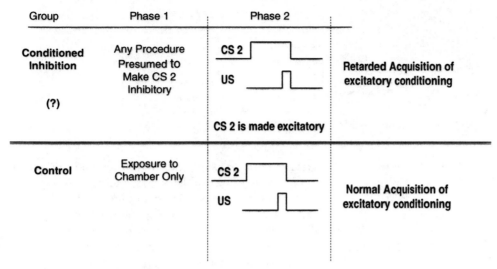

FIGURE 3.15   The retardation test for inhibitory learning.

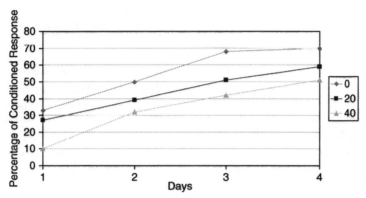

FIGURE 3.16   Use of the retardation test to demonstrate latent extinction.
(Adapted from Lubow, 1965)

> ■ Distinguish between excitatory and inhibitory learning. Describe direct
> and indirect methods for demonstrating inhibitory learning.

## Occasion Setting

A stimulus may be excitatory or inhibitory only under a restricted range of conditions. B. F. Skinner (1938), one of the major figures in the study of control learning, introduced the term **occasion setter** to refer to a stimulus that signals whether
a specific behavior will be followed by a particular consequence. The term has
more recently been applied in predictive learning to stimuli that provide information about the situations in which another stimulus is excitatory or inhibitory.
A **positive occasion setter** is a stimulus that signals that another stimulus is

**Occasion Setter**

A stimulus signaling
whether a CS is predictive.

**Positive Occasion Setter**

A signal that a stimulus is
excitatory (i.e., predicts the
occurrence of an event). For
example, a hotdog signals that
mustard will taste good.

**PREDICTIVE LEARNING**

|  | Occurrence | Nonoccurrence |
|---|---|---|
| Appetitive | Excitatory Appetitive | Inhibitory Appetitive |
| Aversive | Excitatory Aversive | Inhibitory Aversive |

**FIGURE 3.17**    Predictive learning relationships.

**Negative Occasion Setter**

A signal that a stimulus is inhibitory (i.e., predicts the absence of an event). For example, a leash indicates that a large dog will not jump on you.

excitatory (Ross & Holland, 1981). For example, how you respond to mustard might depend on whether it is on top of a hot dog or a hamburger. A **negative occasion setter** signals that another stimulus is inhibitory (Holland, 1984). For example, how you respond to a large dog might depend on whether or not it is on a leash. In Chapter 10, we return to the issue of how occasion setters (there described as discriminative stimuli and warning stimuli) relate to such important concerns as human personality, socialization, and culture.

*Food good...Fire bad!*

**The monster, *Bride of Frankenstein***

**Appetitive Event**

A stimulus that an individual approaches (e.g., food when hungry, water when thirsty).

**Aversive Event**

A stimulus that an individual avoids (e.g., electric shock, extreme heat or cold).

We can now provide an overview of predictive learning, distinguishing between appetitive events and aversive events. **Appetitive events** are those we seek out (e.g., food when hungry, water when thirsty) and **aversive events** are those we wish to avoid (e.g., electric shock, extreme heat or cold). Combining this distinction with that between excitatory and inhibitory learning results in four possibilities: predict occurrence of appetitive event, predict nonoccurrence of appetitive event, predict occurrence of aversive event, and predict nonoccurrence of aversive event (see Figure 3.17).

## Summary

Ivan Pavlov developed classical conditioning procedures to study animals when an event could be predicted but not controlled. We reviewed the historic and contemporary procedures used to measure classical conditioning along with the following basic phenomena: acquisition, extinction, spontaneous recovery, external inhibition, disinhibition, renewal, stimulus generalization, and discrimination. The phenomena of higher-order conditioning and sensory preconditioning demonstrate that acquisition of a conditioned response does not require pairing a stimulus with another biologically significant stimulus. Pavlov demonstrated that animals not only could learn that one event would be followed by another (i.e., excitatory learning), but also that one event would not be followed by another (i.e., inhibitory learning). Therefore, classical conditioning is a far more pervasive process than Pavlov's original procedures might suggest. Classical conditioning may be described as a process through which individuals acquire the ability to predict the occurrence and nonoccurrence of appetitive and aversive events in their environment.

# References

Bouton, M. E. (1984). Differential control by context in the inflation and reinstatement paradigms. *Journal of Experimental Psychology: Animal Behavior Processes, 10*, 56–74.

Bouton, M. E. (2004). Context and behavioral processes in extinction. *Learning and Memory, 11*, 485–494.

Bouton, M. E., & King, D. A. (1983). Contextual control of the extinction of conditioned fear: Tests for the associative value of the context. *Journal of Experimental Psychology: Animal Behavior Processes, 9*, 248–265.

Estes, W. K. (1944). An experimental study of punishment. *Physiological Monographs, 57* (3, Whole No. 263).

Estes, W. K., & Skinner, B. F. (1941). Some quantitative properties of anxiety. *Journal of Experimental Psychology, 29*, 390–400.

Hilgard, E. R., & Marquis, D. G. (1940). *Conditioning and learning.* New York: Appleton-Century-Crofts.

Holland, P. C. (1984). Differential effects of reinforcement of an inhibitory feature after serial and simultaneous feature negative discrimination training. *Journal of Experimental Psychology: Animal Behavior Processes, 10*, 461–475.

Kimble, G. A. (1961). *Hilgard and Marquis' conditioning and learning* (2nd ed.). New York: Appleton-Century-Crofts.

Kirsch, I., Lynn, S. J., Vigorito, M., & Miller, R. R. (2004). The role of cognition in classical and operant conditioning. *Journal of Clinical Psychology, 60*, 369–392.

Lubow, R. E. (1965). Latent inhibition. *Journal of Comparative and Physiological Psychology, 60*, 454–457.

Moore, J. W. (1972). Stimulus control: Studies of auditory generalization in rabbits. In A. H. Black & W. F. Prokasy (Eds.), *Classical conditioning II: Current research and theory.* New York: Appleton-Century-Crofts

Pavlov, I. P. (1927). *Conditioned reflexes: An investigation of the physiological activity of the cerebral cortex.* Oxford, Eng.: Oxford University Press.

Reberg, D., & Black, A. H. (1969). Compound testing of individually conditioned stimuli as an index of excitatory and inhibitory properties. *Psychonomic Science, 17*, 30–31.

Schneiderman, N., Fuentes, I., & Gormezano, I. (1962). Acquisition and extinction of the classically conditioned eyelid response in the albino rabbit. *Science, 136*, 650–652.

Skinner, B. F. (1938). *The behavior of organisms.* Englewood Cliffs, NJ: Prentice Hall.

Staats, A. W., Staats, C. K., & Heard, W. G. (1961). Denotative meaning established by classical conditioning. *Journal of Experimental Psychology, 61*, 300–303.

Staats, C. K., & Staats, A. W. (1957). Meaning established by classical conditioning. *Journal of Experimental Psychology, 54*, 74–80.

Tolman, E. C. (1932). *Purposive behavior in animals and men.* New York: Appleton-Century.

## Chapter 4

# Predictive Learning: Basic Variables and Theoretical Issues

I n Chapter 3, we reviewed methods used to study predictive learning as well as several basic phenomena. In this chapter, we review research findings regarding different variables that influence the predictive learning process as well as theoretical issues regarding the nature of classical conditioning and the extinction process. In the next chapter, we will consider applications of predictive learning principles to the human condition.

## VARIABLES INFLUENCING PREDICTIVE LEARNING

The major variables influencing the strength of predictive learning include the following:

- Sequencing of events
- Timing of events
- Intensity of events
- Scheduling of events

## Sequencing of Events

The conventional classical conditioning terminology for different sequences of events is as follows:

- Delay conditioning (standard pairing)
- Trace conditioning
- Simultaneous conditioning
- Backward conditioning
- Temporal conditioning
- Long-delay conditioning

Figure 4.1 portrays time lines for these different sequences.

Predictive learning can occur only if one event precedes another. **Delay conditioning** occurs when a neutral stimulus (eventually a conditioned stimulus, CS) precedes and stays on until an unconditioned stimulus (US) is presented. This is the most effective procedure for predictive learning. For example, Pavlov could have kept the tone on until the food was presented.

**Trace conditioning** is similar to delay conditioning except that the CS comes on and goes off a consistent amount of time prior to the introduction of the US. In this instance, Pavlov could have turned the tone on and off before presenting the food. In both procedures, the time between onset of the CS and US is referred to as the **interstimulus interval (ISI)**. The **trace interval** refers to the time gap between offset of the CS and onset of the US in trace conditioning. Trace conditioning can be an effective procedure. However, the length of the trace interval negatively impacts predictive learning (Smith, Coleman, & Gormezano, 1969).

**Simultaneous conditioning** is a special example of what we referred to previously as a compound stimulus. The two events come on and go off at the same time.

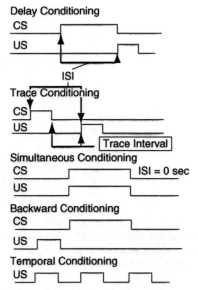

**FIGURE 4.1**  Time lines for different sequences of CS and US.

---

**Delay Conditioning**

A classical conditioning procedure in which a novel stimulus (eventually a CS) precedes and stays on until an unconditioned stimulus (US) is presented.

**Trace Conditioning**

A procedure similar to delay conditioning except that the CS comes on and goes off a consistent amount of time prior to the onset of the US. For example, a tone comes on for 5 seconds and goes off followed by food 10 seconds later. The gap between the offset of the tone and onset of the food is the trace interval.

**Inter Stimulus Interval (ISI)**

The time between the onset of the CS and onset of the US.

**Trace Interval**

Refers to the time gap between offset of the CS and onset of the US in trace conditioning.

**Simultaneous Conditioning**

A classical conditioning procedure in which a CS and a US overlap in time.

**Backward Conditioning**

A classical conditioning procedure in which the US precedes the CS.

**Temporal Conditioning**

A classical conditioning procedure in which there is no external novel stimulus (e.g., a light or a tone). Instead, the US comes on after passage of a constant amount of time (e.g., every minute).

**Long-Delay Conditioning**

A procedure combining the elements of delay and temporal conditioning in which the CS comes on and stays on for a constant extended period of time until the US occurs (e.g., a light comes on and stays on for 1 minute followed by food). Usually, with training the individual increasingly delays making a response (e.g., salivation) until the time is almost up.

That is, there is no interstimulus interval (ISI = 0). In this instance, predictive learning cannot occur.

In **backward conditioning**, the US precedes the CS. We will discuss backward conditioning under CS/US Correlation. For now, think of what the CS predicts in this sequence. Remember, it comes on after the US in this procedure. What do you think the individual learns?

**Temporal conditioning** involves no external novel stimulus (e.g., a light or a tone). Instead, the US comes on after passage of a constant amount of time (e.g., Pavlov could have presented food every minute). If you have ever had the opportunity to observe an infant adjusting to a feeding schedule, you are aware that humans appear to come into this world with a sense of time. The infant is very likely to let you know if feeding is delayed.

A procedure combining the elements of delay and temporal conditioning is called **long-delay conditioning**. As the name describes, the CS comes on and stays on for an extended period of time until the US occurs. Lynch (1973) used a 40-sec long-term delay conditioning procedure with dogs to demonstrate changes in the strength and timing of the CR with experience (see Figure 4.2). Shock was the US, and the dependent variable was the mean percentage of trials with a maximum leg flex (the CR). As we examine the results, we see two distinct changes occurring over the trial blocks. First, as expected, the percentage of CRs increased with trials. An interesting change in the timing of the responses also occurred. During the first trial block, if a response occurred, it was likely to be within the first 10-sec interval (designated "a" on the graph). As trials progressed, the pattern changed, with an increasing percentage of responses occurring during the last interval ("d"). The animals were clearly learning to predict, not only that they would be shocked, but the time shock would occur.

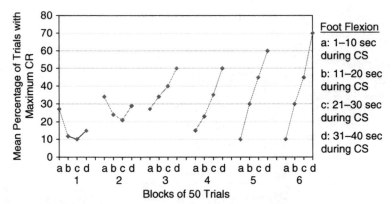

**FIGURE 4.2**   Long-delay conditioning. Mean percentage of maximum paw flexes occurring within the first 10 seconds (a), second 10 seconds (b), third 10 seconds (c), or fourth 10 seconds as a function of trial blocks. As acquisition progresses, the percentage of conditioned responses increases, and they become more likely to occur late in the interval.   (Adapted from Lynch, 1973)

## Timing of Events—The Law of Temporal Contiguity

Human beings have speculated about the learning process since at least the time of the early Greek philosophers. In the fourth century B.C., Aristotle proposed three laws of association that he believed applied to human thought and memory. The law of contiguity stated that objects or events occurring close in time (temporal contiguity) or space (spatial contiguity) become associated. The law of similarity stated that we tend to associate objects or events having features in common such that thinking of one would produce thought of another. The law of frequency stated that the more often we experience objects or events, the more likely we would be to remember them. In a sense, Pavlov created a methodology permitting empirical testing of Aristotle's laws. The law that applies in this section is the law of temporal contiguity. Indeed, we will see throughout this book how this principle consistently plays a significant role in adaptive learning.

**EYEBLINK AND HEART RATE CONDITIONING**    Timing effects, like many variables studied scientifically, lend themselves to parametric studies in which the independent variable consists of different values on a dimension. Figure 4.3 combines the results of several studies examining human eyelid conditioning as a function of the ISI. The optimal ISI is approximately ½ second (500 milliseconds). The percentages of CRs occurring at shorter or longer intervals drop off relatively quickly. Temporal contiguity appears critical in human eyelid conditioning with tenths of a second making a difference. Eyelid conditioning has been studied in several other species with similar results. For example, in a parametric study, the optimal ISI was determined to be ¼ sec in rabbits (cf., Schneiderman & Gormezano, 1964).

Some studies with other species and procedures have produced longer ISIs. For example, heart rate conditioning in dogs appears to work well with intervals between 5 and 10 seconds (Black, Carlson, & Solomon, 1962), and conditioned suppression in rats appears most effective with ISIs of 10 seconds (Yeo, 1974). The optimal ISI for heart rate conditioning in humans appears to be 13 seconds (Hastings & Obrist, 1967).

The overall evidence on optimal ISIs is consistent with Aristotle's assumption that temporal contiguity is necessary for learning associations between events. We will

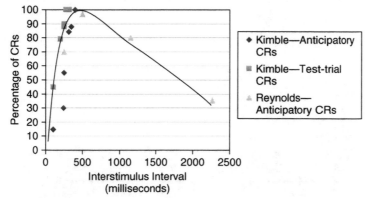

**FIGURE 4.3**    The optimal interstimulus interval in human eyelid conditioning.    (Adapted from Kimble & Reynolds, 1967)

see that this applies to instrumental conditioning (response-event) as well as classical conditioning (event-event) relations when we consider the role of timing in control learning in Chapter 7.

**Acquired Taste Aversion**

A classical conditioning procedure in which the CS is food and the US is a stimulus resulting in sickness.

**AN EXCEPTION—ACQUIRED TASTE AVERSION    Acquired taste aversion** is the only apparent exception to the necessity of temporal contiguity. This exception can be understood as an evolutionary adaptation to protect animals from food poisoning. Figure 4.4 shows the results of a study in which rats were randomly assigned to 16 groups (Smith & Roll, 1967). Half of the groups were exposed to X-rays producing gastrointestinal distress at 8 intervals from immediately to 24 hours after drinking sweetened water. The other groups received a "sham" procedure in which they were placed in the apparatus at the same intervals but not actually exposed to X-rays. These time intervals represent a different scale from the studies previously considered in which ISIs varied by, at most, seconds. All the rats were given a choice between dippers containing ordinary tap water or sweetened water. The results from the sham conditions indicated that these rats had a strong preference for the sweet water, drinking it approximately 80% of the time. Those exposed to X-rays had been drinking mostly sweet water prior to becoming sick up to 24 hours later. If a rat became sick within ½ hour of being exposed to X-rays, sweet-water drinking was totally eliminated. With intervals of 1 to 6 hours, it was reduced from 80% to 10%. Evidence of less drinking of sweet water was seen even after a 24-hour delay! There is no way one of Pavlov's dogs would associate a tone with presentation of food an hour later, let alone 24 hours. This is obviously either an exception to the law of temporal contiguity or contiguity on a time scale of different orders of magnitude (hours rather than seconds). It is as though animals inherit the tendency to conclude that *if they become sick to their stomachs, it must have been something they ate.*

J. Garcia, the researcher who first investigated acquired taste aversion (Garcia, Ervin, & Koelling, 1966), demonstrated the effect of the relationship between the type of predictive stimulus (CS) and the type of aversive event (US) on learning (Garcia & Koelling, 1966). As with Smith and Roll's experiment, rats had a choice between two water dippers. Two of the groups could choose ordinary tap water or sweet water. The other groups could choose ordinary tap water or water accompanied by lights and tones

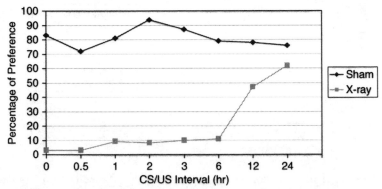

**FIGURE 4.4** Acquired taste aversion with different time intervals.   (Adapted from Smith & Roll, 1967)

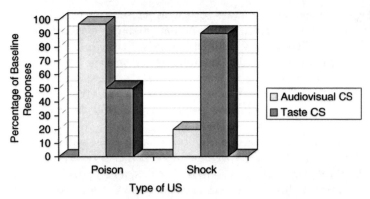

**FIGURE 4.5**   CS/US relevance test results. Poison as a US had practically no effect when it was paired with an audiovisual CS (i.e., there was little change in the level of baseline responding) but a substantial effect when paired with a taste CS. The reverse was true for the effect of shock as the US.   (Adapted from Garcia & Koelling, 1966)

("bright, noisy water"). One of each of these pairs of groups received a sickness-inducing drug and the other received a shock. The results indicated that the pairing made a difference (see Figure 4.5). The dependent variable was the percentage of baseline responding to the stimulus followed by the aversive event. For example, if a rat consumed 4 oz of sweet water during baseline and 2 oz when tested, that would be 50% of baseline responding. We see that rats poisoned after drinking sweet water reduced their consumption by 50%, whereas rats poisoned after drinking the bright, noisy water did not reduce their consumption at all. The opposite pattern was obtained with shock. Rats shocked after drinking sweet water reduced their consumption by only 10%, whereas as those shocked after drinking bright, noisy water reduced their consumption by 80%. This is an example of an interaction between independent variables, whereby the effect of one variable depends upon the level of the other. In this instance, the effect of getting sick or being shocked depended upon whether it was preceded by taste or audiovisual cues. Species-specific characteristics affect the acquisition of taste aversions. Rats associate sickness with taste but not with visual cues, whereas the opposite is true for quail (Wilcoxin, Dragoin, & Kral, 1971). People are similar to rats in this regard. Many of us have had the experience of feeling sick after a meal and finding it difficult to eat the same food, even when we know that the food had nothing to do with feeling sick (e.g., we had the flu). We do not associate feeling sick with the dinnerware, people we were eating with, and so on, only with the taste and smell of the food. If we touch a hot plate (or even hot food for that matter), it does not affect our food consumption, although we may reach carefully the next time we are served.

Summing up, the evidence considering the effect of timing of events on predictive learning indicates that temporal contiguity is necessary in practically all instances. The only known exception is the highly specialized and adaptive ability to acquire taste aversions.

## Intensity of Events

The intensity of events influences the likelihood of their being noticed and of a predictive relationship being learned. Traditionally, classical conditioning procedures have involved an arbitrary, relatively low-intensity stimulus, serving as the first event (CS) and a biologically significant stimulus serving as the second event (US). This tradition is probably responsible for the common misconception that classical conditioning must involve biologically significant stimuli and reflexive behaviors. We have already seen that the phenomena of higher-order conditioning and sensory preconditioning indicate that predictive relationships can be learned in the absence of biologically significant events. Predictive learning may occur whenever one event is reliably followed by another, regardless of their significance to the individual. Still, the intensity of the events does influence the ease of predictive learning.

**Salient**

A stimulus stands out from its background.

Predictive learning opportunities always occur within an environmental context. One is most likely to attend to events that are **salient** (i.e., that stand out from the background). Obviously, this is not an issue when a biologically significant stimulus is involved. However, an otherwise noticeable tone might not be noticed if a bright light is simultaneously flashing. The issue of salience applies to internal as well as external sources of stimulation. Thoughts and feelings are part of an individual's environment, although they are not observable to others. If one is "buried in thought" or extremely hungry, that same tone might also go unnoticed. **Overshadowing** refers to the instance when only an intense component of a compound stimulus gains one's attention. We will return to the issue of what determines the effective components of a stimulus complex in the next chapter.

**Overshadowing**

Only the more intense element of a compound CS is associated with the US and elicits a CR.

## Scheduling of Events

Figure 4.6 portrays the acquisition and extinction graphs for five groups in a human eyelid conditioning study. The groups differed in the percentage of acquisition trials on which the puff of air occurred during acquisition (the first 12 trial blocks prior to the vertical line). One group was presented a novel stimulus by itself (0%), and the others were presented with the novel stimulus followed by a puff of air to the eye on

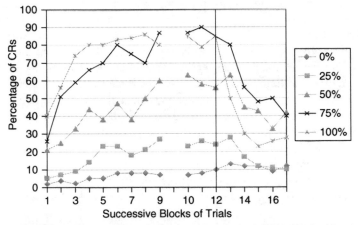

**FIGURE 4.6** The effect of percentage of CS/US pairing on acquisition and extinction. The pace and level of responding during acquisition increased directly as a function of the percentage of trials on which the CS and US were paired. The pace of the reduction in responding during extinction was most rapid after continuous pairing during acquisition. (Adapted from Grant & Schipper, 1952)

25%, 50%, 75%, or 100% of the trials. Not surprisingly, we see that the rate (indicated by the steepness of the line) and strength (indicated by the eventual peak) of conditioning varied directly as a function of the percentage of trials on which the stimuli were presented in a predictive relationship. Overall, the 25% group improved at a lower rate and reached a lower performance level than the 50% group, and so on. What might be surprising is the extinction pattern starting with trial 13. The 100% condition, which rose the fastest during acquisition, declined the fastest during extinction. Overall, the rates of decline during extinction were mirror images of the rate increases during acquisition. You might think about these findings and speculate as to why this occurs. In control learning, this same finding is called the partial reinforcement extinction effect (PREE). We will consider theoretical explanations of the PREE when we study control learning.

> ■ Describe how the following variables influence the classical conditioning (predictive learning) process: CS/US sequence, timing (CS/US interstimulus interval), CS and US intensity, and CS/US pairing schedule (effects on acquisition and extinction).

## THEORETICAL ISSUES

### Is Extinction Unlearning or Inhibitory Learning?

Pavlov was an excellent example of someone who today would be considered a **behavioral neuroscientist**. In fact, the full title of his classic book (1927) is *Conditioned Reflexes: An Investigation of the Physiological Activity of the Cerebral Cortex*. Behavioral neuroscientists study behavior in order to infer underlying brain mechanisms. Thus, Pavlov did not perceive himself as converting from a physiologist into a psychologist when he abandoned his study of digestion to explore the intricacies of classical conditioning. As implied by his "psychic secretion" metaphor, he believed he was continuing to study physiology, turning his attention from studying the digestive system to studying the brain.

**Behavioral Neuroscientist**
A scientist who makes inferences regarding neurological mechanisms based upon behavioral observations.

      One question of interest to Pavlov was the nature of the extinction process. Pavlov assumed that acquisition produced a connection between a sensory neuron representing the conditioned stimulus and a motor neuron eliciting salivation. The reduction in responding resulting from the extinction procedure could result from either breaking this bond (i.e., unlearning) or counteracting it with a competing inhibitory response (see Figure 4.7).

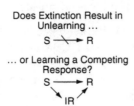

**FIGURE 4.7**  Possible mechanisms for the extinction process.

If you recall three basic classical conditioning phenomena from Chapter 3, you will be able to decide between these two possibilities. Spontaneous recovery refers to the likelihood of a conditioned response increasing during the extinction process if an extended time is permitted to lapse between trials (see Figure 3.9). This could not occur if extinction destroyed the connection between the CS and CR. One might argue that extinction results in a gradual destruction of the connection and that the time lapse permits sufficient "healing" to take place in order for the response to reappear. The phenomena of disinhibition and renewal contradict this interpretation. Disinhibition refers to an increased likelihood of a CR occurring during extinction when a novel stimulus is presented simultaneously with the CS. Presenting a novel stimulus could not physically "repair" a severed neural connection. Neither could changing the context from the one in which extinction was conducted (i.e., the renewal effect). This combination of results leads to the conclusion that extinction itself is a type of learning process. The individual gradually learns that one stimulus no longer predicts another, resulting in the acquisition of an inhibitory repose preventing the previously acquired response from occurring. The conclusion that extinction does not permanently eliminate a previously learned association has important practical and clinical implications. It means that someone who has received treatment for a problem and improved is not the same as a person who never required treatment in the first place (cf., Bouton, 2000; Bouton & Nelson, 1998). For example, someone who has quit smoking has a greater likelihood of relapsing than a nonsmoker has of acquiring the habit. We discuss experiences likely to result in relapse as well as relapse prevention strategies when we deal with control learning applications in Chapter 8.

> ■ Describe the basis for concluding that extinction is an inhibitory as opposed to an unlearning process.

**Stimulus Substitution Model**

Pavlov's model of classical conditioning describing the CS as becoming a substitute for the US.

## Pavlov's Stimulus Substitution Model

For most of the 20th century, Pavlov's originally proposed **stimulus substitution model** of classical conditioning was widely accepted. Pavlov viewed conditioning as a mechanistic (automatic) result of pairing neutral and biologically significant events in time. He believed that the established conditioned stimulus became a substitute for the original unconditioned stimulus. Three assumptions underlie this stimulus substitution model:

- Temporal contiguity between a neutral stimulus (NS) and a US is necessary for the NS to become a CS.
- Temporal contiguity between a NS and US is sufficient for the NS to become a CS.
- The CR will always resemble if not be identical to the unconditioned response (UR).

In Chapter 3, we reviewed the evidence for Pavlov's first assumption and determined that temporal contiguity was necessary for classical conditioning to occur. The only known exception is acquired taste aversion. Here, we examine more recently obtained evidence regarding the other two assumptions. This will lead to modifying our understanding of the classical conditioning process in a manner consistent with our definition of adaptive learning provided in Chapter 1. That is, it is a process through which an individual acquires the ability to predict environmental events.

**IS TEMPORAL CONTIGUITY SUFFICIENT?**

**CS/US Correlation**     Before we examine an important experiment that bears on this issue conducted by Robert Rescorla (1966), it will be helpful to describe how the (usually) statistical terms *positive correlation*, *negative correlation*, and *no (zero) correlation* apply to CS/US temporal relationships (see Figure 4.8). A perfect **positive correlation** between CS and US is depicted. Every time a CS occurs, the US immediately follows. Note that it is possible to have a positive correlation without such perfect correspondence. It is only necessary that the US occur more reliably after the CS than without the CS. The second panel indicates a **negative correlation**. The CS predicts the nonoccurrence of the US or the CS occurs immediately after the US has ended (i.e., as in backward conditioning). Finally, **no (zero) correlation** exists when the US is as likely to occur in the presence of the CS as in its absence. You might recall Pavlov's distinction between excitatory and inhibitory conditioning. A positive correlation between the CS and the US establishes excitatory conditioning (i.e., *if this occurs, then that occurs*), and a negative correlation results in inhibitory conditioning (i.e., *if this occurs, then that does not occur* or, in the instance of backward conditioning, *if this occurs, then that has already occurred*). Positive and negative correlations involve predictive relationships. Learning a predictive relationship is not possible in the instance of no correlation between events.

**Positive Correlation**
One stimulus predicts that another will occur.

**Negative Correlation**
A stimulus predicts that another will not happen or has already occurred.

**No (zero) Correlations**
Two stimulus events are unrelated.

Rescorla (1966) had four groups of rats undergo a conditioned emotional response procedure. As shown in Figure 4.9, the four groups were identical in that the probability of the US (shock) in the presence of a CS (tone) was 40%. They differed only with respect to the likelihood of being shocked when the tone was not present. One group was never shocked without the tone (0%), a second group was shocked 10% of the time in its absence, a third group 20%, and the fourth group was shocked as often in the absence of

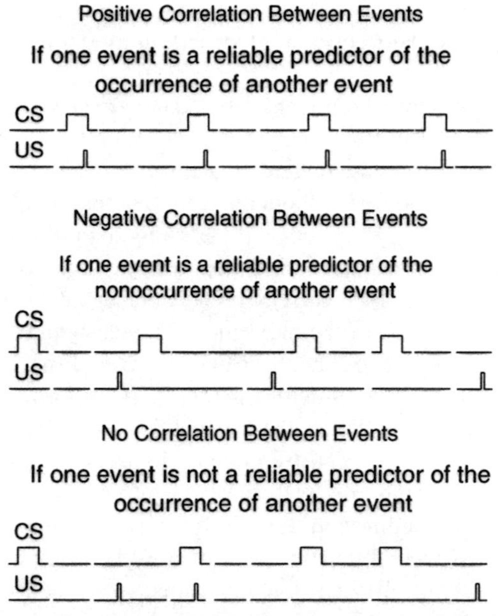

**FIGURE 4.8**     Positive, negative, and no correlation between the CS and the US.

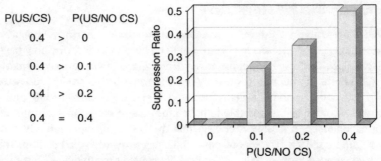

| P(US/CS) | | P(US/NO CS) |
|---|---|---|
| 0.4 | > | 0 |
| 0.4 | > | 0.1 |
| 0.4 | > | 0.2 |
| 0.4 | = | 0.4 |

**FIGURE 4.9** Rescorla's (1966) experiment showing differences in conditioning despite temporal contiguity. All four groups were shocked (US) 40% of the time in the presence of a tone (CS). The only difference between the groups was in the percentage of times they were shocked when the tone was not present (0%, 10%, 20%, 40%). Conditioning to the tone was strongest (i.e., the suppression ratio was lowest) when shock occurred only in the presence of the tone (the 0 group). The group that was shocked the same percentage of the time (40%) when the tone was present and absent demonstrated no conditioning (i.e., the suppression ratio was 0.5).

the tone as in its presence (40%). Therefore, all four groups received temporal contiguity on 40% of the trials between tone and shock. They differed, however, with regard to the correlation between tone and shock. The 0 group had a positive correlation, because it was shocked only in the presence of the tone. The 0.1 and 0.2 groups also had positive correlations, but they were progressively weaker. In the 0.4 group, the tone and shock were not correlated at all.

If, as Pavlov assumed in the second assumption, temporal contiguity was sufficient for predictive learning to occur, the four groups should produce the same results. Recall that suppression ratios range from 0.5, indicating no change in responding when the tone is present, to 0, indicating total suppression of responding. Rescorla found a range of suppression ratios, depending upon the frequency of shock during the non-tone intervals. These shocks do not affect tone/shock contiguity. They are extra shocks occurring in the absence of the tone. According to Pavlov, these shocks should not affect the amount of learning, but clearly they do. Rescorla demonstrated that although temporal contiguity is necessary, it is not sufficient. The correlation between the tone and shock determined the amount of suppression. In the group never shocked without the tone (0 group), total suppression occurred (suppression ratio = 0). In the group shocked the same amount (40%) regardless of the presence of the tone, no suppression occurred (suppression ratio = 0.5).

Another way of describing the correlation between events is to consider how helpful one is in predicting the other. If the only time one gets shocked is in the presence of the tone, then it is predictive of the shock. If one is shocked the same amount whether or not the tone is present, the tone provides no predictive information. As the information value of the tone was degraded in the 0.1 and 0.2 conditions, the amount of suppression was correspondingly reduced (remember, lower suppression values represent greater suppression). The results of the Rescorla (1966) study suggest a very different understanding of classical conditioning than Pavlov's stimulus substitution model. It is not a mechanistic process whereby temporal contiguity between events is sufficient for them to be associated. Rather, they become associated when the first event is correlated with (i.e., predictive of) the second event (see also Rescorla, 1968).

**Blocking**   Leon Kamin (1969) provides additional support for the predictiveness model of classical conditioning. This study relates to an issue we considered when reviewing the effect of intensity of events on predictive learning. We saw then that with a compound stimulus, overshadowing would occur whereby a more intense component would be attended to rather than a less intense component. If you are reading and enjoying this text, you probably aren't noticing the usual background noises provided by people, fans, traffic, and so on. However, if one of those stimuli increased in intensity, despite the fact that you are engaged in my writing, you would probably redirect your attention. Kamin showed that a similar effect, called **blocking**, could occur as the result of prior learning rather than intensity. The blocking group in his study received a tone (CS 1) followed by shock (US) in the first phase, and a control group was simply placed in the chamber (see Figure 4.10). The groups were identical from then on. During the second phase, a compound stimulus consisting of the light and a tone (CS 2) was followed by shock. During a test phase, each component was presented by itself to determine the extent of conditioning.

**Blocking**
The interfering effect of prior experience on learning an association between a CS and a US.

In the blocking group, conditioning occurred to the tone and not to the light. Conditioning occurred to both elements of the compound in the control group. It is as though the prior experience with the tone resulted in the blocking group subjects not paying attention to the light in the second phase. The light was redundant. It did not provide additional information.

A novel and fun demonstration of blocking in college students (Arcediano, Matute, & Miller, 1997) involved a computerized video game in which subjects tried to protect the earth from invasion by Martians with a laser gun (in the form of the space bar). Unfortunately, the enterprising Martians had developed an anti-laser shield; if subjects fired when the shield was in place, their laser gun would be ineffective, permitting a bunch of Martians to land and do their mischief. A flashing light preceded implementation of the laser shield for subjects in the blocking group. A control group did not experience a predictive stimulus for the laser shield. Subsequently, both groups

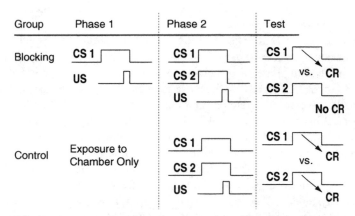

**FIGURE 4.10**   Test for blocking. A group previously receiving a shock in the presence of a tone (CS 1) did not acquire a conditioned response to a light (CS 2) when it was later presented in compound with the tone (i.e., blocking occurred). A group not receiving prior experience with the tone acquired responses to both elements.   (Adapted from Kamin, 1969)

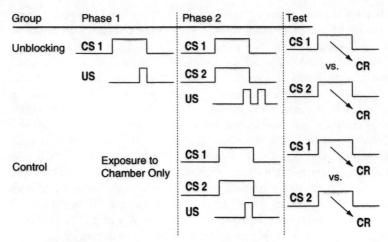

**FIGURE 4.11** Unblocking procedure. If the second element of a compound is predictive of a different event, blocking does not occur.

experienced a compound stimulus consisting of the flashing light and a complex tone. The control group associated the tone with activation of the laser shield whereas the blocking group did not as a result of its prior history with the light. For them, the tone was redundant.

The interpretation that blocking occurs as the result of a redundant CS during the second phase is supported by the results obtained when an unblocking procedure (Dickinson & Mackintosh, 1976) is implemented (see Figure 4.11). The difference between the blocking and unblocking procedures is that a different US occurs in the second phase of unblocking. A double shock is shown in the diagram, but other differences (e.g., in intensity) would work as well. Responding would be demonstrated to both components of the compound stimulus with the unblocking procedure. In this instance, the second component is not redundant. It provides new information—that a double shock rather than a single shock is predicted.

The blocking procedure is a second example demonstrating that temporal contiguity between events, even in a predictive relationship, is not sufficient for learning to occur. In the second phase of the blocking procedure, the compound stimulus precedes the US. According to Pavlov, because both components are contiguous with the US, both should become associated with it and eventually elicit CRs. The combination of Rescorla's (1966) and Kamin's (1969) findings lead to the conclusion that learning occurs when individuals obtain new information enabling them to predict events they were unable to previously predict. Kamin suggested that this occurs only when we are surprised. That is, as long as events are proceeding as expected, we do not learn. Once something unexpected occurs, individuals search for relevant information. Many of our activities may be described as "habitual" (Kirsch, Lynn, Vigorito, & Miller, 2004) or "automatic" (Aarts & Dijksterhuis, 2000). We have all had the experience of riding a bike or driving as though we are on "auto pilot." We are not consciously engaged in steering as long as events are proceeding normally. Once something unexpected occurs, we snap to attention and focus on the immediate environmental circumstances.

This provides the opportunity to acquire new information and is a much more active and adaptive understanding of predictive learning than that provided by Pavlov's stimulus substitution model (see Rescorla, 1988).

**MUST THE CR RESEMBLE THE UR?**    We now examine the third assumption of Pavlov's model, that the conditioned response always resembles the unconditioned response. Meat powder reflexively elicits salivation, and Pavlov observed the same reaction to a conditioned stimulus predictive of meat powder. Puffs of air reflexively elicit eyeblinks, and taps on the knee elicit knee jerks. The conditioned responses are similar to the unconditioned responses in research involving puffs of air and knee taps as unconditioned stimuli. It is understandable that Pavlov and others believed for so long that the conditioned response must resemble if not be identical to the unconditioned response. However, in 1937, Zener took movies of dogs undergoing salivary conditioning and disagreed with this conclusion. He observed, "Despite Pavlov's assertions, the dog does not appear to be eating an imaginary food. It is a different response, anthropomorphically describable as looking for, expecting, the fall of food with a readiness to perform the eating behavior which will occur when the food falls" (Zener, 1937, p. 393).

Kimble (1961, p. 54) offered the possible interpretation that "the function of the conditioned response is to prepare the organism for the occurrence of the unconditioned stimulus." Research by Shepard Siegel (1975, 1977, 1984, 2005) has swung the pendulum toward widespread acceptance of this interpretation of the nature of the conditioned response. Siegel's research involved administration of a drug as the unconditioned stimulus. For example, rats were injected with insulin in the presence of a novel stimulus (Siegel, 1975). Insulin is a drug that lowers blood sugar level and is often used to treat diabetes. Eventually, a conditioned response was developed to the novel stimulus (now a CS). However, rather than lowering blood sugar level, the blood sugar level increased to the CS. Siegel described this increase as a **compensatory response** in preparation for the effect of insulin. He argued that it was similar to other **homeostatic** mechanisms designed to maintain optimal levels of biological processes (e.g., temperature, white blood cell count, fluid levels). Similar compensatory responses have been demonstrated with morphine, a drug having analgesic properties (Siegel, 1977) and with caffeine (Siegel, 2005). Siegel (2008, p. 242) has gone so far as to suggest that "the learning researcher is a homeostasis researcher." We will consider a fascinating and important extension of Siegel's basic research in the chapter on predictive learning applications.

Drug-induced compensatory responses are consistent with the interpretation that the conditioned response constitutes preparation for the unconditioned stimulus. In a review article providing a functional (i.e., adaptive) perspective of classical conditioning, Domjan (2005a) described additional examples supporting the same interpretation. **Preparatory responses** were acquired in studies involving caloric intake and digestion, poison avoidance, breast-feeding, and sexual conditioning (see also Hollis, 1997). Combining this interpretation with the conclusions reached regarding the necessity of predictiveness for classical conditioning to occur leads to the following alternative to Pavlov's stimulus substitution model: *Classical conditioning is an adaptive process whereby individuals acquire the ability to predict future events and prepare for their occurrence.* This is consistent with the definition of adaptive learning provided in Chapter 1.

**Compensatory Response**

A CR that counteracts the biological effect of a US.

**Homeostasis**

The maintenance of an optimum level of a biological state (e.g., blood sugar level, temperature).

**Preparatory Response**

A conditioned response that enables an individual to respond appropriately to the occurrence of a subsequent event (US). For example, salivation is an appropriate response in preparation for food, an eyeblink is an appropriate response in preparation for a puff of air, an increase in blood sugar level is an appropriate response in preparation for a lowering of blood sugar level, and so on.

> ▪ State the assumptions underlying Pavlov's stimulus substitution model of classical conditioning. Describe the research findings addressing each of the assumptions. Show how the research findings are consistent with the description of classical conditioning as an adaptive learning process.

### The Rescorla-Wagner Model

$$\lambda - V = \text{Surprise!!}$$

Pavlov's stimulus substitution model was based on Aristotle's associative law of temporal contiguity. We now know that although necessary in practically all instances, temporal contiguity between a CS and a US is not sufficient for learning to occur. Classical conditioning may be better understood as an adaptive process in which individuals learn about correlations between events and are thus better able to prepare for their occurrence. Research findings disconfirming Pavlov's stimulus substitution model of classical conditioning led to the formulation of alternative models consistent with this adaptive learning interpretation.

Rescorla and Wagner (1972) developed an extremely influential mathematical model of classical conditioning designed to predict trial-by-trial changes in associative (i.e., predictive) learning based on three assumptions. As proposed by Kamin, the model assumes that predictive learning between a CS and a US occurs only when an individual is surprised by the US, and the degree of learning depends on the degree of surprise. The second assumption was that the salience of the CS and the US affect predictive learning. Presumably, once surprised, the likelihood of detecting the correlation between a CS and a US is a function of their salience. The third assumption was that if the CS were a compound stimulus, the total predictive value of the compound would be equal to the sum of the predictive values of the elements.

**Rescorla-Wagner Model**

An influential mathematical model of the classical conditioning process. It assumes that the amount of learning on an individual trial is related to the degree an individual is surprised by the occurrence of an unexpected event (see Surprise factor).

When expressed mathematically, the **Rescorla-Wagner model** is described by the following formula for a compound $CS_{AX}$ consisting of elements $A$ and $X$:

$$\Delta V_A = [\alpha_A \beta_1] (\lambda_1 - V_{AX})$$

and

$$\Delta V_X = [\alpha_X \beta_1] (\lambda_1 - V_{AX})$$

where

$$V_{AX} = V_A + V_X$$

When presented in this form, my students have shown various reactions. Some immediately go into what may be described as an advanced case of "symbol shock" characterized by a combination of feelings of anxiety and helplessness. Others' eyes glaze over, and they appear to enter a trance state resembling sleep. A relatively small number appear enthusiastic and curious about the meaning of this formula. If you were in the second category, I assume you have come out of your trance and are ready to pick up your reading where you left off. If you were in the first category, I wish to reassure you that the bark of this formula is worse than its bite.

You were probably intimidated by the model's presentation as three equations using letters from the Greek alphabet. The reason for the three equations is that the model is designed to explain not only classical conditioning to a simple (i.e., one element) CS but also to compound stimuli. The first two equations are the same, the first applying to change in the predictive value to one element of the compound ($A$) and the other to the other element ($X$). The third equation simply combines the cumulative predictive values results for the two elements to obtain the predictive value of the compound ($AX$).

The model's most important and most difficult concept is the **surprise factor** ($\lambda - V$). The Greek letter lambda ($\lambda$) stands for the maximum amount of predictive value possible between a particular CS (compound $CS_{AX}$ in the example) and US. V stands for the total predictive value that has been accumulated from prior pairings of the CS and US. Thus, $\lambda_1 - V_{AX}$ stands for the difference between the greatest possible predictive strength and the current level of predictive value of the CS. The greater this difference, the more the individual is surprised on that trial. Here's a translation of the Rescorla-Wagner equations leaving out the Greek symbols. It may help to imagine concrete examples with the equations by thinking of $CS_A$ as a light, $CS_X$ as a tone, and $CS_{AX}$ as a compound consisting of the light and tone.

**Surprise Factor ($\lambda - V$)**
This part of the Rescorla-Wagner equation determines the degree of surprise on an individual trial by subtracting the amount of predictive value accumulated on previous trials from the maximum degree of surprise possible with a particular US.

## Equation 1 for $CS_A$

Change in Predictive Value of $CS_A$ on a trial = the salience of $CS_A$ multiplied by the salience of the US multiplied by the surprise factor (the Maximum Predictive Value – the Total Predictive Value of both elements of $CS_{AX}$)
and

## Equation 2 for $CS_X$

Change in Predictive Value of $CS_X$ on a trial = the salience of $CS_X$ multiplied by the salience of the US multiplied by the surprise factor (the Maximum Predictive Value – the Total Predictive Value of both elements of $CS_{AX}$)
where

## Equation 3 for $CS_{AX}$

Total Predictive Value of $CS_{AX}$ = Total Predictive Value of $CS_A$ + $CS_X$

So far this may not seem like a big improvement, but hang in there. The first two formulas consist of the multiplication of three values to determine the expected change in predictive value for each element separately ($CS_A$ and $CS_X$), and the third equation is simply those two predictive value results added to determine the predictive value of the compound ($CS_{AX}$).

The Rescorla-Wagner model proposes that the amount of change in predictive value to a compound $CS_{AX}$ (e.g., a light and tone) on an individual trial depends on the salience of each of the elements of the CS (i.e., the brightness of the light and loudness of the tone), the salience of the US (e.g., the quantity of food), and the degree to which the individual is surprised on that trial. The surprise factor is calculated by subtracting the total accumulated predictive value built up over previous trials from the maximum predictive value possible for the US. That is, surprise decreases as one is repeatedly exposed to CS/US pairings. The maximum predicted value for the US is based on its properties (i.e., a larger or more intense US will have a higher maximum value). For example, if the maximum predictive value is 100 (e.g., cc of saliva, percentage of trials on which a CR occurs, amplitude of an eyeblink) and the accumulated predicted value is 30, then the surprise factor is 70.

In classical conditioning research, the change in predictive value of a CS is measured by the change in the strength of the CR on a trial-by-trial basis. Because the three factors are multiplied, if any one of them is zero, no learning would be predicted. That is, if the CS or US is not salient (i.e., equals 0), or the individual is expecting the US (i.e., the surprise factor is 0), then the strength of the CR should not rise on that trial. For our example, if the CS is a light/tone compound and neither one of the elements is salient (i.e., they are both 0), then no learning will take place. Similarly, even if the CS is very salient, if the US is insufficiently intense (e.g., a salience value of 0), then no learning will occur. Finally, even if the CS and US are both salient, if the individual already expects the US to occur (i.e., the surprise factor is 0 resulting from the Total Predictive Value reaching the maximum), then no learning is predicted.

The first time the individual experiences the CS followed by the US is totally unexpected and will result in the greatest surprise. When there is no prior history with any of the CS elements and a US, then nothing is subtracted from the Maximum Predictive Value in calculating the surprise factor. This results in the greatest degree of learning possible on a trial. As the individual experiences trials with the CS followed by the US, the Total Predictive Value of $CS_{AX}$ increases. Subtracting these totals from the Maximum Predictive Value reduces the overall surprise factor. That is, as the ability to predict the US increases, surprise decreases correspondingly and less learning should occur on that trial. This means that changes in predictive value will be greatest at the beginning when the individual is surprised the most and will gradually decrease as the individual is less surprised. Thus, the Rescorla-Wagner model predicts the typical negatively accelerated classical conditioning learning curve with most learning occurring at the beginning and diminishing learning thereafter.

Since Pavlov's time, it has become clear that other stimuli within an environmental context can impact the effectiveness of a stimulus as a CS. Overshadowing, in which the more salient component of a compound stimulus becomes associated with a US but the less salient component does not, is an example of one such phenomenon. For example, if a compound stimulus consisting of a dim light and a loud tone is paired with food, salivation will be more likely to occur to the tone than to the light. Blocking is another example. It occurs when a previously established CS interferes with another stimulus presented at the same time and prevents it from becoming an effective CS. For example, if a tone is first established as a CS predicting food and then combined with a light, salivation will continue to occur to the tone and not be established to the light (i.e., the prior experience with the tone blocks the light becoming a CS).

The Rescorla-Wagner model does an excellent job of explaining the overshadowing and blocking phenomena. Overshadowing by one element of a compound stimulus is predicted as the result of the salience factors in the equations. For example, if the tone is loud (e.g., with a salience value of .90), it will increase in predictive value 9 times as rapidly as a dim light with a low salience value of .1. As the predictive value of the compound increases over trials, it will be composed almost exclusively of the predictive value of the tone, resulting in overshadowing.

Blocking is accounted for by changes in the surprise value of the initial CS. The model dictates that once a US (e.g., food) is predicted by a single CS element (e.g., a light), eventually it will no longer be surprised by that same stimulus element, even if presented in compound with another (e.g., a light/tone compound). Therefore, no further learning will take place to the other stimulus element (the tone). The **US pre-exposure effect**, another phenomenon, is similar to blocking. If a US (e.g., food) is repeatedly presented in a particular context, the individual will no longer be surprised by its occurrence within that context. This will retard or prevent associating another stimulus (e.g., a light) with the US in the same context.

As a result of its testability, the Rescorla-Wagner model has generated an enormous amount of research since it was proposed in 1972. In addition to explaining acquisition, overshadowing, blocking, and US pre-exposure, the model successfully predicts a phenomenon called the **overexpectation effect**. This occurs when two CSs are separately conditioned to the point that each no longer surprises the individual. If the elements are then presented in compound with the same US, the model predicts that the association value of each element presented by itself should decrease because the maximum total cannot exceed the value of the combined elements. Interestingly, this counterintuitive finding has been replicated several times (e.g., Kremer, 1978; Lattal & Nakajima, 1998; Rescorla, 1970).

Despite these successes, the model is not able to explain all classical conditioning phenomena (Miller, Barnet, & Grahame, 1995). For example, it cannot account for latent inhibition (CS pre-exposure). The Rescorla-Wagner model emphasizes the role of surprise by the occurrence of the US in the predictive learning process and assumes that CS stimulus salience remains constant. Thus, the model has no way of accounting for the fact that exposing an individual to a CS without it being followed by a surprising US retards the acquisition process to that CS. Alternative models emphasizing attention to the CS were developed to address such effects (Mackintosh, 1975; Pearce-Hall, 1980). These models assume that the likelihood of forming a predictive relationship between a CS and a US requires paying attention to the CS, which depends on its salience. They also assume, unlike Rescorla and Wagner, that salience changes as the result of experience. Prior repeated exposure to a stimulus in the absence of any important subsequent stimuli presumably decreases its salience, perhaps through habituation or learned irrelevance (discussed in Chapter 10), slowing down the learning process. In the same way as it is adaptive to react to a surprising stimulus, it is adaptive to ignore uninformative stimuli until they could potentially predict an important event. Returning to the common experience of driving or riding a bike, we seemingly are not paying attention to familiar stimuli until something unexpected occurs.

**US Pre-Exposure Effect**

This refers to the finding that prior exposure to a US makes it more difficult for an individual to later associate it with a CS. The Rescorla-Wagner model explains this as a form of blocking in which pre-exposure results in predictive value accruing to the context in which the US was presented.

**Overexpectation Effect**

A phenomenon that occurs when two CSs are separately conditioned to the point that the individual is no longer surprised by either. If the elements are then presented in compound with the same US, the CR is reduced to each of the elements presented separately.

Since the Rescorla-Wagner model was introduced, research testing of mathematical models of the predictive learning process continues to be refined and developed (Harris, 2011; Thein, Westbrook, & Harris, 2008). At this time, no one model can account for all classical conditioning phenomena.

> ■ Describe how the Rescorla-Wagner model of classical conditioning accounts for the effects of surprise on acquisition, overshadowing, blocking, and US pre-exposure but cannot account for latent extinction (CS pre-exposure).

## Summary

Application of the scientific method to the study of predictive learning led to the understanding of many reliable phenomena described in the previous and current chapters. The phenomena of spontaneous recovery, disinhibition, and renewal indicate that the extinction procedure does not result in unlearning. Rather, an inhibitory response is acquired that counteracts the previously acquired behavior.

As sciences progress, they attempt to formulate theoretical models to integrate and explain phenomena in a meaningful and constructive way. For decades, learning theorists accepted the assumptions underlying Pavlov's stimulus substitution model of the classical conditioning process. It was believed that temporal contiguity was necessary and sufficient for conditioning to occur and that the conditioned response necessarily resembled the unconditioned response. With the possible exception of acquired taste aversion, whereby an association may be formed between a consumed substance and illness with hours separating the events, temporal contiguity is necessary for conditioning to occur (i.e., the CS and US must occur within seconds of each other). Rescorla's research investigating the role of CS/US correlation and Kamin's blocking research indicate that although necessary, temporal contiguity is not sufficient. Learning only occurs when a stimulus provides new information about a subsequent event. If the stimulus is uninformative (as in Rescorla's 40%/40% condition) or redundant (as in Kamin's blocking group), learning does not occur. Siegal's research in which drugs served as the US demonstrated that the CR does not necessarily resemble the UR. Often, when drugs are used, a compensatory response counteracting the US effect is acquired.

These findings are consistent with an understanding of classical conditioning as an adaptive process in which an individual acquires the ability to predict and prepare for the occurrence of an event. The Rescorla-Wagner model of classical conditioning assumes that learning takes place only when an individual is surprised. The model successfully accounts for acquisition, overshadowing, blocking, US pre-exposure, and overexpectation, but it cannot account for the fact that CS pre-exposure retards acquisition. The Rescorla-Wagner model has been modified and alternative models developed in the attempt to develop a comprehensive theory of classical conditioning (predictive learning).

## References

Aarts, H., & Dijksterhuis, A. (2000). Habits as knowledge structures: Automaticity in goal-directed behavior. *Journal of Personality and Social Psychology, 78,* 53–63.

Arcediano, F., Matute, H., & Miller, R. R. (1997). Blocking of Pavlovian conditioning in humans. *Learning and Motivation, 28,* 188–199.

Black, A. H., Carlson, N. J., & Solomon, R. L. (1962). Exploratory studies of the conditioning of automatic responses in curarized dogs. *Psychological Monographs, 76* (1, Whole No. 29).

Bouton, M. E. (2000). A learning theory perspective on lapse, relapse, and the maintenance of behavior change. *Health Psychology, 19* (Supplement), 57–63.

Bouton, M. E., & Nelson, J. B. (1998). The role of context in classical conditioning: Some implications for cognitive behavior therapy. In W. T. O'Donohue (Ed.) *Learning and behavior therapy* (pp. 59–84). Needham Heights, MA: Allyn & Bacon.

Dickinson, A., Hall, G., & Mackintosh, N. J. (1976). Surprise and the attenuation of blocking. *Journal of Experimental Psychology: Animal Behavior Processes, 2*(4), 313–322.

Domjan, M. (2005). Pavlovian conditioning: A functional perspective. *Annual Review of Psychology, 56,* 179–206.

Garcia, J., Ervin, F. R., & Koelling, R. A. (1966). Learning with prolonged delay of reinforcement. *Psychonomic Science, 5,* 121–122.

Garcia, J., & Koelling, R. (1966). Relation of cue to consequence in avoidance learning. *Psychonomic Science, 4,* 123–124.

Harris, J. (2011). The acquisition of conditioned responding. *Journal of Experimental Psychology: Animal Behavior Processes, 37,* 151–164.

Hastings, S. E., & Obrist, P. A. (1967). Heart rate during conditioning in humans: Effect of varying inter-stimulus (CS-UCS) interval. *Journal of Experimental Psychology, 74,* 431–442.

Hollis, K. L. (1997). Contemporary research on Pavlovian conditioning: A "new" functional analysis. *American Psychologist, 52,* 956–965.

Kamin, L. J. (1969). Predictability, surprise, attention, and conditioning. In B. A. Campbell & R. M. Church (Eds.), *Punishment and aversive behavior.* New York: Appleton-Century-Crofts.

Kimble, G. A. (1961). *Hilgard and Marquis' conditioning and learning* (2nd ed.). New York: Appleton-Century-Crofts.

Kimble, G. A., & Reynolds, B. (1967). Eyelid conditioning as a function of the interval between conditioned and unconditioned stimuli. In G. A. Kimble (Ed.), *Foundations of conditioning and learning.* New York: Appleton-Century-Crofts.

Kirsch, I., Lynn, S. J., Vigorito, M., & Miller, R. R. (2004). The role of cognition in classical and operant conditioning. *Journal of Clinical Psychology, 60,* 369–392.

Kremer, E. F. (1978). The Rescorla-Wagner model: Losses in associative strength in compound conditioned stimuli. *Journal of Experimental Psychology: Animal Behavior Processes, 4,* 22–36.

Lattal, K. M., & Nakajima, S. (1998). Overexpectation in appetitive Pavlovian and instrumental conditioning. *Animal Learning and Behavior, 26,* 351–360.

Lynch, J. J. (1973). Pavlovian inhibition of delay in cardiac and somatic responses in dogs: Schizokenesis. *Psychological Review, 32,* 1339–1346.

Mackintosh, N. J. (1975). A theory of attention: Variations in the associability of stimuli with reinforcement. *Psychological Review, 82,* 276–298.

Miller, R. R., Barnet, R. C., & Grahame, N. J. (1995). Assessment of the Rescorla-Wagner model. *Psychological Bulletin, 117,* 363–386.

Pavlov, I. P. (1927). *Conditioned reflexes: An investigation of the physiological activity of the cerebral cortex.* Oxford: Oxford University Press.

Pearce, J. M., & Hall, G. (1980) A model for Pavlovian learning: Variations in the effectiveness of conditioned but not of unconditioned stimuli. *Psychological Review, 87,* 532–552.

Rescorla, R. A. (1966). Predictability and number of pairings in Pavlovian fear conditioning. *Psychonomic Science, 4,* 383–384.

Rescorla, R. A. (1968). Probability of shock in the presence and absence of CS in fear conditioning. *Journal of Comparative and Physiological Psychology, 66,* 1–5.

Rescorla, R. A. (1970). Reduction in the effectiveness of reinforcement after prior excitatory conditioning. *Learning and Motivation, 1,* 372–381.

Rescorla, R. A. (1988). Classical conditioning: It's not what you think it is. *American Psychologist, 43,* 151–160.

Rescorla, R. A., & Wagner, A. R. (1972). A theory of Pavlovian conditioning: Variations in the effectiveness of reinforcement and nonreinforcement. In A. H. Black & W. E Prokasy (Eds.), *Classical conditioning II: Current research and theory* (pp. 64–99). New York: Appleton-Century-Crofts.

Schneiderman, N., & Gormezano, I. (1964). Conditioning of the nictitating membrane of the rabbit as a function of CS-US interval. *Journal of Comparative and Physiological Psychology, 57,* 188–195.

Siegel, S. (1975). Conditioning insulin effects. *Journal of Comparative and Physiological Psychology, 89,* 189–199.

Siegel, S. (1977). Morphine tolerance acquisition as an associative process. *Journal of Experimental Psychology: Animal Behavior Processes, 3,* 1–13.

Siegel, S. (1984). Pavlovian conditioning and heroin overdose: Reports by overdose victims. *Bulletin of the Psychonomic Society, 22,* 428–430.

Siegel, S. (2005). Drug tolerance, drug addiction, and drug anticipation. *Current Directions in Psychological Science, 14,* 296–300.

Siegel, S. (2008). Learning and the wisdom of the body. *Learning and Behavior, 36,* 242–252.

Smith, J. C., & Roll, D. L. (1967). Trace conditioning with X-rays as an aversive stimulus. *Psychonomic Science, 9*, 11–12.

Smith, M. C., Coleman, S. R., & Gormezano, I. (1969). Classical conditioning of the rabbits' nictitating membrane response. *Journal of Comparative and Physiological Psychology, 69*, 226–231.

Thein, T., Westbrook, R. F., & Harris, J. (2008). How the associative strengths of stimuli combine in compound: Summation and overshadowing. *Journal of Experimental Psychology: Animal Behavior Processes, 34*, 155–166.

Wilcoxin, H. D., Dragoin, W. B., & Kral, P. A. (1971). Illness-induced aversions in rat and quail: Relative salience of visual and gustatory cures. *Science, 171*, 826–828.

Yeo, A. G. (1974). The acquisition of conditioned suppression as a function of interstimulus interval duration. *Quarterly Journal of Experimental Psychology, 26*, 405–416.

Zener, K. (1937). The significance of behavior accompanying conditioned salivary secretion for theories of the conditioned response. *American Journal of Psychology, 50*, 384–403.

## Chapter 5

# Predictive Learning: Applications

## BASIC AND APPLIED SCIENCE

It is a common belief that science always is, or should be, a search for the solution to human problems. As an extreme example, the "Golden Fleece Award" was given by a U.S. senator facetiously (and critically) for proposing research projects that have no obvious practical application. In reality, however, most science is "basic" rather than applied, attempting to discover lawful relationships in nature. Frequently, but not always, understanding lawful relationships enables the development of practical technologies impacting significantly on the human condition. Again, think of the contrasting lives led by you and by the Nukak child. Technologies such as commercial food production, plumbing, electricity, and inoculation against disease would not be possible without the basic sciences of physics, chemistry, and biology. Indeed, there would be no rocket ships without "rocket science." Manhattan Island would still look the way it did when Henry Hudson arrived there.

Wilhelm Wundt, Edward Titchner, and other practitioners of the structuralist approach to psychology were dedicated to basic science, demonstrating little interest in application beyond the laboratory. In contrast, as one might expect from the nature of the approaches, those adhering to the functionalist and behavioral perspectives often described the societal implications of their research. For example, John Dewey was one of the foremost leaders in progressive approaches to public education. The functionalist/behaviorists John Watson and B. F. Skinner were recognized for their emphases upon the applications of psychology to understand and improve the human condition.

Functionalism describes the human condition as consisting of continual adaptation to environmental conditions. At the beginning of this book there was a picture of a Nukak child in the Amazonian rain forest. The adaptive challenges this child faces are very different from those you and I face on a day-to-day basis. This child, growing up in a nomadic stone-age culture, faces the same challenges his ancestors have been facing for more than 10,000 years! In his prescient book *Future Shock* (1970), Alvin Toffler argued that technologically advanced societies were progressing at such rapid paces that they were experiencing multiple instances of the equivalent of culture shock throughout their lives. This pace of change has accelerated such that several life-transforming technologies have been developed since Toffler's book. Among these are the personal computer, the growth of the internet, and the international availability of cell phones. It is hard to imagine, but in the mid-19th century prior to the industrial revolution, the great majority of American children grew up on farms. Their lives were in many ways more similar to the lives of current Nukak children than to ours. We will see how the principles of adaptive learning provide a helpful perspective to appreciate the different ways in which humans currently live on our planet.

In the previous two chapters, we explored the methods used to study predictive learning along with the major findings and theoretical conclusions. Much of this material was dry, technical, and abstract. However, it constitutes the basic science leading to principles and technologies having important applications. We now consider several examples of the application of predictive learning principles to the understanding of the human condition.

## DIRECT CLASSICAL CONDITIONING OF EMOTIONS

We start this section on predictive learning applications with Watson's attempt to apply classical conditioning procedures to establish a fear in a young child. John Watson and Rosalie Rayner's (1920) famous (some consider it infamous) attempt to make a child fear a white rat was a reaction to an influential case study published by Sigmund Freud (1955, originally published in 1909). Freud, based upon correspondence with a 5-year-old's father, concluded that the child's fear of horses was the result of the psychodynamic defense mechanism of projection. Freud thought that the horses, wearing black blinders and having black snouts, symbolically represented the father who wore black-rimmed glasses and had a mustache. Freud interpreted the fear as the result of an unconscious Oedipal conflict, despite the knowledge that Little Hans, as the boy was called, witnessed a violent accident involving a horse soon before the onset of the fear.

Watson and Rayner read this case history and considered it enormously speculative and unconvincing. They thought that Pavlov's research in classical conditioning provided principles that could more plausibly account for the onset of Little Hans's fear. They set out to test Pavlov's hypothesis with the 11-month-old son of a wet nurse working in the hospital where Watson was conducting research with white rats. The boy is frequently facetiously referred to as Little Albert, after the subject of Freud's case history.

**FIGURE 5.1**  Watson and Rayner conditioning Little Albert to fear the white rat.

Watson had an interest in child development and eventually published a successful book on this subject. He knew that infants innately feared very few things. Among them were painful stimuli, a sudden loss of support, and a startling noise. Classic videos of Watson and Rayner's demonstration with Albert are available. Albert initially demonstrated no fear and actually approached the white rat. Watson struck a steel rod (the US) from behind Albert while he was with the rat (the CS) 7 times (see Figure 5.1). This was sufficient to result in Albert's crying and withdrawing (CRs) from the rat when the animal was subsequently presented. It was also shown that Albert's fear generalized to other objects including a rabbit and, horror of horrors, Watson in a Santa Claus mask! One can just imagine Albert crying and screaming on some unsuspecting Santa's lap in the future. Freud witnessed the event, making the observation that Albert's father was wearing a white shirt. Naturally he concluded that this was another example of projection when we all know Watson did it with his little hammer! Unfortunately, Albert's mother moved before Watson could undo whatever damage he might have caused. A comical speculative article asked the question "Whatever Happened to Little Albert?" (Harris, 1979).

Mary Jones, one of Watson's students, had the opportunity to undo a young child's extreme fear of rabbits (Jones, 1924). The child, Peter, was fed his favorite food while the rabbit was gradually brought closer and closer to him. Eventually, he was able to hold the rabbit on his lap and play with it. We consider this procedure in the later section Desensitization and Sensitization Procedures. It is important to note that classical conditioning does not apply only to aversive USs and negative emotions such as fear and anxiety. For decades, mothers had advised their daughters that "The way to a man's heart is through his stomach." The strategy is to have the unsuspecting suitor gaze into the daughter's eyes while eating his favorite meal. Mothers obviously understood the potential application of classical conditioning. We will see later that politicians and advertisers also apply classical conditioning principles to achieve their objectives.

## INDIRECT CLASSICAL CONDITIONING OF EMOTIONS

Research continues to support the role of classical conditioning in anxiety disorders (e.g., Mineka, 2008). Many people with extreme fears (phobias) insist that they never experienced a traumatic event in relation to the object of their fear. Others report having experienced such a traumatic event but not becoming fearful. Fear of some objects seems easy to establish despite their rarity (e.g., snakes), whereas fear of other common objects (e.g., electrical outlets) seems difficult to establish. If we are to accept the classical conditioning model of fear acquisition, we need to account for these occurrences in research meeting the criteria of internal and external validity. Indirect classical conditioning through observation or language has been demonstrated to constitute a plausible explanation. Albert Bandura developed a comprehensive model of observational learning that we will consider in Chapter 10. In his classic text *Principles of Behavior Modification* (1969, p. 167), Bandura suggests that

**Vicarious**

Experiencing an event indirectly through observation of another individual's behavior.

both direct and vicarious conditioning processes are governed by the same principle of associative learning, but they differ in the source of the emotional arousal. In the direct prototype, the learner himself is the recipient of pain- or pleasure-producing stimulation, whereas in **vicarious** forms somebody else experiences the reinforcing stimulation and his affective expressions, in turn, serve as the arousal system for the observer.

Observational learning of emotional responses has frequently been demonstrated in human adults (cf., Berger, 1962; Green & Osborne, 1985). In these studies, people witness others appearing to be shocked in the presence of an obvious external stimulus. Susan Mineka and her colleagues have studied the observational learning of fear of snakes in monkeys in a research program extending over 30 years. Mineka observed that rhesus monkeys reared in the wild in India and transported to the United States as laboratory research subjects demonstrated an extreme fear of snakes that was extremely resistant to extinction procedures (Mineka, Davidson, Cook, & Keir, 1984; Mineka, Keir, & Price, 1980). Monkeys reared in the laboratory did not exhibit a fear of snakes. Mineka believed it unlikely that every monkey reared in the wild had an unpleasant experience with snakes and suspected a type of "social contagion" whereby non-fearful snakes observed the emotional reactions of fearful models. She tested this possibility experimentally by having lab-reared monkeys observe their fearful wild-reared counterparts in the presence of snakes. Sure enough, five out of six of the observer monkeys acquired an extreme fear of snakes. A subsequent study (Mineka & Cook, 1986) demonstrated that monkeys could be "immunized" against acquiring a snake fear by first observing other fearless monkeys prior to being exposed to the fearful ones.

It was suggested that humans (similar to monkeys) were especially prone (prepared) to develop fears of objects that pose threats under our early, pre-technological environmental conditions (Seligman, 1971). Ratings of common phobias for preparedness were consistent with this interpretation (de Silva, Rachman, & Seligman, 1977). That is, for millennia humans most likely came into contact with snakes, but only recently with electrical outlets. These overall findings provide compelling support for the indirect acquisition of emotional behaviors and provide information for the conditions under which they are likely or not likely to be obtained. Cook and Mineka (1990) have demonstrated the acquisition of a fear of snakes to videotaped model monkeys. This suggests that current media forms (e.g., TV, video games, recordings) may play a powerful role in humans' emotional learning. One concern has been the potential desensitizing effects of violent video games and the possible link to aggressive behaviors. Several recent studies have indeed indicated such an effect and linkage in college students (Arriaga, Benedicta, & Esteves, 2011; Engelhart, Bartholow, Kerr, & Bushman, 2011; Krahé, Moller, Huesmann, Kirwil, Felber, & Berger, 2011). Observational learning principles will be discussed in depth in Chapter 12.

## DESENSITIZATION AND SENSITIZATION PROCEDURES

We previously described the procedure used by Jones to reduce a child's fear of rabbits. This was an example of the combined use of desensitization and counterconditioning procedures. The gradual increase in the intensity of the feared stimulus constituted the **desensitization** component. This procedure was designed to extinguish fear by permitting it to occur in a mild form with no distressing following event. Feeding the child in the presence of the feared stimulus constituted **counterconditioning** of the fear response by pairing the rabbit with a powerful appetitive stimulus that should elicit a competing response to fear. Direct in vivo (i.e., in the actual situation) desensitization is an effective technique for addressing anxiety disorders, including shyness and social phobias (Donohue, Van Hasselt, & Hersen, 1994), public speaking anxiety (Newman, Hofmann, Trabeert, Roth, & Taylor, 1994), dental phobias (Haukebo et al., 2008), and even panic attacks (Clum, Clum, & Surls, 1993).

Direct in vivo treatment of an anxiety disorder may not be possible (e.g., fear of extremely rare or dangerous events) or may be inconvenient (e.g., the fear occurs in distant or under difficult-to-control circumstances). In such instances, it is possible to administer **systematic desensitization** (Wolpe, 1958), whereby the person imagines the fearful event under controlled conditions (e.g., in the therapist's office). The person is usually taught to relax as a competing response while progressing through a hierarchy (i.e., ordered list) of realistic situations. Sometimes an underlying dimension can serve as the basis for the hierarchy. Jones used distance from the rabbit when working with Peter. Steps on a ladder could be used to treat a fear of height. Time from an aversive event can sometimes be used to structure the hierarchy. For example, someone who is afraid of flying might be asked to relax while thinking of planning a vacation for the following year involving flight, followed by ordering tickets 6 months in advance, picking out clothes, packing for the trip, and so on. Such imaginal systematic desensitization has been recognized for decades as being surprisingly effective for a variety of problems including severe test anxiety (Wolpe & Lazarus, 1966), fear of humiliating jealousy (Ventis, 1973), and anger management (Smith, 1973). An early review of the systematic desensitization literature concluded that "for

**Desensitization**

A procedure exposing individuals to increased intensities on a stimulus dimension. For example, one may be exposed to larger and larger dogs, higher steps on the rungs of a ladder, and so on.

**Counter-Conditioning**

A procedure designed to substitute a desirable for an undesirable behavior (i.e., substituting relaxation for anxiety).

**Systematic Desensitization**

A counterconditioning procedure designed to reduce anxiety by teaching an individual to relax while being exposed to a hierarchy (ordered list) of anxiety-eliciting events, starting with the least anxiety provoking event. The procedure may be administered in vivo (under the actual circumstances) or through one's imagination.

the first time in the history of psychological treatments, a specific treatment reliably produced measurable benefits for clients across a wide range of distressing problems in which anxiety was of fundamental importance" (Paul, 1969).

In vivo and imaginal desensitization are both direct predictive learning procedures because they involve an individual's interaction with actual or imagined events. The ethical concern involving research on establishing a strong fear does not apply to research designed to reduce already existing fears. In a classic series of studies (Bandura, Grusec, & Menlove, 1967; Bandura & Menlove, 1968), children afraid of dogs were shown films of other children interacting with dogs demonstrating progressively threatening behaviors. This indirect observational learning procedure was successful in reducing or eliminating the children's fears.

**Sensitization/ Aversion Therapy**

A counterconditioning procedure designed to change an appetitive stimulus into an aversive stimulus. For example, emetics (drugs causing one to feel sick) have been paired with alcohol in order to reduce excessive consumption.

In some instances, it would be adaptive to change an appetitive stimulus into an aversive stimulus through counterconditioning. In such instances, **sensitization** procedures, sometimes referred to as aversion therapy, may be effective. For example, procedures using drugs causing one to feel sick (emetics) have been used for many years to reduce excessive consumption of alcohol (Lemere & Voegtlin, 1950; Raymond, 1964; Voegtlin, Lemere, Broz, & O'Hollaren, 1941; Wiens & Menustik, 1983). They have resulted in abstinence rates greater than 60% for the period of a year. Indirect covert sensitization techniques in which the person is asked to imagine getting sick have produced mixed results (Cautela, 1966; Elkins, 1980; Wilson & Tracey, 1976). In the classic film *A Clockwork Orange,* an extremely violent individual is given drugs causing him to become sick while he is forced to watch incidences of violence. It is paradoxical that in order to produce empathy for this criminal, a sensitization procedure is vividly portrayed to indirectly sensitize the audience to the use of sensitization procedures!

---

■ Describe applications of desensitization and sensitization procedures to address human concerns.

---

## CLASSICAL CONDITIONING OF WORD MEANING

*Sticks and stones may break your bones But words will never hurt you*

We all understand that in a sense this old saying is true. We also recognize that words can inflict pain greater than that inflicted by sticks and stones. How do words acquire such power? Pavlov (1928) believed that through classical conditioning, words acquired the capacity to serve as an indirect "second signal system" distinct from direct experience.

Ostensibly, the meaning of many words is established by pairing them with different experiences. That is, the meaning of a word consists of the learned responses to it (most of which cannot be observed) resulting from the context in which the word is learned. For example, if you close your eyes and think of an orange, you can probably "see," "smell," and "taste" the imagined orange. Novelists and poets are experts at using words to produce such rich imaginal experiences (DeGrandpre, 2000).

Let us return to the example of a child about to stick her/his hand in an electric outlet. The parent might say "No!" and slap the child on the wrist, producing a withdrawal response. Now it would theoretically be possible to use the word *no* to attach meaning to another word through higher-order conditioning. For example, the child might be reaching for a pot on a stove and the parent could say "Hot, no!" The word *hot* should now elicit a withdrawal response despite never being paired with a slap on the wrist. This would be an example of what Pavlov meant by a **second signal system** with words substituting for direct experience.

Different types of evidence support the classical conditioning model of word meaning. Razran (1939), a bilingual Russian American, translated and summarized early research from Russian laboratories. He coined the term **semantic generalization** to describe a different type of stimulus generalization from that which was described in Chapter 3. One study showed that a conditioned response acquired to a blue light occurred to the word *blue* and vice versa. In these instances, generalization was based on similarity in meaning rather than similarity on a physical dimension. In an American study (Foley & Cofer, 1943), responses acquired to a word occurred to synonyms (words having the same meaning) but not to homophones (words sounding the same), another example of semantic generalization.

In a series of studies, Arthur and Carolyn Staats and their colleagues experimentally established meaning using classical conditioning procedures (Staats & Staats, 1957, 1959; Staats, Staats, & Crawford, 1962; Staats, Staats, & Heard, 1959, 1961; Staats, Staats, Heard, & Nims, 1959). In one study (Staats et al., 1962), subjects were shown a list of words several times, with the word *LARGE* followed by either a loud sound or shock. This resulted in heightened galvanic skin responses (GSRs) and higher ratings of unpleasantness to the word. The unpleasantness rating was related to the GSR magnitude. These studies provide compelling support for classical conditioning, a predictive learning procedure, being the basis for establishing word meaning. In Chapter 10, we will consider the importance of word meaning in our overall discussion of language as an indirect learning procedure.

## CLASSICAL CONDITIONING OF ATTITUDES

We have seen classical conditioning principles used to explain the acquisition of emotional responding and word meaning. Now we will see how the same principles can help us understand the formation of attitudes. Figure 5.2 provides an example of the classical conditioning of the emotional component of an attitude (prejudice, in this case). We can see how children can come to dislike or hate an individual or ethnic group based upon the emotional responses of their parents. Similarly, as in establishing word meaning, the out-group members can be described in negative terms such as immoral, dirty, and lazy. Razran (1938, 1940) demonstrated that ratings of political slogans could be affected in opposite directions by pairing them with either food or noxious odors.

**Second Signal System**

Through classical conditioning, words acquire the capacity to serve as indirect CSs and USs, functioning much as direct experience. For example, one can be told that eating mushrooms can make you sick resulting in feeling nauseous (a CR) to the thought or presence of mushrooms.

**Semantic Generalization**

Stimulus generalization based on similarity in meaning rather than similarity on a physical dimension (i.e., a conditioned response acquired to a blue light occurs to the word *blue* and vice versa).

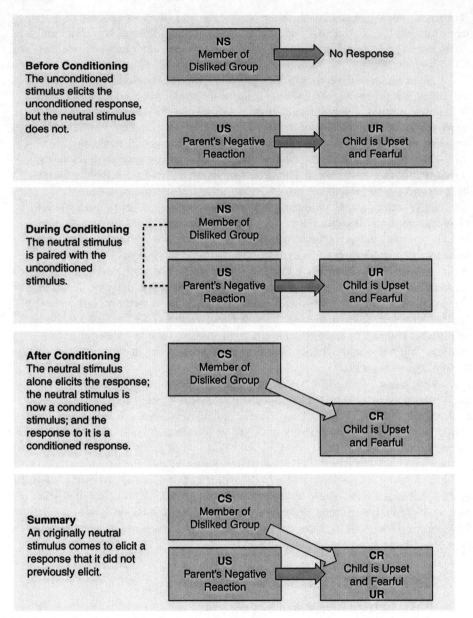

**FIGURE 5.2** Classical conditioning and prejudice.

Similarly, Staats and Staats (1958) showed that attitudes toward national names (e.g., Dutch, Swedish) or even personal names (e.g., Tom, Bill) could be influenced by pairing them with positively or negatively charged words. It is important to recognize the potency of these procedures, because they are so frequently used in an attempt to influence behavior. For example, advertisers pair their products with attractive images (see Figure 5.3), and political candidates frequently "dress themselves in the flag" and "sling mud" at opposing candidates.

**FIGURE 5.3** Classical Conditioning and Advertising. Manufacturers often try to sell their products by associating them with sexual images.

## Evaluative Conditioning

**Evaluative conditioning** is a term applied to the major research area examining how likes and dislikes are established by pairing objects with positive or negative stimuli in a classical conditioning paradigm (Walther, Weil, & Dusing, 2011). Jan De Houwer and his colleagues have summarized more than 3 decades of research documenting the effectiveness of such procedures in laboratory studies and in applications to social psychology and consumer science (De Houwer, 2007; De Houwer, Thomas, & Baeyens, 2001; Hofmann, De Houwer, Perugini, Baeyens, & Crombez, 2010). Pairing aversive health-related images with fattening foods resulted in such foods being considered more negatively and in subjects becoming more likely to choose fruit than snack foods (Hollands, Prestwich, & Marteau, 2011). Similar findings were obtained with alcohol and drinking behavior (Houben, Havermans, & Wiers, 2010). A consumer science study demonstrated that pairing a particular pen with positive images was effective in getting college students to prefer that pen when forced to choose among pens (Dempsey & Mitchell, 2010). Celebrity endorsers are effective, particularly with an appropriate connection between the endorser and the product (Till, Stanley, & Priluck, 2008). For example, basketball players are especially effective when endorsing basketball shoes as opposed to non-basketball-related items.

    It has even been shown that pairing the word *I* with positive trait words increased self-esteem to the extent that individuals were not affected by negative intelligence feedback (Dijksterhuis, 2004). That is, subjects with positive "I-associations" did not experience reduced self-esteem when informed that they performed poorly on intelligence tests.

**Evaluative Conditioning**

Using classical conditioning procedures to establish likes and dislikes by pairing neutral objects with positive and negative stimuli.

> ■ Describe how classical conditioning procedures explain how objects come to elicit emotional reactions, words acquire meaning, and people develop prejudices.

## CLASSICAL CONDITIONING OF DRUG TOLERANCE

Shepard Siegel has developed a fascinating and influential model of drug tolerance and overdose effects based upon his previously described findings concerning the acquisition of compensatory responses (Siegel, 1983). Siegel suggested that many so-called heroin overdoses are actually the result of the same dosage being consumed differently or in a different environment. Such an effect has actually been demonstrated experimentally with rats. Whereas 34% of rats administered a higher than usual dosage of heroin in the same cage died, 64% administered the same dosage in a different cage died (Siegel, Hinson, Krank, & McCully, 1982). As an experiment, this study has high internal validity but obviously could not be replicated with human subjects. In a study with high external validity, Siegel interviewed survivors of suspected heroin overdoses. Most insisted they had taken the usual quantity but indicated that they had used a different technique or consumed the drug in a different environment (Siegel, 1984). This combination of high external validity and high internal validity results makes a compelling case for Siegel's learning model of drug tolerance and overdose effects.

This concludes our treatment of predictive learning applications. We have seen how traditional classical conditioning procedures help us understand the acquisition and elimination of emotional responding, as well as the development of word meaning and attitudes. When we think of adaptive behavior, we ordinarily do not think of emotions, word meaning, or attitudes. Instead, we usually think of these as conditions that motivate or energize the individual to take action. We now turn our attention to control learning, the type of behavior we ordinarily have in mind when we think of adaptation.

## Summary

In this chapter, we reviewed many important classical conditioning phenomena related to the human condition. Objects come to elicit emotional reactions, words acquire meaning, and attitudes are acquired as the result of events occurring in direct or indirect predictive relationships. In vivo (i.e., overtly experiential) and imaginal (i.e., covertly experiential) desensitization procedures have proved extremely powerful in reducing fears and addressing anxiety disorders. Sensitization procedures have been used to make appetitive substances (e.g., alcohol) aversive by pairing them with noxious stimuli (e.g., drugs that make one feel sick to one's stomach). Siegel's compensatory response findings have been extended to the understanding of drug tolerance and apparent overdoses as experientially based phenomena.

## References

Arriaga, P., Benedicta, M., & Esteves, F. (2011). Effects of playing computer games on emotional desensitization and aggressive behavior. *Journal of Applied Social Psychology, 41*, 1900–1925.

Bandura, A. (1969). *Principles of behavior modification.* New York: Holt, Rinehart, and Winston.

Bandura, A., & Menlove, F. L. (1968). Factors determining vicarious extinction of avoidance behavior through symbolic modeling. *Journal of Personality and Social Psychology, 8*, 99–108.

Bandura, A., Grusec, J. E., & Menlove, F. L. (1967). Vicarious extinction of avoidance behavior. *Journal of Personality and Social Psychology, 5*, 16–23.

Berger, S. (1962). Conditioning through vicarious instigation. *Psychological Review, 69*, 450–466.

Cautela, J. (1966). Treatment of compulsive behavior by covert sensitization. *Psychological Record, 16*, 33–41.

Clum, G. A., Clum, G. A., & Surls, R. (1993). A meta-analysis of treatment for panic disorder. *Journal of Consulting and Clinical Psychology, 61*, 317–326.

Cook, M., & Mineka, S. (1990). Selective associations in the observational learning of fear in monkeys. *Journal of Experimental Psychology: Animal Behavior Processes, 16*, 372–389.

De Houwer, J. D. (2007). A conceptual and theoretical analysis of evaluative conditioning. *The Spanish Journal of Psychology, 10*, 230–241.

De Houwer, J. D., Thomas, S., & Baeyens, F. (2001). Associative learning of likes and dislikes: A review of 25 years of research on human evaluative conditioning. *Psychological Bulletin, 127*, 853–869.

de Silva, P., Rachman, S., & Seligman, M. (1977). Prepared phobias and obsessions: Therapeutic outcomes. *Behavior Research and Therapy, 15*, 65–78.

DeGrandpre, R. (2000). A science of meaning. *American Psychologist, 55*, 721–739.

Dempsey, M. A., & Mitchell, A. A. (2010). The influence of implicit attitudes on choice when consumers are confronted with conflicting attribute information. *Journal of Consumer Research, 37*, 614–625.

Dijksterhuis, A. (2004). I like myself but I don't know why: Enhancing implicit self-esteem by subliminal evaluative conditioning. *Journal of Personality and Social Psychology, 86*, 345–355.

Donohue, B., van Hasselt, V. B., & Hersen, M. (1994). Behavioral assessment and treatment of social phobia: An evaluative review. *Behavior Modification, 18*, 262–288.

Elkins, R. (1980). Covert sensitization and alcoholism: Contributions of successful conditioning to subsequent abstinence maintenance. *Addictive Behaviors, 5*, 67–89.

Engelhardt, C. R., Bartholow, B. D., Kerr, G. T., & Bushman, B. J. (2011). This is your brain on violent video games: Neural desensitization to violence predicts increased aggression following violent video game exposure. *Journal of Experimental Social Psychology, 47*, 1033–1036.

Foley, J. P., & Cofer, C. N. (1943). Mediated generalization and the interpretation of verbal behavior: II. Experimental study of certain homophone and synonym gradients. *Journal of Experimental Psychology, 32*, 168–175.

Freud, S. (1955). The analysis of a phobia in a five-year-old boy. In J. Strachey (Editor and translator), *The Standard Edition of the Complete Psychological Works of Sigmund Freud (Vol. 10)*. London: Hogarth (originally published 1909).

Foley, J. P., & Cofer, C. N. (1943). Mediated generalization and the interpretation of verbal behavior: II. Experimental study of certain homophone and synonym gradients. *Journal of Experimental Psychology, 32*, 168–175.

Green, G., & Osborne, J. (1985). Does vicarious instigation provide support for observational learning theories? A critical review. *Psychological Bulletin, 97*, 3–17.

Haukebo, K., Skaret, E., Öst, L., Raadal, M., Berg, E., Sundberg, H., & Kvale, G. (2008). One- vs. five-session treatment of dental phobia: A randomized controlled study. *Journal of Behavior Therapy and Experimental Psychiatry, 39*, 381–390.

Harris, B. (1979). Whatever happened to Little Albert? *American Psychologist, 34*, 151–160.

Hofmann, W., De Houwer, J., Perugini, M., Baeyens, F., & Crombez, G. (2010). Evaluative conditioning in humans: A meta-analysis. *Psychological Bulletin, 136*, 390–421.

Hollands, G. J., Prestwich, A., & Marteau, T. M. (2011). Using aversive images to enhance healthy food choices and implicit attitudes: An experimental test of evaluative conditioning. *Health Psychology, 30*, 195–203.

Houben, K., Havermans, R. C., & Wiers, R. W. (2010). Learning to dislike alcohol: Conditioning negative implicit attitudes toward alcohol and its effect on drinking behavior. *Psychopharmacology, 211*, 79–86.

Jones, M. C. (1924). The elimination of children's fears. *Journal of Experimental Psychology, 7*, 382–390.

Krahé, B. M., Moller, I., Huesmann, L. R., Kirwil, L., Felber, J., & Berger, A. (2011). Desensitization to media violence: Links with habitual media violence exposure, aggressive cognitions, and aggressive behavior. *Journal of Personality and Social Psychology, 100*, 630–646.

Lemere, F., & Voegtlin, W. (1950). An evaluation of the aversion treatment of alcoholism. *Quarterly Journal of Studies on Alcohol, 11*, 199–204.

Mineka, S. (2008). The relevance of recent developments in classical conditioning to understanding the etiology and maintenance of anxiety disorders. *Acta Psychologica, 127*, 567–580.

Mineka, S., & Cook, M. (1986). Immunization against the observational learning of snake fears in rhesus monkeys. *Journal of Abnormal Psychology, 95*, 307–318.

Mineka, S., Davidson, M., Cook, M., & Keir, R. (1984). Observational conditioning of snake fear in rhesus monkeys. *Journal of Abnormal Psychology, 93,* 355–372.

Mineka, S., Keir, R., & Price, V. (1980). Fear of snakes in wild- and lab-reared rhesus monkeys. *Animal Learning and Behavior, 8,* 653–663.

Newman, M. G., Hoffman, S. G., Trabert, W., Roth, W. T., & Taylor, C. B. (1994). Does behavioral treatment of social phobia lead to cognitive changes? *Behavior Therapy, 25,* 503–517.

Paul, G. L. (1969). Outcome of systematic desensitization: II. Controlled investigations of individual treatment, technique variations, and current status. In C. M. Franks (Ed.), *Behavior therapy: Appraisal and status* (pp. 105–159). New York: McGraw-Hill.

Pavlov, I. P. (1928). *Lectures on conditioned reflexes.* New York: International Publishers.

Raymond, M. J. (1964). The treatment of addiction by aversion conditioning with apomorphine. *Behavior Research and Therapy, 1,* 287–291.

Razran, G. H. (1938). Conditioning away social bias by the luncheon technique. *Psychological Bulletin, 36,* 693. (Abstract)

Razran, G. H. (1939). A quantitative study of meaning by a conditioned salivary technique (semantic conditioning). *Science, 90,* 89–90.

Razran, G. H. (1940). Conditioned response changes in rating and appraising sociopolitical slogans. *Psychological Bulletin, 37,* 481. (Abstract)

Seligman, M. E. P. (1971). Phobias and preparedness. *Behavior Therapy, 2,* 307–320.

Siegel, S. (1983). Classical conditioning, drug tolerance, and drug dependence. In Y. Israel, F. B. Glaser, H. Kalant, R. E. Popham, W. Schmidt, & R. G. Smart (Eds.), *Research advances in alcohol and drug problems* (vol. 7, pp. 207–246). New York: Plenum Press.

Siegel, S. (1984). Pavlovian conditioning and heroin overdose: Reports by overdose victims. *Bulletin of the Psychonomic Society, 22,* 428–430.

Siegel, S., Hinson, R. E., Krank, M. D., & McCully, J. (1982). Heroin "overdose" death: The contribution of drug-associated environmental cues. *Science, 216,* 436–437.

Smith, R. E. (1973). The use of humor in the counterconditioning of anger responses: A case study. *Behavior Therapy, 4,* 576–580.

Staats, A. W., & Staats, C. K. (1958). Attitudes established by classical conditioning. *Journal of Abnormal and Social Psychology, 57,* 37–40.

Staats, A. W., & Staats, C. K. (1959). Effect of number of trials on the language conditioning of meaning. *Journal of General Psychology, 61,* 211–223.

Staats, A. W., Staats, C. K., & Crawford, H. L. (1962). First-order conditioning of meaning and the paralleled conditioning of a GSR. *Journal of General Psychology, 67,* 159–167.

Staats, A. W., Staats, C. K., & Heard, W. G. (1959). Language conditioning of meaning to meaning using a semantic generalization paradigm. *Journal of Experimental Psychology, 57,* 187–192.

Staats, A. W., Staats, C. K., & Heard, W. G. (1961). Denotative meaning established by classical conditioning. *Journal of Experimental Psychology, 61,* 300–303.

Staats, A. W., Staats, C. K., Heard, W. G., & Nims, L. P. (1959). Replication report: Meaning established by classical conditioning. *Journal of Experimental Psychology, 57,* 64.

Staats, C. K., & Staats, A. W. (1957). Meaning established by classical conditioning. *Journal of Experimental Psychology, 54,* 74–80.

Till, B. D., Stanley, S. M., & Priluck, R. (2008). Classical conditioning and celebrity endorsers: An examination of belongingness and resistance to extinction. *Psychology and Marketing, 25,* 179–196.

Toffler, A. (1970). *Future shock.* New York: Random House.

Ventis, W. L. (1973). Case history: The use of laughter as an alternative response in systematic desensitization. *Behavior Therapy, 4,* 120–122.

Voegtlin, W. L., Lemere, F., Broz, W. R., & O'Hollaren, P. (1941). Conditioned reflex therapy of chronic alcoholism. *Quarterly Journal of Studies on Alcohol, 2,* 505–511.

Walther, E., Weil, R., & Dusing, J. (2011). The role of evaluative conditioning in attitude formation. *Current Directions in Psychological Science, 20,* 192–196.

Watson, J. B., & Raynor, R. (1920). Conditioned emotional reactions. *Journal of Experimental Psychology, 3,* 1–14.

Wiens, A. N., & Menustik, C. E. (1983). Treatment outcome and patient characteristics in an aversion therapy program for alcoholism. *American Psychologist, 38,* 1089–1096.

Wilson, G. T., & Tracey, D. A. (1976). An experimental analysis of aversive imagery versus electrical aversive conditioning in the treatment of chronic alcoholics. *Behaviour Research and Therapy, 14,* 41–51.

Wolpe, J. (1958). *Psychotherapy by reciprocal inhibition.* Stanford, CA: Stanford University Press.

Wolpe, J., & Lazarus, A. A. (1966). *Behavior therapy techniques: A guide to the treatment of neurosis.* New York: Pergamon.

**PART III   CONTROL LEARNING**

*Chapter 6*

# Control Learning: Basic Principles and Phenomena

## THORNDIKE AND SKINNER

Just as predictive learning had a pioneer at the turn of the 20th century in Ivan Pavlov, control learning had its own in Edward Thorndike. Whereas Pavlov would probably be considered a behavioral neuroscientist today, Thorndike would most likely be considered a **comparative psychologist**. He studied several species of animals including chicks, cats, and dogs and published his doctoral dissertation (1898) as well as a book (1911) entitled *Animal Intelligence*.

> **Comparative Psychologist**
>
> A scientist who studies the behavior of different species of animals.

Thorndike referred to the learning studied by Pavlov as associative shifting (interestingly similar to the idea of stimulus substitution) and contrasted it to trial-and-error (or trial-and-success) learning (1911). B. F. Skinner became an even more influential contributor to the study of control learning later in the century. Skinner (1938) used the terms *respondent conditioning* and *operant conditioning*, and Hilgard and Marquis (1940) introduced the more popular terms *classical conditioning* and *instrumental conditioning* to make the same distinction as Thorndike did.

**Respondent Conditioning**

A term introduced by Skinner to describe acquisition of a behavior elicited by a specific stimulus (see also classical conditioning; predictive learning).

It is instructive to try to infer what the researchers were emphasizing as the crucial differences between the two types of learning. Thorndike seemed to suggest that one type of learning involves shifting an association between an unconditioned stimulus (US) and an unconditioned response (UR) to another conditioned stimulus (the CS), whereas no stimulus elicits a response in the other type of learning. The individual must discover the required response through a random or deliberate exploratory process. Skinner was suggesting that **respondent conditioning** involves responding to a specific stimulus, whereas **operant conditioning** involves operating on the environment to produce a specific stimulus. The term classical conditioning provides no insight into what is being learned, but the term instrumental conditioning implies that the behavior brings about a particular event. Also implied in the terms used was a difference in the type of behavior learned. "Associative shifting" and "respondent" imply reflexive (nonvoluntary) behavior, whereas "trial-and-error" and "operant" imply non-reflexive (voluntary) behavior.

**Operant Conditioning**

A term introduced by Skinner to describe acquisition of a behavior that operates on the environment (see also instrumental conditioning; control learning).

**Predictive Learning**

Acquiring the ability to anticipate an event.

The terms **predictive learning** and **control learning** have been suggested in this text as substitutes for classical and instrumental conditioning. Prediction and control comprise the two possibilities for adaptive learning. If one is unable to predict or control, one is unable to adapt. In some circumstances, one is able to predict but not control events. In other circumstances, one is able to exert a degree of control. The terms *prediction* and *control* are descriptive of the processes and consistent with our current understanding of the two types of learning. It is also possible to describe adaptive learning as consisting of acquiring the ability to predict one's environment with control learning applying to instances when one is acting upon the environment. The distinction between predictive and control learning will continue to be make, along with the use of "classical" terminology when appropriate.

**Control Learning**

Acquiring the ability to change the environment (see also operant conditioning; instrumental conditioning).

## APPARATUSES USED TO STUDY CONTROL LEARNING

The apparatuses to study control learning and the corresponding response measures (dependent variables) are listed here. Unlike the procedures used to study predictive learning, a response is required in these apparatuses in order for an event to occur:

- Discrete Trial
    Puzzle box—time to solution
    Maze—time to goal box; number of errors
    Runway—time to goal box
    Shuttle box—time to respond; percentage of successful responses

- Free Operant
    Operant chamber (Skinner box)—rate of responding

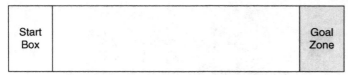

**FIGURE 6.1** Runway.

We saw a picture of one of Thorndike's puzzle boxes at the end of Chapter 2 and discussed Tolman and Honzik's maze-learning study in Chapter 1. **Runways** are typically long rectangular alleyways (see Figure 6.1) with infrared sensors enabling precise timing of when a subject leaves the start area and arrives at the goal area.

**Shuttle boxes** consist of separate compartments that permit an individual to move from one to the other (see Figure 6.2).

Puzzle boxes, mazes, runways, and shuttle boxes are **discrete trial apparatuses**. That is, the subject is placed in the apparatus and observed until the requisite behavior is performed. In the **operant chamber** (more popularly referred to as a Skinner box), the subject can repeatedly make a response (see Figure 6.3). Rate of responding is the most common dependent variable in studies conducted in this apparatus. Skinner boxes have many applications and are in widespread use not only to study predictive and control learning, but also to study perception, motivation, animal cognition, psychophysiology, and psychopharmacology. Perhaps their best-known application is the study of different schedules of reinforcement, which will be treated in depth in Chapter 9. The operant chamber, use of rate of responding as a response measure, and study of reinforcement schedules are three significant contributions Skinner made to the study of control learning. Another major contribution is the schema he developed as an overview of this process.

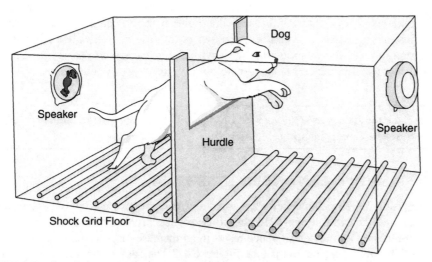

**FIGURE 6.2** Shuttle box.

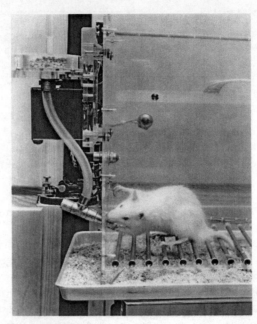

**FIGURE 6.3** Rat in a Skinner box.

As summarized at the end of Chapter 3, research in predictive learning involves detecting the *correlation* between environmental events. Individuals acquire the ability to predict the occurrence or nonoccurrence of appetitive or aversive stimuli. According to Skinner (1938), research in control learning (i.e., instrumental or operant conditioning) involves detecting **contingencies** between one's behavior and subsequent events. This is the same distinction made in Chapter 2 between correlational and experimental research. Correlational research involves systematic observation of patterns of events as they occur in nature. Experimental research requires active manipulation of nature in order to determine if there is an effect. It is as though the entire animal kingdom is composed of intuitive scientists detecting correlations among events and manipulating the environment in order to determine cause and effect. This capability enables adaptation to our diverse environmental niches.

**Contingencies (i.e., Consequences)**

The relationship between one's behavior and subsequent events (e.g., reinforcement and punishment).

■ Describe the apparatuses and procedures used for studying instrumental conditioning (control learning) in appetitive and aversive situations.

## SKINNER'S CONTINGENCY SCHEMA

**Positive Reinforcement**

A consequence in which adding an appetitive stimulus results in an increase in the frequency of behavior.

Skinner developed a schema organizing possible behavioral contingencies based on two considerations: Did the consequence involve adding or removing a stimulus? Did the consequence result in an increase or decrease in the frequency of the preceding behavior (see Figure 6.4)? The four possibilities are **positive reinforcement** in which adding a (presumably appetitive) stimulus increases

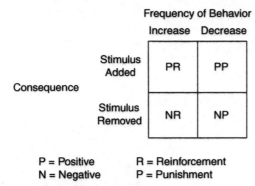

Frequency of Behavior

Increase    Decrease

Consequence

Stimulus Added    PR    PP

Stimulus Removed    NR    NP

P = Positive        R = Reinforcement
N = Negative        P = Punishment

**FIGURE 6.4**  Behavioral contingencies.

the frequency of behavior, **positive punishment** in which adding a (presumably aversive) stimulus decreases the frequency of behavior, **negative reinforcement** in which removing a (presumably aversive) stimulus increases the frequency of behavior, and **negative punishment** in which removing a (presumably appetitive) stimulus decreases the frequency of behavior.

From our human perspective, positive reinforcement is what we ordinarily think of as receiving a reward for a particular behavior (*If I do this, something good happens*). Positive punishment is what we usually think of as a negative result of an action (*If I do this, something bad happens*). Negative reinforcement is often confused with punishment, but, by definition, it results in an increase in behavior. It is what we usually consider to be an **escape** response or an **avoidance** response for an aversive event (*If I do this, something bad is removed*, or *If I do this, something bad does not happen*). Examples of negative punishment would be **response cost** (e.g., a fine) or **time out** (*If I do this, something good is removed*, or *If I do this, something good does not happen*). Everyday examples include the following: A child is given a star for cleaning up after playing and keeps cleaning up (positive reinforcement); a child is yelled at for teasing and the behavior decreases (positive punishment); a child raises an umbrella after (escape) it starts to rain or before (avoidance) stepping out into the rain (both negative reinforcement); a child's allowance is taken away for fighting (response cost), or a child is placed in the corner for fighting while others are permitted to play (time out) and fighting decreases (both negative punishment).

Skinner's "carrots and sticks" schema of contingencies between behaviors and consequences is familiar and intuitive. These principles are arguably the most powerful explanatory tools the discipline of psychology has provided for human behavior. They have been applied with a diversity of individuals and groups (e.g., autistic children, schizophrenic adults, normal schoolchildren) in a diversity of settings (e.g., hospitals, schools, industry) for every conceivable behavior (toilet training, academic performance, wearing seat belts, etc., etc., etc.). We will consider examples of control learning applications in Chapter 8.

Skinner's distinction between positive and negative is similar to Pavlov's distinction between excitatory and inhibitory. Rather than a specific stimulus predicting the occurrence or nonoccurrence of an event, a specific behavior predicts

**Positive Punishment**

A consequence in which adding an aversive stimulus results in a decrease in the frequency of behavior.

**Negative Reinforcement**

A consequence in which removing (escape) or postponing (avoidance) an aversive stimulus results in an increase in the frequency of behavior.

**Negative Punishment**

A consequence in which removing (response cost) or preventing (time out) an appetitive stimulus results in a decrease in the frequency of behavior.

**Escape**

A response that removes an aversive event; for example, a bar press might terminate shock.

**Avoidance**

A response that postpones or eliminates contact with an aversive event; for example, if bar pressing results in not being shocked.

**Response Cost**

Removal of an appetitive stimulus (e.g., a fine for speeding).

**Time Out**

Removal from circumstances in which an appetitive stimulus is available (e.g., being sent to one's room without dessert for teasing a sibling).

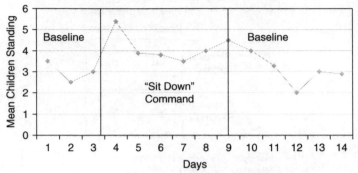

**FIGURE 6.5**   The effect of teacher scolding on children leaving their seats.   (Adapted from Madsen et al., 1970)

the occurrence or nonoccurrence of an event. Unfortunately, Skinner's terminology sometimes causes confusion because of the common usage of the terms *positive* and *negative*, and *reinforcement* and *punishment*. For example, how can punishment be positive or reinforcement be negative? Skinner defined the terms *reinforcement* and *punishment* based upon the direction of behavior change. However, reinforcement is often thought to be synonymous with reward, whereas punishment is assumed to always suppress behavior. As an example of the confusion this causes, Figure 6.5 shows the reversal-design results for a study testing the effects of the verbal scold "sit down" on the number of children standing in a classroom (Madsen, Becker, Thomas, Koser, & Plager, 1970). Surprisingly (and I am sure, disappointing to the teacher), the scold led to an increase in the number of children out of their seats. Technically, therefore, saying "sit down" served as positive reinforcement.

The results of the Madsen et al. (1970) study exemplify an important message. To paraphrase an old saying, "One person's reinforcer can be another person's punisher." This is undeniably true and must be kept in mind when applying these principles. In applied settings, one can never assume that expected reinforcers and punishers will have the intended effects. This must always be established empirically (i.e., tested) for each individual.

> ▪ Describe Skinner's schema for categorizing contingencies between behavior and consequences.

## ADAPTIVE LEARNING OVERVIEW

Figure 6.6 is a control learning version of Skinner's schema. It is similar to the predictive learning table provided in Chapter 3 for Pavlov's excitation and inhibition terminology. In this case, rather than defining reinforcement and punishment based on behavior change, the terms are defined by the nature of the stimulus presented—whether it is appetitive or aversive. Thus, positive reinforcement is shown when an appetitive stimulus occurs after a behavior; positive punishment is shown when an aversive stimulus occurs after a behavior; negative punishment is shown when an appetitive stimulus does not occur after

**Control Learning**

| | Occurrence | Nonoccurrence |
|---|---|---|
| Appetitive | Positive Reinforcement | Negative Punishment |
| Aversive | Positive Punishment | Negative Reinforcement |

**FIGURE 6.6**   Control learning contingencies.

**Adaptive Learning**

| | Predict | | Control | |
|---|---|---|---|---|
| | Occurrence | Nonoccurrence | Occurrence | Nonoccurrence |
| Appetitive | Excitatory Appetitive | Inhibitory Appetitive | Positive Reinforcement | Negative Punishment |
| Aversive | Excitatory Aversive | Inhibitory Aversive | Positive Punishment | Negative Reinforcement |

**FIGURE 6.7**   Adaptive learning schema.

a behavior; and negative reinforcement is shown when an aversive stimulus does not occur after a behavior. The same caveat mentioned earlier for the terms *reinforcement* and *punishment* must be applied to the terms *appetitive* and *aversive*. That is, they can never be assumed but must be tested on an individual basis.

An advantage to the predictive and control learning terminology is that it can incorporate the separate classical and instrumental conditioning terminology in a coherent manner. Figure 6.7 depicts an overview of adaptive learning as acquiring the ability to predict and control the occurrence and nonoccurrence of appetitive and aversive events. Figure 6.8 also shows how this overview relates to traditional Pavlovian and Skinnerian terminology.

This adaptive learning overview provides an intuitively plausible, if simplistic, portrayal of the human condition. Referring back to the Frankenstein monster's observation, some things feel good (like food) and some things feel bad (like fire). We are constantly trying to maximize feeling good and minimize feeling bad. This requires being able to predict, and when possible control, events in our lives. We will now try to understand the details and amplify upon this very basic answer to the human's question in Hardin's cartoon, "What's it all about?"

> ▪ Describe how an adaptive learning perspective integrates basic Pavlovian and Skinnerian principles.

## LEARNED AND UNLEARNED APPETITIVE AND AVERSIVE STIMULI

As Hardin reminds us, we share with the rest of the animal kingdom the need to eat and survive long enough to reproduce if our species is to continue. Just as Pavlov distinguished between unconditioned stimuli (biologically significant events) and conditioned

## Unconditioned Reinforcers

Reinforcers that acquire their effectiveness through genetic mechanisms (e.g., food, water).

## Conditioned Reinforcers

Reinforcers that acquire their effectiveness through experience, either being paired with or exchangeable for other reinforcers; for example, a coupon exchangeable for a particular item, a star provided for a correct answer.

## Generalized Reinforcers

Conditioned reinforcers paired with or exchangeable for a variety of other reinforcers (e.g., tokens and money).

stimuli, Skinner differentiated between **unconditioned reinforcers** (and punishers) and **conditioned reinforcers** (and punishers). Factors related to survival such as food, water, sexual stimulation, removal of pain, and temperature regulation are reinforcing as the result of heredity. We do not need to learn to "want" to eat, although we need to learn what to eat. However, what clearly differentiates the human condition from that of other animals, and our lives from the lives of the Nukak, is the number and nature of our conditioned (learned) reinforcers and punishers.

Early in infancy, children see smiles and hear words paired with appetitive events (e.g., nursing). We saw in Chapter 4 how this would lead to visual and auditory stimuli acquiring meaning. These same pairings will result in the previously neutral stimuli becoming conditioned reinforcers. That is, children growing up in the Colombian rain forest or cities in the United States will increase behaviors followed by smiles and pleasant sounds. The lives of children growing up in these enormously different environments will immediately diverge. Even the feeding experience will be different, with the Nukak child in the rain forest being nursed under changing, sometimes dangerous, and uncomfortable conditions, whereas the American child is nursed or receives formula under consistent, relatively safe, and comfortable conditions. We will examine differences between our lives and the lives of the Nukak in more depth in Chapters 12 and 13. For now, we concentrate on the establishment of grades as powerful conditioned reinforcers that play a large role in your life, but not the life of a Nukak child.

Grades and also money are examples of **generalized reinforcers**. That is, they are paired with or exchangeable for a variety of other reinforcers. Grades probably have been paired with praise and perhaps extrinsic rewards as you grew up. They also provide information (feedback) concerning how well you are mastering material. In Chapter 8, we will review research involving token economies, which are based on the establishment of generalized reinforcers. It will be seen that tokens are very effective in motivating individuals to perform to the best of their ability. In a sense, our economy is a gigantic example of the application of generalized reinforcement.

As a college student, grades probably play a significant role in your life. Most likely, much of your time and effort are dedicated to your coursework. You may not appreciate how important it is to who you are and who you will become that you care about your grades. It was previously mentioned that we have known for decades that if low-performing elementary school students are rewarded after correct answers, they score higher on IQ tests than if they are simply instructed to do their best (Clingman & Fowler, 1976; Edlund, 1972). High-performing students do not demonstrate this difference. These findings were related to Tolman and Honzik's (1930) latent learning study described in Chapter 1. Obviously, these low-performing students had the potential to perform better on the tests but were not sufficiently motivated by the instructions. Without steps taken to address this motivational difference, it is likely that these students will fall further and further behind and not have the same educational and career opportunities as those who are taught early to always do their best in school.

Teaching low-performing students to care about their grades on tests and in classes would be one way to address this concern. My wife was principal of an elementary school in an urban area serving economically disadvantaged minority students. Increasing emphasis has been placed on standardized test performance in recent years. She tried to approach test taking as a "game" and to take advantage of school spirit to motivate the students. Students wore school tee shirts and had practice exercises in test taking. They were rewarded for effort, not results. The attempt was to create a nonthreatening environment in which students would perform to the best of their abilities. Forgive me for bragging, but in 2005 my wife was named as 1 of 50 principals of National Title 1 Distinguished Schools based upon the performance of students in closing the achievement gap on standardized tests.

Parents can also play an enormous role in helping their children acquire the necessary attitudes and skills to succeed in and out of school. It is not necessary to provide extrinsic rewards for performance, although such procedures definitely work when administered appropriately. We can use language and reasoning to provide valuable lessons such as "You get out of life what you put into it" and "Anything worth doing is worth doing well." Doing well in school, including earning good grades, is one application of these more generic guiding principles. In Chapter 8, we will review Kohlberg's model of moral development and discuss the importance of language as a vehicle to provide reasons for desired behavior.

## DISCRIMINATIVE STIMULI AND WARNING STIMULI

The applied Skinnerian operant conditioning literature, called **Applied Behavior Analysis (ABA)**—not to be confused with the reversal design with the same acronym, often refers to the **ABCs**: *a*ntecedents, *b*ehaviors, and *c*onsequences. Adaptation usually requires not only learning what to do, but under what conditions (i.e., the antecedents) to do it. The very same behavior may have different consequences in different situations. For example, whereas your friends may pat you on the back and cheer as you jump up and down at a ball game, reactions will most likely be different if you behave in the same way at the library. We will address the topic of stimulus control in depth in Chapter 10 and see how it helps us understand the development of personality and culture. Now we lay the groundwork by defining related terminology.

In the same way that occasion setters described in Chapter 3 signaled the conditions under which a predictive stimulus is excitatory or inhibitory, antecedents may signal the possibility of appetitive or aversive events. A **discriminative stimulus** signals that a particular behavior will be reinforced (i.e., followed by an appetitive stimulus), whereas a **warning stimulus** signals that a particular behavior will be punished (followed by an aversive event). In the previous example, the ballpark is a discriminative stimulus for jumping up and down, whereas the library is a warning stimulus for the same behavior.

## STIMULUS-RESPONSE CHAINS

Note that the procedures for establishing discriminative stimuli and warning stimuli are the same procedures that establish stimuli as conditioned reinforcers and punishers. Thus, the same stimulus may have more than one function. This is most apparent in a **stimulus-response chain**, a sequence of behaviors in which each response alters the environment and produces the discriminative stimulus for the next response. A popular animal laboratory exercise involves teaching a rat to

**Applied Behavior Analysis (ABA)**
A treatment approach based upon the Skinnerian operant conditioning literature.

**ABCs**
Applied behavior analysis acronym for antecedents, behaviors, and consequences.

**Discriminative Stimulus**
A stimulus that signals that a particular behavior will be reinforced (i.e., followed by an appetitive stimulus). For example, a light might signal the availability of food.

**Warning Stimulus**
A signal that a particular behavior will be punished (followed by an aversive event).

**Stimulus-Response Chain**
A sequence of behaviors in which each response alters the environment producing the discriminative stimulus for the next response. For example, an animal could learn to push a rod to turn on a light and then press a bar to obtain food.

push a rod to turn on a light and then press a bar for food. Here, pushing the rod changes the environment by turning on the light, which is the discriminative stimulus for pressing the bar. Establishing this chain is accomplished by first teaching the rat to press the bar. Once the rat is reliably pressing the bar, the light is randomly turned on and off for different lengths of time. It is usually best to keep it off longer than it is on. The rat is already pressing the bar so, in effect, the difficult part is learning not to press when the light is off. Eventually the rat will press the bar only when the light is on. Once this occurs, the animal can be taught another response (e.g., to push a rod) to turn on the light. Once lit, the rat can complete the response chain by pressing the bar to receive food. In this chain,

**Backward Chaining**

Establishing the components of a stimulus-response chain in reverse order; for example, first teaching a rat to press a bar for food in the presence of a light, then to push a rod to turn on the light.

the light serves two functions: It is a conditioned reinforcer for pushing the rod and a discriminative stimulus for pressing the bar. This procedure is called **backward chaining** because the links are established in reverse order. It is only by proceeding backward that one can take advantage of previously established conditioned reinforcers to add links to chains that can go on indefinitely (e.g., teach a rat to cross a bridge, to swim a moat, to climb a ladder, to raise your school flag for FOOD).

Our daily routines consist of many stimulus-response chains, for example:

- Using the phone: sight of phone—pick up receiver; if dial tone—dial; if busy signal—hang up; ring—wait; sound of voice—respond
- Driving a car: sight of seat—sit; sight of keyhole—insert key; feel of key in ignition—turn key; sound of engine—put car in gear; feel of engaged gear—put foot on accelerator

We can also describe larger units of behavior extending over longer time intervals as consisting of stimulus-response chains, for example:

- Graduating college: Studying this book—doing well on exam; doing well on all exams and assignments—getting good course grade; getting good grades in required and elective courses—graduating
- Getting into college: preparing for kindergarten; passing kindergarten; passing first grade, and so on
- Life: getting fed; getting through school; getting a job; and so on, and so on

If only it were so simple!

We have seen how the basic principles of control learning may be applied to understand the human condition in environments as diverse as the Colombian rain forest and the urban United States. We will now see how some of the same phenomena discussed under predictive learning relate to control learning.

> ■ Describe how common everyday sequences of behaviors as well as behaviors extending over years may be understood as consisting of stimulus-response chains.

## BASIC CONTROL LEARNING PHENOMENA

### Acquisition—Appetitive Control

Acquisition of a control response is different from acquisition of a predictive response. In predictive learning, two correlated events are independent of the individual's behavior. In control learning, a specific response is required in order for an event to occur. In predictive learning, the response that is acquired is related to the second event (e.g., a preparatory response such as salivation for food). In control learning, the required response is usually arbitrary. For example, there is no "natural" relationship between bar pressing and food for a rat or between much of our behavior and its consequences (e.g., using knives and forks when eating). This poses the question, how does the individual "discover" the required behavior? Indeed, you may recall that Thorndike, the pioneer of the study of control learning, described it as a trial-and-error process.

From an adaptive learning perspective, a Skinner box has much in common with Thorndike's puzzle box. The animal is in an enclosed space, and a specific arbitrary response is required to obtain an appetitive stimulus. Still, the two apparatuses pose different challenges and were used in different ways by the investigators. Thorndike's cats and dogs could see and smell large portions of food outside the box. The portion of food in the Skinner box is tiny and released from a mechanical device hidden from view. Thorndike was interested in acquisition of a single response and recorded the amount of time it took for it to be acquired. Skinner developed a way to speed up acquisition of the initial response and then recorded how different variables influenced its rate of occurrence. Skinner's studies of the effects of schedules of reinforcement on the rate of responding will receive separate treatment in Chapter 9. In this section we will be focusing upon acquisition of the first response.

Thorndike's and Skinner's subjects were made hungry by depriving them of food before placing them in the apparatus. Thorndike's animals could see and smell the food outside the puzzle box; thus, they were immediately motivated to determine how to open the door to get out. It usually took about 2 minutes for one of Thorndike's cats to initially make the necessary response. Unless there is residue of a food pellet in the food magazine (food chamber) in a Skinner box, there is no reason for a rat to engage in food-related behavior. One would need to be extremely patient to wait for a rat to discover that pressing the bar on the wall will result in food being delivered in the food magazine. In order to speed up this process, the animal usually undergoes **magazine training**, in which food pellets are periodically dropped into the magazine. This procedure accomplishes two important objectives: Rats have an excellent sense of smell, so they are likely to immediately discover the location of food, and a distinct click is associated with the operation of the food delivery mechanism that can be associated with the availability of food in the magazine. This makes it much easier for the animal to know when food is dispensed. Magazine training is completed when the rat, upon hearing the click, immediately goes to the food. Once magazine training is completed, it is possible to use the **shaping** procedure to "teach" bar pressing. This involves dispensing food after successive approximations to bar pressing. Food is not provided until the rat is in the vicinity of the bar. Then, the rat would need to be closer, center itself in front of the bar, lift its paw, touch the bar, and finally press the bar before food is dispensed. Common examples of behaviors frequently established through shaping with humans are tying shoes, toilet training, bike riding, printing, reading, and writing.

In applied settings (and sometimes in the lab), it is possible to accelerate the shaping process by **prompting** the required behavior. A prompt is any stimulus that increases the likelihood of a desired response. It can be physical, gestural, or verbal. It is often effective to use these in sequence. For example, if we were

**Magazine Training**

A process designed to facilitate an animal's learning the location of food as well as the sound of the food delivery mechanism in a Skinner box.

**Shaping**

Reinforcing successive approximations to a desired response. For example, first reinforcing a rat for approaching a bar, then staying in front of the bar, then touching the bar, and so on.

**Prompting**

The use of a stimulus to increase the likelihood of a desired response. For example, one might physically roll a dog over (physical prompt), move one's arm to signal "roll over" (gestural prompt), or say "roll over" (verbal prompt).

**Fading Procedure**

A procedure involving gradual elimination of one stimulus in order to establish control by another. For example, one might prompt a dog to roll over by physically producing the response and then gradually reducing the amount of pressure.

trying to get a dog to roll over upon hearing the verbal command, you might start by saying "roll over" and physically roll the dog over. Then, you might gradually eliminate the physical prompt, referred to as the **fading procedure**, by saying "roll over" and using less force until you are simply gesturing. Imitative prompts, in which the gesture matches the desired response, are particularly common and effective with children (e.g., the game "peek-a-boo"). Getting back to our dog example, eventually, you could use fading on the gesture. Then, it would be sufficient to simply say "roll over." The combination of shaping, prompting, and fading is a very powerful teaching strategy for nonverbal individuals. Once words have been acquired for all the necessary components of a skill, it can be taught exclusively through the use of language. For example, "Please clean up your room by putting your toys in the chest and your clothes in the dresser." Believe it or not, that can work. Skinner (1986) describes the importance of speech to human accomplishments and considers plausible environmental contingencies favoring the evolutionary progression from physical to gestural to verbal prompts. Such factors include that "sounds are effective in the dark, around corners, and when listeners are not looking." The same is not true for visual prompts (e.g., gestures or sign language).

The example of the transition from physical to gestural to verbal control of action is also consistent with the sociocultural model of human development proposed by the Russian psychologist Lev Vygotsky (1962, 1978). Vygotsky's enormously influential scholarship was conducted in the 1920s and 1930s. He described child development as the transition from socially shared activities to internalized processes. Through interactions with parents and other adults within a community, the child acquires speech patterns and written language. Initially, during the language acquisition phase, he/she speaks out loud. Eventually, speech is internalized and modified to serve as the basis for

**Zone of Proximal Development**

Vygotsky proposed that during instruction, adults must take a child's readiness into consideration.

**Scaffolding**

Vygotsky introduced this term to describe the process of supporting the development of a child's behavior.

thought and adaptation. Consistent with the shaping process, Vygotsky proposed that a **zone of proximal development** existed, whereby learning must start at a particular level and required adult support to reach the highest level. He introduced the term **scaffolding** to describe this support. Prompting and fading may be considered scaffolding techniques and frequently involve indirect learning. Much human learning is indirect, based upon observational learning and the use of language. These topics will be considered in depth in Chapter 12.

Prompting has been used to address several behaviors related to driving. In 1980, Geller and colleagues (Geller, Casali, & Johnson, 1980) identified seat belt usage as an important behavioral objective for study. Since that time, there have been several demonstrations of the effectiveness of visual and verbal prompting in increasing seat belt use (cf., Austin, Alvero, & Olson, 1998; Cox, Cox, & Cox, 2000; Engerman, Austin, & Baily, 1997; Geller, Bruff, & Nimmer, 1985; Thyer, Geller, Williams, & Purcell, 1987) and safe behavior by bicycle and motorcycle riders (Okinaka & Shimazaki, 2011). Other demonstrations have shown the effectiveness of prompts in getting people to stop at stop signs (cf., Austin, Hackett, Gravina, & Lebbon, 2006), yield at crosswalks (Crowley-Koch, Van Houten, & Lim, 2011), and decrease cell phone usage while driving (cf., Clayton, Helms, & Simpson, 2006). When crossing the street at a busy intersection, you may want to apply the results of a recent prompting study (Crowley-Koch et al., 2011) that found that raising your hand or extending your arm increased the likelihood of motorists yielding at a crosswalk. Keep in mind, however, that even with prompting, motorists yielded only about 50% of the time!

> ■ Describe an example incorporating prompting and fading within the shaping procedure to establish verbal control.

## Acquisition—Aversive Control

Until now we have been discussing acquisition of a response followed by an appetitive stimulus, for which the nonhuman and human research literatures are extensive. Losing an appetitive stimulus is unpleasant and an example of what is called **aversive control**. Very few studies involve an appetitive stimulus being removed (response cost) or prevented (time out) in nonhumans. The Skinner box cannot be modified so that a rat or pigeon (the two most common subjects) can observe food being removed. It is possible to include a retractable bar or to darken the chamber to signal a period in which food is not available, but this is rarely done. Response cost (e.g., fines) and time out procedures have, however, been demonstrated to be effective with humans (cf., Levy, 1978; O'Donnell, Crosbie, Williams, & Saunders, 2000). In my study, college students were told they were interacting with three individuals located in other rooms. By pressing different buttons, the students could give each other person 1, 3, or 5 cents, take away the same amounts, or ignore the person. Subjects were instructed that those in the other rooms had the same options. Lights over each of the buttons indicated the other person's response (i.e., giving or taking 1, 3, or 5 cents, or ignoring). In fact, subjects were interacting with three programs: One gave them money 90% of the time and ignored them 10% of the time; another took away money 90% of the time and ignored them 10% of the time; the third matched their behavior. Interestingly, the third program resulted in the "friendliest" responding (i.e., rewarding the most money). Apparently, rather than following the Golden Rule, it is a more effective strategy to do unto others as they do unto you!

A substantial nonhuman and human literature involves the removal (escape) or prevention (avoidance) of an aversive event. Figure 6.8 diagrams a combined escape and avoidance laboratory procedure. A warning stimulus (signal) comes on for 10 sec

> **Aversive Control**
> The effects of punishment and negative reinforcement.

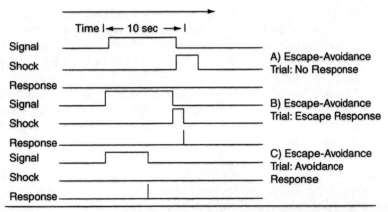

**FIGURE 6.8**  Escape-avoidance contingencies. In the example, a response must be made within 10 sec to avoid shock or during shock to shorten the duration (i.e., escape). In the first panel (A), no response occurs and the animal receives the full duration of the shock. In the second panel (B), the animal escapes the shock. In the third panel (C), the animal avoids shock altogether.

and is followed by 5 seconds of shock if no response (indicated by a vertical tick) occurs (panel A). In panel B, a response occurs after the shock starts, immediately terminating it before the full 5 seconds has elapsed. This constitutes a successful escape response. Panel C depicts a successful avoidance response occurring while the warning stimulus is still on. Note that in addition to not receiving shock, the warning stimulus itself is immediately terminated. As we will see in Chapter 7, this is an important part of the procedure.

> ■ Describe the procedures used to study escape and avoidance learning in the laboratory.

## SPECIES-SPECIFIC CHARACTERISTICS AND ADAPTIVE LEARNING

**Sign Tracking**

Following or responding to stimuli paired with appetitive stimuli. For example, pigeons will peck a lit key if it had previously been paired with food.

**Species-Specific Characteristics**

Inherited behaviors characteristic of all the members of a species.

**Species-Specific Defense Reactions (SSDR)**

Inherited behaviors likely to result under dangerous conditions. For example, when in danger of being shocked, many animals will run or freeze.

We have seen one instance of appetitive control learning, **sign tracking**, whereby a subject's **species-specific characteristics** influence the ease of acquiring a response. All that is necessary to "teach" a pigeon to peck a key is to light it immediately prior to presenting food. It is unnecessary to administer magazine training and shaping as it is with training a rat to press a bar. The importance of species-specific characteristics is heightened in aversive control when animals are threatened with or actually receive aversive events. In an important theoretical paper, Bolles (1970) suggested that the most important variable influencing the acquisition of an avoidance response is its consistency with **species-specific defense reactions (SSDR)**. For example, it is very easy to teach a rat to freeze or flee in a runway or shuttle box but difficult to teach it an arbitrary bar press. Similarly, it is easy to teach a pigeon to flap its wings to avoid shock (MacPhail, 1968) but enormously difficult to teach it to press a key (Schwartz, 1973). Key pecking relates to eating and wing flapping relates to danger for the pigeon.

According to Bolles (1970),

> The parameters of the natural environment make it impossible for there to be any learning of defensive behaviors. Thus, no real-life predator is going to present cues before it attacks. No owl hoots or whistles five seconds before pouncing on a mouse. And no owl terminates his hoots or whistles just as the mouse gets away so as to reinforce the avoidance response. Nor will the owl give the mouse enough trials for the necessary learning to occur. What keeps our little friends alive in the forest has nothing to do with avoidance learning as we normally conceive of it or investigate it in the laboratory. (1970, pp. 32–33)

It is paradoxical, but the avoidance-learning literature may be an instance of research findings with nonhumans applying more to humans than the species studied. Natural selection favors animals inheriting the tendency to sense and avoid danger in their environmental niches. Much of the animal kingdom survives based upon these inherited tendencies. There are few places on earth where humans can survive based exclusively upon their inherited characteristics. The previously recommended book *Guns, Germs, and Steel* (Diamond, 2005) describes how the development of agriculture and animal husbandry enabled humans during the past 13,000 years to spread to different parts of the globe. During this time, many inventions have transformed the human condition to the extent that, other than the few remaining indigenous tribes, we are adapting to a human-constructed world. Our world is similar to the arbitrary one we create to study learning in other animals. Therefore, we have the counterintuitive situation in which the findings from the nonhuman learning literature have more to tell us about our own adaptation than the adaptation of the species being investigated.

> ■ Describe the relationship between species-specific characteristics and control learning in the laboratory. Address the issue of external validity with respect to understanding human learning.

The final form of aversive control learning involves the contingent presentation of an aversive stimulus, what we ordinarily speak of as punishment. We will see in Chapter 7 that this procedure can result in immediate suppression of responding. However, in addition to ethical concerns, effective implementation poses real-world challenges and there may be problematic side effects.

## OTHER BASIC CONTROL LEARNING PHENOMENA

In addition to acquisition, all of the other basic predictive learning phenomena have their control learning counterparts. The extinction process for a response maintained by presentation of an appetitive stimulus involves no longer following the response by that stimulus. This results in a reduction in the frequency of responding. It is as though the individual learns *what used to happen does not happen anymore*. Similarly, spontaneous recovery, external inhibition, disinhibition, and renewal all occur in control learning environments. Stimulus generalization and discrimination will be discussed under the topic of stimulus control in Chapter 12. In higher-order conditioning (see Figure 3.11), a previously established predictive stimulus (CS) was used in place of the second stimulus in another predictive relationship. A stimulus-response chain, in which a previously established discriminative stimulus is used as a conditioned reinforcer for another response, is the control learning equivalent. In sensory pre-conditioning (see Figure 3.12), a previously established predictive relationship between two stimuli was demonstrated by pairing the second stimulus with a biologically significant stimulus (US). The latent learning phenomenon is equivalent in that an appetitive stimulus is used to demonstrate prior control learning (Tolman & Honzik, 1930).

## Summary

In control learning, unlike predictive learning, an individual acts upon and affects the environment. Skinner devised a schema for categorizing the consequences of such acts based upon two considerations: Did the consequence involve the occurrence (positive) or nonoccurrence (negative) of an event? Did the consequence result in an increase (reinforcement) or decrease (punishment) of the preceding behavior? In the attempt to integrate Skinnerian and Pavlovian concepts, an adaptive learning schema was introduced. Learning was described as acquiring the ability to predict and control the occurrence or nonoccurrence of appetitive and aversive events.

Reinforcers (appetitive stimuli) and punishers (aversive stimuli) can acquire their effectiveness through genetic (unconditioned or primary) or experiential (conditioned or secondary) means. A discriminative stimulus signals that a specific behavior will be reinforced. A warning stimulus signals that a specific behavior will be punished. Sequences of behavior extending over short or lengthy time periods may be understood as consisting of stimulus-response chains in which responses alter the environment resulting in discriminative stimuli for subsequent responses.

In predictive learning, the learned response prepares the individual for the second event. There is no necessary relationship between the environment and many control responses. The similarity of a required control response to the individual's genetic predispositions influences the ease of learning the response. Most human learning in technology-enhanced cultures requires the acquisition of arbitrary behaviors. Therefore, perhaps surprisingly, the issue of external validity is often addressed in research involving other animals in specialized apparatuses. In order to establish arbitrary behaviors in the laboratory, it is often efficient to use the procedures of prompting, fading, and shaping. In the natural environment, proceeding in this fashion from physical to gestural to verbal prompts is a powerful sequence for having behavior come under the control of language.

# References

Austin, J., Alvero, A. M., & Olson, R. (1998). Prompting patron safety belt use at a restaurant. *Journal of Applied Behavior Analysis, 31*, 655–657.

Austin, J., Hackett, S., Gravina, N., & Lebbon, A. (2006). The effects of prompting and feedback on drivers' stopping at stop signs. *Journal of Applied Behavior Analysis, 39*, 117–121.

Bolles, R. C. (1970). Species-specific defense reactions and avoidance learning. *Psychological Review, 77*, 32–46.

Clayton, M., Helms, B., & Simpson, C. (2006). Active prompting to decrease cell phone use and increase seat belt use while driving. *Journal of Applied Behavior Analysis, 39*, 341–349.

Clingman, J., & Fowler, R. (1976). The effects of primary reward on the I.Q. performance of grade-school children as a function of initial I.Q. level. *Journal of Applied Behavior Analysis, 9*, 19–23.

Cox, B. S., Cox, A. B., & Cox, D. J. (2000). Motivating signage prompts safety belt use among drivers exiting senior communities. *Journal of Applied Behavior Analysis, 33*, 635–638.

Crowley-Koch, B. J., Van Houten, R., & Lim, E. (2011). Effects of pedestrian prompts on motorist yielding at crosswalks. *Journal of Applied Behavior Analysis, 44*, 121–126.

Diamond, J. (2005). *Guns, germs, and steel.* New York: W. W. Norton & Company.

Edlund, C. (1972). The effect on the test behavior of children, as reflected in the I.Q. scores, when reinforced after each correct response. *Journal of Applied Behavior Analysis, 5*, 317–320.

Engerman, J. A., Austin, J., & Bailey, J. S. (1997). Prompting patron safety belt use at a supermarket. *Journal of Applied Behavior Analysis, 30*, 577–579.

Geller, E. S., Bruff, C. D., & Nimmer, J. G. (1985). Flash for life: Community-based prompting for safety belt promotion. *Journal of Applied Behavior Analysis, 18*, 309–314.

Geller, E. S., Casali, J. G., & Johnson, R. P. (1980). Seat belt usage: A potential target for applied behavior analysis. *Journal of Applied Behavior Analysis, 13*, 669–675.

Hilgard, E. R., & Marquis, D. G. (1940). *Conditioning and learning.* New York: Appleton-Century-Crofts.

Levy, J. C. (1978). Effects of contingencies of reinforcement on same-sexed and cross-sexed interpersonal interactions. *Psychological Reports, 43*, 1063–1069.

MacPhail, E. M. (1968). Avoidance conditioning in pigeons. *Journal of the Experimental Analysis of Behavior, 11*, 625–632.

Madsen, C. H., Becker, W. C., Thomas, D. R., Koser, L., & Plager, E. (1970). An analysis of the reinforcing function of "sit down" commands. In R. K. Parker (Ed.), *Readings in educational psychology* (pp. 265–278). Boston, MA: Allyn & Bacon.

O'Donnell, J., Crosbie, J., Williams, D. C., & Saunders, K. J. (2000). Stimulus control and generalization of point-loss punishment with humans. *Journal of the Experimental Analysis of Behavior, 73*, 261–274.

Okinaka, T., & Shimazaki, T. (2011). The effects of prompting and reinforcement on safe behavior of bicycle and motorcycle riders. *Journal of Applied Behavior Analysis, 44,* 671–674.

Schwartz, B. (1973). Maintenance of keypecking in pigeons by a food avoidance but not a shock avoidance contingency. *Animal Learning and Behavior, 1,* 164–166.

Skinner, B. F. (1938). *The behavior of organisms.* Englewood Cliffs, NJ: Prentice Hall.

Skinner, B. F. (1986). The evolution of verbal behavior. *Journal of the Experimental Analysis of Behavior, 45,* 115–122.

Thorndike, E. L. (1898). Animal intelligence. An experimental study of the associative processes in animals. *Psychological Review Monographs, 2*(8).

Thorndike, E. L. (1911). *Animal intelligence.* New York: Macmillan.

Thyer, B. A., Geller, E. S., Williams, M., & Purcell, E. (1987). Community-based "flashing" to increase safety belt use. *Journal of Experimental Education, 55,* 155–159.

Tolman, E. C., & Honzik, C. H. (1930). Introduction and removal of reward, and maze performance in rats. *University of California Publications in Psychology, 4,* 257–275.

Vygotsky, L. S. (1962). *Thought and language.* Cambridge, MA: MIT Press. (Original work published 1934)

Vygotsky, L. S. (1978). *Mind in society: The development of higher psychological processes* (M. Cole, V. John-Steiner, S. Scribner, & E. Souberman, Eds.). Cambridge, MA: Harvard University Press.

## Chapter 7

# Control Learning: Basic Variables and Theoretical Issues

## VARIABLES INFLUENCING CONTROL LEARNING

The list of major variables influencing control learning is similar to that for predictive learning:

- Deprivation
- Timing of consequence
- Intensity of consequence
- Scheduling of consequences
- Contingency between response and consequence

## Deprivation

In order for appetitive stimuli to be most effective, the individual usually must have experienced recent **deprivation**. The simplest procedure to accomplish this is to manipulate the amount of time since the individual consumed the stimulus (e.g., food, water). A complicated but more sensitive procedure is to maintain the individual at a percentage of the weight it reaches when provided free access to the stimulus. For example, if a rat's **free-feeding body-weight** is 500 grams and it was to be kept at 80% of this weight, its food intake would be reduced until it reached 400 grams. Please recognize that the U.S. government and the American Psychological Association have strict ethical guidelines for conducting research with nonhuman subjects. These guidelines apply to deprivation procedures as well as those involving aversive stimuli. Laboratory animals typically have much safer and comfortable environments than those living in the wild. For example, rats and pigeons do not have free access to food in nature and are usually in a state of mild, if not severe deprivation most of the time. The level of deprivation maintained in the lab is typically low, just enough to ensure that the animal will work for the substance.

Deprivation of an appetitive stimulus has four important effects: It increases general activity level, it increases the vigor of a control response, behavior becomes more goal directed, and behavior becomes resistant to punishment.

In an early parametric study, Collier (1969) manipulated rats' weights by depriving them of food or water. Figure 7.1 shows the relationship between the percentage of

**Deprivation**

Manipulating the amount of time until an individual can consume a stimulus (e.g., food, water).

**Free-Feeding Body-Weight**

The weight an animal attains after being allowed constant access to food.

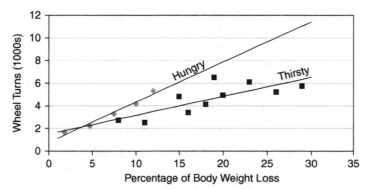

**FIGURE 7.1**  Deprivation and activity level. As deprivation for food or water increases, animals become more active.   (Adapted from Collier, 1969)

free-feeding body-weight loss and the number of turns on a running wheel, an apparatus you are probably familiar with if you ever observed a pet hamster. As both hunger and thirst increase, the amount of activity on the running wheel increases. Note that wheel running does not result in obtaining food or water in this study. The rats simply become more active as a function of deprivation level. At first glance, this may seem maladaptive. One might expect animals to conserve energy if deprived of food or water. With this type of counterintuitive finding, it is often productive to consider how the behavior might be adaptive in nature. In the running wheel, despite its best efforts, the animal "goes nowhere fast." This is not the case in nature, where movement from place to place will increase the likelihood of discovering the appetitive stimulus.

The results of studies in two apparatuses demonstrate the effect of deprivation on the vigor of the control response. In a study manipulating hours of deprivation from 1 to 24, Clark (1958) found a tripling in rats' rate of bar pressing in a Skinner box (see Figure 7.2). In a study manipulating hours of deprivation from 2 to 48, Weiss (1960) found that rats' speed increased significantly from the beginning to the end of a runway (see Figure 7.3). Naturally, the rats slowed down toward the end of the runway as they approached food in the goal box.

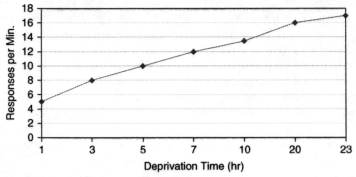

**FIGURE 7.2**   Deprivation and response rate. As deprivation increases, animals work harder for food.   (Adapted from Clark, 1958)

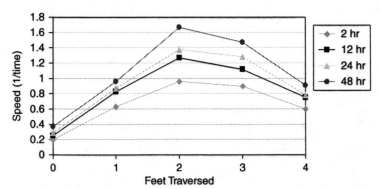

**FIGURE 7.3**   Deprivation and speed of response. As deprivation increases, animals run faster for food.   (Adapted from Weiss, 1960)

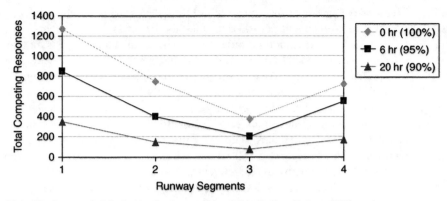

Note: Each curve is labeled by the hours of food deprivation (0,6, and 20) and the correlated percentage of free-feeding weight (100%, 95%, and 90%).

**FIGURE 7.4**  Deprivation and competing responses. As deprivation increases, competing behaviors are reduced.   (Adapted from Porter et al., 1968)

Rats in different laboratory apparatuses frequently engage in various behaviors such as sniffing, grooming, and exploring the apparatus. When this occurs in a control learning situation, such behaviors are considered to be competing with the required control response. In a study manipulating hours of food deprivation (0, 6, and 20) and relating that to percentage of free-feeding weight (100%, 95%, and 90%), Porter, Madison, and Senkowski (1968) demonstrated a reduction in competing responses as a function of deprivation at different points in a runway (see Figure 7.4). Their behavior became more goal directed. That is, when the rats were hungrier, they were less likely to take "the scenic route" and more likely to take the direct route to the food.

Research examining the effects of contingent presentation of an aversive stimulus (punishment) always involves placing an individual in an **approach/ avoidance conflict**. That is, the individual must be motivated to make a response in order to determine whether punishment suppresses it. Deprivation of an appetitive stimulus increases this motivation. Figure 7.5 shows the effect of punishment with shock on the key pecking of a single pigeon at different levels of food deprivation (Azrin, Holz, & Hake, 1963). The graph shows the cumulative

> **Approach/ Avoidance Conflict**
>
> A situation in which a behavior is followed by both an appetitive and an aversive stimulus. For example, a rat may receive both food and shock at the end of a runway.

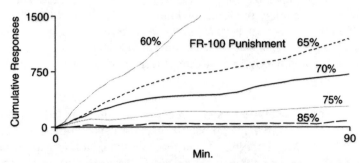

**FIGURE 7.5**  Effect of deprivation on punished responding. As the level of deprivation increases from 85% to 60% of free-feeding weight, the pigeon responds more frequently for food despite being shocked for every 100th.   (Adapted from Azrin, Holz, & Hake, 1963)

number of responses made over the course of a 90-minutes session in which the pigeon was intermittently reinforced and punished for making the response. Cumulative graphs are different from ordinary (i.e., non-cumulative) graphs, as the name implies, in that the total for each data point is added to the previous one. In Chapter 9, we will review several cumulative response graphs when we discuss intermittent schedules of reinforcement. At 85% of its free-feeding weight, punishment almost totally suppressed key pecking with the pigeon responding less than once per minute (pigeons can peck a key several times a second). However, the pigeon responded at substantially higher rates as a function of deprivation. At 60% of its free-feeding weight, the pigeon was responding approximately 30 times per minute (i.e., it responded 1500 times in less than 50 minutes). Later, we will review other variables influencing the effectiveness of the punishment procedure. At this point, you might consider the real-world implications of the fact that deprived individuals will continue to work for reinforcement despite the possibility of being punished.

## Timing of Consequence

In Chapter 4, we saw that with the exception of acquired taste aversion, temporal contiguity is necessary for predictive learning to take place. In some instances, tenths of seconds make a difference, and in most instances, seconds matter. It should come as no surprise that temporal contiguity between response and consequence is also critical in control learning. In the Theoretical Issues section, we will review a substantial body of research addressing the role of temporal contiguity in avoidance learning. For now, we consider its role in presentation of an appetitive stimulus (positive reinforcement), termination of an aversive stimulus (negative reinforcement—escape), and presentation of an aversive stimulus (positive punishment).

**POSITIVE REINFORCEMENT**   Classic evidence investigates the importance of temporal contiguity between presentation of an appetitive stimulus and a response. For example, Watson (1917) failed to find a difference between permitting immediate eating or 30-second delayed eating in rats learning to dig through sawdust for food. However, he observed the delay subjects remaining in the vicinity of the food cup where they could smell the food. Errors in a maze tend to be eliminated starting from the end, nearest the goal box (De Montpellier, 1933). Delays as short as 5 seconds interfered with learning a simple T-maze (Wolfe, 1934) or a black-white discrimination problem (Grice, 1948). Grice emphasized the importance of eliminating possible cues (conditioned reinforcers) that could replace the primary reinforcer and mask delay effects. No doubt, this is what occurred in Watson's study with the smell of the food serving to bridge the time gap until it was actually available. Figure 7.6 indicates how even brief delays in delivery of food in a Skinner box substantially decrease the rate of responding in rats (Azzi, Fix, Keller, & Rocha e Silva, 1964).

**NEGATIVE REINFORCEMENT—ESCAPE**   In escape learning, the individual terminates an aversive stimulus. Figure 7.7 portrays the result of delaying the offset of shock in a runway (Fowler & Trapold, 1962). Upon reaching the goal box, the shock went off immediately for the 0-second group and stayed on for up to 16 seconds for the other five conditions. The results of the first few trials are most informative because they are where initial learning of the escape response takes place. From the very beginning, the rats in

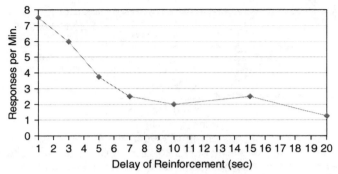

**FIGURE 7.6** Delay of positive reinforcement and response rate. Even delays of a few seconds substantially reduce responding. (Adapted from Azzi et al., 1964)

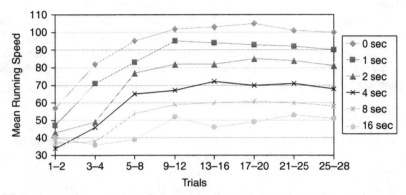

**FIGURE 7.7** Delay of negative reinforcement and speed. As with positive reinforcement, even delays of a few seconds substantially reduce the speed of escaping shock. (Adapted from Fowler & Trapold, 1962)

the 0-second delay group were running considerably faster than even the group with a 1-second delay. The speed decreased for the other groups as a function of the length of the delay. Thus, temporal contiguity applies to the removal of an aversive event in the same way it applies to presentation of an appetitive stimulus.

**PUNISHMENT** As one would expect, temporal contiguity is also important with punishment. Figure 7.8 is a suppression ratio study showing the effect of a 30-second delay in presentation of shock on bar pressing for food (Camp, Raymond, & Church, 1967; Church, 1969).

Recall that a suppression ratio of .5 indicates no effect (i.e., no change in the rate of bar pressing for food), whereas a suppression ratio of 0 indicates total cessation of bar pressing. Immediate punishment almost totally eliminated bar pressing with suppression ratios close to 0. From the rat's perspective, a 30-second delay in punishment was indistinguishable from random noncontingent presentations of shock. Note that there is evidence of slight suppression in the 30-second delay and noncontingent shock conditions. This and other aversive control side effects will be discussed in the Theoretical Issues section.

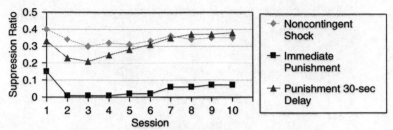

**FIGURE 7.8** Effect of delay of punishment. This figure depicts suppression of responding by immediate punishment, punishment after a 30-second delay, and noncontingent delivery of shock. Delivering shock contingently after a delay of 30 seconds is functionally no different from noncontingent delivery. (The two punishment curves are adapted from Camp et al., 1967. The noncontingent shock curve is adapted from Church, 1969)

Temporal contiguity is important in enabling an individual to detect the contingency between a behavior and an outcome. That is, it facilitates adaptive learning. Delaying reinforcement (positive or negative) not only makes learning more difficult, it has a motivational effect as well. Delayed reinforcers are worth less to an individual (i.e., they are "discounted"). The importance of this fact will be treated in depth under the topic of self-control in Chapter 14.

## Intensity of Consequence

**POSITIVE REINFORCEMENT**   Previously, we saw that deprivation of an appetitive stimulus resulted in increased vigor of a control response. The same is true with respect to the quality or quantity of an appetitive stimulus. Figure 7.9 indicates that rats bar press at six times the rate for sweet water (one-third concentration of sucrose) in comparison to ordinary tap water.

**POSITIVE PUNISHMENT**   Intensity of an aversive stimulus also exerts a powerful effect. Figure 7.10 indicates that the suppressive effect of contingent shock increases directly as a function of intensity. A very mild shock (0.1 milliampere) hardly suppresses responding, whereas an intense shock (2 amperes) almost totally eliminates responding for food.

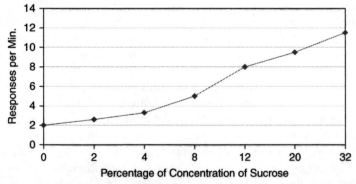

**FIGURE 7.9** Magnitude of reward and response rate. Response rate increases as a function of the sweetness of water. (Adapted from Guttman, 1954)

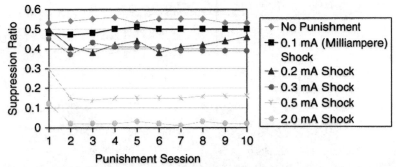

**FIGURE 7.10** Intensity of punishment and suppression. The suppressive effect of punishment increases directly as a function of shock intensity.    (Adapted from Camp et al., 1967)

> ■ Describe how the following variables influence the instrumental conditioning (control learning) process: deprivation, timing between behavior and consequence, and intensity of consequence.

## Scheduling of Consequences

In Chapter 4, we saw that the schedule of pairing two events during acquisition affected the rate of decline of responding during an extinction phase (Grant & Schipper, 1952; see Figure 4.8). In control conditioning, this phenomenon is known as the **partial reinforcement extinction effect (PREE)**. Figure 7.11 compares the average cumulative number of responses during extinction for a group of rats that had been continuously reinforced (i.e., received food after every response) with a group intermittently reinforced (i.e., given food periodically for responding). The partial-reinforcement group made five times as many responses during extinction (approximately 2500 vs. 500)! I previously asked you to suggest an explanation for this effect. In the Theoretical Issues section, we will consider a couple of possibilities that have generated a lot of research.

> **Partial Reinforcement Extinction Effect (PREE)**
>
> Intermittently reinforced responses are more resistant to extinction than continuously reinforced responses (see frustration tolerance).

A similar phenomenon to the PREE may be observed with punishment. In a two-group runway study, Banks (1966) first gave both groups of rats food

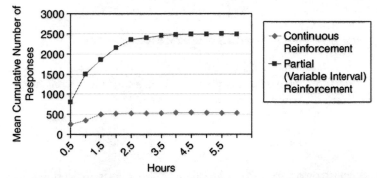

**FIGURE 7.11** Partial reinforcement extinction effect. Intermittently reinforced responses are more resistant to extinction than continuously reinforced responses.    (Adapted from Jenkins, McFann, & Clayton, 1950).

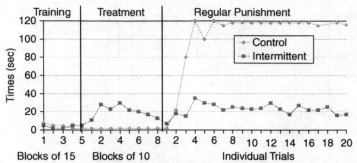

**FIGURE 7.12** Effect of intermittent punishment on later exposure to continuous punishment. During training, both groups are given food rewards for running down the runway. One group is given food and intermittent punishment during training. Finally, both groups receive food and continuous punishment. Exposure to intermittent punishment weakened the effectiveness of continuous punishment. (Adapted from Banks, 1966)

at the end of the runway, measuring the time it took to reach the end (see Figure 7.12). In the second (treatment) phase, the control group members continued to receive only food, whereas the intermittent punishment group continued to always receive food but was also randomly shocked on half the trials. This slowed them down considerably, but they continued to run to the end of the runway in about 20 seconds. In the third (regular punishment) phase, both groups received food and shock on every trial. After their first two trials of shock, the control group did not respond within the 2 minutes allotted on almost all the remaining trials. The intermittent punishment group continued to run to the end of the maze in about 20 seconds. Thus, exposure to intermittent punishment made the rats resistant to the effect of continuous punishment. This finding has important implications with respect to the applicability of punishment procedures in free-living environments. This, along with other issues related to the use of punishment, will be considered in the Theoretical Issues section.

> ■ Describe how intermittent reinforcement influences resistance to extinction (the PREE) and how intermittent punishment influences the effectiveness of continuous punishment.

## Contingency Between Response and Consequence

> God grant me the serenity to accept the things I cannot change; courage to change the things I can; and wisdom to know the difference.
>
> **Reinhold Niebuhr**

**POSITIVE REINFORCEMENT** From an adaptive learning perspective, there is much wisdom in the serenity proverb. In our continual quest to survive and to thrive, physical, behavioral, educational, cultural, economic, political, and other situational factors limit

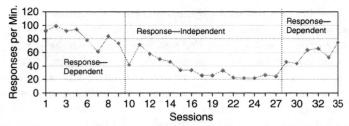

**FIGURE 7.13** Contingency and response rate. When food delivery is dependent upon responding, the pigeon pecks the key approximately 80 times per minute. During the second phase, when food is delivered at the same rate but independent of responding, the rate of key pecking drops to approximately 25 times per minute. Reverting to dependent delivery of food results in a return to the initial response rate. (Adapted from Herrnstein, 1966)

our options. Research findings suggest that the inability to affect either appetitive or aversive outcomes can have detrimental effects. Figure 7.13 indicates that removing the contingency between key pecking and receiving food results in a substantial reduction in responding in pigeons (Herrnstein, 1966). This is akin to what is sometimes described as "spoiling" a child by providing unearned rewards or gifts.

**NEGATIVE REINFORCEMENT—LEARNED HELPLESSNESS**   Figure 7.14 portrays the even more devastating effect of not having control over aversive events (Seligman & Maier, 1967). Dogs were initially placed in a restraining harness with a panel in front of them. One group did not receive shock. A second group received an escape learning contingency in which pressing the panel turned off the shock. A third group served as a **yoked-control** to the second group and received shock at precisely the same time but could do nothing to control it. This was the inescapable shock group. In the second phase, subjects were placed in a shuttle box where they could escape shock by jumping over a hurdle from one side to the other. Dogs not receiving shock or exposed to escapable shock failed to escape on only 10% of the trials, whereas those exposed to inescapable shock failed to escape on

**Yoked-Control**

An experimental procedure in which what happens to one subject is determined by the behavior of another. For example, one animal might receive food when another completes a ratio requirement.

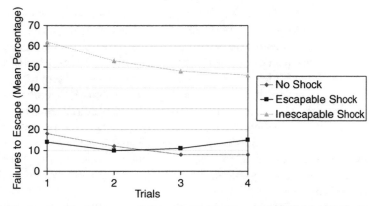

**FIGURE 7.14**   Learned helplessness. Prior exposure to inescapable shock interferes with acquiring the ability to escape shock when it is possible. (Adapted from Seligman & Maier, 1967)

**Learned Helplessness**

When individuals do not have control over significant events in one situation, they may not assert control in other situations in which control is possible. This experience can also result in depressive symptoms (e.g., crying, loss of weight).

more than 50% of the trials. Seligman observed that many of these dogs displayed symptoms similar to those of depressed humans, including lethargy, crying, and loss of appetite. Based upon his findings and observations, Seligman formulated a very influential **learned helplessness** model of clinical depression. He suggested that events such as loss of a loved one or losing a job could result in failure to take appropriate action in nonrelated circumstances as well as development of depressive symptoms. In very readable articles and books, Seligman describes how his learned helplessness model helps us understand the etiology (i.e., cause), treatment (Seligman, Maier, & Geer, 1968), and prevention of depression (Seligman, 1975, 1990). We will review the implications and applications of the learned helplessness model of depression in Chapter 8.

The key factor in the learned helplessness phenomenon is prior exposure to uncontrollable events. Goodkin (1976) demonstrated that prior exposure to uncontrolled food presentations would produce similar detrimental effects to uncontrolled shock presentations on the acquisition of an escape response.

**Spoiling Effect**

Prior exposure to uncontrolled food presentations produces similar detrimental effects to uncontrolled shock presentations on the acquisition of an escape response (see learned helplessness).

The **spoiling effect** with appetitive events has also been demonstrated under laboratory conditions using the learned helplessness model. Pigeons exposed to noncontingent delivery of food were slower to acquire an autoshaped key pecking response and demonstrated a lower rate of key pecking once it was acquired (Wasserman & Molina, 1975). It is clear from these studies and others that the serenity proverb applies to other animals as well as humans. Successful adaptation requires learning when one does and does not have the ability to control environmental events.

---

- Describe the effect of contingency between behavior and positive reinforcement.
- Describe the procedures used to demonstrate learned helplessness.

---

## THEORETICAL ISSUES

### What Maintains Avoidance Responding?

In an ideal world, we would never experience aversive events. There would be no pain, illness, or suffering. Unfortunately, into every life a little rain (and pain, etc.) must fall. Fortunately, by taking precautionary measures, we can often eliminate or substantially reduce experiencing such aversive events. Figure 7.15 portrays the results of an avoidance learning study involving higher shock intensity than ordinarily employed (Solomon & Wynne, 1953). Upon a change in illumination, dogs had 10 seconds to jump over a barrier in order to avoid shock. After receiving shock on the first seven trials, this representative dog avoided shock from then on. Note how quickly the dog made the response. Even though it had 10 seconds, it typically responded in about 2 seconds. The dog was not taking any chances and avoided 100% of the remaining possible shocks. In comparison, in most avoidance studies using milder shock, subjects maintain an avoidance rate of approximately 80%.

In every other contingency involving appetitive and aversive stimuli, the law of temporal contiguity applies. Unless the behavior is soon followed by a consequence, learning does not occur. In avoidance, by definition, it appears that nothing occurs

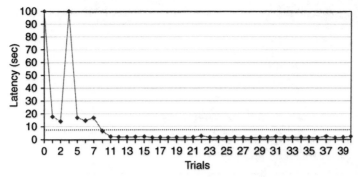

**FIGURE 7.15** Avoidance learning with an intense aversive stimulus. An intense shock resulted when dogs did not respond within 10 seconds. They quickly learned to make the avoidance response much faster than necessary.    (Adapted from Solomon & Wynne, 1953)

after a successful response. This creates the question known as the **avoidance paradox**: How can nothing maintain responding? The result appears to violate the need for temporal contiguity between a response and an environmental event.

**TWO-FACTOR THEORY    Two-factor theory** involving classical and instrumental conditioning was proposed by O. H. Mowrer (1947) in order to address the avoidance paradox. Essentially, the theory converted avoidance into escape. During the early trials prior to acquisition of an avoidance response, the individual is shocked in the presence of the warning stimulus. As with Little Albert, this should lead to the conditioning of fear to the warning stimulus. Mowrer suggested that after the avoidance response was learned, it would be followed by a reduction in fear that maintained the response. Thus, Mowrer converted avoidance of shock into escape from fear. Schoenfeld (1950) modified Mowrer's version of the two-factor theory by emphasizing the importance of the warning stimulus and its offset. When studied in the lab, avoidance responses typically result in offset of the warning stimulus as well as avoidance of the aversive event. Schoenfeld argued that it was actually the warning stimulus itself, not fear, that the individual escaped. We have already seen with suppression ratios that a stimulus paired with shock will reduce the frequency of ongoing instrumental responding. Consistent with Schoenfeld, it has been demonstrated that animals will work to escape from the side of a shuttle box paired with shock (e.g., Miller, 1948).

Physiological data support Mowrer's interpretation for the first few avoidance responses. Upon presentation of the warning stimulus, heart rate increased for dogs. After a successful avoidance response, heart rate decreased. However, once the dog was proficient at making the avoidance response, heart rate stabilized (Black, 1959; Kamin, Brimer, & Black, 1963). This makes perfect sense in that the warning stimulus is no longer being followed by shock. This should result in extinction of the fear response. Thus, fear reduction may be important while the animal is learning the avoidance response but is not the reinforcer that maintains the behavior. Kamin (1957) tested Schoenfeld's version by delaying offset of the warning stimulus after a successful avoidance response. The design is similar to the study described previously in which delayed offset of shock was found to impede escape learning (Fowler & Trapold, 1962). If the warning stimulus is aversive in

**Avoidance Paradox**

The apparent violation of the law of temporal contiguity whereby a response is maintained by the absence of an event.

**Two-Factor Theory**

A theory involving classical and instrumental conditioning to address the avoidance paradox. This theory converted avoidance into escape by assuming that after the warning stimulus was paired with shock, avoidance was followed by a reduction in fear (Mowrer) or termination of the warning stimulus (Schoenfeld).

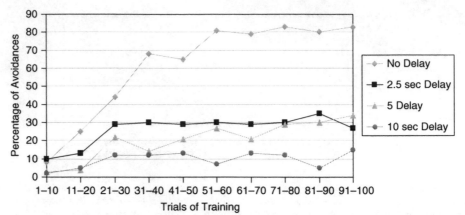

**FIGURE 7.16** Delay of warning stimulus offset and avoidance learning. Even a short delay of the warning stimulus offset substantially reduces avoidance learning. (Adapted from Kamin, 1957)

the same way shock is aversive, then delaying its offset should impede avoidance learning in the same manner that delayed shock offset impeded escape. Figure 7.16 indicates that even a delayed offset of 2.5 seconds for the warning stimulus significantly impeded avoidance responding, supporting Schoenfeld's version of the two-factor theory.

**Nonsignaled Avoidance**

The study of avoidance conditioning in a Skinner box without an external warning stimulus. Avoidance might require making a response within a particular time period.

**S-S (Shock-Shock) Clock**

After failing to avoid shock, the amount of time within which a response must occur to avoid the next shock. If the animal did not press the bar at all, it would be shocked according to the S-S (shock-shock) clock (see nonsignaled avoidance).

**R-S (Response Shock) Clock**

After successfully avoiding shock, the amount of time within which a response must occur to avoid the next shock (see nonsignaled avoidance).

Sidman (1953) studied avoidance conditioning in a Skinner box without an external warning stimulus, that is, **nonsignaled avoidance**. Two clocks determined shock frequency. If the animal did not press the bar, it would be shocked according to the **S-S (shock-shock) clock**. If it pressed the bar before the S-S clock timed out, the clock would be reset according to the **R-S (response-shock) clock**. Sidman manipulated the S-S and R-S intervals. For example, the S-S clock might be set for 20 seconds and the R-S clock for 10 seconds. If the subject did not respond at all, it would be shocked every 20 seconds. Once it pressed the bar in time, it had 10 seconds to avoid the next shock. If it always pressed the bar in less than 10 seconds, it never received shock. Bar pressing, unlike running down a runway or jumping over a hurdle, is not a species-specific defense reaction. Avoidance learning is comparatively slow in the Skinner box, particularly when there is no external warning stimulus. However, animals do eventually learn to avoid the majority of shocks (Sidman, 1953).

The fact that animals learn nonsignaled avoidance would appear to contradict Schoenfeld's version of the two-factor theory. If there is no warning signal, there can be no offset to maintain the avoidance response. The long-delay conditioning and temporal conditioning predictive learning procedures demonstrate that animals are able to estimate time intervals. Anger (1963) suggested that internal cues related to the passage of time could serve the same function as the warning stimulus and its offset. Thus, the fact that animals learn nonsignaled avoidance is not necessarily considered contradictory to the two-factor theory. Additional research by Sidman (1955), however, has caused us to rethink the role of warning stimulus offset. Rats received a hybrid signaled/nonsignaled avoidance procedure. A light indicated the rat had a specific amount of time to avoid shock. After a successful avoidance response, the rat could avoid experiencing the

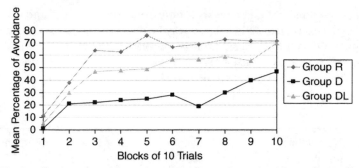

**FIGURE 7.17** Feedback and avoidance learning. Group R received immediate offset of the warning stimulus (tone) after a successful avoidance response. The D group received delayed offset of the tone. The DL condition received delayed offset of the tone but immediate onset of a light (feedback stimulus). Providing feedback reduced the effect of delaying warning stimulus offset. (Adapted from Bower et al., 1965)

warning stimulus (light) by pressing the bar in time. According to Schoenfeld, warning stimulus offset is the reinforcer for avoidance responding. Thus, by definition, the rats should work to keep it off. This is not what they did, however. Instead, they waited until the light came on and then pressed the bar. Kamin's (1957) results indicated that the timing of warning stimulus offset was critical to avoidance responding. Sidman's hybrid findings indicated that offset was not a reinforcer. If warning stimulus offset is critical to avoidance responding but not a reinforcer, what is it?

Bower, Starr, and Lazarowitz (1965) addressed this issue in a three-group runway study similar to Kamin's design. A regular (R) avoidance group terminated a tone upon reaching the goal box in time to avoid shock. The tone remained on for 8 seconds in a delayed (D) offset group. The third, delayed offset/light (DL) group was the same as the D group except that a light came on immediately when the rat reached the goal box in time. Figure 7.17 indicates that the DL group performed similarly to the R group for most of the study, catching up at the end. Bower et al. (1965) interpreted their findings to suggest that individuals require environmental **feedback** to inform them that they have made a successful avoidance response. Usually, in the laboratory, warning stimulus offset serves this role. However, any stimulus occurring in temporal contiguity to the response could serve as an effective substitute.

**Feedback**
An environmental change occurring after a behavior.

In retrospect, learning theorists may have ignored relevant information from predictive appetitive learning research in posing the avoidance paradox. We saw that magazine training designed to teach rats that food is available after a loud click precedes shaping the bar press. Otherwise, it would be enormously difficult for the rat to learn the response. Food is the reinforcer that maintains responding, but it is actually the click that provides the necessary feedback. Similarly, shock avoidance is the reinforcer for making the response with offset of the warning stimulus (or a substitute) providing immediate feedback.

Let us return to where we started our discussion of avoidance learning in order to appreciate its significance to the human condition. Solomon and Wynne (1953) demonstrated that dogs would respond indefinitely to avoid an intense shock. Obviously, this is adaptive in the same way a child needs to always "look both ways before crossing." One mistake could be dangerous. Persistent avoidance can have its costs, however.

There is an anecdote about a person with obsessive-compulsive disorder (OCD) who continually clicks his fingers. When asked why he does this, he replies it keeps away the lions and tigers. When told there are no lions or tigers in the vicinity, he replies "See, it works!" We would witness the same phenomenon if Solomon and Wynne disconnected the shocker. The subjects would continue to make the avoidance response, never discovering that shock no longer occurs.

---

■ Describe the evidence pro and con for the two-factor theory of avoidance conditioning. What is our current understanding of the role of offset of the warning stimulus?

---

**Cognitive Theory of Avoidance**

A theory explaining avoidance learning as the result of acquisition of two expectancies: A specific response results in nonoccurrence of an aversive event, and failure to make the response results in occurrence of the aversive event. Avoidance responding continues as long as the first expectancy is confirmed (see avoidance paradox).

**Flooding**

The process of requiring an individual to remain in an anxiety-provoking situation in order to reduce the anxiety.

**COGNITIVE THEORY OF CONTROL LEARNING** How do we account for such seemingly stubborn and unnecessary behavior? Seligman and Johnson (1973) proposed a **cognitive theory of avoidance** consistent with Tarpy's (1982) structural/functional definition of learning and the adaptive learning approach of this text. The theory stipulates that avoidance learning results in the acquisition of two expectancies: a specific response results in nonoccurrence of an aversive event, and failure to make the response results in occurrence of the aversive event. Avoidance responding continues indefinitely as long as the first expectancy is confirmed. Eliminating persistent avoidance responding would require disconfirming the first or second expectancy. As a therapeutic strategy, the first option, following a previously successful avoidance response with the aversive event, is undesirable. Instead, procedures such as desensitization and **flooding** (requiring the person to remain in the presumed dangerous situation) are employed to disconfirm the expectancy of an aversive event.

A cognitive theory interpretation of all control learning contingencies is possible by assuming the following expectancies are acquired in each instance:

• Occurrence of an appetitive stimulus (positive reinforcement): Making a specific response results in an appetitive event; not making the response results in nonoccurrence of the event (*If I do this, something good happens; If I don't, it doesn't happen*)

• Nonoccurrence of an aversive stimulus (negative reinforcement): Making a specific response stops (escape) or prevents (avoidance) an aversive event; not making the response results in the event (*If I do this, something bad stops or doesn't happen; If I don't, it happens*)

• Occurrence of an aversive stimulus (positive punishment): Making a specific response results in an aversive event; not making the response results in nonoccurrence of the event (*If I do this, something bad happens; If I don't, it doesn't happen*)

• Nonoccurrence of an appetitive stimulus (negative punishment): Making a specific response stops (response cost) or prevents (time out) an appetitive event; not making the response results in the event (*If I do this, something good stops or doesn't happen; If I don't, it happens*)

This model implies that it may be helpful to probe an individual's expectancies in order to understand his/her behavior. Problematic behaviors can be treated by providing reality-testing assignments in the attempt to establish more accurate expectancies. For example, a person might expect others to feel inconvenienced by simple requests. A simple assertiveness training exercise might consist of asking for a glass of water in a restaurant.

> ▪ Describe the cognitive theory expectancies presumed to develop as the result of positive reinforcement, positive punishment, negative reinforcement, and negative punishment.

## Theoretical Explanations of the PREE

Successful individuals and addicted gamblers are extremely persistent despite extended periods of not being rewarded for their acts. Obviously, such persistence is an important quality and can be a good or bad thing. We previously referred to the fact that intermittently reinforced responses are more resistant to extinction than continuously reinforced responses as the PREE, but we still need to answer this question: Why does intermittent pairing of the CS and the US in predictive learning or intermittent reinforcement in control learning increase resistance to extinction?

**DISCRIMINATION**   Common sense would suggest that it is easier to tell that things have changed when switching from always being rewarded to never being rewarded than when switching from sometimes being rewarded. This constitutes an ease of discrimination explanation of the PREE. However, it has been shown that animals first exposed to intermittent reinforcement followed by continuous reinforcement respond longer during extinction than animals receiving continuous reinforcement all along (Jenkins, 1962). Both groups underwent extinction after a period of continuous reinforcement; therefore, both should have recognized the transition in contingencies.

**FRUSTRATION THEORY**   Clearly, some process other than ease of discrimination must be involved in the PREE. Abram Amsel (1958, 1992; Amsel & Roussel, 1952) proposed the **frustration theory**, which offers explanations for three extinction-related phenomena:

| **Frustration Theory** |
| Explains the partial reinforcement extinction effect (PREE) as resulting from the acquisition of frustration tolerance. |

- Reduction in frequency of the previously reinforced response
- PREE
- Interaction between type of schedule (continuous or intermittent) and magnitude of appetitive stimulus on extinction responding

The assumptions of frustration theory follow:

1. If an individual is not reinforced after emitting a response that has been previously reinforced, frustration results.
2. The magnitude of frustration is a function of the discrepancy between the expected and obtained rewards.
3. The feeling of frustration becomes part of the stimulus complex in which it occurs.
4. Frustration is aversive and the individual will engage in competing behaviors that remove the source.
5. If an individual is reinforced for making a response while in the presence of frustration cues, tolerance is acquired.

We all know the feeling of frustration; like rain, it seems to fall into each of our lives. People frequently curse (or worse) misbehaving candy machines, computers, and so on (assumption 1). Amsel suggests that the extinction process consists of these (and less emotional) competing responses gradually replacing the previously successful response (assumption 4).

**Frustration Tolerance**

The continuation of responding in the absence of reinforcement. It is developed by experiencing reinforcement while feeling frustrated (see PREE).

The PREE is presumed to occur as the result of the acquisition of **frustration tolerance**. During acquisition, continuously reinforced individuals are never frustrated and do not have the opportunity to develop tolerance. Intermittently reinforced individuals experience frustration during acquisition. This frustration carries over to trials on which reinforcement occurs (assumption 3), resulting in the acquisition of tolerance (assumption 5). That is, the individual learns that reward is possible while feeling frustrated. Frustration theory would account for Jenkins's findings as resulting from tolerance being acquired during the initial exposure to intermittent reinforcement. It should not matter that a period of continuous reinforcement followed; the tolerance would carry over to a subsequent extinction procedure.

Continuous reinforcement with large rewards results in less responding during extinction than continuous reinforcement with small rewards. Intermittent reinforcement with large rewards results in more responding during extinction than intermittent reinforcement with small rewards. Amsel explains this interaction by incorporating the second assumption. Individuals continuously reinforced with large rewards during acquisition will experience higher levels of frustration and be more likely to engage in competing behaviors during extinction than those reinforced with small rewards during acquisition. Those intermittently reinforced with large rewards during acquisition will experience greater frustration and therefore acquire greater frustration tolerance than those intermittently reinforced with small rewards during acquisition.

Amsel and Roussel (1952) tested the assumption that frustration is aversive and individuals would be energized to escape frustrating circumstances. Rats were placed in a runway having a goal box in the middle (GB1) and at the end (GB2). During the first phase, they received food in both goal boxes and the time to run from GB1 to GB2 stabilized at 50/1000 minutes (3 seconds). In the second (test) phase, the same rats randomly received food on half the trials. Inspection of Figure 7.18 reveals that the rats ran

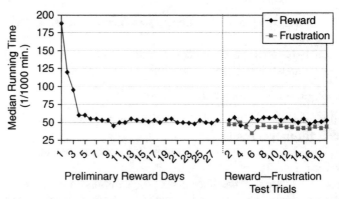

**FIGURE 7.18**  Frustration and running speed. Animals ran faster on trials when they did not received food in the middle of the runway (frustration trials) than when they did (reward trials). This result is consistent with the assumption that animals will work to escape frustrating circumstances.  (Adapted from Amsel & Roussel, 1952)

faster to GB2 when they did not receive food in GB1 (frustration trials). This finding is consistent with the assumption that frustration is aversive and individuals will work to remove themselves from the source of frustration.

**SEQUENTIAL THEORY**   Capaldi (1964, 1966, 1967) offered sequential theory as a cognitive alternative to the motivation-based frustration theory. **Sequential theory** suggests that individuals remember the patterns of reinforcement and nonreinforcement occurring during acquisition and continue to respond during extinction based upon this experience. A key concept is *N*-length, the number of nonreinforced responses followed by a reinforcer. For example the sequence NNRNNR contains two *N*-lengths of two in comparison to NRNNNR, which has *N*-lengths of one and three. Subjects experiencing the second pattern demonstrate more extinction responding than subjects experiencing the first, consistent with the model. The second pattern is variable in addition to including a longer *N*-length. Variability of *N*-lengths also increases extinction responding. Both frustration theory and sequential theory have generated impressive bodies of supportive research. Rather than viewing them as competitive, it is probable that both emotion and memory are involved in the PREE as well as in much of our other behavior. If you've managed to get your coins back by banging on a candy machine a few times in the past, it is likely that if you come upon another malfunctioning candy machine, you will feel frustrated and keep banging away because you recall your prior experiences.

**Sequential Theory**
Explains the PREE as resulting from memory of patterns of reinforcement and nonreinforcement occurring during acquisition (see *N*-length, PREE).

***N*-length**
The number of nonreinforced responses followed by a reinforcer. For example, if reinforcement occurs after the 5th and 15th responses, this would constitute *N*-lengths of 5 and 10.

> ▪ Describe how frustration theory and sequential theory account for the partial reinforcement extinction effect (PREE).

## Is Punishment Effective?

Just as in an ideal world there would be no pain or suffering, it would never be necessary to administer pain or suffering to influence another person. Unfortunately, people can be sufficiently troublesome or dangerous to create the need for drastic measures. The effectiveness of punishment is an empirical question. Whether or not to use punishment is an ethical as well as a practical issue. The ethics of the professional use of punishment are comparable to those governing invasive medical procedures such as surgery. The first objective is to "do no harm." The second objective is to address the condition in the least invasive method possible. For example, a person with a cardiovascular problem might first be put on a diet/exercise regimen before trying a low dosage of a mild drug, followed by increasing dosage and/or strength of drug, before considering the least invasive surgical procedure, and so on. If a child engages in dangerous self-injurious behavior, it is necessary to take action to eliminate the danger. Usually appetitive stimulus-based procedures, including response cost and time out, will be implemented before trying the least invasive aversive procedure. Nonprofessionals would be prudent to apply the same ethical precautionary guidelines when considering the use of punishment.

**PROBLEMS OF IMPLEMENTATION**   Figures 7.5, 7.8, 7.10, and 7.12 indicate that if an individual is not highly motivated to make a response, immediate punishment delivered at a sufficiently high intensity in a consistent fashion can effectively suppress responding. This raises the practical (i.e., external validity) issue of whether it is possible to implement punishment effectively under naturalistic conditions. Punishment is generally regarded as a prerogative of parents and of the criminal justice system. Let us examine a difficult example for each, considering whether it is logistically realistic to apply punishment effectively. We might have a child who picks on a younger sibling as our parenting example and an adult addict who pushes drugs to support his habit as our criminal justice example.

We can approach each example by addressing the variables one at a time. An older child is not as highly motivated to tease or pick on a younger sibling as a deprived addict is to obtain the substance. If administered effectively, punishment will be much more likely to reduce teasing than to suppress pushing drugs to support the addiction. However, is it likely that a parent or other adult will be present almost every time such behaviors occur? If not, we have seen that inconsistent punishment can actually make matters worse (see Figure 7.12). Similarly, in the example of the substance abuser, it would be impossible to catch her/him in the act of pushing drugs on a consistent basis. Even if we did, we would not be able to immediately administer a powerful aversive event. Also, if the abuser is undergoing withdrawal, she/he is like the pigeon at 60% of its free-feeding weight (see Figure 7.5), and even consistent punishment may not be effective.

**PUNISHMENT SIDE EFFECTS**    In addition to being difficult to administer effectively, punishment procedures have other major drawbacks:

- Cue learning
- Avoidance
- Generalized suppression
- Displaced aggression
- Conditioned masochism
- Negative modeling

**Aversive Cue Learning**

The person administering punishment is associated with the aversive event and will become a warning stimulus (cue) as well as a conditioned punisher.

**Generalized Suppression**

When individuals experience aversive stimuli within an environmental context, they will become afraid to respond at all unless they can discriminate the circumstances under which a specific behavior will be punished.

The person administering punishment is associated with the aversive event and will become a warning stimulus as well as a conditioned punisher; this is known as **aversive cue learning**. If one parent is the "good cop" and the other is the "bad cop," a child can become fearful or even hateful toward the punishing parent.

Rather than learning to suppress undesirable behavior individuals often learn how to avoid being punished. For example, an older sibling might first look around to see if a parent is present before teasing his/her younger sibling. The drug pusher is vigilant for signs that she/he may be observed. People may become deceptive and/or dishonest in order to avoid punishment.

We saw in Figure 7.8 that noncontingent punishment had a mild suppressive effect. This is an example of **generalized suppression**. When individuals experience aversive stimuli within an environmental context, they will become afraid to respond at all unless they can discriminate the circumstances under which a specific behavior will be punished. Unfortunately, we often observe this phenomenon in the classroom. Students who have perhaps been embarrassed by teachers or classmates after giving incorrect answers to a question stop answering questions altogether, even when they know the answer. Another example might be when a child punished for being aggressive stops being assertive. It may seem counterintuitive, but assertiveness training has been found to be an effective strategy when working with aggressive individuals (Huey & Rank, 1984). Apparently, one reason individuals may become aggressive is the lack of an alternative means of expressing their needs and desires.

Freud described the phenomenon of **displaced aggression**. Extinction-elicited aggression (Azrin, Hutchinson, & Hake, 1966) and punishment-elicited aggression has been demonstrated in rats (Ulrich & Azrin, 1962) and monkeys (Azrin et al., 1963). In one study, shocked monkeys even attacked a stuffed doll or a tennis ball (Azrin, Hutchinson, & Sallery, 1974). Displaced aggression in humans continues to generate significant research and theoretical analysis (Miller, Pedersen, Earleywine, & Pollock, 2003).

> **Displaced Aggression**
>
> A Freudian term indicating that individuals experiencing frustration or pain are likely to become aggressive toward innocent others.

Well-intentioned people sometimes administer punishment in such a manner as to encourage undesirable behavior. In severe instances, this can result in a process described as **conditioned masochism**. Miller (1960) exposed a "gradual group" of rats to an increasing intensity of shock along with food in a runway goal box. Speed decreased over trials as the shock intensity increased. A second group only received food in the goal box and their speed remained stable. In a second phase, both groups received the same voltage shock the first group was then receiving. The "sudden group," receiving shock for the first time, ran slowly or not at all after a few trials. The gradual group continued to run at the same moderate speed (see Figure 7.19). This procedure is similar to the desensitization procedure previously described as being effective in reducing fear and anxiety. The rats underwent a hierarchy (i.e., gradually increasing intensity) of aversive events followed by an appetitive outcome.

> **Conditioned Masochism**
>
> A procedure in which a behavior is reinforced in the presence of an aversive stimulus that gradually increases in intensity. This can result in the maintenance of responding despite being severely punished. This process is similar to the desensitization procedure effective in reducing fear and anxiety.

The term *masochism* was initially introduced to describe instances of pain-inflicting acts being incorporated into sexual behavior. However, self-destructive acts are not restricted to sex. Abused spouses and children, often starved for attention, frequently return for more abuse. A parent with the best of intentions might softly reprimand a child for misbehaving. When the child continues to misbehave, the parent might scold him/her, followed by a smack on the wrist, followed by a spanking, and so on until

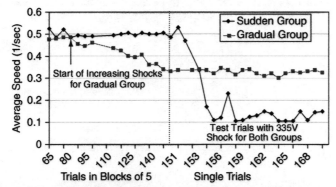

**FIGURE 7.19**  Gradual or sudden presentation of shock. During the first phase, the gradual group is shocked at an increasing intensity. In the second phase, the sudden group is shocked for the first time at the same intensity reached by the gradual group. Gradually increasing the intensity of shock reduced its effectiveness in slowing down responding.   (Adapted from Miller, 1960)

the parent is applying severe corporal punishment or worse. The parent might feel guilty after administering punishment and follow it with attention and affection. This "kiss and make up" pattern in which parent and child (or spouses) fight and then engage in pleasurable behavior is consistent with the conditioned masochism procedure.

Other instances also involve people appearing to voluntarily harm themselves. For example, one U.S. surgeon general described smoking as "slow motion suicide." An individual's initial smoking experience is usually unpleasant. It takes a powerful appetitive stimulus to counteract the aversive properties of cigarettes. Practically all smokers begin in adolescence, when peer pressure and the desire to appear grown up attain enormous importance.

The term *masochism* was not introduced to describe the behavior of other animals. It refers to patterns of human behavior that appear to be motivated by the inclusion of pain. Such behavior seems bizarre and self-destructive. Masochism is often used as a circular pseudo-explanation for behaviors such as those described in these examples. A wife is said to return to an abusing husband because she is masochistic. She is considered masochistic because she returns to the abusive husband. An acceptable psychological explanation must specify genetic and/or experiential causes (independent variables). Describing a behavior as masochistic does not specify the hereditary or experiential factors that cause it to occur. In all the prior examples, aversive events became predictive of appetitive events (sexual behavior, affection, attention, peer acceptance). This constitutes the experiential basis for such unusual, seemingly inexplicable behavior.

**Negative Modeling**

When administering punishment results in an individual demonstrating the same behavior she/he is attempting to suppress.

**Negative modeling** refers to instances when individuals display the same behavior they are attempting to suppress. For example, a parent could hit an older sibling for hitting a younger sibling. Essentially, this is a mixed signal regarding what constitutes acceptable behavior. The direct consequence indicates the behavior is unacceptable while the same behavior is being modeled in a "do as I say but not as I do" fashion.

**DESIRABILITY OF REINFORCING AN ALTERNATIVE RESPONSE** Based on research findings, it seems prudent to avoid using punishment if possible. Punishment is difficult to administer effectively under free-living conditions and has significant undesirable side effects. If punishment is to be used, it is most effective when an alternative means of securing reinforcement is possible. Figure 7.20 shows the cumulative

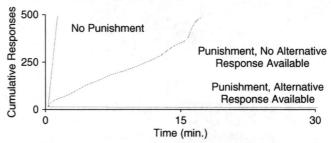

**FIGURE 7.20** Effect of the availability of an alternative response on punishment. The figure shows the cumulative records of responding for cigarettes when there is no punishment, when punishment occurs without an alternative means of obtaining cigarettes, or when punishment occurs with an alternative. Availability of an alternative means of securing reinforcement eliminated the punished response. (Adapted from Azrin & Holz, 1966; after Herman & Azrin, 1964)

response data for human subjects who received no punishment, were punished with an annoying noise with no alternative way of earning the reinforcer, or were punished but could earn the reinforcer with an alternative response. The punished group continued to respond at a slower rate for reinforcement when an alternative response was not available. However, when it was possible to obtain reinforcement with an alternative response, subjects did so and totally suppressed the other behavior (the data line tracks the x-axis on the graph).

In conclusion, we have seen that punishment is problematic and difficult to administer effectively in free-living environments. In Chapter 10, we will describe effective alternatives to punishment that are easier to implement and do not have the same side effects.

> ▪ Describe why it is difficult to administer punishment effectively in a free-living environment as well as the undesirable side effects inherent in the use of punishment.

## Summary

As with predictive learning, application of the scientific method has enabled us to determine how different variables influence control learning. In general, there is consistency in the effects of the variables on both types of learning. For example, temporal contiguity between events is necessary for individuals to detect a predictive relationship. In control learning, the law of temporal contiguity applies to positive reinforcement (controlling the occurrence of an appetitive event), negative reinforcement—escape (controlling the nonoccurrence termination of an aversive event), negative reinforcement—avoidance (controlling the nonoccurrence prevention of an aversive event), and punishment (controlling the occurrence of an aversive event).

At first glance, avoidance appears to violate the law of temporal contiguity in that a successful response results in the absence of an event. The two-factory theory emerged as an attempt to explain avoidance by essentially converting it into escape from either fear (Mowrer) or the warning stimulus (Schoenfeld). Subsequent research led to the conclusion that avoidance learning does not violate the law of temporal contiguity. Immediate feedback is necessary for avoidance learning to occur.

The fact that intermittently reinforced responses are much more resistant to extinction than continuously reinforced responses has been named the partial reinforcement extinction effect (PREE). Frustration theory explains this phenomenon as resulting from the acquisition of tolerance to the emotional experience. Sequential theory accounts for the effect in terms of the memory of patterns of previously experienced reinforcement.

Although punishment can be an effective procedure to suppress behavior, it is difficult to implement under free-living conditions. In order to be effective, it must be delivered at sufficient intensity, immediately, and in a consistent manner. In addition, punishment has problematic side effects: The punishing agent may become aversive; deceptive avoidance behaviors may be acquired; generalized suppression beyond the punished response may occur; aggression may be elicited; conditioned masochism can result from following punishment with reinforcement; and negative modeling may occur, whereby the individual imitates the very behavior one would like to suppress. Punishment is most effective when a desirable alternative behavior is reinforced.

# References

Amsel, A. (1958). The role of frustrative nonreward on noncontinuous reward situations. *Psychological Bulletin, 55*, 102–118.

Amsel, A. (1992). *Frustration theory*. Cambridge, Eng.: Cambridge University Press.

Amsel, A., & Roussel, J. (1952). Motivational properties of frustration. *Journal of Experimental Psychology, 43*, 363–368.

Anger, D. (1963). The role of temporal discrimination in the reinforcement of Sidman avoidance behavior. *Journal of the Experimental Analysis of Behavior, 6*, 477–506.

Azrin, N. H., & Holz, W. C. (1966). Punishment. In W. K. Honig (Ed.), *Operant behavior: Areas of research and application*. Englewood Cliffs, NJ: Prentice Hall.

Azrin, N. H., Holz, W. C., & Hake, D. F. (1963). Fixed-ratio punishment. *Journal of the Experimental Analysis of Behavior, 6*, 141–148.

Azrin, N. H., Hutchinson, R. R., & Hake, D. F. (1966). Extinction-induced aggression. *Journal of the Experimental Analysis of Behavior, 9*, 191–204.

Azrin, N. H., Hutchinson, R. R., & Sallery, R. D. (1964). Pain-aggression toward inanimate objects. *Journal of the Experimental Analysis of Behavior, 7*, 223–228.

Azzi, R., Fix, D. S. R., Keller, F. S., & Rocha e Silva, M. I. (1964). Exteroceptive control of response under delayed reinforcement. *Journal of the Experimental Analysis of Behavior, 7*, 159–162.

Banks, R. K. (1966). Persistence to continuous punishment following intermittent punishment training. *Journal of Experimental Psychology, 71*, 373–377.

Black, A. H. (1959). Heart rate changes during avoidance learning in dogs. *Canadian Journal of Psychology, 13*, 229–242.

Bower, G. H., Starr, R., & Lazarovitz, L. (1965). Amount of response-produced change in the CS and avoidance training. *Journal of Comparative and Physiological Psychology, 59*, 13–17.

Camp, D. C., Raymond, G. A., & Church, R. M. (1967). Temporal relationship between response and punishment. *Journal of Experimental Psychology, 74*, 114–123.

Capaldi, E. J. (1964). Effect of N-length, number of different N-lengths, and number of reinforcements on resistance to extinction. *Journal of Experimental Psychology, 68*, 230–239.

Capaldi, E. J. (1966). Partial reinforcement: A hypothesis of sequential effects. *Psychological Review, 73*, 459–479.

Capaldi, E. J. (1967). A sequential hypothesis of instrumental learning. In K. W. Spence & J. T. Spence (Eds.), *The psychology of learning and motivation* (vol. 1, pp. 67–156). New York: Academic Press.

Clark, F. C. (1958). The effect of deprivation and frequency of reinforcement on variable-interval responding. *Journal of Experimental Analysis of Behavior, 1*, 221–227.

Collier, G. (1969). Body weight loss as a measure of motivation in hunger and thirst. *Annals of the New York Academy of Science, 157*, 594–609.

De Montpellier, G. (1933). An experiment on the order of elimination of blind alleys in maze learning. *Journal of Genetic Psychology, 43*, 123–139.

Fowler H., & Trapold, M. A. (1962). Instrumental escape performance as a function of the intensity of noxious stimulation. *Journal of Experimental Psychology, 60*, 323–326.

Goodkin, F. (1976). Rats learn the relationship between responding and environmental events: An expansion of the learned helplessness hypothesis. *Learning and Memory, 7*, 382–393.

Grant, D. A., & Schipper, L. M. (1952). The acquisition and extinction of conditioned eyelid responses as a function of the percentage of fixed ratio random reinforcement. *Journal of Experimental Psychology, 43*, 313–320.

Grice, G. R. (1948). The relation of secondary reinforcement to delayed reward in visual discrimination learning. *Journal of Experimental Psychology, 38*, 1–16.

Guttman, N. (1954). Equal reinforcing values for sucrose and glucose solutions compared with sweetness values. *Journal of Comparative and Physiological Psychology, 47*, 358–361.

Herman, R. L., & Azrin, N. H. (1964). Punishment by noise in an alternative response situation. *Journal of the Experimental Analysis of Behavior, 7*, 185–188.

Huey, W. C., & Rank, R. C. (1984). Effects of counselor and peer-led group assertive training on Black adolescent aggression. *Journal of Counseling Psychology, 31*, 95–98.

Jenkins, H. M. (1962). Resistance to extinction when partial reinforcement is followed by regular reinforcement. *Journal of Experimental Psychology, 64*, 441–450.

Jenkins, W. O., McFann, H., & Clayton, F. L. (1950). A methodological study of extinction following aperiodic and continuous reinforcement. *Journal of Comparative and Physiological Psychology, 43*, 155–167.

Kamin, L. J. (1957). The gradient of delay of secondary reward in avoidance learning. *Journal of Comparative and Physiological Psychology, 50*, 445–449.

Kamin, L. J., Brimer, C. J., & Black, A. H. (1963). Conditioned suppression as a monitor of fear of the CS in the course of avoidance training. *Journal of Comparative and Physiological Psychology, 56*, 497–501.

Miller, N. E. (1948). Studies of fear as an acquirable drive: I. Fear as motivation and fear reduction as reinforcement in the learning of responses. *Journal of Experimental Psychology, 38*, 89–101.

Miller, N. E. (1960). Learning resistance to pain and fear: Effects of overlearning, exposure, and rewarded exposure in context. *Journal of Experimental Psychology, 60*, 137–145.

Miller, N. U., Pedersen, W. C., Earleywine, M., & Pollock, V. E. (2003). A theoretical model of triggered displaced aggression. *Personality and Social Psychology Review, 7*, 75–97.

Mowrer, O. H. (1947). On the dual nature of learning: A reinterpretation of "conditioning" and "problem-solving." *Harvard Educational Review, 17*, 102–148.

Porter, J. J., Madison, H. L., & Senkowski, P. C. (1968). Runway performance and competing responses as a function of drive level and method of drive measurement. *Journal of Experimental Psychology, 78*, 281–284.

Schoenfeld, W. N. (1950). An experimental approach to anxiety, escape, and avoidance behavior. In P. H. Hock & J. Zubin (Eds.), *Anxiety* (pp. 70–99). New York: Grune & Stratton.

Seligman, M. E. P. (1975). *Helplessness: On depression, development, and death.* San Francisco, CA: Freeman.

Seligman, M. E. P. (1990). *Learned optimism.* New York: Knopf.

Seligman, M. E. P., & Johnston, J. C. (1973). A cognitive theory of avoidance learning. In F.J. McGuigan & D. B. Lumsden (Eds.), *Contemporary approaches to conditioning and learning.* Washington, DC: Winston-Wiley.

Seligman, M. E. P., & Maier, S. F. (1967). Failure to escape traumatic shock. *Journal of Experimental Psychology, 74*, 1–9.

Seligman, M. E. P., Maier, S., & Geer, J. (1968). The alleviation of learned helplessness in the dog. *Journal of Abnormal and Social Psychology, 73*, 256–262.

Sidman, M. (1953). Two temporal parameters of the maintenance of avoidance behavior in the white rat. *Journal of Comparative and Physiological Psychology, 46*, 253–261.

Sidman, M. (1955). Some properties of the warning stimulus and avoidance behavior. *Journal of Comparative and Physiological Psychology, 48*, 444–450.

Solomon, R. L., & Wynne, L. C. (1953). Traumatic avoidance learning: Acquisition in normal dogs. *Psychological Monographs, 67*(354), 19.

Tarpy, R. M. (1982). *Principles of animal learning and motivation.* Glenview, IL: Scott Foresman and Company.

Ulrich, R. E., & Azrin, N. H. (1962). Reflexive fighting in response to aversive stimulation. *Journal of the Experimental Analysis of Behavior, 5*, 511–520.

Wasserman, E. A., & Molina, E. J. (1975). Explicitly unpaired key light and food presentations: Interference with subsequent autoshaped key pecking in pigeons. *Journal of Experimental Psychology: Animal Behavior Processes, 1*, 30–38.

Watson, J. B. (1917). The effect of delayed feeding upon learning. *Psychobiology, 1*, 51–60.

Weiss, R. F. (1960). Deprivation and reward magnitude effects on speed throughout the goal gradients. *Journal of Experimental Psychology, 60*, 384–390.

Wolfe, J. B. (1934). The effect of delayed reward upon learning in the white rat. *Journal of Comparative and Physiological Psychology, 17*, 1–21.

# Chapter 8

# Control Learning: Applications

In Chapter 6, we discussed the ubiquity of adaptive learning in our lives. It is the process through which human beings acquire the ability to predict and control their environment. Therefore, it is the process through which we understand and transform our world and our lives. We reviewed basic control learning phenomena and terminology, seeing how our every day existence may be described in units of short-term and long-term stimulus-response chains. Our days consist of learned adaptations to discriminative and warning stimuli. In this chapter, we review some of the major applications of control learning principles to understanding the human condition. We start with a discussion of speech, because once acquired, it is so crucial to indirect adaptive learning.

# SPEECH AND LANGUAGE (VERBAL SYMBOLIC BEHAVIOR)

Civilization began the first time an angry person cast a word instead of a rock.

**Sigmund Freud**

Spoken language is observed in stone-age hunter/gatherer and technologically advanced cultures. The role of nature and nurture in human language development has been controversial (Chomsky, 1959; Skinner, 1957). Skinner, writing from a functionalist/behavioral perspective, tellingly entitled his book *Verbal Behavior*, not "Using Language." Watson (1930) described a good deal of what we call thinking as "covert speech," and Skinner (1953) referred to "private behavior." As described by Vygotsky (1962), children initially "think out loud" and eventually learn to "think to themselves." Skinner suggested that speaking and thinking were not different in kind from other forms of behavior and that respondent conditioning (predictive learning) and operant conditioning (control learning) could provide the necessary experiential explanatory principles.

We saw in Chapter 5 how predictive learning principles could be applied to the acquisition of word meaning. Basically, Skinner argued that words could serve as overt and covert substitutes for the control learning ABCs (antecedents, behaviors, consequences). As **antecedents**, words could function as discriminative stimuli and warning stimuli. For example, "Here is ice cream" or "Heads up." Words can describe behaviors (e.g., "Give mommy a kiss" or "Be careful crossing the street"). As consequences, words could substitute for reinforcers and punishers (e.g., "Thank you." "Stop that!"). A rule is a common, useful, and important verbal statement that includes each of the control learning ABCs (Hayes, 1989). That is, a rule specifies the circumstances (antecedents) under which a particular act (behavior) is rewarded or punished (consequence). For example, a parent might instruct a child, "At dinner, if you eat your vegetables, you can have your dessert" or "When you get to the curb, look both ways before crossing the street or you could get hit by a car."

> **Antecedents**
> Events taking place prior to a behavior (e.g., discriminative stimuli and warning stimuli).

Chomsky, a psycholinguist, submitted a scathing critique of Skinner's book, emphasizing how human genetics appears to include a **language acquisition device**. The picture in Chapter 1 of the human homunculus, with its disproportional brain space dedicated to the mouth and tongue, certainly suggests that the human being's structure facilitates speech acquisition. The homunculus also implies an adaptive value to spoken language; otherwise, these structures would not have evolved. Proposing a "language acquisition device" to account for speech is a pseudo-explanation. It is circular. The language acquisition device is inferred from the observation of speech; it does not explain speech. Remember, a psychological explanation must specify specific hereditary and/or environmental causes. Chomsky does neither, whereas Skinner is quite specific about the types of experience that will foster different types of verbal behavior. MacCorquodale (1969) wrote a retrospective appreciation of Skinner's book along with a comprehensive response (1970) to Chomsky's critique.

> **Language Acquisition Device**
> According to Chomsky, the mechanism responsible for humans' learning to speak.

It is not as though Skinner denies the role of human structure in the acquisition of speech or its importance as indicated in the following quote: "The human species took a crucial step forward when its vocal musculature came under operant control [described as control learning in this text] in the production of speech sounds. Indeed, it is possible that all the distinctive achievements of the species can be traced to that one genetic change" (Skinner, 1986, p. 117). Neuroscientists and behavioral neuroscientists are actively engaged in research examining how the "all-purpose acquisition device" known as the brain is involved in the learning of speech, reading, quantitative skills, problem solving, and other skills.

Human beings may have started out under restricted geographic and climatic conditions in Africa, but we have spread all over the globe (Diamond, 2005). We have developed different words and languages tailored to our environmental and social circumstances. There is much to be learned from the school of hard knocks, but that is limited to our direct experience and can be difficult or dangerous. Our verbal lives enormously expand learning opportunities beyond our immediate environment to anything that can be imagined. Indirect learning in the form of observation or language often speeds up adaptive learning and eliminates danger. It is not surprising that human parents universally dedicate a great deal of effort to teaching their children to speak. It makes life easier, safer, and better for them as well as their children.

---

■ Describe how control learning principles help us understand verbal behavior.

---

## PARENTING

Children are completely egoistic; they feel their needs intensely and strive ruthlessly to satisfy them.

It is impossible to overlook the extent to which civilization is built upon a renunciation of instinct.

The first requisite of civilization is that of justice.

**Sigmund Freud**

### Parenting Styles and Control Learning

In addition to helping their children acquire safety and survival skills, parents attempt to teach codes of moral conduct (i.e., the difference between right and wrong). Much parenting consists of intentional or nonintentional administration of appetitive and aversive events. In an important and related schema, parenting styles have been categorized on the dimensions of demandingness and responsiveness (Baumrind, 1968, 1971; Maccoby & Martin, 1983). Demanding parents specify clear rules of conduct and require their children to comply. Responsive parents are affectionate and sensitive to their children's needs and feelings. Figure 8.1 lists the four parenting styles resulting from different combinations of high and low demandingness and responsiveness.

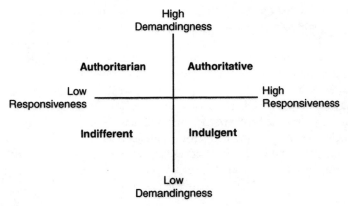

**FIGURE 8.1**  Baumrind's parental styles.

We may consider the implications of control learning principles for these parenting styles. Indifferent parents (low demandingness, low responsiveness) do not specify codes of conduct or respond to their children's needs. If other people (siblings, relatives, peers) do not provide rules and/or consequences, the children will most likely base decisions about what is right and wrong on the outcomes of their actions (if it feels good, it is right; if it feels bad, it is wrong).

Indulgent parents (low demandingness, high responsiveness) do not specify codes of conduct but are affectionate and responsive. They provide "unconditional positive regard" (Rogers, 1957), the type of noncontingent appetitive consequence likely to result in spoiling and a sense of entitlement. This could create problems for the children in other contexts (e.g., school, playgrounds) when others react differently to their behavior.

Authoritarian parents (high demandingness, low responsiveness) specify strict codes of conduct in a nonresponsive manner. If the children ask for reasons, they may reply "because I say so!" In their parents' absence, the children would seek other sources of authority.

Authoritative parents (high demandingness, high responsiveness) specify strict codes of conduct within a context of warmth and sensitivity to the children's needs. They are likely to provide reasons for their codes of conduct, listen to their children's perspective, and at some times negotiate alternative codes.

In Chapter 6, we considered the use of punishment for a child who picks on a younger sibling. It was concluded that it would be very difficult to administer punishment immediately on a consistent basis, and it would not likely work as intended. There was the risk that the older sibling would learn to fear and perhaps avoid the punisher and could actually imitate punishing a weaker individual on other occasions. Indifferent parents are not likely to be present to appropriately administer punishment and will probably be inconsistent. Indulgent parents are less likely to administer punishment than other parents, if they administer it at all. Authoritarian parents ("my way or the highway") might effectively suppress the undesired behavior when present but run the previously mentioned risks. Authoritative parents, taking advantage of their children's verbal and reasoning skills, probably have the greatest likelihood of attaining the desired result.

For example, an older sibling picking on a younger one might be told the following scenario, which includes stipulation of rules of conduct:

There is a difference between a jungle and a society. In the jungle, strong animals often attack weaker animals that receive no protection. Human beings have families and societies in which the strong protect the weak and help them grow stronger. You have to decide whether you want to live in our family and society. If you keep picking on your little brother/sister, we will need to treat you like an animal from the jungle. When we bring dangerous animals near our homes, we put them in a zoo so they can't hurt anyone. If necessary, we will keep you in your room so you can't bother your little brother/sister. If you take care of your little brother/sister, mommy and daddy will let you play together and have fun.

■ Relate control learning principles to Baumrind's parenting styles.

**Pre-Conventional Morality**

When right and wrong are based on extrinsic rewards and punishers. This is the first major stage of Lawrence Kohlberg's (1976) influential model of moral development.

**Conventional Morality**

When right and wrong are based on appeals to an authority figure (e.g., parent, teacher, clergy member) or written source (e.g., the Constitution, Bible) This is the second major stage of Lawrence Kohlberg's (1976) influential model of moral development.

**Post-Conventional Morality**

When right and wrong are based on the application of universal principles such as the Golden Rule (Do unto others as you would have others do unto you). This is the third major stage of Lawrence Kohlberg's (1976) influential model of moral development.

## Parenting Styles and Moral Development

Lawrence Kohlberg (1976) developed an influential stage model of moral development. He distinguishes among three levels ("styles") of reasoning: pre-conventional, conventional, and post-conventional. **Pre-conventional morality** is based on extrinsic rewards and punishers. **Conventional morality** appeals to an authority figure (e.g., parent, teacher, clergy member) or written source (e.g., the Bible, Koran, Constitution). **Post-conventional morality** is based on the application of universal principles such as the Golden Rule (Do unto others as you would have others do unto you). As described earlier, indifferent parenting would appear to be most likely to produce pre-conventional reasoning in children. The authoritarian parenting style would appear likely to result in conventional reasoning and the authoritative style in post-conventional reasoning. Ideally, by providing reasons and explanations in age-appropriate language, our children would internalize principles of moral conduct and apply them appropriately throughout their lives (see Figure 8.2).

| Negligent | Indulgent | Authoritarian | Authoritative |
|---|---|---|---|
| Unavailable to monitor behavior, administer consequences consistently, or provide explanations | Available to administer non-contingent presentation of appetitive events and provide praise | Available to administer contingent presentation of mostly aversive events without explanation | Available to administer contingent presentation of appetitive and aversive events with explanation |
| Pre-conventional morality | Sense of entitlement | Conventional morality | Post-conventional morality |

**FIGURE 8.2**   Parental styles and stages of morality.

■ Relate control learning principles to Kohlberg's stages of moral development.

## Preparing for Adulthood

> Anatomy is destiny.
> Love and work…work and love, that's all there is.
>
> **Sigmund Freud**

For most of our time on earth, variations of the human species survived as nomadic small bands of hunter/gatherers in Africa. Diamond (2005, pp. 36–37) describes fossilized evidence that humans migrated to Southeast Asia approximately 1 million years ago, with Homo sapiens reaching Europe one-half-million years ago. Existing evidence suggests that humans reached the Americas between 14,000 and 35,000 years ago. Diamond (2005, p. 87) provides an overview of the causal factors impacting the human condition. Geographic and climatic conditions affecting the availability of wild plants and animals determined the possibility of the development of agriculture and animal domestication. Localized food production enabled the establishment of more permanent residences and larger communities. Food storage permitted surpluses, freeing people from survival demands on a day-to-day basis. This resulted in development of new "occupations" and technologies.

**PREPARING CHILDREN TO BE HUNTER/GATHERERS**    The portion of the Amazonian rain forest inhabited by the **Nukak** people, consisting almost entirely of marshes and wetlands, does not support a permanent lifestyle based upon domestication of plants and animals (Politis, 2007). There are, however, abundant edible nondomesticated plant, fruit, and vegetable species and some edible animals (e.g., several species of monkeys, peccaries, tortoises, birds, ducks, and fish). The Nukak are one of the few remaining cultures continuing to practice the nomadic hunter/gatherer lifestyle characteristic of the earliest members of our species. They travel in bands composed of approximately five nuclear families with a median of 20–30 individuals. Temporary shelters designed for stays of about 4 days are crafted from posts, tree branches, and leaves to form a camp. Furnishings include hammocks for sleeping and a hearth for cooking.

**Nukak**
One of the few remaining cultures continuing to practice the nomadic hunter/gatherer lifestyle characteristic of the earliest members of our species. This tribe lives in the Colombian Amazon rainforest.

The Nukak, living day to day, have maintained a similar lifestyle for more than 10,000 years. They lack familiarity with government, property, or money. The Nukak do not have a concept of the future and their past history is limited to a few generations. In order to survive under very challenging conditions, the Nukak had to acquire the knowledge and skills to protect themselves from the elements and predators. They had to learn to forage and prepare a nonpoisonous, nutritionally adequate diet.

An adult male almost always leads the daily excursions from the camp, and many such excursions are limited to males. Most of the activities are related to hunting, fishing, and collecting foods (fruits, vegetables, honey, etc.). These trips also involve collecting resources such as cane for blowpipes, leaves for roofs, bark and vines for cords. Because their groups have such low population densities, trips can involve searches for potential mates among other bands. Females often take part in local foraging trips, but most of their time is spent near the shelters caring for young children and preparing food. Time is frequently taken out during the day for men and women to pass on survival skills from generation to generation. Considering this lifestyle, one would not be surprised if a Nukak in Hardin's cartoon was thinking "eat, survive, reproduce" rather than "What's it all about?"

**PREPARING CHILDREN FOR SCHOOL AND WORK**    We live very different lives than the Nukak, resulting from the effects of centuries of civilization and available technologies. Thanks to machinery reducing the need for physical strength and the availability of contraception, anatomy is not necessarily the dominating force in one's destiny that it was in the past. Opportunities for women enormously expanded as we transitioned to an economy based upon service and information.

**Adolescence**

Demarcated by the onset of puberty as males and females become physically capable of reproduction. Adolescence ends with the assumption of adult responsibilities (e.g., financial independence, having a family).

Freud remains current in his observation that the human condition includes the two major developmental tasks of preparing for love and work. The beginning of **adolescence** is demarcated by the onset of puberty as males and females gradually become physically capable of reproduction. Associated is the development of a new and powerful basic drive. Some high school teachers describe their students as "hormones with legs!" The Nukak have no reason to discourage sexuality or delay childbearing. As soon as males and females are ready, they pair off and usually form monogamous relationships. The educational requirements of many current vocations in technologically advanced societies require delaying the start of a family. In 1950, the average age of marriage was 23 for men and 20 for women in the United States. By 2000, these ages had increased to 27 and 25, respectively (Arnett, 2000). The increasing need to delay marriage during emerging adulthood poses a challenge for many contemporary individuals and societies. One result is a birthrate declining to less than what is needed for replacement in some technologically advanced cultures.

Industrialization resulted in people moving from predominantly rural, low-density population, agricultural lifestyles to urban, high-density population, manufacturing lifestyles. Many of the jobs were dangerous and some required advanced intellectual skills. A need and desire for compulsory education arose toward the end of the 19th century. In 1890, 5% of American ages 14–17 were enrolled in high school. By 1970, 90% were enrolled (Tanner, 1972). The same trend has been observed with college attendance. In 1890, fewer than 5% of 18- to 21-year-olds were enrolled (Arnett & Taber, 1994), and by 2011 this number exceeded 68%, according to U.S. Bureau of Labor statistics. No doubt this percentage will continue to increase in the future, and we will observe similar trends in graduate and postgraduate education. Arnett (2000) has suggested the need to add a new developmental phase, **emerging adulthood**, between what we ordinarily consider the end of adolescence (graduation from high school at about the age of 18) and the assumption of adult responsibilities (being financially independent, living apart from one's parents, starting a family, etc.). Arnett found that many college students report feeling "in between" adolescence and adulthood, consistent with the need to consider emerging adulthood an intermediary stage of development. This feeling may be even more pronounced when economic conditions lead to children returning home to live with their parents.

**Emerging Adulthood**

Arnett's (2000) suggested developmental phase between what we ordinarily consider the end of adolescence (graduation from high school at about the age of 18) and the assumption of adult responsibilities (being financially independent, living apart from one's parents, starting a family, etc.).

The Nukak have faced the same environmental demands and parents have transmitted the same survival skills from generation to generation for millennia. The Nukak have essentially two stages of development, childhood and adulthood. Children's toys usually consist of scaled-down versions of survival tools. Children participate in foraging, hunting, and food preparation as soon as they are physically able. This contrasts with the extensive schooling required to create a common knowledge base and prepare the children in technologically advanced cultures for ever-changing vocations. Many countries have compulsory primary and secondary education in order to address these goals. Thus, in addition to teaching a culture's code of conduct, parents in these countries need to prepare their children to attend school.

School represents a different "world" for children with its own set of adaptive requirements. Parents play an important role in preparing their children for school. The authoritative style characterized by high demandingness and high responsiveness has been shown to result in better school performance than the authoritarian style (Pratt, Green, MacVicar, & Bountrogianni, 1992; Hokoda & Fincham, 1995). In school, teachers, rather than parents, are the ones establishing standards and administering consequences. The dimensions of demandingness and responsiveness may be applied to teaching as well as parenting styles. Teachers may hold high or low standards for their students. They may be personable and warm in their classroom interactions or distant and detached. As with parenting, authoritative teaching styles result in better academic and social performance than do authoritarian styles (Walker, 2008).

**The Good Behavior Game**    Children arrive at school with different levels of preparedness and skills. This often results in classroom management challenges for the teacher. Various adaptive learning procedures have been implemented successfully to address such problems. The **Good Behavior Game (GBG)** is a comprehensive program recommended by the Coalition for Evidence-Based Policy (www.evidencebasedprograms.org), a member of the Council for Excellence in Government. The GBG was developed by two teachers and Montrose Wolf (Barrish, Saunders, & Wolf, 1969), one of the founders of the *Journal of Applied Behavior Analysis*, a very readable and practical publication. In order to "play the game," the teacher (it has been implemented as early as preschool) divides the class into two or three teams of students. The GBG is usually introduced for 10-minute sessions, 3 days a week. The session times are gradually increased to a maximum of an hour. A chart is posted in front of the room listing and providing concrete examples of inappropriate behaviors such as leaving one's seat, talking out, or causing disruptions. The teacher identifies any instance of such a behavior (e.g., "Team 1 gets a check because Danielle just talked out without raising her hand"), and a check mark is placed on the chart under the team's name. The teacher also praises the other groups for behaving (e.g., "Teams 2 and 3 are working very nicely"). At the end of the day, the members of the team with the fewest check marks receive school-related rewards such as free time, lining up first for lunch, or stars on a "winner's chart." It is usually possible for all groups to receive rewards if they remain below a specified number of inappropriate behaviors. This number may then be reduced over sessions.

The Good Behavior Game has been tested in two major randomized controlled studies in an urban environment resulting in several publications. It was demonstrated to

**Good Behavior Game (GBG)**

A comprehensive program to address classroom management challenges for the teacher recommended by the Coalition for Evidence-Based Policy, a member of the Council for Excellence in Government. The experimental findings for the effectiveness of the GBG have been so consistent and powerful that it has been recommended as an extremely cost-efficient "universal behavioral vaccine" (Embry, 2002).

reduce aggression (Dolan et al., 1993), increase on-task behavior in first-graders (Brown, 1993), and reduce aggression (Kellam, Rebok, Ialongo, & Mayer, 1994) and the initiation of smoking (Kellam & Anthony, 1998) in middle school students. A follow-up after the sixth grade found that students experiencing the GBG in the first grade had a 60% lower incidence of conduct disorder, 35% lower likelihood of having been suspended, and 29% lower likelihood of having received mental health services. Perhaps most impressively, 14 years after implementation, the GBG was found to result in a 50% lower rate of lifetime illicit drug abuse, a 59% lower likelihood of smoking 10 or more cigarettes a day, and a 35% lower rate of lifetime alcohol abuse for 19- to 21-year-old males (Kellam et al., 2008)! More recently, the Good Behavior Game has been found to significantly reduce disruptive behavior in kindergarteners (Donaldson, Vollmer, Krous, Downs, & Beard, 2011). Tingstrom and colleagues reviewed more than 30 years of research evaluating variations of the Good Behavior Game (Tingstrom, Sterling-Turner, & Wilczynski, 2006). The experimental findings for the effectiveness of the Good Behavior Game have been so consistent and powerful that it has been recommended as an extremely cost-efficient "universal behavioral vaccine" (Embry, 2002).

---

■ Describe control learning applications within school settings.

---

## TREATING BEHAVIORAL PROBLEMS WITH NONVERBAL INDIVIDUALS

**Behavioral Excesses**

Problems resulting from the presence of behavior (e.g., aggressive acts, excessive drinking, tics).

As mentioned in Chapter 1, all psychological (as distinct from medical) treatments depend upon the learning process. An underlying assumption is that no matter what the cause of maladaptive behavior, it can usually be modified by providing appropriate experiences. Rather than simply assigning an American Psychiatric Association diagnosis (e.g., autism, schizophrenia, depression, anxiety disorder), an adaptive learning approach describes problems as consisting of **behavioral excesses** (e.g., aggressive acts, excessive drinking, tics) and **behavioral deficits** (e.g., lack of assertiveness, illiteracy, failure to wear seat belts).

**Behavioral Deficits**

Problems resulting from the absence of performance (e.g., lack of assertiveness, illiteracy, failure to wear seat belts).

### Applied Behavior Analysis with Autistic Children

**Autism**

A severe developmental disorder characterized by extreme behavioral deficits (e.g., an apparent lack of interest in other people, lack of speech) and excesses (e.g., tantrums, self-stimulatory behavior such as rocking back and forth or flapping hands, and self-destructive behaviors such as headbanging).

As an example of the application of the adaptive learning approach to understanding the human condition, we start with the condition of early infantile autism. **Autism** is a severe developmental disorder characterized by an apparent lack of interest in other people, including parents and siblings. The child may throw tantrums and engage in self-destructive behaviors such as head banging (a severe behavioral excess) and self-stimulatory behavior such as rocking back and forth or flapping hands. A behavioral excess such as head banging is not only likely to result in serious injury, but will also interfere with a child's acquiring important linguistic and social skills. That is, an extreme behavioral excess may result in serious behavioral deficits. Autistic children often display excesses and/or deficits of attention. For example, they may stare at the same object for an entire day (stimulus over-selectivity) or seem unable to focus upon anything for more than a few seconds (stimulus under-selectivity). In the absence of treatment, an autistic child may fail to acquire the most basic self-help skills such as dressing or feeding oneself or looking before crossing the street. They require constant attention from caregivers in order to survive, let alone acquire the social and intellectual skills requisite to making friends and preparing for school.

The basic principles of predictive and control learning have predominantly been established under controlled conditions with nonverbal animals. It should therefore come as no surprise that procedures based upon these principles have been applied to nonverbal children having pervasive developmental disorders. Ivar Lovaas (1967) pioneered the creation and assessment of applied behavior analysis as a comprehensive learning program for autistic children that, in the absence of a medical understanding of the disorder, continues to be the most effective available treatment. An excellent summary of this early work (Lovaas & Newsom, 1976) describes his success in reducing self-destructive behavior (e.g., head banging) and teaching language using control learning procedures. A still inspiring film (Lovaas, 1969) portrays this seminal research.

In Lovaas's words,

> What one usually sees when first meeting an autistic child who is 2, 3, or even 10 years of age is a child who has all the external physical characteristics of a normal child—that is, he has hair, and he has eyes and a nose, and he may be dressed in a shirt and trousers—but who really has no behaviors that one can single out as distinctively "human." The major job then for a therapist—whether he's behaviorally oriented or not—would seem to be a very intriguing one, namely the creation or construction of a truly human behavioral repertoire where none exists. (Lovaas & Newsom, 1976, p. 310)

Because autistic children are nonverbal and do not imitate, teaching them can have much in common with training a laboratory animal in a Skinner box. Initially, one needs to rely on direct learning procedures. Unconditioned reinforcers and punishers (i.e., biologically significant stimuli such as food or shock) serve as consequences for behavioral deficits and excesses.

**BEHAVIORAL EXCESSES—REDUCING SELF-INJURIOUS BEHAVIOR**  Some early attempts at eliminating self-injurious behaviors by withdrawing attention (Wolf, Risley, & Mees, 1964) or placing the child in social isolation (Hamilton, Stephens, & Allen, 1967) were successful. However, such procedures tend to be slow acting and risky in extreme cases. In such instances, presentation of an aversive stimulus (a brief mild shock) may be necessary. Lovaas, Schaeffer, and Simmons (1965) were the first to demonstrate the immediate long-lasting suppressive effect of contingent shock on tantrums and self-destructive acts with two 5-year-old children. These findings have been frequently replicated, including with a device developed by collaboration among psychological researchers, engineers, autism advocates, and medical manufacturers known as the **Self-Injurious Behavior Inhibiting System (SIBIS)**. A sensor module that straps onto the head is attached to a radio transmitter. The psychologist can adjust the sensor for different intensities of impact, and shock can immediately be delivered to the arm or leg

**Self-Injurious Behavior Inhibiting System (SIBIS)**

A device developed by collaboration among psychological researchers, engineers, autism advocates, and medical manufacturers. A sensor module that straps onto the head is attached to a radio transmitter. The sensor can be adjusted for different intensities of impact and contingent shock can immediately be delivered to the arm or leg.

if the child exceeds the impact threshold. Rapid substantial reductions in self-injurious behavior were obtained with five previously untreatable older children and young adults using brief mild shocks (Linscheid, Iwata, Ricketts, Williams, & Griffin, 1990).

**BEHAVIORAL DEFICITS—ESTABLISHING IMITATION AND SPEECH** Once interfering behavioral excesses are reduced to being manageable, it is possible to address behavioral deficits and establish the capability of indirect learning through imitation and language. Perhaps the most disheartening aspect of working with an autistic child is her/his indifference to signs of affection. Smiles, coos, hugs, and kisses are often ignored or rejected. Autistic children are typically physically healthy and good eaters. Therefore, Lovaas and his coworkers were able to make obtaining food contingent on specific behaviors.

To address language learning, shaping procedures including prompting and fading were used at first to teach the child to emit different sounds. For example, in teaching the child to say "mama," the teacher would hold the child's lips closed and then let go when the child tried to vocalize. This would result in the initial "mmm." (You can try this on yourself.) Once this was achieved, the teacher would touch the child's lips without holding them shut, asking him/her to say "mmm." Eventually, the physical prompt could be eliminated and the verbal prompt would be sufficient. At this point, the teacher would ask the child to say "ma," holding the child's lips closed while he/she is saying "mmm" and suddenly letting go. This will result in an approximation of "ma" that can be refined on subsequent trials. It is then a straightforward process to have the child repeat "ma," producing the desired "mama." As this procedure is repeated, the child gradually acquires the ability to imitate different sounds and words and the pace of learning picks up considerably.

Once the child is able to imitate what she/he hears, procedures are implemented to teach meaningful speech. Predictive learning procedures are used in which words are paired with the objects they represent, resulting in verbal comprehension. Verbal expression is achieved by rewarding the child for pointing to objects and saying their name. The child is taught to ask questions (e.g., "Is this a book?") and make requests (e.g., "May I have ice cream?"). After a vocabulary of nouns is established, the child learns about relationships among objects (e.g., "on top of," "inside of"), and other parts of speech are taught (e.g., pronouns, adjectives). Eventually, the child becomes capable of describing his/her life (e.g., "I had cereal for breakfast") and creative storytelling.

Lovaas assessed the extent to which the treatment gains acquired in his program were maintained over a 4-year follow-up in other environments. If the children were discharged to a state institution, they lost the benefit of training. Self-injurious behavior, language, and social skills all returned to pretreatment levels. Fortunately, providing "booster" sessions rapidly reinstated the treatment gains. Those children remaining with their parents (who received instruction in the basic procedures) maintained their treatment gains and continued to improve in some instances (Lovaas, Koegel, Simmons, & Long, 1973). Low intellectual functioning often accompanies autism, so it is unrealistic to expect all children to reach the age-appropriate grade level. Still, Lovaas (1987) has achieved this impressive ideal with 50% of the children treated with his comprehensive program when they started prior to 30 months of age. Despite ongoing research to address the biological mechanisms thought to underlie autism, applied behavior analysis remains the most effective treatment approach with this population.

■ Describe how control learning interventions have been used to treat behavioral excesses and deficits with autistic children.

## TREATING BEHAVIORAL PROBLEMS WITH VERBAL INDIVIDUALS

One might think that if it is possible to socialize an autistic child with extreme behavioral excesses and severely limiting behavioral deficits, treating a healthy, verbal, and cooperative adult for a psychological problem would be easy in comparison. However, we need to appreciate the logistic and treatment implementation issues that arise when working with a free-living individual. Lovaas was able to create a highly controlled environment during the children's waking hours. It was possible for trained professionals to closely monitor the children's behavior and immediately provide powerful consequences. In comparison, adult treatment typically consists of weekly 1-hour "talking sessions" and "homework" assignments with which the therapist does not have this degree of access or control. Success depends upon the client following through on suggested actions and accurately reporting what transpires.

### Cognitive-Behavioral Treatment of Depression

As an example, let us consider someone who becomes depressed after losing a job. In Chapter 7, we reviewed Seligman's research suggesting that depression results from a perceived loss of control over significant events. It is as though the person believes that *if I do this, it will not matter*. Depression in humans has been related to **attributions** on three dimensions: internal–external, stable–unstable, and global–specific (Abramson, Seligman, & Teasdale, 1978). With respect to our example, the person is more likely to become depressed if he/she attributes loss of the job to a personal deficiency such as not being smart (internal) rather than to a downturn in the economy (external), the belief that not being smart is a permanent deficiency (stable) rather than temporary (unstable), and that not being smart will apply to other jobs (global) rather than just the previous one (specific).

Therapy consists of exercises designed to reveal and modify these underlying attributions through reality testing. The therapist might challenge the notion that the person is not smart by reminding her/him of past job performance successes. They could review the person's credentials in preparation for a job search. Severe cases of depression might require assignments related to self-care and small-step achievements (e.g., making one's bed, grooming and getting dressed, going out for a walk). An important study determined that the behavioral homework assignments constituted the most important component of the **cognitive-behavioral treatment of depression** (Jacobson et al., 1996). Apparently, therapies are effective to the extent that they result in clients experiencing the consequences of their acts under naturalistic circumstances. This finding is consistent with an adaptive learning model of the psychotherapeutic process. That is, therapy is designed to help the individual acquire the necessary skills to cope with her/his environmental demands.

The therapeutic process frequently consists of determining adaptive **rules**. For example, in treating a severely depressed individual, one might start with

**Attributions**
The assumed causes of events. For example, one may attribute loss of a job to internal factors such as lack of aptitude and skills or to external factors such as a downturn in the economy.

**Cognitive-Behavioral Treatment of Depression**
A treatment approach based on the assumption that feelings and behavior are influenced by one's thoughts (see attributions). Individuals are encouraged to change the attributions for their problems from being internal, global, and permanent to being external, specific, and temporary.

**Rule**
A verbal statement including each of the control learning ABCs specifying the circumstances (antecedents) under which a particular act (behavior) is rewarded or punished (consequence).

"If you get out of bed within 30 minutes after the alarm goes off, you can reward yourself with 30 minutes of TV." This can then be modified to require getting up within 20 minutes, 10 minutes, and 5 minutes. Once this is accomplished, the person may be required to get up and make the bed, get up and make the bed and wash his/her face, and so on. If the person is not severely depressed, it may be sufficient to establish rules such as "After finding appropriate positions in the newspaper, you can reward yourself with reading your favorite section of the paper after you send out your resume."

> ▪ Describe how control learning procedures have been applied to the treatment of depression.

## Contingency Management of Substance Abuse

Let us return to our example of an adult selling illegal drugs to support an addictive disorder. Such an individual is highly motivated to surreptitiously commit an illegal act. A person addicted to drugs could be expected to behave similarly to the food-deprived pigeon described in Chapter 7 (see Figure 7.5; Azrin, Holz, & Hake, 1963). As withdrawal symptoms become increasingly severe, punishment procedures lose their effectiveness. It would be prudent and desirable to enroll the addict in a drug-rehabilitation program involving medically monitored withdrawal procedures or medical provision of

**Contingency Management**

The manipulation of consequences to promote desirable changes in behavior.

a legal substitute. Ideally, this would be done on a voluntary basis, but it could be court mandated. **Contingency management** procedures have been used successfully for years to treat substance abusers. In one of the first such studies, vouchers exchangeable for goods and services were given for cocaine-free urine samples, assessed three times per week (Higgins, Delaney, Budney, Bickel, Hughes, & Foerg, 1991). The hope is that successful treatment of the addiction is sufficient to eliminate the motive for further criminal activity. A contingency management cash-based voucher program for alcohol abstinence has been implemented using combined urine and breath assessment procedures. It resulted in a doubling, from 35% to 69%, of alcohol-free test results (McDonell et al., 2012).

> ▪ Describe how control learning procedures have been applied to treat substance abuse.

## EMPIRICALLY VALIDATED THERAPEUTIC TECHNIQUES

**Empirically Validated Therapeutic Techniques**

Approaches to intervention supported by multiple experimental research findings.

In 1995, Division 12 (Clinical Psychology) of the American Psychological Association published a report recommending training in and promotion of **empirically validated therapeutic techniques** (APA, 1995; Nathan & Gorman, 2002). The great majority of those techniques meeting the criteria for empirical validation (i.e., controlled outcome studies) were behaviorally focused applications of adaptive learning principles. Such procedures have been found to be effective for treatment of anger and aggression in youth (Blake & Hamrin, 2007), attention-deficit/hyperactivity disorder (Chronis & Jones, 2006), borderline personality disorder (Linehan, 1993), depression (Elkin et al., 1989; Jacobsen et al., 1996; McCullough, 2000), hypochondriasis (Barsky & Ahern, 2004), obsessive-compulsive disorder (Foa et al., 1995), panic disorder (Barlow, Craske, Cerny, & Klosko, 1989), sexual offenses (Serran, Fernandez, Marshall, & Mann, 2003), social phobia (Mattick, Peters, & Clarke, 1989), substance abuse (Ouimette, Finney, & Moos, 1997), and suicidal behavior (Rudd, Joiner, & Rajab, 2001). The shift to training clinical graduate students to use empirically validated treatments has been found to improve their treatment outcomes when they become practitioners (Cukrowicz et al., 2005).

It is unfortunate that the logistic problems related to monitoring behavior and effectively administering consequences with free-living individuals have often interfered with implementation of the most effective procedures (cf., Probst, 2008). Successful efforts have been made to improve implementation through **bibliotherapy** (Rapee, Abbott, & Lyneham, 2006), videoconferencing (Bouchard et al., 2004), and computer-assisted delivery (Carroll et al., 2008, 2009). Lovaas was able to motivate autistic children to adapt to an environment he created. The challenge was then to ensure that the training benefits carried over to their home and school environments. Teaching the parents to monitor their children's behavior and administer appetitive and aversive stimuli appropriately facilitated this. The challenge when working with free-living individuals is to successfully use indirect learning procedures to enable them to acquire the skills to adapt to their own idiosyncratic conditions. Books, videos, and computer simulations (including virtual reality) can help. *Research Press* publishes many excellent manuals and videos for parenting, counseling, and working with special education populations.

**Bibliotherapy**
Treatment for a behavioral problem in the form of textual material.

## USING TECHNOLOGY TO TREAT BEHAVIORAL EXCESSES

We have seen that adaptive learning principles may be applied by parents and helping professionals to address many important and serious behavioral problems occurring in home, school, and clinical settings. It is usually possible to rely upon positive reinforcement procedures to treat behavioral deficits. In Chapter 9, we will see that it is also frequently possible to rely upon reinforcement-based procedures to treat behavioral excesses. Such approaches do not have the logistic issues or produce the side effects associated with punishment.

Punitive approaches to behavioral excesses require continuous monitoring of behavior. We saw how a helmet with sensors was developed to address this problem and successfully eliminate head banging in autistic children. It is also necessary to detect instances of undesirable behavior and be able to manipulate the consequences if one is to effectively implement reinforcement-based procedures to reduce behavioral excesses. Ideally, we would be able to identify and eliminate the reinforcer that is maintaining undesirable behavior. Recent technologies are making it theoretically possible to address a wide range of serious behavioral excesses including criminal behavior by enabling the surveillance of behavior and elimination of the reinforcer .

An old saying is that "money is the root of all evil." In reality, the saying is both incorrect and misleading. Some of the most extreme examples of evil such as murder and rape are not usually motivated by profit. In addition, the saying fails to mention that money is the root of much productive work behavior as well. There is no doubt, however, that money is the incentive underlying the drug trade and many other forms of criminal activity including burglary, prostitution, political graft, etc. If it were possible to monitor all financial transactions, it would theoretically be possible to detect practically all instances of illegal trafficking in drugs. Drug traffickers rely upon the availability of cash and money-laundering operations to amass huge fortunes. A cashless society has been discussed for several decades as a way of eliminating the incentive for profit-related crime. Today, most individuals are able to carry out almost all financial transactions with personal checks and credit and debit cards. It is technically feasible to eliminate cash altogether or significantly reduce the denominations (e.g., all bills above $20). Once this occurred, practically all major transactions would produce a traceable record. Some consider a cashless society a severe threat to our privacy rights while recognizing its convenience and safety benefits. There is no doubt that the elimination of cash would significantly impact drug trafficking, illegal weapons sales, prostitution, all instances of smuggling, kidnapping, political graft, the "underground economy," and so on. Surveillance technologies are developing and improving while criminals are becoming increasingly tech savvy and dangerous. One of the defining issues of the first decades of the 21st century is the conflict between the need for security and the right to privacy.

Other examples of the conflict between increasing security and sacrificing privacy relate to widespread use of global position system (GPS) devices and video cameras to monitor where you are and what you are doing. GPS devices are attached to many cars to enable electronic collection of tolls. They are also installed in cell phones and digital cameras.

Increasingly, video cameras are becoming pervasive in stores and malls, at stoplights, stadiums, and in high-crime areas. I asked my students how they would feel about cameras being installed in classrooms to discourage cheating. Many responded that they did not mind because they resent it when students receive inflated grades by dishonest means. Also, apparently growing up in a culture with cell phone cameras and reality TV has desensitized the current generation of college students to being photographed unknowingly. An example of the educational benefit of surveillance was provided in a recent study in which physicians were videotaped while administering preventive care visits to infants (Nyp et al., 2011). Corrective feedback was provided resulting in improved performance on subsequent preventive care visits.

The editors of *Scientific American* (2010) included two uses of surveillance to promote socially beneficial behaviors among their listing of potentially transformative technologies. The first took advantage of the reinforcing power of competitive games by monitoring and making public neighbors' usage of energy and water in homes in order to promote conservation. The second employed GPS technologies to individualize the costs of driving based upon miles driven, times of day, routes taken, and so on. In this way, people could be encouraged to drive less and use routes designed to reduce congestion.

The Orwellian (1949) "Big Brother" watching us is becoming increasingly real and perhaps inevitable and acceptable. As a society, we need to do our best to protect privacy rights as we increasingly rely upon technology-enhanced means of monitoring behavior to increase our security and encourage socially desirable behaviors.

> ▪ Describe how technologies related to surveillance of behavior and financial transactions impact the ability to effectively implement contingencies of control learning.

## RELAPSE PREVENTION

In Chapter 5, we saw that the extinction process does not undo prior learning. Rather, an inhibitory response is acquired that counteracts the previously learned behavior. Adaptive learning procedures have been successful in addressing a wide range of behavioral problems. Successful treatments rely upon the establishment of new behaviors to counteract behavioral excesses and eliminate behavioral deficits. Unfortunately, as Lovaas demonstrated, treatment success does not guarantee sustained benefits. That is, psychological problems are subject to relapse. G. Alan Marlatt has published extensively on the conditions likely to result in relapse and developed a strategy for reducing the risk (Brownell, Marlatt, Lichtenstein, & Wilson, 1986; Marlatt, 1978; Marlatt & Donovan, 2005; Marlatt & Gordon, 1980, 1985). Much of this research relates to addictive disorders that have been shown to undergo remarkably similar relapse patterns. Unless provided with additional training, 70% of successfully treated smokers, excessive drinkers, and heroin addicts are likely to relapse within 6 months (Hunt, Barnett, & Branch, 1971). Marlatt conducted follow-up interviews to track the incidence of relapses and attain information regarding the circumstances (e.g., time of day, activity, location, presence of others, associated thoughts and feelings). Approximately 75% of the relapses were precipitated by negative emotional states (e.g., frustration, anger, anxiety, depression), social pressure, and interpersonal conflict (e.g., with spouse, family member, friend, employer/employee). Marlatt also described the **abstinence violation effect**, in which a minor lapse was followed by a full-blown binge.

**Abstinence Violation Effect**

A minor lapse followed by a full-blown binge. For example, if an individual overeats at one meal and then completely goes off a diet.

**Relapse prevention** methods involve identifying personal high-risk situations and acquiring and practicing coping skills. For example, depending upon one's environmental demands, any combination of the following treatments may be appropriate: relaxation exercises, desensitization for specific fears or sources of anxiety, anger management, time management, assertiveness training, social-skills training, conflict resolution training, and training in self-assessment and self-control. A review of research applying relapse prevention methods to difficult recalcitrant substance abuse problems concluded that it was quite successful (Irvin, Bowers, Dunn, & Wang, 1999).

**Relapse Prevention**

A strategy designed to sustain the benefits of effective intervention. The methods include identifying personal high-risk situations and acquiring coping skills.

An adaptive learning perspective requires an extensive analysis of an individual's environmental demands and coping strategies. Whether in the home, the school, or a free-living environment, there may be a mismatch between the demands and the person's current skill set. Successful treatment provides the necessary skills to cope with not only the current demands, but also to prepare the individual for predictable stressors and setbacks.

> ▪ Describe the conditions most likely to result in relapse as well as procedures found helpful in reducing the likelihood of its occurrence.

## Summary

Every known human culture has spoken language, attesting to its adaptive value. Control learning principles help us understand how speech is acquired and maintained. Spoken words (or thoughts) can function as antecedents and consequences. Verbal rules state the conditions under which specific behaviors are reinforced and punished. Speech enables humans to indirectly acquire knowledge and skills efficiently and safely.

Different parenting styles may be described according to the manner in which consequences are administered. It was suggested that the patterns of moral behavior depicted by Kohlberg's stages relate to these parental styles. All cultures prepare children to mate and adapt to the requirements of their environments. Increasingly, in technologically enhanced societies, this requires extensive schooling. Control learning procedures have been successfully applied to increase the likelihood of success in school and decrease the likelihood of developmental problems.

There is experimental evidence for the efficacy of control learning procedures in addressing a wide range of disorders with human clients of all ages in diverse settings. Applied behavior analysis procedures for treating behavioral excesses (e.g., self-injurious behavior) and deficits (e.g., lack of imitation and speech) in autistic children have proved to be the most successful treatment approach for this population. Cognitive-behavioral approaches to treating depression and contingency-management approaches to treating substance abuse in free-living adults were described. Technological advances in behavioral surveillance and monitoring of financial transactions enable effective administration of control learning procedures under conditions posing logistic challenges with free-living individuals. Societies will struggle to simultaneously maintain security along with the right to privacy. Successful treatment of behavioral problems is not necessarily sustained. The conditions under which relapse is most likely have been identified and it is now possible to prepare individuals for such eventualities.

## References

Abramson, L. Y., Seligman, M. E., & Teasdale, J. (1978). Learned helplessness in humans: Critique and reformulation. *Journal of Abnormal Psychology, 87*, 49–74.

American Psychological Association. (1995). Training in and dissemination of empirically-validated psychological treatments: Report and recommendations. *The Clinical Psychologist, 48*, 2–24.

Arnett, J. J. (2000). Emerging adulthood: A theory of development from the late teens through the twenties. *American Psychologist, 55*, 469–480.

Arnett, J. J., & Taber, S. (1994). Adolescence terminable and interminable: When does adolescence end? *Journal of Youth and Adolescence, 23*, 517–537.

Azrin, N. H., Holz, W. C., & Hake, D. F. (1963). Fixed-ratio punishment. *Journal of the Experimental Analysis of Behavior, 6*, 141–148.

Barlow, D. H., Craske, M. G., Cerny, J. A., & Klosko, J. S. (1989). Behavioral treatment of panic disorder. *Behavior Therapy, 20*, 261–282.

Barrish, H. H., Saunders, M., & Wolf, M. M. (1969). Good behavior game: Effects of individual contingencies for group consequences on disruptive behavior in a classroom. *Journal of Applied Behavior Analysis, 2*, 119–124.

Barsky, A. J., & Ahern, D. K. (2004). Cognitive behavior therapy for hypochondriasis: A randomized controlled trial. *Journal of the American Medical Association, 291*, 1464–1470.

Baumrind, D. (1968). Authoritative vs. authoritarian parental control. *Adolescence, 3*, 255–272.

Baumrind, D. (1971). Current patterns of parental authority. *Developmental Psychology Monographs, 4*(1, Pt. 2).

Blake, C. S., & Hamrin, V. (2007). Current approaches to the assessment and management of anger and aggression in youth: A review. *Journal of Child and Adolescent Psychiatric Nursing, 20*, 209–221.

Bouchard, S., Paquin, B., Payeur, R., Allard, M., Rivard, V., Fournier, T., . . . Lapierre, J. (2004). Delivering cognitive-behavior therapy for panic disorder with agoraphobia in videoconference. *Telemedicine Journal and e-Health, 10*, 13–24.

Brown, C. H. (1993). Statistical methods for preventive trials in mental health. *Statistics in Medicine, 12*, 289–300.

Brownell, K. D., Marlatt, G. A., Lichtenstein, E., & Wilson, G. T. (1986). Understanding and preventing relapse. *American Psychologist, 41*, 765–782.

Carroll, K. M., Ball, S. A., Martino, S., Nich, C., Babuscio, T. A., & Rounsaville, B. J. (2009). Enduring effects of a computer-assisted training program for cognitive behavior therapy: A 6-month follow-up of CBT4CBT. *Drug and Alcohol Dependence, 100*, 178–181.

Carroll, K. M., Ball, S. A., Martino, S., Nich, C., Gordon, M. A., Portnoy, G. A., & Rounsaville, B. J. (2008). Computer-assisted delivery of cognitive behavioral therapy for addiction: A randomized trial of CBT4CBT. *The American Journal of Psychiatry, 165*, 881–889.

Chomsky, N. (1959). Review of Skinner's *Verbal behavior*. *Language, 35*, 26–58.

Chronis, A. M., & Jones, H. A. (2006). Evidence-based psychosocial treatments for children and adolescents with attention-deficit/hyperactivity disorder. *Clinical Psychology Review, 26*, 486–502.

Cukrowicz, K. C., White, B., Reitzel, L. R., Burns, A. B., Driscoll, K. A., Kemper, T. S., & Joiner, T. E. (2005). Improved treatment outcome associated with the shift to empirically supported treatments in a graduate training clinic. *Professional Psychology: Research and Practice, 36*, 330–337.

Diamond, J. (2005). *Guns, germs, and steel*. New York: W.W. Norton & Company.

Dolan, L., Kellam, S. G., Brown, C. H., Werthamer-Larsson, L., Rebok, G. W., & Mayor, L. S. (1993). The short-term impact of two classroom-based preventive intervention trials on aggressive and shy behaviors and poor achievement. *Journal of Applied Developmental Psychology, 14*, 317–345.

Donaldson, J. M., Vollmer, T. R., Krous, T., Downs, S., & Beard, K. P. (2011). An evaluation of the Good behavior game in kindergarten classrooms. *Journal of Applied Behavior Analysis, 44*, 605–609.

Elkin, I., Shea, M. T., Watkins, J. T., Imber, S. D., Sotsky, S. M., & Collins, J. F. (1989). National Institute of Mental Health Treatment of Depression Collaborative Research Program: General effectiveness treatments. *Archives of General Psychiatry, 46*, 971–982.

Embry, D.D. (2002). The good behavior game: A best practice candidate as a universal behavioral vaccine. *Clinical Child and Family Psychology Review, 5*, 273–297.

Foa, E. B., Kozak, M. J., Goodman, W. K., Hollander, E., Jenike, M. A., & Rasmussen, M. D. (1995). DSM-IV field trial: Obsessive-compulsive disorder. *American Journal of Psychiatry, 152*, 90–96.

Hamilton, J., Stephens, L., & Allen, P. (1967). Controlling aggressive and destructive behavior in severely retarded institutionalized residents. *American Journal of Mental Deficiency, 71*, 852–856.

Hayes, S. C. (1989). *Rule-governed behavior: Cognition, contingencies, and instructional control*. New York: Plenum Press.

Higgins, S. T., Delaney, D. D., Budney, A. J., Bickel, W. K., Hughes, J. R., Foerg, F., & Fenwick, J. W. (1991). A behavioral approach to achieving initial cocaine abstinence. *American Journal of Psychiatry, 148*, 1218–1224.

Hokoda, A., & Fincham, F. D. (1995). Origins of children's helpless and mastery achievement patterns in the family. *Journal of Educational Psychology, 87*, 375–385.

Hunt, W. A., Barnett, L. W., & Branch, L. G. (1971). Relapse rates in addiction programs. *Journal of Clinical Psychology, 27*, 455–456.

Irvin, J. E., Bowers, C. A., Dunn, M., & Wang, M. C. (1999). Efficacy of relapse prevention: A meta-analytic review. *Journal of Consulting and Clinical Psychology, 67*, 563–570.

Jacobson, N. S., Dobson, K. S., Truax, P. A., Addis, M. E., Koerner, K., Gollan, J. K., ... Prince, S. E. (1996). A component analysis of cognitive behavioral treatment for depression. *Journal of Consulting and Clinical Psychology, 64*, 295–304.

Kellam, S. G., & Anthony, J. C. (1998). Targeting early antecedents to prevent tobacco smoking: Findings from an epidemiologically-based randomized field trial. *American Journal of Public Health, 88*, 1490–1495.

Kellam, S. G., Brown, C. H., Poduska, J. M., Ialongo, N. S., Wang, W., Toyinbo, P. ... Wilcox, H. C. (2008). Effects of a universal classroom behavior management program in first and second grades on young adult behavioral, psychiatric, and social outcomes. *Drug and Alcohol Dependence, 95*, 5–28.

Kellam, S. G., Rebok, G. W., Ialongo, N., & Mayer, L. S. (1994). The course and malleability of aggressive behavior from early first-grade into middle-school: Result of a developmental epidemiologically-based preventive trial. *Journal of Child Psychology and Psychiatry, 35*, 359–382.

Kohlberg, L. (1976). Moral stages and moralization: The cognitive-development approach. In T. Lickona (Ed.), *Moral development and behavior* (pp. 31–53). New York: Holt, Rinehart and Winston.

Linehan, M. M. (1993). *Cognitive-behavioral treatment of borderline personality disorder*. New York: Guilford.

Linscheid, T. R., Iwata, B. A., Ricketts, R. W., Williams, D. E., & Griffin, J. C. (1990). Clinical evaluation of the self-injurious behavior inhibiting system (SIBIS). *Journal of Applied Behavior Analysis, 23*, 53–78.

Lovaas, O. I. (1967). A behavior therapy approach to the treatment of childhood schizophrenia. In J. P. Hill (Ed.), *Minnesota symposia on child psychology* (Vol. 1, pp. 108–159). Minneapolis, MN: University of Minnesota Press.

Lovaas, O. I. (1969). *Behavior modification: Teaching language to psychotic children.* New York: Appleton-Century-Crofts (Film).

Lovaas O. I. (1987). Behavioral treatment and normal educational and intellectual functioning in young autistic children. *Journal of Consulting and Clinical Psychology, 55*, 3–9.

Lovaas, O. I., Koegel, R. L., Simmons, J. Q., & Long, J. S. (1973). Some generalization and follow-up measures on autistic children in behavior therapy. *Journal of Applied Behavior Analysis, 6*, 131–165.

Lovaas, O. I., & Newsom, C. D. (1976). Behavior modification with psychotic children. In H. Leitenberg (Ed.), *Handbook of behavior modification and behavior therapy* (pp. 303–360). Englewood Cliffs, NJ: Prentice Hall.

Lovaas, O. I., Schaeffer, B., & Simmons, J. Q. (1965). Experimental studies in childhood schizophrenia: Building social behavior in autistic children by use of electric shock. *Journal of Experimental Research in Personality, 1*, 99–109.

Maccoby, E., & Martin, J. (1983). Socialization in the context of the family: Parent-child interaction. In E. M. Hetherington (Ed.), *Handbook of child psychology: Socialization, personality, and social development* (Vol. 4, pp. 1–101). New York: Wiley.

MacCorquodale, K. (1969). B. F. Skinner's *Verbal behavior*: A retrospective appreciation. *Journal of the Experimental Analysis of Behavior, 12*, 831–841.

MacCorquodale, K. (1970). On Chomsky's review of Skinner's *Verbal behavior. Journal of the Experimental Analysis of Behavior, 13*, 83–99.

Marlatt, G. A. (1978). Craving for alcohol, loss of control, and relapse: A cognitive-behavioral analysis. In P. E. Nathan, G. A. Marlatt, & T. Loberg (Eds.), *Alcoholism: New directions in behavioral research and treatment* (pp. 71–117). New York: Plenum.

Marlatt, G. A., & Donovan, D. M. (2005). *Relapse prevention: Maintenance strategies in the treatment of addictive behaviors* (2nd ed.). New York: Guilford

Marlatt, G. A., & Gordon, J. R. (1980). Determinants of relapse: Implications for the maintenance of behavior change. In P. O. Davidson & S. M. Davidson (Eds.), *Behavioral medicine: Changing health lifestyles* (pp. 410–452). New York: Brunner/Mazel.

Marlatt, G. A., & Gordon, J. R. (Eds.). (1985). *Relapse prevention: Maintenance strategies in the treatment of addictive behaviors.* New York: Guilford.

Mattick, R. P., Peters, L., & Clarke, J. C. (1989). Exposure and cognitive restructuring for social phobia: A controlled study. *Behavior Therapy, 20*, 3–23.

McCullough, J. P. (2000). The case of Katrina: Skating on thin ice. *Cognitive and Behavioral Practice, 7*, 510–514.

McDonell, M. G., Howell, D. N., McPherson, S., Cameron, J. M., Srebnik, D., Roll, J. M., & Ries, R. K. (2012). Voucher-based reinforcement for alcohol abstinence using the ethyl-glucuronide alcohol biomarker. *Journal of Applied Behavior Analysis, 45*, 161–165.

Nathan, P. E., & Gorman, J. M. (2002). *Treatments that work* (2nd ed.). New York: Oxford University Press.

Nyp, S. S., Barone, V. J., Kruger, T., Garrison, C. B., Robertsen, C., & Christopherson, E. R. (2011). Evaluation of developmental surveillance by physicians at the two-month preventive care visit. *Journal of Applied Behavior Analysis, 44*, 181–185.

Orwell, G. (1949). *Nineteen eighty-four.* New York: Harcourt, Brace & Company.

Ouimette, P. C., Finney, J. W., & Moos, R. H. (1997). Twelve step and cognitive-behavioral treatment for substance abuse: A comparison of treatment effectiveness. *Journal of Consulting and Clinical Psychology, 65*, 230–240.

Politis, G. G. (2007). *Nukak.* Walnut Creek: University College, London Institute of Archeology Publications.

Pratt, M. W., Green, D., MacVicar, J., & Bountrogianni, M. (1992). The mathematical parent: Parental scaffolding, parenting style and learning outcomes in long-division mathematics homework. *Journal of Applied Developmental Psychology, 13*, 17–34.

Probst, B. (2008). Issues in portability of evidence-based treatment for adolescent depression. *Child & Adolescent Social Work Journal, 25*, 111–123.

Rapee, R. M., Abbott, M. J., & Lyneham, H. J. (2006). Bibliotherapy for children with anxiety disorders using written materials for parents: A randomized controlled trial. *Journal of Consulting and Clinical Psychology, 74*, 436–444.

Rogers, C. (1957). The necessary and sufficient conditions of therapeutic personality change. *Journal of Consulting Psychology, 21*, 95–103.

Rudd, M. D., Joiner, T., & Rajab, M. H. (2001). *Treating suicidal behavior: An effective time-limited approach.* New York: Guilford Press.

Serran, G., Fernandez, Y., Marshall, W. L., & Mann, R. E. (2003). Process issues in treatment: Application to sexual offender programs. *Professional Psychology: Research and Practice, 34*, 368–374.

Skinner, B. F. (1953). *Science and human behavior.* New York: Macmillan.

Skinner, B. F. (1957). *Verbal behavior.* Englewood Cliffs, NJ: Prentice-Hall.

Skinner, B. F. (1986). The evolution of verbal behavior. *Journal of the Experimental Analysis of Behavior, 45*, 115–122.

Tanner, D. (1972). *Secondary education.* New York: Macmillan.

Tingstrom, D. H., Sterling-Turner, H. E., & Wilczynski, S. M. (2006). The good behavior game: 1969–2002. *Behavior Modification, 30*, 225–253.

Vygotsky, L. S. (1962). *Thought and language.* Cambridge, MA: MIT Press. (Original work published 1934).

Walker, J. M. T. (2008). Looking at teacher practices through the lens of parenting style. *The Journal of Experimental Education, 76*, 218–240.

Watson, J. B. (1930). *Behaviorism.* New York: Norton.

Wolf, M. M., Risley, T., & Mees, H. (1964). Application of operant conditioning procedures to the behavior problems of an autistic child. *Behavior Research and Therapy, 1*, 305–312.

World changing ideas: Ten thoughts, trends and technologies that have the power to transform our lives. (2010). *Scientific American, 303*(6), 42–53.

## Chapter 9

# Schedules of Reward and Maintenance of Learned Behavior

In Chapters 3 through 8, we discussed predictive and control learning principles, findings, theoretical issues, and applications. Repeatedly we observed that learning is an adaptive process, and individuals acquire behaviors that result in favorable outcomes or reduce unfavorable ones. It is as though the scientific method is carried in the DNA of much of the animal kingdom! Animals appear genetically prepared to detect predictive correlations and control contingencies in their environmental niches. Once these correlations and contingencies are detected, individuals behave adaptively to attain appetitive stimuli and reduce aversive stimuli.

We also observed that even after learning has occurred, individuals remain sensitive to environmental correlations and contingencies. Previously acquired behaviors will stop occurring if the correlation or contingency is eliminated. This is the extinction process. In Chapter 4, we saw that extinction is not the equivalent of unlearning. The phenomena of spontaneous recovery, disinhibition, and renewal indicate that a previously learned behavior can reappear. In Chapter 8, we saw that autistic children who had benefited from Lovaas's institutionally based intensive teaching program lost these benefits unless placed in a supportive environment (Lovaas, Koegel, Simmons, & Long, 1973).

That is, under some circumstances, despite the potential, previously learned behavior may not occur. Obviously, there is a need to understand the factors that maintain learned behavior.

## SKINNERIAN METHODOLOGY

### The Operant Chamber (Skinner-Box)

Studying the maintenance of learned behavior requires a methodology different from that used to study the initial learning process. In studying learning, it is often sufficient to demonstrate that a specific response occurs once (e.g., reaching the end of a maze without making an error). In order to study maintenance, one needs to observe ongoing behavior for an extended time period. Again it is appropriate to acknowledge the groundbreaking contributions of B. F. Skinner. The maze, runway, and shuttle box are examples of **discrete-trial apparatuses**. That is, by placing the animal in the apparatus, the researcher determines the opportunity to make a single response. After the response occurs, it cannot be made again until the animal is returned to the starting point of the apparatus. In comparison, animals may be left in an operant chamber (Skinner box) indefinitely, and the animal can repeatedly make the response. This **free-operant** situation enables the study of the effects of manipulation of different independent variables (e.g., magnitude of reward, delay of reward, effort of response, schedule of reward) on ongoing behavior. Thus, patterns of environmental events, including scheduling of appetitive events, may be observed to influence patterns of behavior. The combination of the operant chamber with a device known as a **cumulative recorder** enabled automation of the plotting of graphs of an animal's rate of responding over time. Skinner published an interesting and entertaining article describing the different steps and missteps, gadgets, and devices produced in his development of the operant chamber and cumulative recorder (Skinner, 1956).

The Skinner box has undergone remarkably little modification in the past 50 years, a testament to its value as a means of collecting internally and, just as interestingly and important, externally valid behavioral data. The Amazonian rain forest may be described as a complicated operant chamber in which diverse behaviors must be acquired to obtain food and avoid danger. Over the millennia, the Nukak have evolved in an environment that has not changed. Just as a pigeon is predisposed to pecking a lit key, it is likely that the Nukaks' foraging behaviors are easily acquired. Alvin Toffler wrote his prescient book *Future Shock* in 1970, arguing that technologically advanced cultures are changing so rapidly as to repeatedly result in the equivalent of culture shock within one's lifetime. It is impossible for humans to rely upon genetic evolution to adapt to their changing modern conditions. We are more like rats than pigeons in a Skinner box, having to acquire totally arbitrary behaviors in order to adapt to our circumstances. Just as rats do not inherit the tendency to press bars, humans do not inherit the tendency to use computers and cellphones.

### Cumulative Records

Whereas the Skinner box continues to survive and thrive in laboratories all over the world, the cumulative recorder appears on the verge of extinction (the physical, not

**Discrete-Trial Apparatus**

By placing the animal in the apparatus, the researcher determines the opportunity to make a single response. After the response occurs, it cannot be made again until the animal is returned to the starting point of the apparatus. The maze, runway, and shuttle box are examples.

**Free-Operant**

In comparison to discrete-trial apparatuses, animals may repeatedly make a response. The operant chamber (Skinner box) is an example.

**Cumulative Recorder**

An automated graphing device developed by B. F. Skinner. It plots an animal's rate of responding during a session in an operant chamber.

biological or adaptive learning kind). Computers have replaced electromechanical equipment in the control of environmental events and recording of behavioral data. For example, the operant chamber may be programmed to deliver food after every bar press and record the number of responses occurring each minute. Following is a table of hypothetical data for a 10-minute acquisition session in which a subject gradually increases its rate of responding from 0 to 5 responses per minute. The data are plotted as a line graph of responses per minute in Figure 9.1 and of cumulative responses per minute in Figure 9.2.

The first 3 data points, in which the subject is not responding, are the same on both graphs. However, the cumulative graph presents a more descriptive portrayal of the increasing and eventual constant rate of responding than the noncumulative line graph. Also, notice how easy it is to determine the total number of responses and average response rate from the cumulative graph. One merely has to determine the high point for the total number of responses (25 in this example) and divide by the session

| Minute | Responses | Cumulative Responses |
|--------|-----------|----------------------|
| 1 | 0 | 0 |
| 2 | 0 | 0 |
| 3 | 0 | 0 |
| 4 | 1 | 1 |
| 5 | 2 | 3 |
| 6 | 3 | 6 |
| 7 | 4 | 10 |
| 8 | 5 | 15 |
| 9 | 5 | 20 |
| 10 | 5 | 25 |

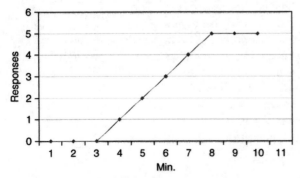

**FIGURE 9.1** Responses per minute.

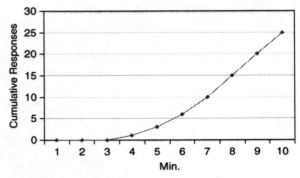

**FIGURE 9.2** Cumulative responses per minute.

| Minute | Cumulative Responses per Minute |
|--------|----------------------------------|
| 1 | 25 |
| 2 | 30 |
| 3 | 35 |
| 4 | 40 |
| 5 | 44 |
| 6 | 47 |
| 7 | 49 |
| 8 | 50 |
| 9 | 50 |
| 10 | 50 |

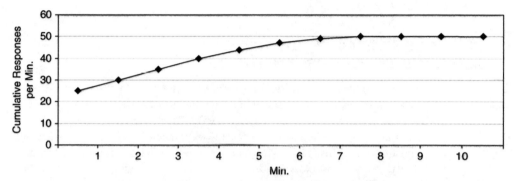

**FIGURE 9.3**  Hypothetical extinction session in which responding tapers off.

length (10 minutes) to calculate the average rate (2.5 responses per minute). For these reasons, cumulative graphs are favored in the presentation of response rate data.

Other examples are provided to assist in the interpretation of cumulative response graphs. Figure 9.3 portrays a cumulative response graph for a hypothetical extinction session in which the response rate gradually declines. Notice that when the subject stops responding, the line does not return to the *x*-axis; it remains at the highest point. Time marches on and so does the cumulative record.

Figure 9.4 shows the data for three subjects responding at constant rates. One responds 3 times per minute (i.e., 30 responses in 10 minutes), a second responds 6 times per minute (60 responses in 10 minutes), and the third responds 9 times per minute (90 responses in 10 minutes). Note that all constant rates of responding result in straight lines with the magnitude of the slope (i.e., angle of incline) increasing as a function of the magnitude of the rate. Thus, the line for the subject responding 9 times per minute

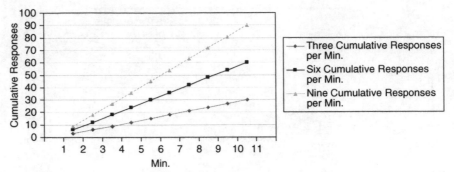

**FIGURE 9.4** Constant cumulative response rates result in straight lines. The magnitude of the rate is indicated by the slope (steepness) of the lines.

is steepest. Next, we consider Skinner's schema for categorizing intermittent schedules of reinforcement. We will see that different schedules produce their own characteristic cumulative response patterns.

## SKINNER'S SCHEMA OF INTERMITTENT SCHEDULES OF REINFORCEMENT

**Intermittent Schedules of Reinforcement**

When some but not all responses are reinforced.

Much of B. F. Skinner's empirical research demonstrated the effects of different **intermittent schedules of reinforcement** on the cumulative response patterns of pigeons and rats (cf., Ferster & Skinner, 1957). There are an infinite number of possible intermittent schedules between the extremes of zero responses and the reinforcement of all responses. How can we organize the possibilities in a meaningful way? Skinner developed a useful schema for their categorization based on two considerations. The most fundamental distinction was between schedules requiring that a certain number of responses be completed (ratio schedules) and those requiring only a single response when the opportunity was presented (interval schedules). I often ask my classes if they can provide "real-life" examples of ratio and interval schedules. One astute ROTC student suggested that officers try to get the students to believe that promotions occur according to ratio schedules (i.e., how often you do the right thing), but, in reality, they occur on the basis of interval schedules (i.e., doing the right thing when an officer happened to be observing or found out about it). Working on a commission basis is a ratio contingency. The more items you sell, the more money you make. Calling one's friend is an interval contingency. It does not matter how often you try if the person is not home. Only one call is necessary if the friend is available. The other distinction

**Fixed Ratio (FR) Schedule**

Reinforcement occurs after a constant number of responses (e.g., an individual on an FR 3 schedule is reinforced after every third response).

Skinner made is based on whether or not the response requirement (in ratio schedules) or time requirement (in interval schedules) is constant. Contingencies based on constants were called "fixed," and those for which the requirements changed were called "variable." These two distinctions define the four basic reinforcement schedules (see Figure 9.5): fixed ratio (FR), variable ratio (VR), fixed interval (FI), and variable interval (VI).

In a **fixed ratio (FR) schedule**, reinforcement occurs after a constant number of responses. For example, an individual on an FR 20 schedule would be

Contingency

|  | Response Dependent | Time Dependent |
|---|---|---|
| Constant Pattern | FR | FI |
| Random Pattern | VR | VI |

F = fixed, constant amount
V = variable, average amount
R = ratio, number of responses
I = interval, amount of time

**FIGURE 9.5** The four basic schedules of intermittent reinforcement.

reinforced after every 20th response. In comparison, an individual on a **variable ratio (VR) schedule** of 20 would be reinforced, on average, every 20th response (e.g., 7 times in 140 responses with no pattern). In a **fixed interval (FI) schedule**, the opportunity for reinforcement is available after the passage of a constant amount of time since the previous reinforced response. For example, in an FI 5-minute schedule, the individual would be reinforced for the first response occurring after 5 minutes elapse since the previous reinforcement. A **variable interval (VI) schedule** of 5 minutes would include different interval lengths averaging 5 minutes between opportunities.

It is possible to describe the emerging behavioral pattern as a function of exposure to an intermittent schedule of reinforcement as an example of control learning. That is, one can consider what constitutes the most effective (i.e., adaptive) pattern of responding to the different contingencies. The most adaptive outcome would result in obtaining food as soon as possible while expending the least amount of effort. Individuals have a degree of control over the frequency and timing of reward in ratio schedules that they do not possess in interval schedules. For example, if a ratio value is 5 (i.e., FR 5), the quicker one responds, the sooner the requirement is completed. If an interval value is 5 minutes, it does not matter how rapidly or how often one responds during the interval. It must lapse before the next response is reinforced. In contrast to ratio contingencies, with interval schedules only one response is required, so lower rates of responding will reduce effort while possibly delaying reinforcement.

Figure 9.6 shows the characteristic cumulative response patterns produced by each of the four basic schedules. We may consider the optimal response pattern for each of these schedules and compare them with what actually occurs under laboratory conditions. High rates of responding in ratio schedules will result in receiving food as soon as possible and maximizing the amount of food received per session. Therefore, it is not surprising that ratio schedules result in higher response rates than interval schedules. At low ratio values (e.g., less than 15 for a rat or 50 for a pigeon), nearly constant high rates of responding occur under both FR and VR schedules. It is possible to gradually

**Variable Ratio (VR) Schedule**

Reinforcement occurs after an average number of responses. For example, an individual on a VR 3 schedule would be reinforced on the average every third response.

**Fixed Interval (FI) Schedule**

The opportunity for reinforcement is available after the passage of a constant amount of time since the previous reinforced response (e.g., an individual on a FI 5-minute schedule is reinforced for the first response occurring after 5 minutes lapse since the previous reinforcement).

**Variable Interval (VI) Schedule**

The opportunity for reinforcement is available after the passage of an average amount of time since the previous reinforced response (e.g., an individual on a VI 5-minute schedule is reinforced for the first response occurring after different intervals averaging 5 minutes since the previous reinforcement).

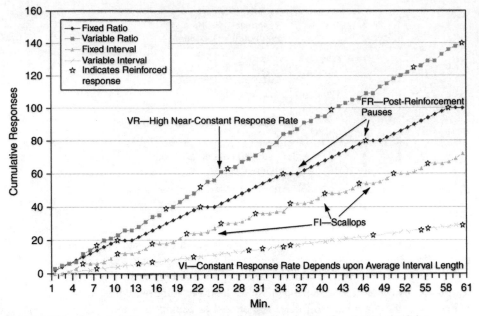

**FIGURE 9.6** Characteristic cumulative response patterns for the four basic schedules.

build up to very high ratio values (100s for rats and 1000s for pigeons). When this is done, FR schedules result in an "all-or-none" pattern with distinct post-reinforcement pauses related to the ratio value. In contrast, shorter pauses typically occur randomly with large-value VR schedules. This difference is due to the predictability of the FR schedule, whereby with experience the individual can develop an expectancy regarding the amount of effort and time it will take to be rewarded. Receiving a reward in an FR schedule indicates that there will be significant effort and delay before receiving the next reward. That is, it would be expected to result in inhibitory learning (*If I have just received food, it will not happen again for a while*). The amount of effort and time required for the next reward is unpredictable with VR schedules; therefore, one does not observe post-reinforcement pauses.

With an FI schedule, it is possible to receive reinforcement as soon and with as little effort as possible by responding once immediately after the required interval has elapsed. For example, in an FI 5-minute schedule, responses occurring before the 5 minutes lapse have no effect on delivery of food. If one waits past 5 minutes, reinforcement is delayed. Thus, there is competition between the desires to obtain food as soon as possible and to conserve responses. The cumulative response pattern that emerges under such schedules has been described as the fixed-interval scallop and is a compromise between these two competing motives. The extended pause that occurs after reinforcement is similar to what occurs with the FR schedule because once again the predictive interval length should result in inhibitory learning. However, unlike the characteristic burst following the pause in FR responding, the FI schedule results in a gradual increase in response rate until responding is occurring consistently when the reward becomes available. This response pattern results in receiving the food as soon as possible and conserving responses. Repetition of the pattern produces the characteristic scalloped cumulative response graph.

With a VI schedule, it is impossible to predict when the next opportunity for reinforcement will occur. Under these conditions, as with the VR schedule, the individual responds at a constant rate. Unlike the VR schedule, the pace is dependent upon the average interval length. As with the FI schedule, the VI pattern represents a compromise between the desires to obtain the reward as soon as possible and to conserve responses. An example might help clarify why the VI schedule works this way. Imagine you have two tickets to a concert and know two friends who would love to go with you. One of them is much chattier than the other. Let us say the chatty friend talks on average for 30 minutes on the phone, whereas the other averages only about 5 minutes. Assuming you would like to contact one of your friends as soon as possible, you would most likely try the less chatty one first and more often if receiving busy signals for both.

---

- Describe the difference between response-dependent (ratio) and time-dependent (interval) schedules of reinforcement.
- Define the four basic schedules of positive reinforcement. Sketch and describe the behavioral patterns portrayed in their characteristic cumulative response graphs.

---

## WHY DO RATIO SCHEDULES PRODUCE HIGHER RESPONSE RATES THAN INTERVAL SCHEDULES?

As described previously, there are two plausible explanations for the fact that ratio schedules produce higher response rates than interval schedules. First is the fact that ratio contingencies enable the individual to be rewarded earlier by responding more rapidly. For example, if the ratio value is 20, the sooner you complete 20 responses, the sooner you are rewarded. The second possibility is that by responding more rapidly under ratio schedules, the individual is reinforced more frequently over the course of a session (Baum, 1973). For example, if one is responding 5 times per minute, it would take 4 minutes to complete 20 responses and one would receive 15 rewards per hour on FR 40 or VR 40 schedules. By responding 10 times per minute, 30 rewards are received per hour.

In order to decide between these possibilities, it is necessary to hold reward frequency constant while permitting the contingency (ratio versus interval) to vary. This may be achieved by using the yoked-control procedure described in Chapter 7. In one study, Killeen (1969) yoked an interval subject to one on an FR 40 schedule by programming the operant chambers so that once the FR 40 subject completed 39 responses, the next response would be reinforced for both subjects. This produced an interval schedule for the yoked subject, with the interval lengths being determined by how long it took the FR subject to complete 39 responses. Despite the fact that this procedure ensured that the frequency and timing of rewards would be almost identical for ratio and interval animals, the ratio animals responded at much higher rates. Therefore, we conclude that it is the ratio contingency itself, not reinforcement frequency, that is responsible for the differences in response rate. Otherwise, the results would have been the same for both groups. In a similar study, Reynolds (1968) found pigeons reinforced on a VR schedule responded at 5 times the rate of yoked VI subjects (see also Reynolds, 1961).

> ■ Describe the results of yoked-control research, assessing whether reinforcement frequency or the relationship between responding and reinforcement is responsible for the higher rates of responding under ratio as opposed to interval contingencies.

## MAINTENANCE OF LEARNED BEHAVIOR

The biographies of high-achieving individuals often describe them as enormously persistent. They seem to engage in a lot of practice in their area of specialization, be it the arts, sciences, helping professions, business, or athletics. Successful individuals persevere, even after many "failures" occur over extended time periods. Legend has it that when Thomas Edison's wife asked him what he knew after all the time he had spent trying to determine an effective filament for a light bulb, he replied "I've just found 10,000 ways that won't work!" When we discussed theoretical interpretations of the partial reinforcement extinction effect (PREE), the development of persistence or frustration tolerance was thought to result from exposure to intermittent schedules of

**Learned Industriousness**

Persistence (i.e., frustration tolerance), the willingness to expend maximum effort, and self-control (i.e., choosing large delayed reinforcers rather than small immediate ones) appear to be related. Improvement on one results in improvement on the other two.

rewards. Eisenberger (1992) reviewed the animal and human research literatures and coined the term **learned industriousness** to apply to the combination of persistence (i.e., frustration tolerance), willingness to expend maximum effort, and self-control (i.e., working for delayed large reinforcers rather than small immediate ones). Eisenberger found that improvement on any one of these characteristics carried over to the other two.

Skinner's schema of intermittent schedules and the findings regarding their effects provide some guidance regarding implementation. If one's objective is to produce "eager beavers" during acquisition and many responses during extinction, ratio schedules would be preferred. A shaping process could be used to gradually increase ratio sizes. If one's objective is to produce steady, moderate responding during acquisition and extended responding during extinction, interval schedules would be chosen. Variable schedules produce more consistent performance during acquisition and more responding during extinction than fixed schedules.

Whether working with children or adults, one needs to be sensitive to the "natural" contingencies existing in the free-living environment. Behavioral trapping, whereby the contingencies are sufficient to sustain learned behaviors, may or may not occur. One must assess the appropriate environments (e.g., home, school, office) to determine the likelihood that current contingencies are sufficient. Additional measures to consider beyond the use of intermittent schedules are to teach and to encourage significant others to reward appropriate behaviors. Lovaas et al. (1973) demonstrated the effectiveness of this strategy with autistic children in their homes and schools. Another, perhaps ideal, approach is to teach the individual self-control techniques.

Perri and Richards (1977) found that college students systematically using behavior-change techniques were more successful than others in regulating their eating, smoking, and studying habits. Self-control findings and procedures will be discussed at length in Chapter 14.

## DIFFERENTIAL REINFORCEMENT SCHEDULES AS ALTERNATIVES TO PUNISHMENT

Thus far, we have discussed intermittent schedules of reward within the context of maintenance of learned behavior. This is appropriate when dealing with behavioral deficits such as the lack of imitation or speech in autistic children. These are behaviors that must be acquired and sustained in order to adapt to our contemporary conditions. As we saw when we first described early infantile autism, behavioral excesses may be equally or more problematic. Self-destructive acts such as head banging can delay or prevent educational programs geared toward behavioral deficits. In such instances, it is crucial to eliminate or substantially reduce these problematic responses. When we are confronted with behavioral excesses, our usual tendency is to consider punishment procedures as the only strategy. Our consideration of the effectiveness of punishment led us to the conclusion that although it can be immediately and permanently effective, it is logistically difficult to implement. In free-living environments, it is usually impossible to immediately detect and punish all instances of behavioral excesses. Inconsistent punishment can make matters worse with the individual becoming resistant to future consistent punishment procedures. In addition, individuals often learn to avoid punishment through deception and may become aggressive. At best, punishment is "addition by subtraction." That is, even when effective, punishment does not teach desirable alternatives. As described at the end of Chapter 7, punishment is most effective when there is an alternative means of securing reinforcement (see Figure 7.15). Ideally, approaches to the treatment of behavioral excesses would promote desirable options and not share the implementation problems and undesirable side effects of punishment. Fortunately, such options exist in the form of differential reinforcement schedules.

In **differential reinforcement schedules**, a specific behavior is targeted for reduction. This may be accomplished in different ways, each possessing its own descriptive acronym: **differential reinforcement of low rates of responding (DRL)**, **differential reinforcement of other (or zero) responding (DRO)**, **differential reinforcement of alternative responding (DRA)**, and **differential reinforcement of incompatible responding (DRI)**. Let us return to our previous example of a child who teases a younger sibling to see how each of these procedures is implemented. In DRL, if a specified amount of time passes without an instance of teasing, upon the next instance the child receives a reward (e.g., candy, a trinket, the chance to play a game). If the child teases before the time is up, the clock resets to zero. Once the child is consistently being reinforced, it is possible to gradually increase the interval length, further reducing responding until it is eliminated or occurring at an acceptable rate. In DRO, if a time interval lapses without teasing, the child is reinforced. It is not necessary

**Differential Reinforcement Schedules**

These are alternatives to punishment procedures as treatment of behavioral excesses. They involve the positive reinforcement of behaviors other than the behavioral excess (see DRA, DRI, DRL, and DRO for examples).

**Differential Reinforcement of Low Rates of Responding (DRL)**

Reinforcing a specific behavior once a specified amount of time passes without an instance (e.g., a reward is provided for waiting an hour between cigarettes).

**Differential Reinforcement of Other (or Zero) Responding (DRO)**

Providing reinforcement if a time interval lapses without a behavior occurring (e.g., if a child has gone a certain amount of time without teasing a sibling).

**Differential Reinforcement of Alternative Responding (DRA)**

Reinforcing a specific behavior other than the one you wish to reduce (e.g., rewarding a child for playing with a sibling rather than fighting).

**Differential Reinforcement of Incompatible Responding (DRI)**
Reinforcing a specific behavior that cannot occur at the same time as the one you wish to reduce (e.g., reinforcing a child who hits himself in the head for holding a soft toy).

that another instance of teasing occur. Once the interval lapses, the child is rewarded for engaging in any behavior other than teasing. Then, another interval is started. DRA and DRI are counterconditioning procedures that involve reinforcing behaviors other than the target. An example of DRA might be reinforcing a child for playing a game with a younger sibling. Although teasing could occur while playing the game, it would presumably be less likely. An example of DRI might be to reinforce a child for reading to the younger sibling. Reading a story to a younger sibling is incompatible with teasing. The two activities cannot occur simultaneously.

Differential reinforcement schedules have been found effective in decreasing sibling conflict (Leitenberg, Burchard, Burchard, Fuller, & Lysaught, 1977), reducing attention-seeking (Austin & Bevin, 2011; Carr & Durand, 1985; Durand & Carr, 1987, 1991), reducing talking out in class (Deitz & Repp, 1973), slowing down eating (Lennox, Miltenberger, & Donnelly, 1987), reducing thumb sucking (Knight & McKenzie, 1974), reducing severe self-scratching (Allen & Harris, 1966; Cowdery, Iwata, & Pace, 1990), and reducing other self-injurious behavior (Mazaleski, Iwata, Vollmer, Zarcone, & Smith, 1993). O'Brien and Repp (1990) published a 20-year review of research investigating the use of differential reward schedules with low-functioning individuals. Differential reinforcement schedules can be effectively combined with extinction of the targeted behavior. For example, in addition to rewarding other responses, one may eliminate the consequence maintaining the problem behavior. This has been found to increase the effectiveness of DRO in reducing self-injurious behaviors in autistic children (Mazaleski et al., 1993).

## EXTINCTION AS AN ALTERNATIVE TO PUNISHMENT

The extinction process is always a preferable and effective alternative to the use of punishment to reduce behavioral excesses. Implementing extinction requires identification of the consequence (i.e., presentation of an appetitive event or removal of an aversive event) that is maintaining the problematic behavior. A **functional analysis** in which the behavior is monitored while potential consequences are systematically removed and reinstated may be used for this purpose. Once the consequence maintaining the problematic behavior is identified, it may often be eliminated (Hanley, Iwata, & McCord, 2003). Examples of when this may be difficult include when the behavior is maintained by its sensory feedback as in the self-stimulatory acts of many autistic children (e.g., rocking back and forth, hand flapping). Often, however, it is possible to eliminate such consequences as inappropriate attention from peers or adults. When this is done consistently, extinction can be very effective. However, the extinction process may require a lot of patience for successful implementation. A common mistake is to "give in," essentially placing the individual on an intermittent schedule and making matters worse. For example, many parents have difficulty withholding attention from their children when they cry at bedtime. In a classic study, parents had to endure a tantrum lasting 45 minutes on the first night of implementation of an extinction procedure. Fortunately, this was reduced to 10 minutes on the second night and the child stopped crying after a week's time (Williams, 1959). The cashless society described in Chapter 8 is an example of the application of extinction to illegal profit-motivated behaviors.

**Functional Analysis**
Behavior is monitored while potential consequences are systematically removed and reinstated. This is implemented to determine what is maintaining a (usually problematic) behavior.

## NONCONTINGENT REINFORCEMENT AS AN ALTERNATIVE TO PUNISHMENT

Noncontingent reinforcement is an oxymoron referring to the noncontingent (usually time-based) delivery of appetitive stimuli. It is an oxymoron because, by definition, reinforcement requires a contingency. This procedure involves systematic presentation of an appetitive stimulus in a manner independent of the occurrence of a problem behavior with the objective of reducing its frequency. Interestingly, a growing literature attests to the efficacious clinical utility of noncontingent delivery as an alternative to punishment, differential reinforcement, and extinction (Carr, Severtson, & Lepper, 2009; Holden, 2005). An advantage of noncontingent delivery in comparison to extinction is that it is not necessary to conduct a functional analysis to determine the reinforcer maintaining a problem behavior. It has been determined that noncontingent delivery of an arbitrary reinforcer is sufficient to reduce the behavior (Fischer, Iwata, & Mazaleski, 1997). Noncontingent reinforcement has even been found effective for reducing problematic stereotyped behaviors (e.g., repeated rocking by autistic children) maintained by their consequent sensory stimulation (Britton, Carr, Landaburu, & Romick, 2002).

---

■ Describe how differential reinforcement schedules, extinction, and noncontingent reinforcement may be used as alternatives to punishment to reduce behavioral excesses.

---

## Summary

Once a behavior has been learned, schedules of consequences will determine the frequency and pattern of occurrence over extended time periods. Skinner devised a schema to organize intermittent behavior-consequence contingencies based on two considerations: Did the contingency require a certain number of responses (ratio schedule) or a single response during a window of opportunity (interval schedule)? Was the number of responses or length of time between opportunities constant (fixed) or inconsistent (variable)? Each of the four basic schedules of positive reinforcement (FR, VR, FI, VI) results in a characteristic response pattern. Fixed contingencies result in post-reinforcement pauses, whereas variable contingencies produce consistent response rates. Ratio contingencies result in higher response rates than interval contingencies. Procedures holding reinforcement frequency constant reveal that the ability to influence how soon reinforcement occurs is responsible for the higher response rates under ratio schedules.

Schedules in which reinforcement is contingent upon a low rate of responding (DRL), the nonoccurrence of a behavior (DRO), and the occurrence of an alternative (DRA) or incompatible (DRI) response are effective alternatives to punishment to reduce behavioral excesses. Functional analysis enables determination of the reinforcer maintaining a behavior. This permits the implementation of extinction to reduce or eliminate the behavior. Noncontingent delivery of appetitive stimuli has also proved effective in reducing problematic behavior.

# References

Allen, K. E., & Harris, F. R. (1966). Elimination of a child's excessive scratching by training the mother in reinforcement procedures. *Behaviour Research and Therapy, 4*, 79–84.

Austin, J., & Bevan, D. (2011). Using differential reinforcement for low rates to reduce children's requests for teacher attention. *Journal of Applied Behavior Analysis, 44*, 451–461.

Baum, W. M. (1973). The correlation-based law of effect. *Journal of the Experimental Analysis of Behavior, 20*, 137–153.

Britton, L. N., Carr, J. E., Landaburu, H. J., & Romick, K. S. (2002). The efficacy of non-contingent reinforcement as treatment for automatically reinforced stereotypy. *Behavioral Interventions, 17*, 93–103.

Carr, E. G., & Durand, V. M. (1985). Reducing behavior problems through functional communication training. *Journal of Applied Behavior Analysis, 18*, 111–126.

Carr, J. E., Severtson, J. M., & Lepper, T. L. (2009). Non-contingent reinforcement is an empirically-supported treatment for problem behavior exhibited by individuals with developmental disabilities. *Research in Developmental Disabilities, 30*, 44–57.

Cowdery, G. E., Iwata, B. A., & Pace, G. M. (1990). Effects and side-effects of DRO as treatment for self-injurious behavior. *Journal of Applied Behavior Analysis, 23*, 497–506.

Deitz, S. M., & Repp, A. C. (1973). Decreasing classroom misbehavior through the use of DRL schedules of reinforcement. *Journal of Applied Behavior Analysis, 6*, 457–463.

Durand, V. M., & Carr, E. G. (1987). Social influences on "self-stimulatory behavior": Analysis and treatment application. *Journal of Applied Behavior Analysis, 20*, 119–132.

Durand, V. M., & Carr, E. G. (1991). Functional communication training to reduce challenging behavior: Maintenance and application in new settings. *Journal of Applied Behavior Analysis, 24* (2), 251–264.

Eisenberger, R. (1992). Learned industriousness. *Psychological Review, 99*, 248–267.

Ferster, C. B., & Skinner, B. F. (1957). *Schedules of reinforcement*. New York: Appleton-Century-Crofts.

Fischer, S. M., Iwata, B. A., & Mazaleski, J. L. (1997). Noncontingent delivery of arbitrary reinforcers as treatment for self-injurious behavior. *Journal of Applied Behavior Analysis, 30*, 239–249.

Hanley, G. P., Iwata, B. A., & McCord, B. E. (2003). Functional analysis of problem behavior: A review. *Journal of Applied Behavior Analysis, 36*, 147–185.

Holden, B. (2005). Non-contingent reinforcement: An introduction. *European Journal of Behavior Analysis, 6*, 1–8.

Killeen, P. (1969). Reinforcement frequency and contingency as factors in fixed-ratio behavior. *Journal of the Experimental Analysis of Behavior, 12*, 391–395.

Knight, M. F., & McKenzie, H. S. (1974). Elimination of bedtime thumb-sucking in home settings through contingent reading. *Journal of Applied Behavior Analysis, 7*, 33–38.

Leitenberg, H., Burchard, J. D., Burchard, S. N., Fuller, E. J., & Lysaght, T. V. (1977). Using positive reinforcement to suppress behavior: Some experimental comparisons with sibling conflict. *Behavior Therapy, 8*, 168–182.

Lennox, D. E., Miltenberger, R. G., & Donnelly, D. (1987). Response interruption and DRL for the reduction of rapid eating. *Journal of Applied Behavior Analysis, 20*, 279–284.

Lovaas, O. I., Koegel, R. L., Simmons, J. Q., & Long, J. S. (1973). Some generalization and follow-up measures on autistic children in behavior therapy. *Journal of Applied Behavior Analysis, 6*, 131–165.

Mazaleski, J. L., Iwata, B. A., Vollmer, T. R., Zarcone, J. R., & Smith, R. G. (1993). Analysis of the reinforcement and extinction components in DRO contingencies with self injury. *Journal of Applied Behavior Analysis, 26*, 143–156.

O'Brien, S., & Repp, A. C. (1990). Reinforcement-based reductive procedures: A review of 20 years of their use with severe or profound retardation. *Journal of the Association of Persons with Severe Handicaps, 15*, 148–159.

Perri, M. G., & Richards, C. S. (1977). An investigation of naturally-occurring episodes of self-controlled behavior. *Journal of Counseling Psychology, 25*, 178–183.

Reynolds, G. S. (1961). Relativity of response rate and reinforcement frequency in a multiple schedule. *Journal of Experimental Analysis of Behavior, 4*, 179–183.

Reynolds, G. S. (1968). *A primer of operant conditioning*. Glendale, IL: Scott, Foresman.

Skinner, B. F. (1956). A case history in scientific method. *American Psychologist, 11*, 221–233.

Toffler, A. (1970). *Future shock*. New York: Random House.

Williams, C. D. (1959). The elimination of tantrum behavior by extinction procedures. *Journal of Abnormal and Social Psychology, 59*, 269.

# PART IV   THE HUMAN CONDITION

## Chapter 10

# Personality, Socialization, and Culture

## MULTIPLE SCHEDULES, PERSONALITY, AND CULTURE

We have frequently mentioned the ABCs of control learning: *a*ntecedents, *b*ehavior, and *c*onsequences. In prior chapters, the acquisition and maintenance of behavior have been discussed without emphasizing the conditions under which behavior occurs. That is, we skipped over "A" in our coverage of "B" and "C." In reality, an important component of adaptation is learning what the consequences of one's acts will be under different conditions. This is the subject matter of (antecedent) stimulus control.

Let us start with an example of Jamie, an attention-seeking child visiting relatives for a holiday get-together. Jamie has attended similar get-togethers in the past and is familiar with the patterns of attention provided by two aunts and an uncle. They typically take turns sitting in an easy chair reading the newspaper. Aunt Lucy is sometimes very resistant to Jamie's pestering; at other times, she gives in right away. Aunt Rose has a strategy whereby she reads an article from beginning to end and waits for the next incidence of pestering that she knows is coming. After playing with Jamie for a while, she reads another article from beginning to end. Uncle Harry is hard of hearing, which in dealing with Jamie is not altogether a bad thing. He turns down the volume in his hearing aids and reads the newspaper without ever paying attention.

When I ask students if they think Jamie will behave the same way toward each of the relatives, almost all say no. They expect different patterns to emerge because of the different ways in which they respond to pestering. I ask the students if the ways in which the adults respond remind them of previously described reinforcement schedules. It is determined that Aunt Lucy, by providing attention after different amounts of pestering was implementing a variable ratio (VR) schedule. Aunt Rose's strategy resulted in a variable interval (VI) schedule with the length of each interval determined by how long it took her to finish an article. Uncle Harry, by not paying attention at all, was applying the extinction procedure. After repeatedly being exposed to these contingencies, Jamie would be expected to respond with the characteristic pattern associated with each reinforcement schedule: continuously pestering Aunt Lucy at a very high rate, consistently pestering Aunt Rose at a moderate rate, and not pestering Uncle Harry at all. The described scenario with Jamie is an example of a **multiple schedule**, whereby different reinforcement contingencies are reliably associated with distinct antecedent stimuli. Another example, provided in Chapter 6, occurs when cheering out loud is reinforced in athletic stadiums but not in the library.

Often we describe people (and even pets) as having distinct traits and personalities. For example, children such as Jamie frequently become identified as "pests." In Chapter 1, we saw that trait labels are often used as pseudo-explanations. This would result in the circular reasoning that Jamie bothers adults because of being a pest rather than being labeled a pest because of bothering adults. This could result in the failure to consider alternative explanations for Jamie's behavior (i.e., the different patterns of attention provided by adults) and in a self-fulfilling prophecy whereby Jamie is treated in a particular way because of being considered a "pest." This example indicates that trait labels, in addition to being nonexplanatory (i.e., they provide no information about genetic or experiential causes of behavior), are inaccurate as descriptions of behavior. Describing an individual as a "pest," or as "aggressive," or as "extroverted" implies cross-situational consistency. That is, in the same way that disease-related symptoms occur no matter where you are, characteristic trait behaviors would be expected under all conditions. Being a pest implies that Jamie is always a pest. Yet, this is not the case. Jamie's pestering varies depending upon who is sitting in the easy chair. Similarly, college students agree that they can be the life of the party with one group of friends, whereas they are quiet and withdrawn with others. Does it make sense to describe an individual as extroverted or introverted if both behavior patterns occur? The example of Jamie reveals how a multiple-schedule, adaptive learning analysis of human personality can accurately describe and explain how behavior can change across situations. It also helps us understand what we mean by culture and socialization. **Culture** refers to consensually agreed-upon rules relating situations (i.e., antecedents), behaviors, and consequences. **Socialization** is the implementation of these rules in parenting, schooling, and other interpersonal relations. For example, in some cultures, children are encouraged to look adults in the eye when they are talking. In other cultures, this same behavior is considered rude.

**Multiple Schedule**

The occurrence of different reinforcement contingencies reliably associated with distinct antecedent stimuli. For example, one may be smiled at when screaming at a football game but not when screaming in the library.

**Culture**

An adaptive learning perspective would describe culture as consensually agreed-upon rules relating antecedents, behaviors, and consequences.

**Socialization**

The implementation of rules regarding antecedents, behaviors, and consequences in parenting, schooling, and other interpersonal relations (i.e., consensually agreed-upon rules).

- Describe how trait labels are inaccurate as descriptions of human behavior in addition to being inadequate as explanations.
- Describe how multiple schedules account for behavioral inconsistencies across situations and relate to human personality, socialization, and culture.

## STIMULUS CONTROL, BASEBALL, AND THE HUMAN CONDITION

In addition to using hitting as an example of antecedent stimulus control, I will now do my best to convince you that baseball is a wonderful metaphor for the human condition and that pitchers are sneaky. Researchers studying **stimulus control** usually define it as the extent to which the value of a stimulus on a dimension affects responding. This is similar to the predictive learning phenomena Pavlov named *stimulus generalization* and *discrimination*. When describing these phenomena, we saw that conditioned responses occur not only to a previously established conditioned stimulus, but also to other physically similar stimuli (i.e., stimulus generalization). We also saw that if, during acquisition, two stimuli were presented with only one followed by an unconditioned stimulus, the individual would respond only to a very narrow range of stimuli on the dimension (stimulus discrimination). The term *stimulus control* subsumes the phenomena of generalization and discrimination into one unifying dimension. The behavior of hitting a baseball demonstrates the advantage of this terminology.

> **Stimulus Control**
>
> This term subsumes the phenomena of generalization and discrimination into one unifying dimension. It measures the extent to which the value of a stimulus affects responding. This is usually assessed with a stimulus control graph plotting the number of responses as a function of value on a continuum (e.g., wavelength of light, frequency of a tone).

Figure 10.1 shows the paths of different pitches in relation to home plate. For a right-handed batter, location 1 is a ball missing the inside corner (i.e., it does not pass over the plate); location 2 is a strike near the inside corner; location 3 is a strike, right down the middle of the plate; location 4 is a strike near the outside corner; and location 5 is a ball missing the outside corner. If you have trouble relating to baseball, imagine that home plate represents a car. The dotted line for location 1 represents the path of a deer approaching the car from the far left, missing the car; location 2 is the deer approaching from the near left, potentially hitting the car; location 3 is the deer approaching from directly in front of you; location 4 is the deer approaching from

The most favorable pitch is down the center of home plate

The other pitches are less favorable

① ② ③ ④ ⑤

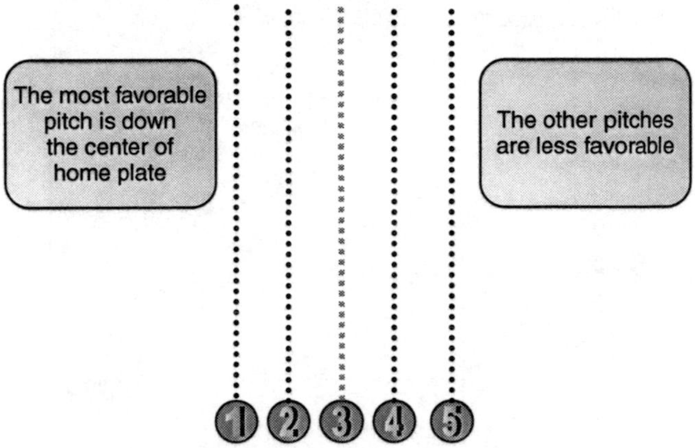

**FIGURE 10.1** A dimension of pitch location.

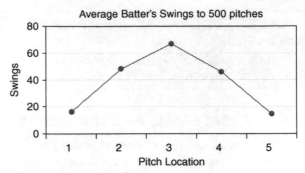

**FIGURE 10.2** Average batter's pattern of swinging.

the near right, potentially hitting the car; and location 5 is the deer approaching from the far right, missing the car.

Most hitters find a pitch over the middle of the plate easiest to hit and are most likely to swing when a pitch is in that location. Similarly, most drivers would be most likely to apply their brakes if an object approaches them directly from the front. The likelihood of swinging (braking) drops off as the pitches (deer) approach from other locations. Figure 10.2 is a stimulus control graph for a hypothetical "average" hitter (driver) experiencing 100 pitches (deer) in each of the five locations. Pavlov considered this gradient to represent stimulus generalization because the response occurred to stimuli other than the original training stimulus. However, the same pattern could be interpreted as indicating stimulus discrimination because the amount of responding is dependent on pitch (or object) location. The term *stimulus control* was introduced to resolve this ambiguity.

Some hitters, often described as "free swingers," do not seem to care where the pitch is located. They are as likely to swing at pitches off the plate as pitches over the plate. Figure 10.3 portrays the stimulus control graph for such a hitter. This would also be the pattern for a driver who brakes equally for deer regardless of their path. Other hitters are very "picky." They have a restricted "happy zone" and rarely swing at pitches outside this zone. Figure 10.4 portrays the stimulus control graph for such a discriminating hitter. This pattern would apply to a driver who brakes only for deer approaching from almost directly in front of the car (i.e., location 3).

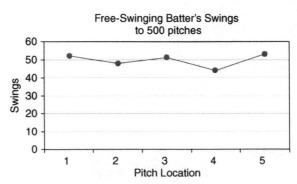

**FIGURE 10.3** Swinging pattern for a nondiscriminating batter (i.e., free swinger).

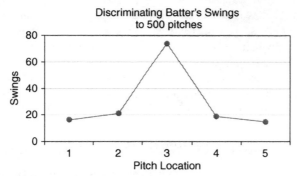

**FIGURE 10.4**   Swinging pattern for a discriminating (i.e., picky) batter.

Recall that stimulus control refers to the extent to which the value of a stimulus on a dimension affects responding. Figure 10.5 combines the graphs for average, free-swinging, and discriminating hitters. It is possible to describe the extent of stimulus control as ranging from none (i.e., pitch location does not matter at all for the free-swinging batter) to a lot (i.e., pitch location is highly related to the swinging of discriminating batters). This removes the ambiguity from the moderate graph obtained by Pavlov. Rather than using the terms "generalization" or "discrimination," this pattern is better described as representing a moderate degree of stimulus control.

Our example with Jamie involved qualitatively different antecedent stimuli (the aunts and uncle), whereas the baseball example involved quantitatively different stimuli (pitch location). Many everyday examples of each can be provided. I know that if my wife has one look in her eye, it means I am in trouble, whereas another look means something very different. If you have a morning class the next day you (hopefully) set the alarm clock for a different time than for days you do not have class. You probably study more for some classes and teachers than others, use a different mouse for laptop and desktop computers, dress differently (hopefully) for school and for fun, and so on. Similarly, the likelihood of your putting on a sweater probably is a function of temperature, the likelihood of your paying attention to someone may be a function of that person's attractiveness, and the likelihood of going to a restaurant a function of its cost.

Now, why do I consider pitchers sneaky? They try to get you to believe that a pitch is going to be over the center of the plate when it is going to be outside (i.e., they throw curve

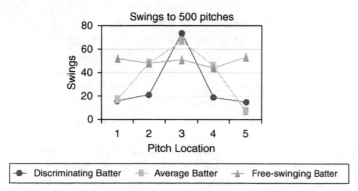

**FIGURE 10.5**   Swinging patterns for three types of batters.

balls), and get you to believe that a pitch will be above your knees when it is going to bounce in the dirt (sliders, splitters, and sinkers). There is no limit to their deception, but pitchers are not satisfied to perform their trickery in space: They also lead you to believe that the ball will arrive now rather than a little later (changes of pace). This is why, having spent a good part of my youth playing baseball, I consider pitchers sneaky. As you well know, every once in a while life throws us a curve ball or change of pace. We rely upon our adaptive learning ability to cope as best we can. Thus, baseball is a wonderful metaphor for the human condition.

## MEASURING STIMULUS CONTROL IN THE LABORATORY

Guttman and Kalish (1956) developed the laboratory procedures used to demonstrate stimulus control in individual animals. Among other applications, such tests produce precise measures of the sensory capacities of other species. Birds, predominantly pigeons, are the most frequent subjects in basic stimulus control research because of interest in the sense of vision, which is so fundamental to human adaptation. As you might expect for animals that fly and must locate food from extreme distances, birds have excellent vision. This includes sensitivity to color. In order to fully understand a stimulus control test on the color dimension, it may be helpful to review the underlying physics of the visual spectrum.

On an intuitive level, colors seem qualitatively as opposed to quantitatively different. That is, we perceive red, orange, yellow, green, blue, indigo, and violet (Roy G Biv) as different from one another in kind, not in quantity. Colors differ, however, in wavelength (measured in nanometers, billionths of a meter) on the electromagnetic dimension. This dimension includes cosmic and gamma rays as its lowest values (billionths of billionths of meters!) and radio waves and broadcast bands at its high end (hundreds, even thousands of miles!). Humans are sensitive to a very narrow band of wavelengths (approximately 390 nm to 750 nm) that we perceive as color. Pigeons are also sensitive to these same wavelengths, as we are able to demonstrate with stimulus control tests.

As described previously, Skinner boxes for pigeons require key pecking rather than bar pressing as the response (see Figure 10.6). Guttman and Kalish used an apparatus having a single key that could be lit with different wavelengths of light through the use of color filters. During the acquisition phase, the pigeon was taught to respond to a particular wavelength (S+ = 580 nm in this case, a yellow-orange). The test phase was conducted on 11 wavelengths, 5 on each side of the training stimulus. During acquisition, the key was sometimes lit (580 nm) and sometimes not lit. When it was lit, the pigeon

**Presence/Absence Discrimination Training Procedure**

A discrimination training procedure in which reinforcement is provided when a stimulus is there (e.g., a lit key) but not when it is not there.

was reinforced for pecking on a VI 1-minute schedule. When the key was not lit, the pigeon was on extinction (i.e., never reinforced). This is called a **presence/absence discrimination training procedure**. You might recognize this procedure as a simple example of a multiple schedule in which reinforcement for key pecking occurs in the presence of one stimulus and not in the presence of another. As you would expect from the example with Jamie, eventually the pigeon pecked when the key was lit and not when it was dark.

Besides producing a constant rate of responding during acquisition, VI schedules result in a very gradual tapering off of responding during extinction. Thus, they are the schedules of choice when requiring stable baselines during acquisition or testing. When measuring stimulus control, it is possible to present different stimuli at random time intervals during extinction without being concerned about unexpected bursts or lapses in responding. Guttman and Kalish presented twelve

**FIGURE 10.6**   Pigeon pecking key in Skinner box.

5-1/2 minute blocks during extinction for a total session length of 66 minutes. The 11 test colors ranged in value from 530 nm to 630 nm in 10-nm increments and were presented in random order for 30 sec during each of the 12 blocks. Essentially, testing determined how much the pigeon learned about color during acquisition. That is, if the pigeon simply learned to peck the lit key, this would result in a flat pattern; if it learned to specifically peck yellow-orange, this would result in the sharply peaked pattern; if it just learned that the key was colored, this would result in a moderate gradient. Guttman and Kalish observed a moderately peaked test gradient (see Figure 10.7).

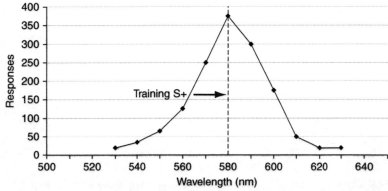

**FIGURE 10.7**   Stimulus control gradient. Pigeons were trained to peck a key lit at 580 nm and tested in the presence of other wavelengths.   (Adapted from Guttman & Kalish, 1956)

# DETERMINANTS OF STIMULUS CONTROL TEST PATTERNS

**Intradimensional Discrimination Training**

Reinforcing responding to one value of a stimulus on a dimension and not reinforcing responding to another value on the same dimension during acquisition. For example, subjects could be reinforced for responding to 580 nm and not reinforced for responding to 620 nm on the visual wavelength dimension or reinforced for responding to 1000 Hz and not 800 Hz on the auditory frequency dimension.

**Peak Shift**

This occurs when intradimensional discrimination training is provided with stimuli close in value on a dimension. The peak of the stimulus control gradient is shifted in the direction opposite the S–. For example, if pigeons are taught to respond to a 1000 Hz tone and not a 950 Hz tone, the peak of the stimulus control gradient will be to a value higher than 1000.

This raises the question of what types of experiences produce the different stimulus control test patterns (Lashley & Wade, 1946). Guttman and Kalish's pigeons weren't given "instructions" that they were taking a test for stimulus control on color or any other dimension. For example, testing could have been conducted on the dimensions of brightness, size, or shape. We know that presence/absence training resulted in the pigeons' learning something about color. Presumably, the same would be true on these other dimensions. Jenkins and Harrison (1960, 1962) provided three types of acquisition experiences prior to testing for stimulus control (see Figure 10.8). Pigeons again served as subjects, but this time acquisition and testing were conducted on the auditory dimension of pitch (frequency of sound waves, measured in Hz). Subjects in all three groups received food for pecking while a 1000 Hz tone sounded. For one group, the tone remained on throughout the entire session; that is, there was no S– (i.e., time when key pecking was not reinforced). A second group received the auditory equivalent of presence/absence discrimination training. When the 1000 Hz tone was on, the pigeon was reinforced for responding. When the tone went off, extinction of key pecking was in effect. The third group received **intradimensional discrimination training** in which it was reinforced for pecking in the presence of the 1000 Hz tone but not in the presence of a tone slightly lower in pitch (950 Hz).

Inspection of Figure 10.8 indicates that the stimulus control gradients were dramatically different for the three conditions. The group that did not receive discrimination training (no S–) produced a flat pattern indicating the absence of stimulus control. The presence/absence condition (S– = silence) produced the same moderately peaked graph centered over the original S+ obtained by Guttman and Kalish. The group receiving intradimensional discrimination training (S– = 950) produced a very narrow, sharply peaked gradient indicating a great degree of stimulus control. Surprisingly, the peak was not centered over the original S+, but it was shifted in the direction opposite the acquisition S–. Pigeons responded more to a frequency of 1050 Hz than to 1000 Hz. This finding, descriptively known as the **peak shift**, has theoretical implications to be considered shortly.

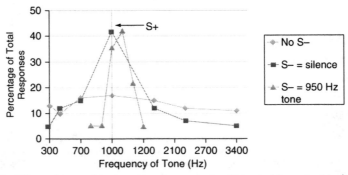

**FIGURE 10.8** Effect of type of S– on stimulus control. (Adapted from Jenkins & Harrison, 1960, 1962)

However, for now, let us see if we can make sense of the overall findings of Jenkins and Harrison's research.

We have seen that animals are constantly seeking information helpful in predicting and controlling events in their lives. They learn only about environmental stimuli that convey nonredundant information about subsequent events. From an adaptive learning perspective, we would expect individuals to pay closer attention to stimuli that are informative about the possibility of obtaining food. In the No S− condition, the tone was always on. It was part of the overall context of the operant chamber in the same way the floor, walls, and ceiling were. In order to receive food, the pigeon did not have to pay attention to any of these stimuli. It needed only to peck the key. In the same way that you probably "tune out" background noises when listening to a lecture, the pigeons in this condition apparently tuned out the tone. This would appear to be an example of the phenomenon of **habituation** that is prevalent throughout the animal kingdom: "Habituation is defined as a behavioral response decrement that results from repeated stimulation and that does not involve sensory adaptation/ sensory fatigue or motor fatigue" (Rankin et al., 2009). Habituation is essentially learned irrelevance: "Nervous systems are constantly evaluating incoming stimuli and filtering out stimuli that are not important as well as cataloguing and using stimuli that are important (i.e., those stimuli that signal things that are good or bad for the survival of the organism)" (Rankin et al., 2009). Habituation is a primitive form of learning appearing in creatures as simple as the sea slug (Siegelbaum, Camardo, & Kandel, 1982) and as early as in the fetus in humans (Morokuma, Fukushima, Kawai, Tomonaga, Satoh, & Nakano, 2004).

**Habituation**

A behavioral response decrement that results from repeated stimulation and that does not involve sensory adaptation/sensory fatigue or motor fatigue. For example, one usually does not "hear" the constant background noises in a room (e.g., a fan).

In a presence/absence discrimination session, the individual has to attend to the occurrence and nonoccurrence of an event in order to determine the availability of food and not waste effort. Apparently, this level of attention is sufficient to learn something about the values of a stimulus on different dimensions, resulting in moderately peaked test gradients. In comparison, in order to respond efficiently when confronted with an intradimensional discrimination, one has to pay very close attention to values of the acquisition S+ and S−. Thus, when tested, one responds only to stimuli very close in value to the original S+, producing the sharply peaked gradient. The Jenkins and Harrison results help us understand the types of experiences that result in the likelihood of paying attention to the value of a stimulus. This determines whether testing produces no, moderate, or substantial stimulus control.

> ▪ Describe how laboratory procedures used to measure the extent of stimulus control demonstrate the important role of the nature of the S−.

## THE PEAK SHIFT AND SPENCE'S MODEL OF DISCRIMINATION LEARNING

The peak shift reliably occurs when intradimensional discrimination training is provided with stimuli close in value on a dimension, as was the case with the S− = 950 condition in the Jenkins and Harrison study. Kenneth Spence (1936) applied Pavlov's concepts of excitation and inhibition in an influential model of instrumental discrimination learning.

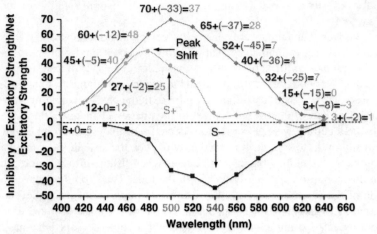

**FIGURE 10.9**   Spence's theory of discrimination and generalization. The upper curve is the presumed excitatory gradient based on reinforced responses to S+. The lower curve is the presumed inhibitory gradient based on nonreinforced responses to S−. The net curve is obtained by subtracting the inhibitory value from the excitatory value at each point on the wavelength dimension. It may be seen that the model predicts a peak shift when S+ and S− are close in value.

## Spence's Discrimination Learning Model

An explanation of discrimination learning based on the Pavlovian concepts of excitation and inhibition. It is assumed that these opposing processes may apply to an individual stimulus with the likelihood of responding to that stimulus being based on the net (i.e., excitatory minus inhibitory) excitatory strength.

**Spence's discrimination learning model** suggested that the counterintuitive peak shift resulted from opposing excitatory and inhibitory tendencies to respond to the S+ and not respond to the S−. When the two stimuli are close in value, these tendencies interact so that the net tendency to respond is greater to a stimulus in the direction opposite the S− because such stimuli would have lower inhibitory values than the S+. The following example (see Figure 10.9) applies Spence's model to a visual discrimination between an S+ of 540 nm (a blue-green) and an S− of 500 nm (green). The upper (red) gradient represents the excitatory strength peaked at the S+ and weakening symmetrically to other stimulus values. The lower (blue) gradient plotted with negative numbers represents the inhibitory strength assumed to be greatest to the S− and weakening symmetrically to other stimulus values. The net curve represents the stimulus control gradient predicted to result from interaction (i.e., summation) of the excitatory and inhibitory gradients. The values for the curve are obtained by subtracting the inhibitory value from the excitatory value at each of the wavelengths, as shown on the graph. Note that a peak shift is predicted because of the tapering off of the inhibitory curve as it moves to the left of the S+.

If Spence's model is correct, it would be possible to eliminate the peak shift if an intradimensional discrimination could be learned without generating inhibition. In this instance, there would be no lower curve and nothing would be subtracted from the excitatory gradient. The enormously practical fading procedure was actually introduced by Terrace (1963a, 1963b) in order to test Spence's model. Terrace reasoned that if the peak shift resulted from inhibition to the S− acquired during acquisition, it would be possible to reduce the amount of inhibition if the subject could acquire the discrimination with few errors (i.e., responses to the S−). We have previously seen that pigeons learn to respond to a lit key immediately by pairing it with food delivery. This can even occur noncontingently through the phenomenon of autoshaping (sign tracking). Therefore, it is possible to establish a lit key as S+ and unlit key as S– very rapidly. Once the pigeon was responding consistently to only the S+, Terrace implemented the fading procedure by gradually increasing the intensity of the S–. For example, if the S+ was blue-green and the S– was green, Terrace would start out with a very dim green. If the pigeon was still responding only when the key was lit blue-green, the brightness level of the green key would be increased. This process would be followed until the S+ and S– were presented at the same brightness level. This resulted in the pigeon hardly ever responding to the S– (green) during acquisition. In fact, in one of Terrace's studies, pigeons trained with the fading procedure made 1% of the errors (i.e., responses to S–) exhibited by pigeons learning the same discrimination with the conventional procedure. Because they hardly ever responded to the S– with the fading procedure, it should not become inhibitory. Consistent with the assumption that the peak shift occurs because of the buildup of inhibition during acquisition, Terrace's pigeons trained with the conventional discrimination training procedure produced a pronounced peak shift; those trained with the fading procedure had the peak of their test gradients directly over the original S+.

Terrace introduced the fading procedure in order to test Spence's model of the peak-shift phenomenon. He had no particular application in mind, but the procedure has become a staple in behavior modification. It is an excellent example of a useful application derived from basic research. In a study cited in Whaley and Malott's classic *Elementary Principles of Behavior* (1971), Meyerson and Michael (1964) administered hearing tests to nonverbal children by first reinforcing them for pressing a lever when a light went on. After this was learned, a tone was presented at the same time as the light. Once the child was consistently responding to the light/tone compound stimulus, the light was gradually decreased in intensity. Eventually, it was possible to present different frequency tones at different amplitudes to determine if the child heard them by whether or not she/he pressed the lever.

At this point you may be asking what all this tells us about baseball. OK, you may not be asking yourself this, but while writing this book, I though it might be another helpful example of fading. If I were trying to prepare a budding Little Leaguer for a world inhabited by sneaky pitchers, I would start by throwing only pitches right down the middle of the plate at regular speed. Pitches to other locations would be thrown very slowly, increasing the likelihood that they would be let go or hit. Gradually, the speed of pitches to these other locations would be increased with the objective of widening the "happy zone." Rather than cursing the darkness (i.e., pitchers), it is better to light candles (i.e., teach our Little Leaguers to become better hitters).

> ■ Describe how the fading procedure enabled a test of Spence's excitatory/inhibitory process theory account of the peak shift.

## ATTENTION THEORY AND DISCRIMINATION LEARNING

A long-standing issue in discrimination learning is whether it is a gradual, continuous process (cf., Hull, 1943; Spence, 1937) or a sudden, discontinuous process (cf., Krechevsky, 1932; Lashley, 1929). The first possibility assumes that by being reinforced or not reinforced, the subject gradually builds up tendencies to respond to the S+ and withhold responses from the S–. The other possibility, often referred to as

## Attention Theory

A description of discrimination learning as first identifying the relevant dimension and then determining the value that leads to reinforcement. The first task is considered more difficult. For example, once it is determined that shape is the relevant dimension, it is easy to select a circle or a square.

**attention theory**, is that discrimination involves a type of hypothesis testing whereby the subject attends to a specific dimension as long as this enables efficient responding. For example, in Terrace's fading procedure, the differences were so obvious on the background dimension (brightness) at first that subjects probably attended to it only to obtain reinforcement. As the brightness levels became more similar, it would reach a point at which it was difficult to tell the S+ and S− apart. The subject might then "discover" and transfer attention to another dimension (color). Touchette (1971) tried to determine whether the transfer from the faded background dimension to the test dimension occurred gradually or suddenly by inserting a probe interval (similar to a predictive learning blank trial) prior to providing the fading cue. If subjects were learning gradually, this would result in a tapering off of responding during the probes. Sudden learning would be implied by consistently responding the same to the S− as to the S+ during probe intervals until at some point in the fading process, the subject stopped responding at all to the S−. Consistent with attention theory, Touchette observed the latter pattern.

Attention theory assumes a two-stage process in which individuals first need to determine the relevant dimension in a situation and then learn the correct value on the dimension (Mackintosh, 1965; Sutherland & Mackintosh, 1971). The first stage is difficult and typically requires a long time, depending upon the complexity of the situation. The second stage is easy, requiring little time. Let us return to the battle between pitcher and hitter for an example. Hitters search for subtle cues to determine the likely speed and location of a pitch. They may focus upon how the pitcher is holding the glove, the release point of the pitch, the spin on the ball, and so on. The relevant dimensions might vary across pitchers. Once a useful dimension is identified, it is relatively easy to determine which glove location, release point, or spin to look for. Just in case you might prefer an example other than baseball, the following lyrics from "A Lover's Question" might make the point:

> *Oh, tell me where the answer lies?*
> *Is it in her kiss or in her eyes?*
> *Well it's a lover's question, I'd like to know*

BY BROOK BENTON AND JIMMIE WILLIAMS

Once you've determined the answer to the question, it should not be difficult to figure out what type of look or kiss to hope for.

Three other discrimination-learning findings consistent with attention theory are the overtraining reversal effect, the easy-to-hard discrimination learning effect, and ease of making intradimensional shifts as opposed to extradimensional shifts. In a demonstration of the **overtraining reversal effect**, Reid (1953) gave three groups of rats a brightness discrimination in a T-maze. One of the groups received 50 and another received 150 additional trials beyond those needed to reach the criterion of correct performance. After completing this phase, the three groups received a reversal discrimination task in which S+ became S− and vice versa. The group receiving 150 additional trials learned the reversal more quickly than the other two groups. Because this group continued to be reinforced for responses to the original S+ longer than the others, it might be expected that it would be more

## Overtraining Reversal Effect

Subjects receiving additional training on a two-choice discrimination task will switch to the other stimulus more rapidly after a change in the contingencies (i.e., S+ becoming S− and S− becoming S+) than subjects receiving less training.

difficult for them to make this switch. This would be the prediction of Spence's model based upon accumulating excitatory and inhibitory tendencies. Attention theory, on the other hand, would expect the additional training to improve the ability to attend to the brightness dimension. This would make switching to another value on the same dimension even easier, consistent with Reid's results.

Lawrence (1952) demonstrated that rats learning a black-white discrimination first had much less difficulty learning a difficult discrimination involving shades of gray than a group starting with the difficult discrimination. Presumably, experience with the easy discrimination established attention to the brightness dimension, facilitating transfer to different values on the same dimension. This same result was obtained more recently with both rats and humans learning difficult auditory discriminations (Liu, Mercado, Church, & Orduna, 2008). This **easy-to-hard discrimination effect** provides another tool for combating sneaky pitchers in this world. That is, we can start out teaching Little Leaguers to hit with very slow pitches that are over the plate and wait until they are consistently hitting the ball hard whenever they swing. At this point, it may be possible to introduce pitches off the plate and at higher speeds.

Also consistent with the assumptions of attention theory are the findings comparing the results of discrimination transfer tasks that involve the same dimension, that is, **intradimensional shifts**, or different dimensions, that is, **extradimensional shifts** (Mackintosh, 1964; Mackintosh & Little, 1969). Figure 10.10 portrays such a study involving the dimensions of color and shape. The intradimensional condition starts out with a red/green color discrimination followed by blue/yellow. The extradimensional condition starts on the shape dimension (circle/square) prior to being shifted to the same blue/yellow color discrimination. Intradimensional shifts have consistently been found to be learned more rapidly than extradimensional shifts as attention theory would predict.

**Easy-to-Hard Discrimination Effect**

The finding that training on an easy discrimination (e.g., black vs. white) facilitates learning a difficult discrimination (e.g., between two shades of gray).

**Intradimensional Shift**

Learning a discrimination on a dimension (e.g., red vs. green) followed by learning another discrimination on the same dimension (e.g., blue vs. yellow). Consistent with the assumptions of attention theory, this is easier than a transfer task on a different dimension (see attention theory; extradimensional shift).

**Extradimensional Shift**

Learning a discrimination on a dimension (e.g., red vs. green) followed by learning a discrimination on another dimension (e.g., circle vs. square). Consistent with the assumptions of attention theory, this is more difficult than a transfer task on the same dimension (see attention theory; intradimensional shift).

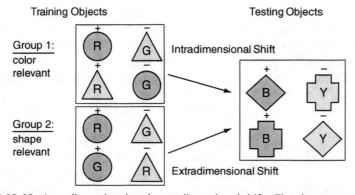

**FIGURE 10.10** Intradimensional and extradimensional shifts. The shapes are colored either red (R), green (G), yellow (Y), or blue (B); the correct object in each pair is marked (+), and the incorrect object is marked (−). For subjects in the intradimensional-shift group, the correct objects during both training and testing can be identified by their color; for subjects in the extradimensional-shift group, the relevant dimension is shape during training, but color during testing.

> ■ Show how attention theory explains the overlearning reversal effect, easy-to-hard transfer task, and ease of learning intradimensional in comparison to extradimensional shifts.

This concludes our treatment of the "A" in the control learning ABCs. It may be helpful at this time to summarize how control learning relates to our understanding of the human condition. We sometimes have the ability to control our environment. When this is true, we do our best to increase the occurrence of appetitive stimuli and decrease the occurrence of aversive stimuli. Often, the likelihood of being able to increase appetitive and decrease aversive stimuli is related to the circumstances under which they occur. Adaptive learning is the process through which we adapt to and, when possible, alter the human condition to our advantage.

## Summary

Adaptive learning principles have been demonstrated to be powerful explanatory tools for understanding and modifying the human condition. Adaptation usually requires not only learning how to behave but also when (or under what circumstances) to emit a specific behavior. The same behavior may be appropriate under some conditions but not others. Thus, it is not surprising that describing human personality as consisting of traits may be inaccurate in addition to being nonexplanatory (pseudo-explanations). Typically, behavior is not as consistent across situations as trait labels imply. A multiple schedule involves implementing different reinforcement schedules in the presence of different stimuli. Behavior will eventually change to reflect these differences. This process explains how the same individual's behavior may vary as a function of the setting in which it occurs. Socialization of children by parents and caretakers consists of implementing contingencies of reinforcement and punishment in order to achieve desired behavioral outcomes. A culture consists of consensually agreed upon socialization practices and desired behavioral outcomes.

Differential responding to antecedents has been studied in the laboratory under the topic of stimulus control. Usually, responses are reinforced in the presence of a specific stimulus and not in its absence (presence/absence training), or to one value on a dimension and not to another (intradimensional discrimination training). The degree of stimulus control is reflected in the amount of responding to different values on the dimension during test trials. If an individual is simply reinforced in the presence of a stimulus, habituation (learned irrelevance) will result in responding equally to other values on its different dimensions (e.g., shape, color, size). Differential reinforcement is necessary in order to establish stimulus control. Even simply reinforcing responding in the presence of a stimulus but not in its absence is sufficient to establish a moderate degree of stimulus control. Discrimination training with different values on the same dimension produces sharper stimulus control gradients. Research supports two stimulus control learning processes. A model based upon the summation of excitatory strength to the S+ and inhibitory strength to the S− provides the best account of the peak-shift phenomenon. Attention theory assumes that stimulus control requires first determining a relevant dimension before responding to a particular value on that dimension. This model best accounts for the overlearning reversal effect, easy-to-hard effect, and ease of learning intradimensional in comparison to extradimensional shifts.

# References

Guttman, N., & Kalish, H. I. (1956). Discriminability and stimulus generalization. *Journal of Experimental Psychology, 51*, 79–88.

Hull, C. L. (1943). *Principles of behavior.* New York: Appleton-Century-Crofts.

Jenkins, H. M., & Harrison, R. H. (1960). Effects of discrimination training on auditory generalization. *Journal of Experimental Psychology, 59*, 246–253.

Jenkins, H. M., & Harrison, R. H. (1962). Generalization gradients of inhibition following auditory discrimination learning. *Journal of the Experimental Analysis of Behavior, 5*, 435–441.

Krechevsky, I. (1932). "Hypotheses" in rats. *Psychological Review, 39*, 516–532.

Lashley, K. S. (1929). *Brain mechanisms and intelligence.* Chicago: University of Chicago Press.

Lashley, K. S., & Wade, M. (1946). The Pavlovian theory of generalization. *Psychological Review, 53*, 72–84.

Lawrence, D. H. (1952). The transfer of a discrimination along a continuum. *Journal of Comparative and Physiological Psychology, 45*, 511–516.

Liu, E. H., Mercado, E., Church, B. A., & Orduna, I. (2008). The easy-to-hard effect in human (Homo sapiens) and rat (Rattus norvegicus) auditory identification. *Journal of Comparative Psychology, 122*, 132–45.

Mackintosh, N. J. (1964). Overtraining and transfer within and between dimensions in the rat. *Quarterly Journal of Experimental Psychology, 16*, 250–256.

Mackintosh, N. J. (1965). Selective attention in animal discriminative learning. *Psychological Bulletin, 64*, 124–150.

Mackintosh, N. J., & Little, L. (1969). Intradimensional and extradimensional shift learning by pigeons. *Psychonomic Science, 14*, 5–6.

Meyerson, L., & Michael, J. (1964). Hearing by operant conditioning procedures. *Proceedings of the International Congress on Education of the Deaf, 1964*, 238–242.

Morokuma, S., Fukushima, K., Kawai, N., Tomonaga, M., Satoh, S., & Nakano, H. (2004). Fetal habituation correlates with functional brain development. *Behavioral Brain Research, 153*, 459–463.

Rankin, C. H., Abrams, T., Barry, R., Bhatnagar, S., Clayton, D. F., Colombo, J. … Thompson, R. F. (2009). Habituation revisited: An updated and revised description of the behavioral characteristics of habituation. *Neurobiology of Learning and Memory, 92*, 135–138.

Reid, G. S. (1953). The development of noncontinuity behavior through continuity learning. *Journal of Experimental Psychology, 46*, 107–112.

Siegelbaum, S. A., Camardo, J. S., & Kandel, E. R. (1982). Serotonin and cyclic AMP close single K+ channels in Aplysia sensory neurons. *Nature, 299*, 413–417.

Spence, K. W. (1936). The nature of discrimination learning in animals. *Psychological Review, 43*, 427–449.

Spence, K. W. (1937). The differential response in animals to stimuli varying within a single dimension. *Psychological Review, 44*, 430–444.

Sutherland, N. S., & Mackintosh, N. J. (1971). *Mechanisms of animal discrimination learning.* New York: Academic Press.

Terrace, H. S. (1963a). Discrimination learning with and without "errors." *Journal of the Experimental Analysis of Behavior, 6*, 1–27.

Terrace, H. S. (1963b). Errorless transfer of a discrimination across two continua. *Journal of the Experimental Analysis of Behavior, 6*, 223–232.

Whaley, D. L., & Malott, R. W. (1971). *Elementary principles of behavior.* New York: Appleton-Century-Crofts.

## Chapter 11

# Becoming Human and Transforming the Human Condition

As implied in Hardin's cartoon in Chapter 1, the types of learning we have treated so far occur throughout the animal kingdom. We, along with the Nukak and animals such as squirrels, try to determine the locations of preferred foods. Whereas the Nukak and squirrels forage under naturalistic conditions, we typically "forage" in supermarkets and restaurants. In this chapter, we discuss types of learning that are far more characteristic of humans than other animals. An understanding of these types of learning is essential to understanding the potential of the human being to transform nature and alter the human condition.

## CONCEPT LEARNING

In the previous chapter, under the topic of stimulus control, we saw how animals can learn to behave differently based upon the qualitative or quantitative properties of stimuli. Depending upon who is pitching in a baseball game (a qualitative stimulus), a hitter might look for a particular release point (a quantitative stimulus) in order to determine whether to swing. Based upon whom you are with (a qualitative concept), you may be observing the size of the person's pupils (a quantitative stimulus supposedly indicative of interest). In each of these instances, stimulus control relates to the presence of a particular stimulus. Much of what we learn about the world applies to different variations of discrete stimuli. For example, it could be possible that the release point is important with all left-handed pitchers. In this case, handedness would be an important variable to consider. Handedness, however, is not a particular stimulus. Rather, it is a shared property of a number of different stimuli. **Concept learning** is the term used for the acquisition of the ability to respond in the same way to all instances of a stimulus class (i.e., a collection of stimuli sharing at least one common property).

**Concept Learning**
The acquisition of the ability to respond in the same way to all instances of a stimulus class (i.e., a collection of stimuli sharing at least one common property such as circle or red).

## Qualitative and Quantitative Concepts

Much of our knowledge base consists of concepts. For example *circle* and *boy* are qualitative concepts; *middle-sized* and *tenth* are quantitative concepts. Typically, parents try to teach such concepts soon after their children begin to speak. How would a parent go about teaching the concept *circle* and know if the child understands? When I ask my students this question, they usually suggest that the parent say the word "circle" while pointing to circular objects in the environment. You may recall our discussion of this procedure under the topic of predictive learning. This is a classical conditioning procedure in which a sound ("circle") is associated with many stimuli sharing the property. A control learning discrimination training procedure could be used to establish and assess conceptual responding to circles. The child would receive an appetitive stimulus for saying the word "circle" while pointing to appropriate examples differing in size, color, and other properties. The child would never be reinforced for saying "circle" to other shaped stimuli. Eventually, the child should be able to appropriately generalize the response to new instances of circles.

The same procedure could be used with quantitative concepts. When I was a graduate student, the research literature on **transposition** (i.e., relational responding) suggested that nonhumans and young children were unable to apply the middle-sized relation beyond sets of stimuli very close in value (see Reese, 1968, for a comprehensive review). In my doctoral dissertation (Levy, 1975), I demonstrated near-perfect middle-sized transposition on two very different arrays by nursery school children first taught to point to squares in a consistent order before being required to select the middle-sized one. The "in-order" condition was taken to a criterion of five consecutive ordering sequences on arrays 1,2,3 and 4,5,6 (see Figure 11.1). The "out-of-order" condition was taken to the same criterion but in a sequence inconsistent with the sizes (e.g., 1,3,2 and 4,6,5). A third group was taught to order three same-sized squares in sequence according to their brightness (i.e., shade of gray). Control subjects received no pre-training.

**Transposition**
The transfer of responding from one circumstance to another on the basis of stimulus relationships (e.g., picking out the middle-sized object from different arrays).

After pre-training, all subjects were taken to a criterion of five consecutive responses to the middle-sized stimulus (stimulus 2) in the first array. The subjects in the size-ordering and brightness-ordering groups were instructed to order the stimuli prior to selecting one. After this training, all subjects received 12-trial test blocks without feedback on arrays 4,5,6 and 7,8,9. All 10 children in the "in-order" condition demonstrated transposition to array 4,5,6 (i.e., responded to stimulus 5), and 9 out of 10 transposed to the large array (i.e., chose stimulus 8), which they had not seen before.

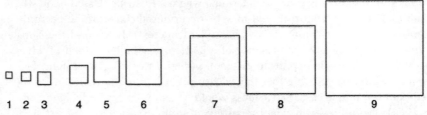

**FIGURE 11.1**   Three arrays of three squares similar to those used in Levy (1975). Children taught to order the first two arrays in sequence and choose the middle-sized stimulus in the first array (i.e., stimulus 2) transposed to the larger arrays (i.e., chose stimulus 5 in the second array and stimulus 8 in the large array).

Interestingly, 9 out of 10 children in the "out-of-order" group transposed to 4,5,6 and 5 transposed to 7,8,9. That is, it did not matter if the order was consistent with the sizes as long as the same sequence was used for the training and transfer arrays of three stimuli. Only 3 out of 20 children in the brightness-ordering and control groups transposed to array 4,5,6 and 1 transposed to 7,8,9.

The results of the size-ordering groups support the conclusion that transposition occurs when an individual sequentially orders the stimuli in an array prior to making a discriminative choice response. After being taught to count, it becomes possible to establish relational responding (i.e., transposition) based upon any quantity. For example, a child could be asked to point to the fifth largest triangle. This would require sequentially ordering all the triangles in an array based on size and then counting to five starting from the smallest one. Although in my study, the ordering sequence did not have to be consistent with the sizes, it was much easier for the children to learn to point to the sizes in order, suggesting prior familiarity with the size dimension. Coleman Paul, one of my mentors and the father of a precocious young daughter, brought this point home to me by suggesting I could have obtained the same result by using pictures of bears rather than squares and asking the children to point to the "mama bear" in each array.

## Natural Concepts

Even pigeons readily learn visual concepts such as *triangle* and *square* (Towe, 1954) and can distinguish between letters of the alphabet (Blough, 1982). Using a Skinner box permitting presentation of slides, researcher have demonstrated that pigeons easily learn such abstract natural concepts as *tree, water,* or even *person* (Herrnstein & Loveland, 1964; Herrnstein, Loveland, & Cable, 1976). Apparently, excellent vision, not a large cortex, is necessary for such learning (i.e., pigeons have "bird brains"). Skinner (1960), humorously, describes an interesting, previously classified World War II project in which pigeons were taught to identify the defining characteristics of Axis-power military ships. The objective was to respond to the invasion of Pearl Harbor with our own squadron of "kamikaze pigeons."

The Nukak people of the Colombian rain forest have language, and no doubt there is an overlap between many of our and their concepts related to basic needs (e.g., food, water, shelter, temperature, danger, pain). One way of understanding the enormous differences in our human conditions, however, would be to examine a lexicon of our concepts. For example, the Nukak will have a much more extensive vocabulary for types of rain and types of forestry than we will. We will have more extensive vocabularies regarding planes, trains, and automobiles. When I was very young, my mother taught me

Sickle from approximately 3000 B.C.

Egyptian cave painting of a plow.

"red car," "blue car," "green car," and so on. My father taught me "coupe," "convertible," and "sedan," and eventually "Chevy," "Chrysler," "Ford," and so on.

Unlike the rain forest, some climates and geographies support domestication of plants and/or large animals. Such environmental conditions enabled the development of agriculture and animal husbandry, permitting humans to abandon their nomadic lifestyle. New vocabularies developed related to the essential concepts for these life-transforming activities. When humans were able to permanently settle in a location, larger and larger communities evolved, creating the need for concepts related to increasingly complex interpersonal relations. Food surpluses brought opportunities for people to dedicate their time and creative efforts to the development of new tools, technologies, and occupations. Eventually, communities, economic arrangements, governments, and formal religions evolved. Along with these developments, the collective human knowledge base and vocabulary expanded. It was after the last Ice Age, approximately 13,000 years ago, that the agricultural lifestyle became the predominant human condition. For the great majority, this stage of human history probably had more in common with Stone Age nomadic cultures than our contemporary conditions. Literacy was not essential, and survival needs took up most of the daily activities. This remained true for millennia but changed with the industrial revolution and the institution of compulsory education.

We have seen how the ability to use speech to communicate a continually expanding vocabulary of adaptive concepts has enabled humans to live very differently and control their fates far more than the rest of the animal kingdom. Until relatively recently, however, only the privileged acquired the ability to read, write, and perform mathematic operations (i.e., learn the three Rs). This meant that the great majority of humans, even in the relatively advanced Western societies, were unable to profit from or contribute to the accumulating knowledge recorded on the written page. John Adams, one of America's Founding Fathers stated,

> A memorable change must be made in the system of education, and knowledge must become so general as to raise the lower ranks of society nearer to the higher. The education of a nation, instead of being confined to a few schools and universities for the instruction of the few, must become the national care and expense for the formation of the many. (McCullough, 2001, p. 364)

As Adams's call for universal education was eventually realized, an increasing number of people became literate, creating an expanding pool to contribute to the ever-evolving knowledge base. Resulting new technologies continue to transform the human condition at an accelerating pace.

> ■ Describe the procedures for determining if a nonverbal individual understands a concept.

**Learning Sets**

The provision of a series of experiences having something in common. It can result in acquisition of a strategy useful for all related experiences. The term is sometimes used to refer to the experiences (i.e., the independent variable) and sometimes to the effect (i.e., dependent variable) of those experiences. For example, Harlow demonstrated that with experience, chimps became more and more proficient at solving examples of two-choice discrimination problems.

**Win-Stay Lose-Shift Strategy**

The ideal performance pattern with two-choice discrimination problems. If correct, one would continue to choose the same stimulus; if incorrect, one would switch to the other possibility.

## LEARNING TO LEARN

The ability to transform the human condition involves more than concept learning. Also critical are the abilities to solve problems and to create tools. We begin our discussion of problem solving by describing Harlow's (1949) classic research into chimpanzee's acquisition of learning sets. **Learning sets** refer to the independent or dependent variable, to a number of experiences that have something in common, or to the effect of those experiences (as in being "set up"). Harlow provided his subjects with more than 300 two-choice visual discrimination problems. For example, the first problem might have required choosing between a circle and a square, the second problem might have consisted of a red triangle and a green triangle, the third problem a large diamond and a small diamond, and so on. Different stimuli and dimensions were relevant across the problems. The chimps were given up to 25 trials to reach a criterion of six consecutive correct responses on each problem. Figure 11.2 shows the average percentage of correct responses on the first six trials as the subjects progressed through the sets of problems (1–8, 9–16, 25–32, etc.). Because each problem includes only two possible choices (left or right position is never correct), the likelihood of being correct on the first trial by chance was 50%. An alert human adult could be correct on trial 2 and thereafter because the necessary information would be provided on the first trial. If correct, he/she would continue to choose the same stimulus; if incorrect, he/she would switch to the other possibility. Harlow and others described this ideal performance pattern as a **win-stay, lose-shift strategy**.

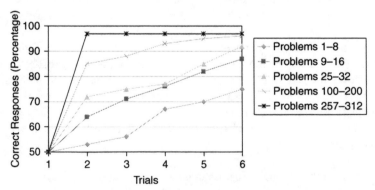

**FIGURE 11.2** Learning sets. Each line shows the average number of correct responses for the problem numbers shown. Chimpanzees' ability to solve two-choice discriminations improved as a function of experience with problem examples. (Adapted from Harlow, 1949)

Inspection of the chimps' performance over the first 32 problems (i.e., the bottom three lines in the graph) suggests a gradually improving incremental learning process in which the chimps slowly get better and better within and across problems. This appears qualitatively, rather than quantitatively, different from the strategy characteristic of human adults. However, the top two lines, covering problems 100 through 312, suggest that something very different is occurring. The win-stay, lose-shift strategy emerges with experience so that the performance of the chimps on the last 55 trials is quite humanlike. Thus, it appears that in the same way that pigeons are able to learn concepts by "abstracting out" the common characteristics of a collection of visual stimuli, chimpanzees are able to abstract out an approach to solving all two-choice visual discrimination problems, regardless of the stimuli involved. That is, they have been "set" (i.e., have learned how to learn) to solve a particular type of problem. Warren (1965) has compared the trial 2 results of different species of animals on learning sets, finding that more complex species (e.g., types of monkeys) improve more rapidly and eventually achieve higher levels of performance than less complex species (e.g., rodents).

> ■ Describe how acquiring concepts and learning sets may be described as abstractive processes.

## BASIC RESEARCH IN PROBLEM SOLVING

We frequently describe challenges in life as problems. A problem exists when there is a discrepancy between the way things are and the way one would like them to be. The solution consists of acquiring the information and ability to eliminate the discrepancy. Kittens and infants play with toys for extended periods of time with no apparent external reward other than the sensory stimulation. Monkeys will learn a response in order to gain the opportunity to look through a window (Butler, 1953). Human adults appear to find intrinsic reinforcements in solving complex problems. How else could we understand the creation of crossword puzzles and recreational games such as chess? Two-choice discriminations are as simple as problems get. One piece (i.e., bit) of information is all that is required to solve the problem and obtain the reward. Crossword puzzles and chess are far more complicated. Perhaps we seek complexity because such experience is adaptive. Unfortunately, many problems in life are extremely difficult to address and to solve. Issues related to health, interpersonal relationships, and finances often top such a list. It would be good preparation to acquire skills and strategies that apply in such circumstances. Many have likened life to a game of chess—posing problems having many possible options and requiring extensive planning for future possibilities. In fact, some have described life as consisting of one problem followed by another.

Psychologists have studied problem solving in humans and other animals almost since the founding of the discipline. As described previously, Thorndike studied a few species in puzzle boxes, describing the problem-solving process as involving trial-and-error (or success) learning. In his classic *The Mentality of Apes* (translated in 1925), the Gestalt psychologist Wolfgang Kohler argued that the puzzle box, by its very nature requires a "blind" (i.e., trial-and-error) learning process because the required behaviors cannot be determined by observing the environment. Wertheimer (1945) published

**FIGURE 11.3**   One of Kohler's "How do I reach the banana?" problems.

a "how to" book entitled *Productive Thinking* that extended Gestalt concepts to childhood education.

Kohler created a number of naturalistic problems for his subjects, primarily chimpanzees, and characterized the problem-solving process as the attainment of **insight**. Gestalt psychologists primarily studied perceptual phenomena (e.g., the phi phenomenon), so it is not surprising that Kohler considered insight to be a process requiring reorganization of the perceptual field in order to attain "closure." One famous example of Kohler's problems required that the chimpanzee insert a thin bamboo stick within a wider one in order to create a tool long enough to reach a banana outside the cage. Kohler also administered a variation of the two-stick problem requiring stacking boxes in order to reach a banana suspended from the ceiling (see Figure 11.3). Another required combining sticks to reach a banana hanging from above. Kohler amusingly anthropomorphizes (i.e., attributes human characteristics to another species) as he describes the chimp's initial unsuccessful attempts culminating in the "Aha!" moment when he runs over to connect the sticks or stack the boxes.

### Facilitative Effects of Prior Experience

Other researchers believed that Kohler underemphasized the role of prior experience in problem solving. The subjects in Kohler's primate colony were reared in the wild, not in captivity. The prevalence of bamboo sticks in that environment made it likely that the chimpanzees had handled them previously, increasing the likelihood of solving the two-stick problem. Birch (1945) provided five previously unsuccessful chimps with sticks to play with for 3 days. They were observed to gradually use the sticks to poke, shovel, and pry objects. When again provided with the two-stick problem, all five discovered the solution within 20 sec, demonstrating the importance of prior experience. Kohler also administered a variation of the two-stick problem requiring stacking boxes in order to reach a banana suspended from the ceiling.

Based on Harlow's observation of learning to learn, one can imagine Kohler's chimps entering their cages, looking for the banana, and asking themselves "OK, what does Kohler want me to do today?" In a humorous simulation of the box stacking problem (Epstein, Kirshnit, Lanza, & Rubin, 1984), pigeons needed to move a box under a plastic banana and then step on the box in order to peck the banana to receive food. Some pigeons were shaped to move the box to wherever a spot appeared on the floor, others were shaped to stand on the box and peck the plastic banana, and a third group was taught both responses. Only the group taught both components of the required behavior displayed insight, confirming the importance of prior learning experiences in problem solving.

## Interference Effects of Prior Experience

Prior experience can impede, as well as facilitate, problem solving. Luchins (1942) gave college students a series of arithmetic problems to solve (see Figure 11.4). They were asked to provide the most direct way of obtaining a certain amount of liquid from jars holding different quantities.

In the example, subjects were shown how it was possible to obtain 20 units of water by filling a 29-unit container and spilling 3 units into a separate container, 3 times (i.e., 29 – 3 times 3, or A – 3B, using the jar labels). After the example, a control group was administered the last problem (C1), which could be solved using two (the direct solution, A – C) or all three jars (the indirect solution, B – A – 2C). An experimental group was given five problems that could be solved with the B – A – 2C formula prior to being given the last problem. The experimental subjects were much more likely than the control subjects to use the less-efficient indirect method. This sort of "rigidity" is counterproductive. Thus, although it is often helpful to rely upon past experience in approaching problems, there is also value in considering each problem separately. Otherwise, we may be very unlikely to "think outside the box." Figure 11.5 shows the solution to the well-known nine-dot problem in which one is instructed "Without lifting your pencil from the paper, draw exactly four straight, connected lines that will go through all nine dots, but through each dot only once." Here, the solution literally requires thinking outside the box.

| Problem | Given Jars of the Following Sizes | | | Obtain the Amount |
|---------|---|---|---|---|
|         | A | B | C |   |
|         | 29 | 3 |   | 20 |
| E1 | 21 | 127 | 3 | 100 |
| E2 | 14 | 163 | 25 | 99 |
| E3 | 18 | 43 | 10 | 5 |
| E4 | 9 | 42 | 6 | 21 |
| E5 | 20 | 59 | 4 | 31 |
| C1 | 23 | 49 | 3 | 20 |

Note: E = Experimental Group; C = Control Group

**FIGURE 11.4**  Luchin's water jar problems. Subjects were instructed to obtain a specific amount of liquid as directly as possible by using jars holding specified quantities.

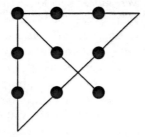

**FIGURE 11.5**  "Think outside the box."

**FIGURE 11.6** Functional fixedness. Subjects were unlikely to perceive the paintbrush as a weight to be tied to the end of a string.

**Functional Fixedness**

A special case of the phenomenon of "set" in which prior experience interferes with problem solving. In this instance, previous experience with the use of an object (e.g., a brick) interferes with its being used in another way (e.g., as a door stop).

A special case of being blinded by past experience has been demonstrated with the use of physical objects, a phenomenon called **functional fixedness**. N. R. F. Maier was one of the pioneers investigating human problem solving. One of the tasks he created is called the two-string problem (Duncker, 1945; Maier, 1930, 1931). Subjects (usually college students) are placed in a room with two strings suspended from the ceiling (see Figure 11.6). The strings are not long enough to be tied together easily. The solution requires tying an object to the bottom of one string and setting it in motion (i.e., creating a pendulum). Then, it is possible to grab the other string and bring it over, wait for the original one to swing back to the point where it can be caught, and tie the ends of the two strings together.

Maier and Janzen (1968) found that college students were much more likely to use some objects rather than others to tie the strings together. For example, they were more likely to tie a ruler than a bar of soap to the bottom of a string. Presumably, the usual function of soap interferes with consideration of it for another use, even within a different context. Birch and Rabinowitz (1951) demonstrated this effect experimentally. Two groups of college students were first provided experience using either a relay or a switch to complete electrical circuits. When they were given the two-string problem to solve, subjects given the relay were far more likely to use the switch as the weight whereas subjects provided prior experience with the switch were more likely to use the relay.

The Gestalt psychologists emphasized the tendency to perceive objects as meaningful wholes. Functional fixedness appears to be an inevitable result of this tendency. An implication of this perspective is that counteracting this tendency should reduce the likelihood of functional fixedness. This has been found to be the case when college students were asked to engage in a task similar to the introspection procedure employed by the structuralists as they attempted to analyze conscious experience (McCaffrey, 2012). A "generic parts technique" was employed in which subjects were asked to break down objects into their component parts without consideration of how they were used.

For example, the subject might describe a brick as being hard, heavy, having specific dimensions, and so on.

The **unusual uses test** (Guilford & Guilford, 1980; Guilford, Merrifield, & Wilson, 1958) is a popular assessment of creativity based upon the concept of functional fixedness. One is asked to list as many uses as possible for different objects (e.g., "What can you do with a brick?"). Responses may be counted or scored for originality. It is conceivable that training on the genetic parts technique could increase creativity scores on this test.

> **Unusual Uses Test**
>
> A popular assessment of creativity based upon the concept of functional fixedness. One is asked to list as many uses as possible for different objects (e.g., "What can you do with a brick?").

> ▪ Describe how prior experience can either facilitate or interfere with problem solving.

## THE GENERAL PROBLEM-SOLVING PROCESS

Goldfried and Davison (1976) include a **general problem-solving process** in their book describing clinical behavior therapy procedures. Based upon research findings, they divide problem solving into five distinct stages: (1) general orientation, (2) problem definition and formulation, (3) generation of alternatives, (4) decision making, and (5) verification (p. 187).

> **General Problem-Solving Process**
>
> A five-stage strategy consisting of (1) general orientation, (2) problem definition and formulation, (3) generation of alternatives, (4) decision making, and (5) verification.

The general orientation stage encourages individuals to define conditions eliciting unpleasant emotions as problems. As stated before, many of life's major problems relate to health, interpersonal relationships, and financial concerns. Such circumstances can be devastating to an individual, possibly resulting in debilitating anxiety and/or depression. I developed and implemented a behavioral approach to weight maintenance within a medically supervised clinic. Frequently, emotionality related to unrealistic societal ideals for appearance interfered with a client's adhering to a prudent lifestyle. It was helpful to reduce the emotionality related to one's appearance by adopting a scientific approach to weight control and body shape (stage 1). Then, the problem was defined as a discrepancy between one's current weight and dimensions and a more desired profile (stage 2). This permitted a relatively detached brainstorming discussion of different nutritional and exercise modifications designed to affect caloric input and output (stage 3). The likely benefits and drawbacks of implementing the different approaches were discussed with the goal of deciding upon a strategy that could be sustained (stage 4). The decided-upon strategy was implemented, with objective (weight and measurements) and subjective (ease of implementation, satisfaction) progress consistently monitored (stage 5). A **TOTE (test-operate-test-exit)** approach was implemented to determine the need for fine-tuning or changing the strategy (Miller, Galanter, & Pribram, 1960). Similar to the use of a thermostat, the individual would test the environment (i.e., determine current weight and measurements), operate on the environment (i.e., "turn on" the nutritional and exercise program), and continue to assess progress (test) until achieving the desired objective (and exiting). This same process would be sustained in order to maintain the desired end state.

The same thermostat approach could be applied to financial matters. The problem could be defined as a discrepancy between a family's income and

> **TOTE (Test-Operate-Test-Exit)**
>
> An acronym for a problem-solving process in which one assesses the environment (test) to determine whether to implement a procedure (operate), and assess (test) again to determine whether to continue the operation or terminate implementation upon solution (exit). A thermostat is a useful metaphor for the process.

expenditures. Brainstorming would be conducted to list possible ways to increase income or reduce costs. A strategy would be decided upon, implemented, and continually assessed. Adoption of a problem-solving approach is particularly helpful with interpersonal problems, which are almost always emotionally charged. It is difficult, but possible, to teach individuals or couples to respond objectively to the substance of what someone says while ignoring provocative language. Once this is achieved, difficulties and solutions can be mutually defined and strategies for addressing them can be negotiated prior to implementation and assessment (D'Zurilla & Goldfried, 1971).

---

▪ Describe how one would apply the stages of the general problem-solving process to a meaningful problem.

---

## TOOLS, TECHNOLOGY, AND THE HUMAN CONDITION

### The Law of Accelerating Returns

The general problem-solving process represents a higher level of abstraction than the win-stay lose-shift strategy that applies only to two-choice discrimination problems. This generic process emerges from learning-set type experiences with a variety of problems and then may be applied to all others. The premise of this text is that the abilities to predict and control our environment, including problem solving and creating tools, have enabled the transformation of the human condition. It is a mistake to believe that this occurred quickly or in a linear progression (i.e., equally spaced in time). To paraphrase Charles Dickens's opening to *A Tale of Two Cities* (2003/1859): It is the fastest of times, it is the slowest of times; it is the age of the internet, it is the age of the blowpipe.

Gordon Moore (1965) calculated that since the invention of the integrated circuit in 1958, the number of transistors that could be contained on a computer chip doubled approximately every year. Now known as **Moore's law**, this geometric relationship has been shown to hold with regard to computing speed as well as memory. Raymond Kurzweil (2001), inventor and futurist, proposed that Moore's law was simply one example of the generic **law of accelerating returns** that applies to the pace of all evolutionary biological and technological change.

**THE STONE AGE, BRONZE AGE, AND IRON AGE**   Many archeologists divide the time period prior to recorded history into three ages. During the Stone Age, it took tens of thousands of years for the occurrence of such **paradigm shifts** (i.e., life-transforming events) as the use of stone tools, the control of fire, and the invention of the wheel. It took until the Bronze Age (3300–1200 B.C.) and **Iron Age** (1200–900 B.C.) for tools to be manufactured, as opposed to being handmade from items found in nature. For example, rather than using stones attached to parts of trees as weapons, metal swords were forged from basic materials. Skipping to the first millennium A.D., advances such as the use of paper for writing and toiletry, inventions such as the quill and fountain pens, guns and gunpowder, and the creation of the first public library were occurring every hundred years or so.

Ancient stone wheel, circa 4000 B.C.

**THE INDUSTRIAL REVOLUTION AND THE MODERN ERA**    In the 19th century, major advances occurred every few years. Toward the end of the century, the industrial revolution increased the pace, laying the groundwork for our current human condition. The steam locomotive and automobile replaced the horse as the fastest way to travel on land, permitting travel across the continent; the steamboat and submarine enabled speedy travel on and beneath the sea. The reaper, steel plow, and refrigerator improved the yield and storage of food. The telegraph and telephone enabled instant communication over long distances. The light bulb prolonged work and recreation time, and phonographs and cameras enabled the recording of audio and visual media. The revolver, repeating rifle, and machine gun changed self-defense and warfare, altering the balance of power among cultures and nations.

Early steam locomotive.

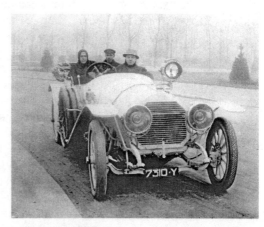

Early automobile.

The Wright brothers testing the first powered airplane.

These technologies were enhanced and in some instances replaced during the 20th century. Orville and Wilbur Wright's initial flight in 1903 was followed by the development of the airplane as the favored mode of transportation over long distances. Cross-country trips that took months by horse and days by train took hours by plane. Intercontinental flights replaced ships as the only possible way to traverse oceans. During the industrial revolution, people left farms for employment in large cities. Highway development and the proliferation of cars reversed the trend, and suburban living became a preferred lifestyle for many. Improved agricultural and meat-processing techniques led to large, highly efficient industries. Within 150 years, people went from producing their own food, to shopping at small markets, to shopping at large supermarkets. Radio enabled everyone with electricity to listen to the same event at the same time culminating in talk shows with audience participation. Television extended this phenomenon to the visual world and soon a common culture was created, consisting of news, sports, variety shows, comedies, soap operas, and reality shows. Communication satellites in space and optical fibers beneath the sea connected the continents, enabling and encouraging globalization.

While foraging, the Nukak sometimes build small bridges to pass over small bodies of water. The bridge is a wonderful metaphor as well as a feat of engineering for connecting peoples and places. The Nukak live in bands of approximately 15 individuals (usually the children and adults of three to five families). The tribe consists of approximately 20 bands living in different parts of a small region in the Amazon rain forest. That is their world. At the beginning of the 19th century, most people lived on farms in small villages. That was their world. Technological innovations in transportation and communication have potentially connected every person on the planet. Within the span of 200 years, we have moved from communication by word of mouth and written letters to wireless phones and e-mail. We have landed a rocket ship on the moon and are currently exploring Mars for signs of life. These are our worlds!

The telephone then.

The telephone now.

Listening to the radio then.

Listening to the radio now.

Watching TV then.

Watching TV now.

The computer then.

The computer now.

The advances over the past 2 centuries have also led to a dramatic change in human life expectancy (see Figure 11.7):

> *In the eighteenth century, we added a few days every year to human longevity; during the nineteenth century we added a couple of weeks each year; and now we're adding almost a half a year every year. With the revolutions in genomics, proteomics, rational drug design, therapeutic cloning of our own organs and tissues, and related developments in bio-information sciences, we will be adding more than a year every year within ten years. So take care of yourself the old fashioned way for just a little while longer, and you may actually get to experience the next fundamental paradigm shift in our destiny.* (Kurzweil, 2001)

The dramatic increases in human life expectancy over the past 150 years are primarily the result of improved sanitary conditions and inoculations against such

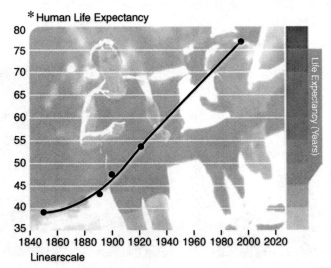

**FIGURE 11.7**  Increase in human life expectancy since 1850.  (From Kurzweil, 2001)

diseases as smallpox, polio, rubella, diphtheria, and influenza. In current technologically advanced cultures, the major reasons for loss of life are lifestyle related. For example, more than 400,000 Americans die each year from smoking-related disorders. Heart disease and cancer, which combine for a half of all deaths on an annual basis, are significantly related to nutritional and exercise habits. **Health psychology** has emerged as a subdiscipline of psychology dedicated to "the prevention and treatment of illness, and the identification of etiologic and diagnostic correlates of health, illness and related dysfunction" (Matarazzo, 1980, p. 815). Hopefully, the knowledge acquired through this discipline will enable the development of lifestyle-related technologies essential to the continuation of the upward trend in human life expectancy.

**Health Psychology**

An emerging subdiscipline of psychology dedicated to the prevention and treatment of illness through behavior change methods.

However, technology is a two-edged sword. It may be used to improve the human condition for the betterment of all or lead to our own extinction. The basic science of biology resulted in improvement in sanitary conditions and inoculations against major diseases. The same knowledge has been applied to create potentially devastating biological weapons. Chemistry has enabled the development of plastics and plastic explosives. Physics has enabled nuclear energy and nuclear weapons. Humans are the most creative and destructive force on this planet. It is the hope of this author that the science of psychology can contribute to our survival and enable us to realize the potential of our species.

Clearly, the automobile, airplane, telephone, radio, television, personal computer, cell phone, and World Wide Web have each transformed the human condition. How do we reconcile these advances occurring within such a short period of time with the concurrent Stone Age existence of the Nukak? Once again, I will quote from Kurzweil's extraordinary essay:

> *Technology goes beyond mere tool making; it is a process of creating ever more powerful technology using the tools from the previous round of innovation. In this way, human technology is distinguished from the tool making of other species. There is a record of each stage of technology, and each new stage of technology builds on the order of the previous stage.* (Kurzweil, 2001)

The recording of progress is responsible for the distinction between tool making in other species and human technological change, according to Kurzweil. This same explanation can be applied to the distinction between the human conditions for the Nukak and for us. I have emphasized the speeding up of the pace of technological change during the past 2 centuries. It is easy to forget the glacial pace of change during the Stone Age. The Nukak survive under geographic and climatic conditions limited to a hunter/gatherer lifestyle. They have learned to make fires by rubbing sticks together, to make blowpipes from cane, and to tip darts with the paralyzing drug curare. The inability to store foods or domesticate large animals makes it impossible to produce food surpluses. Life is a day-to-day struggle for survival. There is no time or opportunity to create the technologies that transformed the human condition in cultures originating in the Fertile Crescent, a region of fertile soil and rivers currently consisting of Israel, Lebanon, Jordan, Syria, and Iraq.

---

■ Describe and give examples of the law of accelerating returns applied to technological innovations.

## THE PHONETIC ALPHABET AND ARABIC NUMBERING SYSTEM

In the following chapter, we will examine indirect learning through observation and symbolic communication. It is through indirect learning that the benefits of direct learning, including tool making and technological change, are recorded and disseminated among humans. This is as true for the Nukak as it is for us. The Nukak have language and adults socialize children and teach survival skills. Before we discuss indirect learning, however, it is important to recognize the enormous contribution of two other human inventions: the phonemic alphabet and the Arabic numbering system.

**Phonetic Alphabet**

Visual symbols representing sounds, permitting written representation of any pronounceable word in a language.

**Arabic Numbering System**

System of written representation of any quantity, real or imagined, that is fundamental to mathematics and the scientific method, which rely on quantification and measurement.

As previously mentioned, it is language in its written form that has enabled the rapid and widespread dissemination of knowledge within and between cultures. It is also the medium of recording our evolving advances in knowledge and technology. Early forms of Bronze Age writing were based on symbols or pictures etched in clay. Later Bronze Age writing began to include phonemic symbols that were precursors to the Iron Age Phoenician alphabet consisting of 22 characters representing consonants (but no vowels). The Phoenician alphabet was adopted by the Greeks and evolved into the modern Roman alphabet. The **phonetic alphabet** permitted written representation of any pronounceable word in a language.

The **Arabic numbering system** was originally invented in India before being transmitted to Europe in the Middle Ages. It permits written representation of any quantity, real or imagined, and is fundamental to mathematics and the scientific method, which rely on quantification and measurement. The alphabet and Arabic numbers permit words to become permanent in comparison to their transitory auditory form. This written permanence made it possible to communicate with more people over greater distances and eventually to build libraries. The first great library was established in Alexandria, Egypt, in approximately 300 B.C.

Gutenberg's printing press.

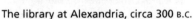

The library at Alexandria, circa 300 B.C.

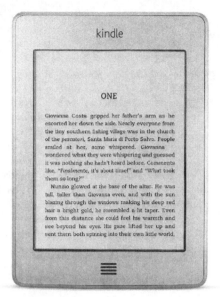

The "library" now.

Scrolls of parchment and papyrus were stored on the walled shelves of a huge concrete building. Gutenberg's invention of the printing press in 1439 enabled mass publication of written material throughout Western Europe. Today, e-books are available for electronic readers that can be held in the palm of your hand! In a study of college students, individual differences in knowledge correlated with their amount of exposure to print (Stanovich & Cunningham, 1993). Advances in the dissemination of knowledge will continue to contribute to the accelerating pace of technological development described by Kurzweil.

> ▪ Describe how written language underlies the law of accelerating returns.

## Summary

Conceptual behavior involves responding in the same way to different stimuli sharing a common property. As humans adapt to their environmental circumstances, they establish lexicons of helpful concepts. Much of our vocabularies relate to qualitative concepts such as color and shape names and quantitative concepts such as size relationships and numbers. Adaptation may often be described as a problem-solving process in which an individual attempts to discover a strategy for attaining a specific objective. Researchers have demonstrated that prior experience can facilitate or impede problem solving. Over the millennia, humans have combined their ability to learn with their ability to create tools to solve adaptive problems.

The law of accelerating returns describes how the pace of significant technological innovations has quickened over time. Written language based on alphabets and numbering systems enabled the recording and spread of technology described by this law.

# References

Birch, H. G. (1945). The role of motivational factors in insightful problem-solving. *Journal of Comparative Psychology, 38*, 295–317.

Birch, H.G., & Rabinowitz, H. S. (1951). The negative effect of previous experience on productive thinking. *Journal of Experimental Psychology, 41*, 121–125.

Blough, D. S. (1982). Pigeon perception of letters of the alphabet. *Science, 218*, 397–398.

Butler, R. A. (1953). Discrimination learning by rhesus-monkeys to visual-exploration motivation. *Journal of Comparative and Physiological Psychology, 46*, 95–98.

D'Zurilla, T. J., & Goldfried, M. R. (1971). Problem solving and behavior modification. *Journal of Abnormal Psychology, 78*, 107–126.

Duncker, K. (1945). On problem solving. *Psychological Monographs, 58*(5).

Epstein, R., Kirshnit, C. E., Lanza, R. P., & Rubin, L. C. (1984). "Insight" in the pigeon: Antecedents and determinants of intelligent performance. *Nature, 308*, 61–62.

Goldfried, M. R., & Davison, G. C. (1976). *Clinical behavior therapy*. New York: Holt, Rinehart, and Winston.

Guilford, J. P., & Guilford, J. (1980). *Alternative uses manual*. Orange, CA: Sheridan Psychological Services.

Guilford, J. P., Merrifield, P. R., & Wilson, R. C. (1958). *Unusual uses test*. Orange, CA: Sheridan Psychological Services.

Harlow, H. F. (1949). The formation of learning sets. *Psychological Review, 56*, 51–65.

Herrnstein, R. J., & Loveland, D. H. (1964). Complex visual concept in the pigeon. *Science, 146*, 549–551.

Hernstein, R. J., Loveland, D. H., & Cable, C. (1976). Natural concepts in pigeons. *Journal of Experimental Psychology: Animal Behavior Processes, 2*, 285–302.

Kohler, W. (1925). *The mentality of apes* (E. Winter, Trans.). New York: Harcourt Brace.

Kurzweil, R. (2001). The law of accelerating returns. Retrieved from *KurzweilAI.net*, http://www.kurzweilai.net/the-law-of-accelerating-returns

Levy, J. C. (1975). The effects of sequential ordering training on middle-size transposition in preschool children. *Child Development, 46*, 416–423.

Luchins, A. S. (1942). Mechanization in problem solving. *Psychological Monographs, 54*, Whole 24B.

Maier, N. R. F., & Janzen, J. C. (1968). Functional values as aids and distractors in problem solving, *Psychological Reports, 22*, 1021–1034.

Maier, N. R. F. (1930). Reasoning in humans I: On direction. *Journal of Comparative Psychology, 10*, 115–143.

Maier, N. R. F. (1931). Reasoning in humans II: The solution of a problem and its appearance in consciousness. *Journal of Comparative Psychology, 12*, 181–194.

Matarazzo, J. D. (1980). Behavioral health and behavioral medicine: Frontiers for a new health psychology. *American Psychologist, 35*, 807–817.

McCaffrey, T. (2012). Innovation relies on the obscure: A key to overcoming the classic problem of functional fixedness. *Psychological Science, 23*, 215–218.

McCullough, D. (2001). *John Adams*. New York: Simon & Schuster.

Miller, G. A., Galanter, E., & Pribram, K. H. (1960). *Plans and the structure of behavior*. New York: Holt.

Moore, G. E. (1965). Cramming more components onto integrated circuits. *Electronics, 38*, 1–4.

Reese, H. W. (1968). *The perception of stimulus relations*. New York: Academic Press.

Skinner, B. F. (1960). Pigeons in a Pelican. *American Psychologist, 15*, 574–591.

Stanovich, K. E., & Cunningham, A. E. (1993). Where does knowledge come from? Specific associations between print exposure and information acquisition. *Journal of Educational Psychology, 85*, 211–229.

Towe, A. L. (1954). A study of figural equivalence in the pigeon. *Journal of Comparative and Physiological Psychology, 47*, 283–287.

Warren, J. M. (1965). Primate learning in comparative perspective. In A. M. Schrier, H. F. Harlow, & F. Stollnitz (Eds.), *Behavior of nonhuman primates* (Vol. 1). New York: Academic Press.

Wertheimer, M. (1945). *Productive thinking*. New York: Harper.

# Chapter 12

# Becoming Human Through Indirect Social Learning

In order to appreciate the differences between the lives of nonhuman animals, present-day hunter/gatherer groups such as the Nukak, and technologically enhanced humans, it is necessary to consider the role and extent of indirect social learning that involves others of the same species. Observational learning has been evidenced in many species of animals including birds (Zentall, 2004), but approximations to speech appear practically unique to humans. Paul Revere famously ordered a lantern signal of "one if by land and two if by sea" during his Revolutionary War midnight ride through the streets of Massachusetts. This is not functionally different from the distinct alarm calls emitted by vervet monkeys in the presence of eagles, snakes, and leopards (Seyfarth, Cheney, & Marler, 1980; Strushaker, 1967). Through observational learning, young vervets learn to respond to different screeches for "heads up," "heads down," and "look around!" Vervets hide under trees to the eagle warning, rear on their hind paws to the snake warning, and climb the nearest tree to the leopard warning. This is the closest thing we see to social learning of speech in other animals. Meltzoff and Moore (1977, 1983) demonstrated unambiguous examples of imitation in infant humans as young as 12 to 21 days old, leading to the conclusion that humans normally do not need to be taught this mode of learning. Skinner (1986) contributed an interesting but admittedly post hoc speculative theoretical article describing possible evolutionary scenarios for the adaptive learning of imitation and the use of language.

# BANDURA'S FOUR-STAGE MODEL OF OBSERVATIONAL LEARNING

Albert Bandura is to the study of **observational learning** what Pavlov is to the study of predictive learning (classical conditioning) and what Thorndike and Skinner are to the study of control learning (instrumental or operant conditioning). Bandura conducted some of the pioneering research demonstrating observational learning in children and developed a comprehensive theory of social learning (Bandura, 1962, 1965, 1969, 1971, 1973, 1977a, 1977b, 1978, 1986; Bandura, Ross, & Ross, 1961, 1963a, 1963b; Bandura & Walters, 1963). Much of his empirical research relates to the four-stage model of observational learning he proposed to analyze and organize the voluminous literature (1986, p. 52). The four logically necessary observational learning processes are attention, retention, production, and motivation. That is, in order for an observer to imitate a model, it is essential that the observer attends to the model's behavior, retains information regarding the important components, has the ability to produce the same actions, and is motivated to perform. This is a "chain as strong as its weakest link." If any stage is missing, imitation (but not necessarily learning) does not occur. As we will see later, children may learn by observing a model but will not necessarily imitate the act (Bandura, 1965). We now review some of the major variables related to the model and the observer found to influence each of these stages.

## Attention

Much of what we have learned about the role of attention in direct predictive and control learning applies to observational learning as well. When we considered the determinants of the effective component of a compound predictive stimulus, we listed preferred sense modality, stimulus salience (overshadowing), and the role of prior learning (blocking). Under the topic of antecedent stimulus control, we saw that individuals pay attention to the features providing information concerning important consequences.

Human beings predominantly rely upon the senses of vision and hearing to adapt to environmental demands. This applies to observational as well as direct learning. In order to imitate what we see or hear, we must be attending to critical elements of modeled behavior. Factors such as intensity, attractiveness, and emotionality will enhance the salience of a stimulus, increasing the likelihood of imitation (Waxler & Yarrow, 1975).

Prior learning experience significantly affects the probability of attending to different models in one's environment. Perceived similarity to self, especially in sex (i.e., male or female) and gender (i.e., masculine or feminine), but also in age, race, ethnicity, and social class, plays an important role. Girls and boys are universally treated differently. They are dressed differently, given different hair styles, and encouraged to behave differently from birth. When children first start to speak, they soon learn to categorize the world into "mama," "dada," and boys and girls, and they assign themselves gender and age identities. These assignments (and others) impact their choices of models throughout their lives. Selective indirect learning experiences influence family responsibilities in all cultures and education and career opportunities in technologically enhanced cultures. One of the pronounced effects of technological advances has been the reduction and elimination of such gender differences. Transition from strength-driven to skills-driven and information-driven occupations, as well as availability of contraceptives, is reducing the role of biology on women's destinies.

In addition to attending to those similar to themselves, people are most likely to attend to others designated as "authority figures" or "role models," whether these designations are earned or assigned. A Stone Age culture such as the Nukak has very few potential models. Elders are most likely to be considered authority figures. Certain elders may be considered to have special powers or abilities. Every day in our culture, we come into contact with a large number of potential models based on kinship, grade level, occupation, organization membership, friendship, among others. In addition to these real-life examples, we are exposed to a countless number of potential models on the radio, TV, internet, and other media. The likelihood of paying attention to a model can be based upon perceived functional value. For example, one may seek out a particular relative or friend or search for a particular website in order to obtain knowledge or skills that relate to a current problem. Sources of authority may include elders, teachers, clergy, experts, or celebrities.

## Retention

Memory and forgetting have been favored topics in psychology since the start of the discipline. Hermann Ebbinghaus (1885) generated the first learning and forgetting curves using himself as the subject. He invented the three-letter nonsense syllable (e.g., GUX, VEC.) for this purpose in order to eliminate the effects of prior familiarity. Memory research led to the demonstration of two sources of interference based on prior experience. **Retroactive interference** occurs when learning new materials reduce the ability to recall previously learned material. **Proactive interference** is the reduction of memory of new materials resulting from prior learning (Slamecka & Ceraso, 1960). For example, if a student learned Spanish in high school and French in college, the new French vocabulary might interfere with remembering the former Spanish vocabulary. This is retroactive interference. Spanish interfering with the recall of French would be proactive interference.

Bartlett (1932) conducted memory research with meaningful materials such as stories or fables. He found that in retelling stories, people tended to alter them in systematic ways. He concluded that memory is a reconstructive rather than a reproductive process involving **leveling** (simplification), **sharpening** (exaggeration of specific details), and **assimilation** (incorporation into existing schemas). Thus, when we observe a model, we are not storing a "videotape" of what we see and hear but rather encoding our observations in such a manner that we can reconstruct what occurred at a later time. For example, if someone is demonstrating how to open a combination lock, we will probably try to memorize verbal instructions (e.g., turn clockwise past 0 to 14, turn counterclockwise past 0 to 28). Breaking this complex behavior down into manageable units and repeatedly presenting these instructions at a slow pace will decrease the likelihood of encoding errors, thereby improving retention. Overtly and covertly (i.e., silently) rehearsing the instructions will also improve memory, increasing the likelihood of successfully opening the lock. Adults who verbally coded modeled events and actively rehearsed afterward were much better at imitating what they observed than were adults who did not code the events or were prevented from rehearsing (Bandura & Jeffrey, 1973).

**Retroactive Interference**

The reduction of memory of old information resulting from subsequent learning. For example, learning to drive in England will slow down the return to driving in the United States.

**Proactive Interference**

The reduction of memory of new information resulting from prior learning. For example, first learning to drive in the United States will slow down learning to drive in England where the steering wheel is to the right of the car and people drive in the left lane.

**Assimilation, Leveling, Sharpening**

Bartlett found that in retelling stories, people tended to alter them in systematic ways. He concluded that memory is a reconstructive, rather than a reproductive, process that involves leveling (simplification), sharpening (exaggeration of specific details), and assimilation (incorporation into existing schemas).

### Response Capability

When I was a child, I loved the TV character Superman. I would join my friends with a towel draped around my neck and try to fly. I have yet to take off. Obviously, I had attended to Superman and remembered what he did. As I grew up, I continued to watch TV and have role models. Many of these, like Superman, possessed natural abilities that escaped my genes or skills that escaped my learning history. In the former case, I was forced to be serene. In the latter, with "courage" I could acquire the component responses necessary to imitate the model. In Chapter 14, we will consider the topic of self-control and I will describe a research-based process for changing one's behavior in a desired fashion. Still, I wouldn't suggest trying to fly.

### Motivation

We can see people doing pretty much anything on the internet. Fortunately, it is not necessarily the case that "people see, people do." In our complicated, open, media-dominated world, we are constantly exposed to models performing undesirable, illegal, or dangerous acts. We do not automatically try to imitate everything we observe. Often, the outcome is an example of latent observational learning. The rats in Tolman and Honzik's (1932) group that did not initially receive food at the end of the maze learned the correct route but did not show that they had learned it until motivated by food. We often attend to models, remember what they performed, and possess the ability to imitate their actions but do not in the absence of an incentive.

In a classic study, Bandura (1965) showed boys and girls a film depicting a child displaying unusually aggressive acts with a Bobo doll punching bag (e.g., hitting the doll with a hammer, see the accompanying photograph). In one version of the film, an adult observed the child and punished his aggressive acts. In a second version, the adult praised and provided candy to the boy. There was no consequence in a third condition. Afterward, the children were placed in a room with a Bobo doll and observed to see

Child hitting "Bobo" doll. (Bandura, 1965)

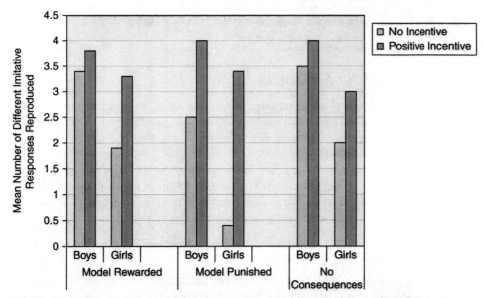

**FIGURE 12.1**   Mean number of different matching responses reproduced by children as a function of response consequences to the model and positive incentives.   (Adapted from Bandura, 1965)

how often they displayed the aggressive acts. The findings indicated that boys committed more of these aggressive acts than girls in all three conditions. Both boys and girls were more likely to imitate the model who was rewarded at the end of the film than the model who was punished. Then, children in the three groups were offered treats to imitate what they observed in the film. As was true in Tolman and Honzik's group that was switched from non-reward to reward, there was a dramatic increase in the number of aggressive acts by the children. Clearly, the children had learned and retained what they observed. The likelihood of imitation was influenced by both the consequences displayed in the film as well as by the contingencies implemented in the playroom (see Figure 12.1).

When we discussed the control learning acquisition process in Chapter 6, presentation of a behavior to imitate was described as a particularly powerful form of gestural prompting. In Chapter 8, we saw that teaching autistic children to imitate is an important precursor to initiating a comprehensive language training program. Games including imitation are used starting in infancy and early childhood to teach children (e.g., "I'll touch my nose and then you touch your nose," singing the ABC song, and playing Simon says). The following guidelines summarize what we have learned about effective observational learning techniques. In order to increase the likelihood of imitation:

- Use peers, significant others, or authority figures as models.
- Break down behavior into manageable units and present it at a slow pace.
- Use language to direct attention to key elements and explain their significance.
- Use prompting and fading if necessary.
- Provide accurate feedback for the observer under realistic conditions.
- Reward successive approximations to ideal performance.

> ■ Describe how different variables influence the attention, retention, production, and motivation stages of observational learning.

## SPEECH AND LANGUAGE

**Language**
A consensually agreed-upon collection of arbitrary symbols used to represent objects, actions, relationships, thoughts, and feelings.

This is a text about adaptive behavior in human beings. Research with other animals is reviewed with the objective of helping us understand human behavior. There is controversy regarding the extent to which other animals use or can be taught to use **language** (cf., Linden, 1974). With our focus on human behavior, we can avoid this controversy. For those interested, again I recommend the excellent book *Next of Kin* (Fouts, 1997). Spoken language appears in every human culture currently known. The Nukak have an extensive language, different even from those of nearby tribes in the Amazon rain forest.

### Hockett's Features of Language

If we are to understand human behavior, we must understand how language is acquired and its impact upon subsequent adaptive learning. Before we proceed, we must consider what we mean by language. Charles Hockett (1960) listed 13 features that he considered essential to language:

1. Vocal-auditory channel. We saw in Chapter 1 that the human being's brain, with its disproportional amount of space dedicated to the tongue, facilitates the acquisition of speech. Sign language, involving a manual-visual channel, is mostly restricted to people with hearing difficulties and those wishing to communicate with them.
2. Broadcast transmission and directional reception. Sound is sent out in all directions while being received in a single place. This provides an adaptive advantage in that people can communicate with others out of their line of sight.
3. Rapid fading (transitoriness). Sounds are temporary. Writing and audiorecordings are techniques used to address this limitation of speech (and alas, lectures).
4. Interchangeability. One must be able to transmit and receive messages.
5. Total feedback. One must be able to monitor one's own use of language.
6. Specialization. The organs used for language must be specially adapted to that task. Human lips, tongues, and throats meet this criterion.
7. Semanticity. Specific signals can be matched with specific meanings. Different sounds exist for different words.
8. Arbitrariness. A connection is not necessary between a meaningful unit (e.g., word) and its reference.
9. Discreteness. There are distinct basic units of sound (phonemes) and meaning (words).
10. Displacement. One must be able to communicate about objects that are not present. One must be able to symbolically represent the past and the future.
11. Productivity. The units of sound and meaning must be able to be combined to create new sounds and meaningful units (sentences).
12. Duality of patterning. The sequence of meaningful units must matter (i.e., there must be a syntax).
13. Traditional transmission. Specific sounds and words must be learned from other language users.

Although all of Hockett's features are frequently cited as the defining characteristics of language, the first three elements are restricted to speech. These features do not apply to sign language, letter writing, and other examples of non-vocal/auditory modes of symbolic communication.

| ▪ Describe Hockett's major characteristics of language. |
| --- |

## Language Acquisition

Let us examine how principles of predictive and control learning help us understand the acquisition of language and the role it plays in subsequent human adaptation. At a few months of age, infants start to babble and are able to make all the possible human sounds. Eventually, as the child is increasingly exposed to the sounds of her/his social unit, some of the sounds are "selected," and others removed from the repertoire. Routh (1969) demonstrated that infants are able to make subtle discriminations in sounds. The frequency of speaking either vowels or consonants could be increased if selectively reinforced with tickles and "coos." The mother's vocal imitation of a child's verbalizations is also an effective reinforcer (Pelaez, Virues-Ortega, & Gewirtz, 2011).

Children may learn their first word as early as age 9 months. Usually, the first words are names of important people ("mama," "dada"), often followed by greetings ("hi," "bye") and favored foods. As described in Chapter 5, classical conditioning procedures may be used to establish word meaning. For example, the sound "papa" is consistently paired with a particular person. Children are encouraged to imitate the sound in the presence of the father. It may be the source of humor (or embarrassment) when a child overgeneralizes and uses the word for another male adult. With experience, children learn to attend to the relevant dimensions and apply words consistently and exclusively to the appropriate stimuli or actions (e.g., "walk," "run," "eat"). Similarly, words are paired with the qualities of objects (e.g., "red," "circle") and actions (e.g., "fast," "loud"). Children learn to abstract out the common properties through the process of concept formation. Words are also paired with quantities of objects. In the same way that "redness" may be a quality of diverse stimuli having little in common, "three-ness" applies to a particular number of diverse stimuli.

Much of our vocabulary applies to nonobservable objects or events. It is important to teach a child to indicate when "hurt" or "sick" or "happy" or "sad." In these instances, an adult must infer the child's feelings from his/her behavior and surrounding circumstances. For example, if you see a child crying after bumping her head, you might ask if it hurts. As vocabulary increases, meaning can be established through higher-order conditioning using only words. For example, if a child is taught that a jellyfish is a "yucky creature that lives in the sea and stings," he will probably become fearful when swimming in the ocean.

Different languages have different word orders for the parts of speech. As a result, syntax (i.e., grammatical order) must be learned. At about 18 to 24 months, children usually start to combine words and by 30 months, they are forming brief (not always grammatical) sentences. With repeated examples of their native language, children are able to abstract out schemas for forming grammatical sentences (e.g., "the car is blue," "the square is big"). It is much easier to learn grammatical sequences of nonsense words

**Schema Learning**

The acquisition of a coherent structure capable of incorporating separate entities having definable characteristics. For example, children acquire a schema that enables them to differentiate grammatical from nongrammatical groups of words.

(e.g., The maff vlems oothly um the glox nerfs) than nongrammatical sequences (e.g., maff vlem ooth um glox nerf). This indicates the role of **schema learning** in the acquisition of syntax (Osgood, 1957, p. 88). Children usually acquire the intricacies of grammar by about age 6.

Vocabulary size is an important predictor of success in school (Anderson & Freebody, 1981). Major factors influencing vocabulary size include socioeconomic status (SES) and the language proficiencies of significant others, particularly the mother. In a monumental project, Hart and Risley (1995) recorded the number of words spoken at home by parents and 7-month- to 36-month-old children in 42 families over a 3-year period. They found that differences in the children's IQ scores, language abilities, and success in school were all related to how much their parents spoke to them. They also found significant differences in the manner in which low- and high-SES parents spoke to their children. Low-SES parents were more likely to make demands and offer reprimands, whereas high-SES parents were more likely to engage in extended conversations, discussion, and problem solving. Whereas the number of reprimands given for inappropriate behavior was about the same for low- and high-SES parents, high-SES parents administered much more praise.

Speech becomes an important and efficient way of communicating one's thoughts, wishes, and feelings. This is true for the Nukak as well as for us. Given the harshness of their living conditions and the limits of their experiences, the Nukak have much in common with low-SES children within our society. Declarative statements (e.g., "the stick is sharp," "the stove is hot," "pick up the leaves," "don't fight with your sister," "I am happy," "you are tired") become the primary basis for conducting much of the everyday chores and interactions. Language becomes a primary supplement to direct experience and observation as a means of adapting to one's environmental circumstances.

> ▪ Describe how control learning principles apply to the acquisition of language.

## PREPARING FOR SCHOOL AND THE 3 RS

In technologically advanced societies, much of childhood is dedicated to activities in preparation for school. Children enjoy listening to rhymes. Children enjoy singing. Children REALLY enjoy singing rhymes! It is not unusual for adults to start singing the alphabet song to children as young as age 2. The alphabet is an example of a serial list in which items always appear in a particular order. **Serial learning** was one of the first types of memory studied by Ebbinghaus. One usually learns the items at the beginnings and ends of lists before learning items in the middle, the so-called **serial-position effect** (Hovland, 1938). The alphabet song divides the 26 letters into four manageable chunks based on rhyming sounds. This makes learning the entire sequence fun and relatively easy, even for a very young child. Once this is accomplished, it is possible to match the sounds to their written forms, an important precursor to learning to read.

**Serial Learning**

Recalling items in a specific order (e.g., the letters of the alphabet, numbers).

**Serial-Position Effect**

People usually learn the items at the beginnings and ends of serial lists before learning the items in the middle.

Counting represents another fundamental serial learning task for children. It is different from the alphabet in that the sequence of items is not arbitrary. That is, there is no reason "a" has to be the first letter of the alphabet and precede "b." However, "1" has to be first, and "2" second. Counting, therefore, requires additional learning in which the numbers are spoken in the presence of the appropriate quantities of different objects. Eventually, the child "abstracts out" the dimension of quantity and the different values. Similar to letters, the sounds are eventually associated with their written forms, an important precursor to learning arithmetic.

Previously, I cited implementation of compulsory education around the turn of the 20th century as an enabling factor for subsequent scientific and technological advances. In order for individuals and for a society to receive the full benefits of compulsory education, children must be prepared for the first years of schooling. The richness of their experiences and extensive vocabularies provides many children with the basic knowledge and skills required to excel in preschool and beyond. Unfortunately, as revealed in Hart and Risley's findings, not all children currently receive the level of preparation necessary to immediately acquire the ability to read, write, and perform quantitative operations. Hopefully, parent education and preschool programs such as Head Start will reduce the continuing achievement gap among different segments of our population.

Kurzweil attributed the difference in technological achievements between humans and other animals to the recording of prior successes. Without this recording, individuals and cultures would not be able to profit from prior advances. The phonetic alphabet, the basis for reading, has served as the major means of recording human knowledge since the time of the Phoenicians. There is certainly much truth to the statement that "reading is fundamental."

Learning to read is an excellent example of the importance of the perspective endorsed by the early Gestalt psychologists. Reading may be broken down into a sequence of steps establishing larger and larger meaningful units (i.e., gestalts). Eye-movement recordings reveal that individual letters are not initially perceived as units. With increased experience, we are able to integrate the components into a relatively small number of distinct letters followed by integration of letters into words. We perceive the letters of words simultaneously (i.e., as a gestalt) not sequentially (Adelman, Marquis, & Sabatos-DeVito, 2010). Eventually, we are able to read aloud fluently by scanning phrases and sentences (Rayner, 1998).

Learning to write requires establishing larger and larger behavioral units through shaping and chaining. As soon as a child is able to grasp a pencil or pen, parents often encourage her/him to "draw." Once a certain level of proficiency is achieved, it is possible to teach the writing of letters and numbers. This may begin by having the child trace the appropriate signs and then fading them out so that eventually the appropriate symbol can be formed without visual assistance. Fluency of writing letters, followed by words, followed by phrases and complete sentences is eventually achieved. As they advance through the grades, children are assigned tasks requiring more extensive reading and writing.

Learning basic arithmetic is an extension of counting. It is possible to visually differentiate between small numbers of items (e.g., to tell the difference between 3 and 4). This is not possible once a threshold is passed (e.g., trying to see the difference between 10 and 11 items, or 20 and 21, or 120 and 121). It is necessary to accurately apply verbal counting to the actual number of objects in order to perform such tasks. Once a child is able to count objects, it is possible to begin teaching basic mathematics, including addition and subtraction, the base-10 system, multiplication and division, and fractions. For an early comprehensive treatment of the application of predictive and control learning principles to reading, writing, and arithmetic, I recommend Staat's excellent book *Learning, Language, and Cognition* (1968). One cannot overstate the fundamental importance of compulsory education to societal development and economic progress. Rindermann and Thompson (2011) conducted sophisticated statistical analyses demonstrating the powerful relationship of cognitive ability, particularly in the STEM fields (science, technology, engineering, and math), to wealth in 90 countries. The top 5% in cognitive ability contribute significantly, often in the form of scientific and technological advances.

> ▪ Describe how control learning principles apply to preparing children for school.

## Summary

We opened this chapter with the statement that in order to appreciate the differences among the lives of nonhuman animals, hunter/gatherers such as the Nukak, and technologically enhanced humans, it is necessary to consider the role and extent of indirect social learning. Many other species appear capable of observational learning, and one, the vervet monkey, uses this process to teach its young three distinct predator warnings. However, with this limited exception, the rest of the animal kingdom is restricted to direct and indirect learning experiences involving their immediate environments. They acquire the ability to predict and control based on their own interactions with the environment or by observing others directly interacting with the environment.

Bandura described observational learning as requiring attention to the details of a model's behavior, retention of the information necessary to repeat the behavior, the physical skills necessary to perform the behavior, and the motivation to do so. Perceived similarity to self and reinforcement value are powerful variables influencing the likelihood of attending to a model. Human memory was described as a reconstructive as opposed to a reproductive process. Imitation often occurs as the result of rehearsing, storing, and retrieving verbal codes.

As indicated in Hockett's list of the features of language, speech may be used to represent past experiences and describe alternate futures. Language creates a symbolic reality for human beings enabling us to escape the here and now. The Nukak and other remaining Stone Age hunter/gatherer tribes, all of whom have language, demonstrate that the human advances and inventions occurring over the past 13,000 years were not inevitable. Our species by necessity maintains a nomadic existence unless agriculture and domestication of large animals are possible. The Amazon and other extreme environments on earth are unsuitable to year-round agriculture. There may be no indigenous large animals, or those that exist may be dangerous. The Nukak and others living under such conditions remain in a day-to-day struggle to survive.

The human being is by necessity a social animal. Our children require protection and care in order to survive. In the absence of a village, it takes several adults assisting one another on a daily basis in order for the group to survive. The Nukak, as nomads, live in small bands throughout their lives because they are constantly on the move. The development of agriculture and domestication of large animals enabled humans to meet their nutritional needs while remaining in one location for extended periods. This stability permitted communities to increase in size, and food surpluses enabled people to engage in activities other than those required for survival. Necessity may be "the mother of invention," but invention could occur only when people had the time and opportunity.

# References

Adelman J. S., Marquis, S. J., & Sabatos-DeVito, M. G. (2010). Letters in words are read simultaneously, not in left-to-right sequence. *Psychological Science, 21*, 1799–1801.

Anderson, R. C., & Freebody, P. (1981). Vocabulary knowledge. In J. Guthrie (Ed.), *Comprehension and teaching: Research reviews* (pp. 77–117). Newark, DE: International Reading Association.

Bandura, A. (1962). Social learning through imitation. In M. R. Jones (Ed.), *Nebraska Symposium on Motivation, 10*, 211–274.

Bandura, A. (1965). Influence of model's reinforcement contingencies on the acquisition of imitative responses. *Journal of Personality and Social Psychology, 1*, 589–595.

Bandura, A. (1969). *Principles of behavior modification.* New York: Holt, Rinehart, and Winston.

Bandura, A. (1971). Vicarious and self-reinforcement processes. In R. Glaser (Ed.), *The nature of reinforcement* (pp. 228–278). New York: Academic Press.

Bandura, A. (1973). *Aggression: A social learning analysis.* Englewood Cliffs, NJ: Prentice Hall.

Bandura, A. (1977a). *Social learning theory.* Englewood Cliffs, NJ: Prentice Hall.

Bandura, A. (1977b). Self-efficacy: Toward a unifying theory of behavioral change. *Psychological Review, 84*, 191–215.

Bandura, A. (1978). The self system in reciprocal determinism. *American Psychologist, 33*, 344–358.

Bandura, A. (1986). *Social foundations of thought and action.* Englewood Cliffs, NJ: Prentice Hall.

Bandura, A., & Jeffrey, R. W. (1973). Role of symbolic coding and rehearsal processes in observational learning. *Journal of Personality and Social Psychology, 26*, 122–130.

Bandura, A., Ross, D., & Ross, S. (1961). Transmission of aggressions through imitation of aggressive models. *Journal of Abnormal and Social Psychology, 63*, 575–582.

Bandura, A., Ross, D., & Ross, S. (1963a). Imitation of film-mediated aggressive models. *Journal of Abnormal and Social Psychology, 66*, 3–11.

Bandura, A., Ross, D., & Ross, S. (1963b). Vicarious reinforcement and imitative learning. *Journal of Abnormal and Social Psychology, 67*, 601–607.

Bandura, A., & Walters, R. H. (1963). *Social learning and personality development.* New York: Holt, Rinehart & Winston.

Bartlett, F. C. (1932). *Remembering: A study in experimental and social psychology.* New York: Macmillan.

Ebbinghaus, H. (1885, translated 1913). *Memory: A contribution to experimental psychology* (H. A. Ruger & C. E. Bussenius, Trans.). New York: Teachers College, Columbia University, Bureau of Publications.

Fouts, R. (1997). *Next of kin.* New York: Avon Books.

Hart, B., & Risley, R. T. (1995). *Meaningful differences in the everyday experience of young American children.* Baltimore: Paul H. Brookes.

Hockett, C. F. (1960). The origin of speech. *Scientific American, 203*, 88–111.

Hovland, C. I. (1938). Experimental studies in rote learning theory: III. Distribution of practice with varying speeds of syllable presentation. *Journal of Experimental Psychology, 25*, 622–633.

Linden, E. (1974). *Apes, men, and language.* New York: Penguin Books.

Meltzoff, A. N., & Moore, M. K. (1977). Imitation of facial and manual gestures by human neonates. *Science, 198*, 75–78.

Meltzoff, A. N., & Moore, M. K. (1983). Newborn infants imitate adult facial gestures. *Child Development, 54*, 702–709.

Osgood, C. E. (1957). A behavioristic analysis of perception and language as cognitive phenomena. In J. S. Bruner (Ed.), *Contemporary approaches to cognition* (pp. 75–117). Cambridge, MA: Harvard University Press.

Pelaez, M., Virues-Ortega, J. & Gewirtz, J. L. (2011). Reinforcement of vocalizations through contingent vocal imitation. *Journal of Applied Behavior Analysis, 44*, 33–40.

Rayner, K. (1998). Eye movements in reading and information processing: 20 years of research. *Psychological Bulletin, 124*, 372–422.

Rindermann, H., & Thompson, J. (2011). Cognitive capitalism: The effect of cognitive ability on wealth, as mediated through scientific achievement and economic freedom. *Psychological Science, 22*, 754–763.

Routh, D. (1969). Conditioning of vocal response differentiation in infants. *Developmental Psychology, 1*, 219–225.

Seyfarth, R., Cheney, D., & Marler, P. (1980). Monkey responses to three different alarm calls: Evidence of predator classification and semantic communication. *Science, 210*, 801–803.

Skinner, B. F. (1986). The evolution of verbal behavior. *Journal of the Experimental Analysis of Behavior, 45,* 115–122.

Slamecka, N. J., & Ceraso, J. (1960). Retroactive and proactive inhibition of verbal learning. *Psychological Bulletin, 57,* 449–475.

Staats, A. W. (1968). *Learning, language, and cognition.* New York: Holt, Rinehart & Winston.

Strushaker, T. (1967). Auditory communication among vervet monkeys (Cercopithecus aethiops). In S. A. Altmann (Ed.), *Social communication among primates* (pp. 281–324). Chicago: University of Chicago Press.

Tolman, E. C., & Honzik, C. H. (1930). Introduction and removal of reward, and maze performance in rats. *University of California Publications in Psychology, 4,* 257–275.

Waxler, C. Z., & Yarrow, M. R. (1975). An observational study of maternal models. *Developmental Psychology, 11,* 485–494.

Zentall, T. T. (2004). Action imitation in birds. *Learning and Behavior, 32,* 15–23.

# Chapter 13

# Adaptive Learning and Self-Actualization

The final two chapters demonstrate how principles of adaptive learning enable us to appreciate cultural differences in the human condition and how these principles may be applied to achieve personal goals. Abraham Maslow (1943), a humanistic psychologist, proposed a **hierarchy of human needs** often portrayed in textbooks as a pyramid (see Figure 13.1).

Basic physiological needs form the base of the pyramid, followed by safety and security, sense of belonging (love and interpersonal relationships), **self-esteem** (feeling good about oneself), and **self-actualization** (fulfilling one's personal goals and potential). Maslow's hierarchy is a perceptive and constructive schema for organizing and prioritizing aspects of the human condition. It provides a meaningful lens through which to view the differences between the Stone Age cultures such as

**FIGURE 13.1**   Maslow's hierarchy of human needs.

that of the Nukak of the Amazonian rain forest and our adaptive learning needs. According to Maslow, the objective of human adaptation is to rise through the pyramid ultimately achieving self-actualization. In order to appreciate this task, it is necessary to understand the requirements to succeed at each of the levels for Stone Age and technologically advanced cultures.

## THE NUKAK'S PHYSIOLOGICAL NEEDS

The Nukak are anatomically and physiologically the same as we are. They share the need to breathe, eat, drink, sleep, and maintain biological homeostasis. Necessary for survival of the species, though not for individual survival, they also engage in sexual activity.

For thousands of years, the Nukak have been adapting to the demands and resources of the Amazonian rain forest. These demands result from poor soils for cultivating plants, a scarcity of animals for hunting, a difficult terrain prohibiting rapid transportation, and isolation from technologically advanced cultures. Over that time period, the Nukak have learned to rub sticks together to make fire, dig holes to obtain fresh water, hunt local wild animals (mostly monkeys and birds), and gather edible plants to obtain food.

### Hunting and Gathering

"Every Nukak knows how to make virtually everything he or she will need during his or her lifetime, and the basic material for making these items can be found within the band's territory" (Politis, 2007, p. 229). The **blowpipe**, fashioned from cane, is the primary hunting tool. Darts made from palm trees are shaped, sharpened, and tipped with the paralyzing drug curare obtained from the bark of the parupi vine. Nukak men spend considerable time making 7- to 10-foot-long

Rubbing sticks together to make a fire.

Nukak man approaching prey
before shooting dart with blowpipe.

blowpipes and caring for and maintaining them. Men frequently test their blowpipes for accuracy and firing distance. Smaller blowpipes (less than 6 feet long) are constructed for young boys to play with and acquire expertise. Male adolescents often accompany their fathers on foraging trips with scaled-down (6- to 8-feet long) blowpipes. Young men and adult males also use wood bows with palm fiber bow strings to fire palm harpoons at fish.

Child playing with blowpipe and darts.

Man fishing with harpoon.

Women and girls are responsible for grinding various fruit and seeds. The mortars are created from sections of tree trunks and the pestle is a straight stick with one end flattened. Women also fashion clay pots for the storage and transport of fruits and liquids, fiber hammocks, and baskets of different sizes made from vines (Politis, 2007, p. 210–217).

Woman grinding with mortar and pestle.

Girl with clay pot.

| Time | Distance | Activity |
|------|----------|----------|
| 7:49 | 0.00 km | Departure. |
| 8:05 | 0.62 km | Stopped to eat moriche fruit in a low zone. |
| 8:38 | 2.06 km | Short stop in an abandoned camp. |
| 9:00 | 2.45 km | Stopped to defecate off the path. |
| 9:36 | 4.64 km | Crossed a creek with high water level. |
| 9:41 | 4.87 km | Stopped in abandoned camp. Checked young papaya and achiote plants that were growing on the floor. |
| 10:10 | 5.62 km | Passed through an abandoned camp with puyu and seje plants. |
| 10:59 | 7.35 km | Hunted two pavas (birds) with blowpipe. |
| 11:15 | 7.45 km | Started the return journey. |
| 11:20 | 7.54 km | Hunted three birds. One juaine (which he threw away) and two iooro. |
| 11:50 | 8.53 km | Stopped at an abandoned camp (the same at which he had stopped at 10:10); collected puyu and seje plants. |
| 12:41 | 12.30 km | Hunted three small squirrel monkeys during heavy rain. |
| 15:45 | 16.20 km | Arrived back at camp. |

**FIGURE 13.2**   A foraging trip for an adult male.   (Politis, 2007)

Politis (2007) and his associates accompanied members of the Nukak on several foraging trips. Figure 13.2, taken from Politis's book (2007, pp. 344–345), summarizes a typical trip for Kanilo, one of the adult males.

After foraging over a distance of approximately 5 miles each way for 8 hours, Kanilo returned with four birds (two pavas and two iooro), three squirrel monkeys, and some small puyu and seje plants.

Foraging trips usually include several individuals. Figure 13.3 summarizes a foraging expedition conducted by Kanilo, bringing a machete and metal axe obtained from colonists living on the border of the rain forest; Ute (an adult man), taking a machete; Krit'ti and Kodiban (adult women), each bringing a basket and bowl; and Dit'ta (a young woman), bringing a basket.

After foraging over a distance of approximately 3.5 miles each way for almost 9.5 hours, the total products brought into the camp included 2 kg of plantillo in a basket by Dit'ta, 1 kg of honey in a basket by Dit'ta, 6 kg of parupi' in a basket by Dit'ta, 10 kg of parupi' in a basket by Krit'ti, 1.5 kg of honey in a basket by Krit'ti, 10 kg of honey in a sling by Kanilo, a 10-kg land turtle by Kanilo, 8 kg of parupi' in a basket by Ute, and 3 kg of honey wrapped in leaves by Ute.

These Nukak foraging trips are representative of those made for the past thousands of years. While others are foraging, most elderly adults, young women, and children remain in the camp. As described earlier, older children may accompany their fathers and mothers in hunting and gathering. Young children collect water from nearby watering holes as their contribution to the survival needs of the camp.

| Time | Distance | Activity |
|------|----------|----------|
| 7:35 | 0.00 km | Departure. |
| 8:05 | 0.97 km | Kanilo attempted to hunt a bird by throwing his machete, but he missed. |
| 8:22 | 1.22 km | Cut a vine. |
| 8:47 | 2.16 km | Cut palms. |
| 9:24 | 2.89 km | Dug up a tuber. |
| 9:54 | 3.79 km | A beehive was found, burned, brought down, and opened. All group members ate honey and made hidromiel. |
| 11:27 | 5.15 km | Cut a vine. Glanced over a dead sloth at the foot of a tree. |
| 11:52 | 6.06 km | Cut palms and gathered their fruit. Stopped to eat fruit. |
| 12:45 | 7.45 km | Started the return journey. |
| 13:05 | 7.15 km | Burned another beehive and collected honey. |
| 15:39 | 8.72 km | Kanilo captured a land turtle. |
| 16:20 | 9.20 km | Collected plantillo fruit. |
| 16:54 | 11.09 km | Arrived back at camp. |

**FIGURE 13.3**   A foraging trip conducted by two pairs of adult men and women and a young woman.   (Politis, 2007, pp. 348–349)

## THE NUKAK'S SHELTER AND SAFETY NEEDS

### Building a Campsite

The Nukak pick up and move every 4 to 5 days, constructing between 70 and 80 campsites each year, almost never reoccupying an abandoned camp. One benefit of this mobility pattern is the creation of future sources of edible plants. The seeds left from previous occupancy result in larger and denser patches of fruit than typically occur in the rain forest. Thus, the Nukak practice a form of **migratory agriculture**, literally laying the seeds for future foraging trips (Politis, 2007, pp. 114–119).

**Migratory Agriculture**

The practice by some Amazonian nomadic tribes of planting seeds when abandoning campsites, resulting in the creation of future sources of edible plants. The seeds left from previous occupancy result in larger and denser patches of fruit than typically occur in the rain forest.

Campsites are located next to resources that are abundant at various times during the year. For example, fish are more abundant during the dry season, so during those months campsites are usually established near waterways and streams (Politis, 2007, pp. 281–283).

A campsite consists of an average of four functional units, each accommodating a nuclear family and perhaps one or two close relatives. Every functional unit includes at least one central hearth, providing heat for cooking, tool crafting, and warmth. Hammocks are hung from the trunks of medium-sized and small trees. In the rainy season (8 months of the year), roofs are constructed of platanillo and seje leaves (Politis, 2007, pp. 100–103).

The Nukak perform most daily activities near the hearth while seated in the hammocks. Women weave baskets and bracelets, spin plant fibers, hollow out palm tree

Man and woman eating while sitting in their hammocks around the hearth.

trunks to make mortars used for the grinding of plantain seeds, and perforate the teeth of (predominantly) monkeys to make necklaces. Men work on their blowpipes; make darts and harpoons; and craft breechcloths, their only articles of clothing. They start fires to harden and sharpen the points on stone tools and spears and to boil curare for their dart points. Children observe and imitate all these activities to the best of their abilities. All members of the family assist in body and facial painting. Meal-related activities, including food processing and eating, are usually conducted while sitting in the hammocks (Politis, 2007, pp. 132–136).

Children usually play in spaces set aside within, or immediately outside, the campsite. Miniature replicas of a camp are sometimes built, and the children mimic adult behavior. Children create or find toys unrelated to adult roles, including bark hammocks, fruit spinning tops, large vine rings, and rounded stones. They also play with discarded or broken adult artifacts, such as axes, machetes, vessels, and pestles. Adults also fashion scaled-down tools such as blowpipes, bows, harpoons, spears, baskets, and pottery vessels as toys (Politis, 2007, pp. 222–223). Small monkeys are kept as pets. Although not always within sight, children remain within hearing range of adults or older children. At about age 7 or 8, children's games become more gender specific and they assume more responsibilities, including taking care of younger children. An isolated, small domed structure is sometimes created for menstruating girls and for conducting female rituals (Politis, 2007, pp. 156–159).

The leader of a band is usually the best hunter and an emotionally stable individual, but this is not a powerful position with many prerogatives. Other adult men and women are also important decision makers (Politis, 2007, p. 80). The leader usually determines the location and timing of moves. He and his wife are also the first to position their hammocks. Establishing a new camp takes no more than a couple of hours and is mostly conducted by the men.

Nukak camps are designed for providing warmth when needed, effective ventilation, and cover during the rainy season. They are not designed for protection from predatory animals or other humans. There are no known instances of attacks by jaguars or other carnivores (Politis, 2007, p. 124). Spats between couple members appear to be the only examples of Nukak "violence" (e.g., breaking of blowpipes, pottery, hammocks).

The Nukak believe the world consists of three flat circular "plates." They live in the "intermediate world," with the heavens located in the "world-of-above." The "world-of-below" is believed to be occupied by powerful spirits and may be visited only in dreams (Politis, 2007, pp. 84–87). According to Politis,

> One of the overriding causal factors that influence the residential camp design is the need to be close together to provide mutual protection against supernatural spirits. This is crucial at night when people dream and there are many more spirits roaming the intermediate world. The camp is designed so that the individual shelters housing the separate families are inter-connected without separating walls. This permits the members of the band to protect each other from spirits at night. It also eliminates privacy, resulting in most intimate sexual activity occurring during the day on foraging trips. (Politis, 2007, p. 124)

The Nukak traditionally live almost all of their lives in these small camps located within a 240- to 300-square-mile portion of the Amazonian rain forest (Politis, 2007, p. 163). Living in this manner facilitates communication and sharing of food, water, firewood, and other substances required for survival and comfort. Periodically, the Nukak visit bands, often consisting of kin, located within a wider, tribal region of approximately 600 to 1200 square miles. The population density is such that tribes in the Nukak's region of the Amazonian rain forest do not compete for land or resources. There is no territoriality evidenced by the Nukak or neighboring tribes, and is no evidence of conflict or intertribal aggression (Politis, 2007, p. 180).

## THE NUKAK'S LOVE AND INTERPERSONAL NEEDS

Nukak couples form soon after the members reach puberty and are mostly monogamous (approximately 85 % in two samples taken in the 1990s) with some men having two wives. A cross-cousins (i.e., cousin from a parent's same-sex sibling) is the preferred partner with marriage with a parallel cousin (i.e., cousin from a parent's opposite-sex sibling) being prohibited. Although the stated norm is for the woman to live with the husband's family, in practice living arrangements appeared to be flexible in the 1990s (Politis, 2007, pp. 81–82). This may have been the result of sudden reductions in population resulting from contact with the outside world starting in 1988. When Politis conducted his field research from 1990 to 1996, children under age 10 constituted almost 40% of the total population, and half of the population was younger than age 15 (Politis, 2007, p. 222). Nukak bands travel periodically so that members may visit (frequently kin), search for potential mates, engage in ritual dances, or participate in feasts (Politis, 2007, pp. 80–81).

## THE NUKAK'S ESTEEM NEEDS

Self-esteem refers to an individual's personal assessment of worth. At the end of his book, Politis (2007, p. 343) describes the Nukak as "a clear-cut example of a society all the behavioral patterns of which are oriented toward preventing the development of rank and social complexity." A male's expertise in the use of the blowpipe is an important source of prestige and status among Nukak band members (Politis, 2007, pp. 196–202). Hunting ability often determines leadership in a band. However, as mentioned previously, other adult band members have significant input, and no substantial rewards accompany the leadership role. There is minimal competitiveness among band members as all are encouraged to identify with the group. An example is given of a hunter chastising another for not sharing his game. The Nukak show no interest in accumulating food or possessions. Acceptance of their assigned roles and lack of competition for status and material goods appears to result in the Nukak having high self-esteem. Every member of the tribe feels she/he is making a significant contribution.

**Body painting** using plant dyes serves as a means of indicating gender and band identity, both significant to an individual's self-esteem. It is thought that the paint may act as an insect repellent. Body painting is more extensive and elaborate in preparation for meetings and ceremonies (Politis, 2007, p. 83). Many of the Nukak wear necklaces fashioned of monkey teeth connected by palm fibers through holes in the teeth. Children of both genders wear necklaces consisting of 20 to 30 teeth. Adults usually wear necklaces with only 3 or 4 teeth. Should a child die, the necklace is placed in his/her grave (Politis, 2007, p. 221).

### Body Painting

Some Amazonian tribes use plant dyes to serve as a means of indicating gender and band identity. The painting may be more extensive and elaborate in preparation for meetings and ceremonies.

Body paint may act as an insect repellant.

Necklace of monkey teeth.

## THE NUKAK'S SELF-ACTUALIZATION NEEDS

Self-actualization refers to the attainment of one's personal goals and fulfillment of one's potential. It is often assumed that self-actualization is achieved through creative and artistic endeavors. For the most part, the Nukak's personal goals are addressed by survival and family needs. Fulfilling one's potential requires time and opportunity, neither of which is in large supply for the Nukak. As we have seen, almost all of their days are taken up with activities related to survival. These include foraging, food preparation, tool making, moving, and building new shelters. Still, the Nukak manage to demonstrate such distinctly human acts of creativity as face and body painting, wearing jewelry, and fashioning and playing flutes. Three holes are made on the flat side of long jaguar or deer bones to fashion flutes. Mouthpieces are made of beeswax. Flutes have important symbolic and ritual value among many tribes in the Amazon (Politis, 2007, p. 219).

The Nukak have developed a creation story and complicated mythology resulting in the construction of a permanent "house of worship" (the house of the tapir). Being able to fulfill an important mission by contributing to construction of the house of the tapir contributes to a Nukak's self-actualization. The **tapir** is a relatively large (about 3 feet tall and 6.5 feet long) four-legged animal resembling a swine with a long snout. It, along with the deer and jaguar, are the largest animals indigenous to the Amazon. The Nukak are prohibited from killing or eating these animals because they are thought to be like people and to embody spirit-ancestors. The tapir is given special spiritual status among these, and killing one is believed to cause thunder, the spirit-ancestor of a powerful enemy (Politis, 2007, pp. 294–295). The house of the tapir is a relatively large (up to 12 feet by 20 feet), rectangular, wall-less structure with a flat roof. It can take up to 3 days to build and is the most elaborate as well as time-consuming Nukak structure (Politis, 2007, p. 128). Unlike the temporary shelters, it is designed to be permanent and kept fastidiously clean: "Nukak believe that by building an earthly house the tapir will have somewhere to go as it roams the surface-world forest during the night and therefore will not become angry with humans" (Politis, 2007, p. 122).

**Tapir**

A relatively large (about 3 feet tall and 6.5 feet long) four-legged animal resembling a swine with a long snout. It, along with the deer and jaguar, are the largest animals indigenous to the Amazon. The Nukak are prohibited from killing or eating these animals because they are thought to be like people and to embody spirit-ancestors. The tapir is given special spiritual status among these and killing one is believed to cause thunder, the spirit-ancestor of a powerful enemy.

House of the tapir.

## OUR PHYSIOLOGICAL NEEDS IN COMPARISON TO THE NUKAK'S

The Nukak's rain forest conditions, in contrast to our technologically enhanced circumstances, pose very different adaptive learning challenges. For thousands of years, the Nukak have lived in a relatively predictable and controllable environment. They have had time to experience and adjust to the intricacies of the rain forest and transmit their knowledge and skills to one another and their children. We live in an ever-changing environment but have the advantage of continually accumulating knowledge and technologies to assist in prediction and control. Compulsory elementary and secondary education, as well as opportunities for extended higher education, enables us to take advantage of enhancements in knowledge and technology.

Every day, many Nukak band members travel several miles to forage for unknown quantities and varieties of locally available food. In contrast, it would take us less than an hour to shop in a supermarket for a week's worth of food from all over the world!

Instead of having to dig a hole, water is available to us at the nearest faucet or fountain. If we need to urinate or defecate, we go to the nearest bathroom rather than searching for privacy in the bushes. Obviously, the Nukak must dedicate far more time and effort than we do to satisfy the basic survival needs at the base of Maslow's pyramid.

> ▪ Describe differences in how Stone Age and technologically enhanced cultures meet their physical needs.

## OUR SHELTER AND SAFETY NEEDS IN COMPARISON TO THE NUKAK'S

Many of us live for years in enclosed, secure apartments and homes in policed neighborhoods. It is ironic that we may be less safe than the Nukak in their temporary, open camps in the unguarded Amazon. Population densities in the Nukak's section of the rain forest consist of perhaps a few dozen people per square mile. Some of our cities have population densities in the tens of thousands per square mile! The Nukak live amongst their kin and close relations, all of whom depend upon one another to survive. For us, industrialization has resulted in movement from sparsely populated rural areas to crowded urban centers. Increasingly, people live among strangers with a diversity of needs, interests, and values.

Domestication of plants and large animals enabled humans to abandon the nomadic lifestyle and settle in one location. Larger and larger communities formed, leading to increased competition for resources. A need arose for collective security. Hunting weapons originally developed during the Stone Age, such as the axe, spear, and bow and arrow, became tools of self-defense and war. Diamond's (2005) book *Guns, Germs, and Steel* describes the results of this development and the important impact it had on the current human condition for cultures as distinct as the Nukak and us.

The Nukak have recently been introduced to metal tools (e.g., axes and knives) and frequently prefer them to their traditional instruments. However, as a peaceful tribe, their use is restricted to foraging. The story of David and Goliath has contemporary parallels to more competitive and aggressive cultures. From the slingshot to smart missiles, and the stone to nuclear warheads, humans have "improved" the accuracy and distance of the means of delivery and the destructiveness of their weapons. It is now possible for small numbers of individuals to inflict enormous loss of life and damage to the human condition. Diamond (2005, pp. 46–47) argues convincingly that early human beings were responsible for the extinction of several species of large animals in the Americas. Improvements in hunting and fishing techniques over the centuries resulted in the extinction of a variety of other species all over the globe. Relatively recent impacts on the environment resulting from industrialization, such as pollution, habitat degradation, and climate change, have led to the extinction of countless others. The major security challenges of the modern world require protecting ourselves from our own technologies. Let's hope we do not place ourselves on the endangered-species list.

> ▪ Describe differences in how Stone Age and technologically enhanced cultures meet their shelter and safety needs.

## OUR LOVE AND INTERPERSONAL NEEDS IN COMPARISON TO THE NUKAK'S

For several decades, cross-cultural research has indicated that approximately 90% of individuals all over the world eventually get married (Carroll & Wolpe, 1996). This number has remained steady for years but may be decreasing slightly in the United States according to 2011 Pew Research results. Americans are delaying getting married, with marriages occurring later in life than had been the norm in the past. The idea that there is only one perfect spousal match is certainly truer for the Nukak than for us. It is unlikely that there are many cross-cousins of the right age and gender among the Nukak bands in the rain forest, their entire population numbering less than 500. Contrast that with the number of potential partners you might meet on Facebook! Actually, the idea of romantic love as the basis for marriage is relatively recent: "In most cultures throughout history, marriages have been arranged by parents, with little regard for the passionate desires of their children" (Arnett, 2001, p. 267). Buss (1989) conducted a monumental study of more than 10,000 young people in 37 cultures representing all the continents except Antarctica. There was striking consistency across cultures in the most important factors in mate selection. Both males and females considered "love" (i.e., mutual attraction) first, followed in order by "dependable character," "emotional stability and maturity," and "pleasing disposition." It would certainly seem an evolutionary and adaptive learning challenge for two people to find one another given the complexity and difficulty of this search. However, consistent with attention theory, the fact that 90% of us eventually marry suggests that once we settle upon and attend to these critical dimensions, we find it possible to locate potential mates.

Band membership remains relatively stable among the Nukak, often consisting of related nuclear families. Even when members are not biologically related or related by marriage, their lives are so interdependent that they function like an extended family. Visits with other bands typically involve adult ceremonial functions. The equivalents of industrialized world friendship patterns that may start to emerge in schools are not apparent in Nukak interactions. Compulsory education results in classes of similar-aged children being formed as soon as they reach age 6 or so. Thus, unlike those in traditional cultures, industrialized children spend much of the day among unrelated peers rather than with their parents or extended family. As they grow older, time spent with peers spreads to after-school activities, weekends, and summers (Arnett, 2001). This results in extensive adaptive-learning adjustments to different people under different circumstances. Industrialized-world children must learn to get along with their classmates in school, other children in schoolyards, athletic teammates on playing fields and in gymnasiums, and other social group members in other environments (e.g., houses of worship). The control learning ABCs (antecedents, behaviors, and consequences) apply as specific behaviors are rewarded, ignored, or punished by different people under different conditions.

> ■ Describe differences in how Stone Age and technologically enhanced cultures meet their family and friendship needs.

## DEVELOPMENTAL TASKS AND STAGES FOR THE NUKAK AND US

Freud considered the major life tasks to consist of learning to love and to work. For almost all of human history, the only meaningful developmental distinction was between childhood and adulthood. As children, the Nukak are taught to survive in the rain forest. When they reach puberty, they are expected to assume the adult role: find a partner, have children, and provide for the family's and the band's needs.

Prior to the industrial revolution, the great majority of Americans lived on farms. As with the Nukak, childhood was spent learning the necessary survival skills. Soon after puberty, individuals were expected to marry, start families, and establish independent lives. With advances in knowledge and technology, it became necessary to spend increasing time acquiring the necessary skills to perform jobs in industrialized cultures. Prolongation of education has led to increasing delays in couples being able to marry and live independently. Around the turn of the 20th century, states started extending compulsory attendance beyond elementary to secondary education. In 1904, G. Stanley Hall published a seminal textbook describing adolescence (starting with the onset of the physiological changes accompanying puberty) as a distinct developmental phase between childhood and adulthood (when one assumed the responsibilities of independent living). At that time, adolescence was considered to end at about the time of graduation from high school (age 18 or so).

It is becoming increasingly necessary to graduate from college in order to attain desirable occupations in the global economy. This need has created cohorts of individuals seeing themselves as no longer adolescents, but not quite adults, because they may continue to live at home or be financially dependent upon their parents. Arnett (2000) suggested that this reality requires postulating another developmental period for such individuals, one he named **emerging adulthood**. Most college and graduate students see themselves as being in this stage, which may last into the mid- to late-20s.

**Emerging Adulthood**

A developmental period for individuals perceiving themselves as no longer adolescents, but not quite adults, because they may continue to live at home or be financially dependent upon their parents. Most college and graduate students regard themselves as being in this stage, which may last into the mid- to late-20s.

> ▪ Describe the differences in the major developmental tasks and stages for Stone Age and technologically enhanced cultures.

## OUR ESTEEM NEEDS IN COMPARISON TO THE NUKAK'S

One's self-esteem is very much related to the tasks involved in preparing for adulthood. Nukak young women, upon reaching puberty and menstruating, are treated differently by their elders and considered ready to find a mate and assume increased responsibility for survival needs. There is no equivalent biological marker for Nukak young men, and they must demonstrate proficiency as hunters before being treated as adults.

For most American high school students, physical appearance, social acceptance, and school performance are significantly related to self-esteem during those years. The primary adaptive-learning challenges are "looking good," "fitting in," and "moving on." Unlike the Nukak, the self-esteem of adolescents in our culture is probably influenced as much by their peers as by their parents or other adults. As they approach college graduation, however, they have probably become less "outer-directed," and more "inner-directed." That is, what others may think is less important than it was in high school. Although physical appearance and interpersonal relations may still be important, efforts are increasingly dedicated to preparing for a future vocation.

Unlike previous generations, this is probably just as true if for women as for men. Technological advances have transformed the world, decreasing the extent to which "biology is destiny." Within a few generations, women have made enormous strides in many fields of education and in most occupations. It is common to see women physicians, lawyers, and soldiers, as well as teachers, secretaries, and nurses. Whereas "glass ceilings" remain and equality of pay for the same positions has not yet been achieved, progress has occurred. The trend is toward complete equality of opportunity and reward. However, new stresses have been created for women as they continue to perform traditional duties as wives and mothers in addition to their career responsibilities. Many contemporary men seem willing, even happy, to divide the labor in a collaborative fashion.

It was previously believed that improving self-esteem would enhance an individual's ability to succeed. However, findings with respect to school performance suggest the reverse is true. Students who were praised and taught to praise themselves, independent of school success, did not improve in their school performance (Harter, 1990). Their conduct sometimes actually deteriorated in comparison to their more objective peers (Dubois, Bull, Sherman, & Roberts, 1998). In comparison, providing students with the skills to succeed in school improves their self-esteem (Bednar Wells, & Peterson, 1995; Dubois & Tevendale, 1999). These results are exactly what one would expect from what we have learned about the importance of contingencies between behavior and outcome in control learning. The lack of a contingency between performance and success can result in learned helplessness and, presumably, low self-esteem. Success in school can establish industriousness and enhanced self-esteem.

> ▪ Describe differences in how Stone Age and technologically enhanced cultures meet their esteem needs.

## OUR SELF-ACTUALIZATION NEEDS IN COMPARISON TO THE NUKAK'S

Unlike the Nukak, we do not have to dedicate the majority of our time and effort to simply surviving until the next day. We encounter an ever-increasing variety of educational, career, and leisure-time possibilities. Still, many face obstacles in attaining their goals or realizing their potential. What are the prospects for self-actualization in the technologically enhanced world?

First, the importance of the "self" in "self-actualization" must be recognized. That is, "goals" and "one's potential" are subjective and must be defined by each individual for her/himself. This thought is recognized in the most famous quote from the Declaration of Independence: "We hold these truths to be self-evident, that all men are created equal, that they are endowed by their creator with certain unalienable rights, that among these are life, liberty and the pursuit of happiness."

Happiness is an elusive concept. Jonathan Haidt (2006) opens his book *The Happiness Hypothesis* with the questions: "What should I do, how should I live, and whom should I become?" Despite all our technology, there are limitations to what we can do, how we can live, and who we can become. Each of us has our own genetic homunculus resulting in differences in the ease of learning different behaviors. Try as we might, none of us is able to fly like Superman. Some of us find learning mathematics easier than learning to speak a foreign language, whereas the reverse is true for others. Some of us live in environments that are supportive of our behaviors, whereas others are discouraged or find it dangerous to behave in the same way. Some of us grow up in privilege and have a smooth, direct, educational and career path. Others of us grow up under less fortunate circumstances and have a "long and winding road" in life. Some of us face significant obstacles and barriers along this road. Technological advances sometimes create bridges to help us bypass these impediments to reaching our desired destinations.

> ■ Describe differences in how Stone Age and technologically enhanced cultures meet their self-actualization needs.

## BRIDGES, GLOBALIZATION, AND THE HUMAN CONDITION

The Amazonian rain forest includes many streams and creeks. As nomads, it is frequently necessary for the Nukak to construct small bridges for foraging trips or to visit other bands. They accomplish this by knocking down long palm trees that are smooth and free of branches (Politis, 2007, p. 123).

Some of contemporary civilization's greatest feats of engineering include bridges and tunnels connecting bodies of land separated by substantial distances. Many of the recent significant technological advances in travel and communication noted in Chapter 11 address the same needs to connect to other places and people. The Nukak's potential social network consists of a few hundred people at the most. Thomas Friedman, Pulitzer Prize–winning author of *The World Is Flat* (2006), describes how advances in computer technology and installation of optical fiber networks connected the continents. This enabled the social and

*The World Is Flat*

The title of Thomas Friedman's book describing how advances in computer hardware and software and installation of optical fiber networks connecting the continents enabled the social and vocational networking of millions of people, globalization, and the transformation of the human condition for most of the planet.

Man crossing bridge during a daily foraging trip.

vocational networking of millions of people, globalization, and the transformation of the human condition for most of our planet.

Transformation is not necessarily a good thing. Guns, germs, and steel were the factors Diamond (2005) considered responsible for the domination of technologically enhanced cultures over more traditional cultures. He cites the 1532 battle of Cajamarca in which Pizarro and 168 Spanish soldiers slaughtered 7000 Peruvian Inca soldiers and captured Atahuallpa, the emperor, as the first example of such a clash (Diamond, 2005, p. 68). In the preface to his book, Politis (2007) states that his study of the Nukak "probably represents one of the last opportunities to observe a hunter-gatherer society that still lives in a traditional way." The Nukak have since undergone massive changes and are threatened with extinction as the result of contact with the outside world. Tragically, the population has been decimated by diseases to which the Nukak had never been exposed. As a result of the flattening of the world, the same fate appears inevitable for the few remaining nomadic tribes. Let's hope we will not lose the benefit of sharing our planet with people continuing to adapt to our original environmental conditions.

## Summary

Maslow's hierarchy of human needs was used as an organizational schema to compare and contrast the human conditions of nomadic Stone Age and technologically enhanced cultures. In the absence of food surpluses, life becomes a daily struggle to survive using tools made from natural elements. Population densities and social networks are minimal. Advanced learning is unnecessary and there are few examples of artistic creativity.

Technology can free the human being from the struggle to meet basic physical needs. Much of childhood and adolescence can be dedicated to schooling. As increasing percentages of the population acquire reading, writing, and quantitative skills, more individuals can contribute to a culture's knowledge, technology, and creative arts.

The social, vocational, and creative opportunities available to an individual are all influenced by the existing technologies. Life becomes adaptation to a human-constructed world.

# References

Arnett, J. J. (2000). Emerging adulthood: A theory of development from the late teens through the twenties. *American Psychologist, 55,* 469–480.

Arnett, J. J. (2001). *Adolescence and emerging adulthood: A cultural approach.* Upper Saddle River, NJ: Prentice Hall.

Bednar R., Wells, M., & Peterson, S. (1995). *Self-esteem* (2nd ed.). Washington, DC: American Psychological Association.

Buss, D. (1989). Sex differences in human mate preferences: Evolutionary hypothesis tested in 37 cultures. *Behavior and Brain Sciences, 12,* 1–49.

Carroll, J., & Wolpe, P. (1996). *Sexuality and gender in society.* New York: HarperCollins.

Diamond, J. (2005). *Guns, germs, and steel.* New York: W. W. Norton & Company.

DuBois, D., Bull, C., Sherman, M., & Roberts, M. (1998). Self-esteem and adjustment in early adolescence: A social-contextual perspective. *Journal of Youth & Adolescence, 27,* 557–584.

DuBois, D., & Tevendale, H. (1999). Self-esteem in childhood and adolescence: Vaccine or epiphenomenon? *Applied & Preventive Psychology, 8,* 103–117.

Friedman, T. L. (2006). *The world is flat.* New York: Farrar, Straus and Giroux.

Haidt, J. (2006). *The happiness hypothesis.* New York: Basic Books.

Hall, G. S. (1904). *Adolescence: Its psychology and its relation to physiology, anthropology, sociology, sex, crime, religion, and education* (Vols. 1 and 2). Englewood Cliffs, NJ: Prentice Hall.

Harter, S. (1990). Self and identity development. In S. Feldman & G. Elliott (Eds.), *At the threshold: The developing adolescent* (pp. 352–387). Cambridge, MA: Harvard University Press.

Maslow, A. H. (1943). A theory of human motivation. *Psychological Review, 50,* 370–396.

Politis, G. G. (2007). *Nukak.* Walnut Creek, CA: University College, London Institute of Archeology Publications.

## Chapter 14

# Self-Actualization Through Self-Control

W e are nearing the completion of our journey. Let us consider how far we have come and how the remaining topics represent an appropriate place to end. A recurring message of this text is that learning principles constitute powerful explanations for human behavior and help us understand the way we live and why we, more than any other animal, dominate this planet. That was the opening sentence of Chapter 1, and it has been supported throughout the chapters. We have observed how the genetic potential enabling humans to predict and control their environment, to speak and to create tools, has resulted in our development of technologies that transformed our world and the human condition. In the previous chapter, we compared the self-actualization possibilities for humans living under Stone Age and technologically enhanced conditions. I will end by making this personal, considering the implications and applications of the material we have discussed to conducting our own lives and achieving self-actualization. It is first necessary to discuss research in which individuals are provided behavioral options. We will revisit the assumption of determinism with respect to the choices we make and describe an empirically supported process for achieving our personal goals.

## CONCURRENT SCHEDULES AND THE MATCHING LAW

None of the control learning apparatuses described in past chapters provide individual subjects with behavioral options. Subjects could either respond or not respond in a maze, runway, or Skinner box. Psychologists have also extensively studied animals in situations in which they could make different responses at any moment in time. For example, Skinner boxes have been constructed with two or more bars or keys. A **concurrent schedule of reinforcement** includes different response options associated with different types, magnitudes, delays, or schedules of reinforcement. This enables the study of how different variables influence what may be described as preference, choice, or decision making (Rachlin, 1989). For example, rats might be provided with "classic chow" for pressing one bar and new "wonder chow" for pressing another bar. Their degree of preference for one of the brands could be quantified through indication of the ratio of responses to the two options (e.g., a 2:1 preference for wonder chow).

A straightforward relationship, called the **matching law**, has been found to apply under certain conditions with concurrent schedules (Herrnstein, 1961, 1970, 1974). With variable interval (VI) schedules, the frequency of responding to each of the alternatives mirrors (matches) the frequency of reinforcement to that alternative. For example, reinforcement can occur twice as often on a VI 1-minute schedule as on a VI 2-minute schedule. When animals are placed in Skinner boxes with these contingencies, their responding stabilizes at the same ratio of 2:1 responding to the VI 1-minute bar (or key). Matching of response rate to reinforcement rate has been demonstrated with as many as five options for pigeons (Miller & Loveland, 1974). In addition to reinforcement frequency, the matching law has also been found to apply to magnitude of reinforcement (Catania, 1963), duration of reinforcement (Keller & Golub, 1977), and delay of reinforcement (Chung & Herrnstein, 1967). Both the magnitude and quality of reinforcement (level of preference for toys) influenced the amount of time autistic children played with a peer or sibling in a concurrent situation (Hoch, McComas, Johnson, Farander, & Guenther, 2002). The amount of time autistic children allocated to different activities in an educational setting was also found to be influenced by reinforcement frequency in addition to reinforcement quality (Neef, Mace, Shea, & Shade, 1992). The difficulty of arithmetic problems along with reinforcer quality impacted the time allotted in a concurrent task (Mace, Neef, Shade, & Mauro, 1996). Billington and DiTommaso (2003) published a comprehensive review of studies demonstrating applications of the matching law to the effects of reinforcement rate, quality, immediacy, and task difficulty on student engagement in

**Concurrent Schedule of Reinforcement**

A procedure in which different response options are associated with different types, magnitudes, delays, or schedules of reinforcement. This enables the study of how different variables influence preference, choice, and decision making.

**Matching Law**

A straightforward relationship that holds under certain conditions with concurrent schedules of reinforcement. With variable interval (VI) schedules, the frequency of responding to each of the alternatives mirrors (matches) the frequency of reinforcement to that alternative. The matching law has also been found to apply to the magnitude of reinforcement, duration of reinforcement, and delay of reinforcement. It has been shown to apply to humans in the form of probability matching.

school assignments. Interestingly, the matching law has even been shown to apply to the number of 2- and 3-point field goals attempted by college and professional basketball teams (Alferink, Critchfield, & Hitt, 2009) and the number of running and passing plays called in professional football (Reed, Critchfield, & Martens, 2006).

> ■ Describe the matching law of the behavior of individuals under concurrent schedules of reinforcement.

**Probability Matching**

An application of the matching law to humans in situations when events occur with different probabilities. For example, subjects might win money for choosing which of an array of lights will go on. Over a series of trials, the subject's choices tend to match the actual probabilities for each light.

The matching law has also been shown to apply to humans in the form of **probability matching** (Estes, 1964; Koehler & James, 2010; West & Stanovich, 2003). For example, college students may be given a small monetary reward for correct guesses as to which of two lights will come on. The lights may be programmed with different probabilities (e.g., 70% for one, and 30% for the other). Over a large number of trials, despite the fact that it does not represent the optimal strategy, the majority of subjects stabilize at matching their response rates to the probabilities of the two options. A minority of subjects maximize their payoff by always selecting the 70% light, thus being correct 70% of the time. By matching, the likelihood of being correct on an individual trial is reduced to 58% (0.7) (0.7) + (0.3) (0.3). Later we will consider how the matching law can be considered adaptive despite not resulting in maximization of reinforcement.

**Behavioral Economics**

A developing research area empirically investigating economic concepts such as elasticity of demand.

**Elasticity of Demand**

The extent to which an individual's income, the price of an object, deprivation of the object, or availability of a suitable substitute affects the likelihood of its purchase.

Economics is the study of the allocation of scarce resources by individuals and societies. Concurrent schedules can be considered "economic" in that behavior (a scarce resource) is being allocated as a function of different variables. **Behavioral economics** (cf., Bickel, Green, & Vuchinich, 1995; Francisco, Madden, & Borrero, 2009) is the name of a developing research area empirically investigating economic concepts such as **elasticity of demand** (i.e., the extent to which individual income, the price of an object, deprivation of the object, or availability of a suitable substitute affects the likelihood of its purchase). For example, Madden and Bickel (1999) found that smokers were heavily influenced by both deprivation and cost. Those deprived for 5 to 6 hours were willing to work harder to puff cigarettes than those who were not deprived even when cost was increased. Increasing the cost, however, substantially reduced smoking. Findings such as these have important implications and applications with respect to encouraging and discouraging behaviors. Murphy and his colleagues published a series of articles based upon a behavioral economic analysis of college student drinking (Murphy, Barnett, & Colby, 2006; Murphy, Correia, & Barnett, 2007; Murphy, Correia, Colby, & Vuchinich, 2005). The magnitude of the college drinking problem is exacerbated by the convenience and relatively low cost of alcohol on college campuses. The recommendations based on the studies were to increase the cost of alcoholic beverages and to discourage drinking by scheduling morning classes on Fridays. It was also suggested that the range of substitute activities not involving alcohol be increased on campuses. These could include social events as well as academic, career, and service opportunities.

## SELF-CONTROL—MAGNITUDE AND DELAY OF REINFORCEMENT

Rachlin and Green (1972) reported the findings of a seminal study manipulating both magnitude and delay of reinforcement with concurrent schedules (see Figure 14.1). In a sense, they asked the proverbial question, "Which is worth more, a bird in the hand or two in the bush?" They actually asked which is worth more to a bird (pigeon), immediate access to 2 seconds of food or twice as much food after a 4-second delay (see bottom discrimination in Figure 14.1)? The findings were unequivocal. Pigeons almost always chose the red (right) key associated with the small immediate reward rather than the green (left) key associated with the larger delayed reward. Anthropomorphizing, the pigeons appeared **impulsive** rather than displaying **self-control** (i.e., choosing the larger delayed reward over the smaller immediate one). This preference is known as **delay discounting** and has been studied in depth (Mazur, 1987; Richards, Mitchell, de Wit, & Seiden, 1997).

### Commitment

This finding, in and of itself, is interesting. However, Rachlin and Green went one step further by adding a second link. Pigeons were first confronted with two white keys (see left discrimination in Figure 14.1). Pecking the left key 15 times caused it to turn green after 10 seconds. At that point, the pigeon could respond only to the left (now green) key in order to receive 4 seconds of food after an additional 4-second delay. If, instead, the pigeon pecked the right key 15 times, it was presented with the original choice between the left green and right red keys after the 10-second delay. The surprising finding was that the pigeons were twice as likely to press the left key as the right key.

This result is certainly counterintuitive. We know that when confronted with the original choice, the pigeons strongly preferred "red." Why didn't they initially go right, resulting in the opportunity to make that same choice? Or, why

**Impulsive**

A behavioral pattern of choosing a smaller, immediate reward over a larger, delayed one (see self-control).

**Self-Control**

A behavioral pattern of choosing a larger, delayed reward over a smaller, immediate one (see impulsive).

**Delay Discounting**

The preference for choosing smaller immediate rewards over larger, delayed ones.

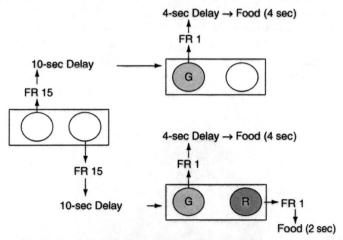

**FIGURE 14.1** Procedures used to study the effect of magnitude and delay of reinforcement on choice (Adapted from Rachlin & Green, 1972). Pigeons behave "impulsively" (i.e., choose an immediate small reward rather than a larger delayed reward) when confronted with the bottom choice. However, when an initial choice response includes a delay (10 seconds in the example), pigeons are more likely to make a "commitment" (i.e., avoid temptation) to self-control (i.e., selecting the delayed larger reward).

didn't they initially go right and then press "green" when provided the original options? The surprising interpretation by Rachlin and Green (1972) is included in the title of their article: "Commitment, Choice, and Self-control." By pressing the left key 15 times, the pigeons in a sense performed a **commitment response** to ensure selecting the delayed reward. By responding in this manner, they were not tempted by the red key that was likely to be followed by a response resulting in a small, immediate reward.

**Commitment Response**

In a self-control context, the act of making a response in advance that increases the likelihood of choosing a larger delayed reward over a smaller immediate reward.

Why, one might ask, is the pigeon able to act less impulsively when provided with the choice between the two white keys than when presented with the choice between the red and green keys? It is usually said that the devil is in the details. This is an instance where the opposite appears true. Something very beneficial is revealed in a detail of the procedures used by Rachlin and Green (1972). It is easy to overlook the 10-second delay that occurred no matter whether the pigeon responded to the left or right white key. At that point in time, the choice is not between 2 seconds of immediate food versus 4 seconds of food after a 4-second delay. It is between 2 seconds of food after a 10-second delay as opposed to 4 seconds of food after a 14-second (10 + 4) delay. Apparently a 10-second delay is an eternity to a pigeon and the "psychological" difference in a delay of 10 versus 14 seconds is far less than the difference between immediacy and 4 seconds. Because there is a long delay (10 or 14 seconds) no matter the choice between the blank keys, the pigeon is more influenced by the magnitude of the reward (4 rather than 2 seconds) at that point in time. As the length of the additional delay was increased, the likelihood of self-control was enhanced. As discussed later, this finding has important practical implications.

### The Marshmallow Test

**Marshmallow Test**

Walter Mischel developed this procedure to study impulsiveness and self-control. Children are given the choice of eating a marshmallow immediately or waiting a period of time for the opportunity to eat two marshmallows.

Walter Mischel developed the **marshmallow test** to study impulsiveness and self-control in children (Mischel & Ebbesen, 1970; Mischel, Ebbesen, & Raskoff Zeiss, 1972; Mischel, Shoda, & Peake, 1988; Mischel, Shoda, & Rodriguez, 1989; Mischel & Yates, 1979; Shoda, Mischel, & Peake, 1990). An adult placed a single marshmallow in front of a child with the instruction that it could be eaten immediately or if the child waited a certain amount of time (e.g., 20 minutes), a second one would be provided. There are many amusing and interesting YouTube videos of children undergoing the marshmallow test and implementing strategies to avoid giving in to temptation. Children who distracted themselves (e.g., by

The marshmallow test.

playing with a toy) were more successful than children who focused upon the marshmallow. An important result was that Mischel and his colleagues found that the ability to delay gratification by 4-year-olds was significantly related to their later success in life as indicated by such measures as school performance, SAT scores, completion of college, and interpersonal competence.

It is possible to learn self-control. Mazur and Logue (1978) first trained pigeons to choose a larger delayed reward over a smaller delayed reward. Over the course of a year, the pigeons were shaped to gradually tolerate increasingly shorter delays of the smaller reward. When tested a year later, the pigeons continued to exhibit a preference for larger delayed rewards over smaller immediate ones (Logue & Mazur, 1981). These same findings were obtained with children provided similar training (Schweitzer & Sulzer-Azaroff, 1988). Given the documented importance of self-control to success later in life, it would appear prudent to incorporate such training as early in life as practicable. See Logue (1995) for a comprehensive review of the self-control literature, including applications to eating disorders, substance abuse, money management, studying, and interpersonal relations.

Many human problems occur as the result of choosing immediate small rewards rather than delayed, but more significant rewards. Examples include eating an ice cream sundae despite trying to lose weight; excessive drinking, threatening one's (and others') safety; smoking a cigarette ("slow-motion suicide" according to a report issued in 1979 by the U.S. secretary of health, education and welfare and the surgeon general); hitting one's spouse or a child to immediately stop them from bothering you, even though much larger, delayed family problems are created; or, horror of horrors, watching TV instead of reading this text! Rachlin and Green's (1972) results suggest that each of these problems can be addressed by committing oneself to a course of action in advance, for example, shop from a list including only nutritious, nonfattening foods; don't drive past the ice cream store; don't go to the bar, or make sure you have a designated driver; stay away from places or events where you are likely to smoke; imagine the behaviors that upset you and rehearse a better coping strategy; or use a daily planner for time management and write the title of this book all over the pages (only kidding).

---

▪ Describe examples of common self-control problems showing how prior
  commitment can facilitate the selection of long-term large rewards rather than
  short-term small rewards).

---

## MATCHING, IMPULSIVENESS, AND ADAPTIVE LEARNING

At this time, you may be asking yourself why people (or other animals) follow the matching law if it results in less reinforcement. Also, why are people so influenced by short-term as opposed to long-term consequences because this is frequently self-destructive? Such questions are usually addressed by pointing to the adaptive (i.e., survival) value of a particular behavior. For example, it is not surprising that animals (including humans) repeat behaviors followed by appetitive stimuli and suppress behaviors followed by aversive stimuli. Obviously, animals with the opposite tendencies are unlikely to survive to transmit their genes to the next generation. The same is true for the phenomenon of acquired taste aversion. Animals inheriting this tendency will be less likely to die as the result of poisoning.

It is not as obvious why the animal kingdom should inherit tendencies to match reinforcement frequencies and discount delayed consequences. Thus, it is necessary to engage in some **post hoc** (i.e., after-the-fact) speculation. Let us imagine squirrels living in a treed suburban neighborhood with a number of private homes. Recent research indicates that the foraging of other rodents (rats) becomes more variable under conditions of reduced reinforcement probability, increasing the likelihood of discovering other sources of reinforcement (Gharib, Gade, & Roberts, 2004; Stahlman & Blaisdell, 2011). Some properties may have more trees than others and thus more nuts available for our little friends. The matching law predicts that squirrels will apportion the amount of time spent in the different yards according to the likelihood of finding nuts. These probabilities are fixed in the laboratory, whereas in nature they are likely to change over time. By foraging in one of the backyards, the squirrel depletes the number of nuts relative to the other yards. In addition, a strong rainstorm or other climatic event might occur, differentially washing away or spoiling nuts in the yards. Under variable naturalistic conditions, it is advantageous to continue sampling the environment. Even if "it ain't broke," it could become so.

**Post Hoc**

Explanations for events provided after they have already taken place.

The foraging environment of Amazonian rain forest inhabitants such as the Nukak is similar to that of squirrels in some respects. The Nukak and animals indigenous to the rainforest are in competition for food. Some natural events are unpredictable and conditions may change considerably as the result of circumstances over which they have no control. In order for the Nukak to discover random changes in resource allocations, they must continue to explore different regions of the forest.

Some events influencing food availability are predictable, such as changing conditions during the rainy and dry seasons that affect the number of fish. The Nukak's pattern of moves is influenced by such factors. As noted previously, the Nukak also take steps to control future food supplies through their discard patterns. Foraging trips include stops to check the development of food patches at previously abandoned camps. It might be interesting to study shopping patterns in supermarkets. Even when shopping from lists, contemporary "foragers" might check here and there for sales.

■ Describe how the matching law may be more adaptive than maximizing rewards under naturalistic conditions.

Like us, the Nukak inherit a preference for sweet foods (e.g., honey and fruits). On foraging trips, they frequently consume some and pack the rest for later, even though they will be returning to the same spot on the return trip. Similarly, the Nukak will hunt down prey as soon as they observe it. For them, a monkey in the basket is worth more than two in the trees. In both of these instances, it is plausible that discounting delayed consequences is adaptive (Kagel, Green, & Caraco, 1986). It is possible, even likely, that food supplies will disappear if not hunted and gathered immediately.

Fruit and honey are not so plentiful in the rainforest that preferring them results in an obesity issue for the Nukak. Besides, they get plenty of exercise! Politis (2007) did not describe any instances of substance abuse among the Nukak. In their environment, unlike ours, the tendency to be more influenced by short-term rather than long-term consequences appears adaptive rather than maladaptive. We evolved as a species to survive in an environment much closer to theirs than to ours. This results in our genetic tendency to discount delayed consequences that often proves maladaptive under our technologically enhanced conditions.

> ■ Describe how the tendency to be influenced by short-term rewards may be adaptive under naturalistic conditions.

## DETERMINISM AND FREEDOM

Throughout this book, we have described the human condition as consisting of adaptive learning challenges. With experience, we acquire the ability to predict and, when possible, control our environment. The human condition may also be described as a series of choices. Moment by moment, similar to the pigeon in a multiple-choice Skinner box, we are confronted by different possibilities. We all have the subjective experience of being free to choose as we wish. How do we reconcile this feeling with the scientific understanding of the human condition attained through the study of adaptive learning?

You may recall that we addressed the assumption of determinism in psychology in Chapter 1. Determinism implies that the subject matter of the discipline is lawful. Thus, through application of the scientific method, we ought to be able to discover reliable relationships between hereditary and environmental variables and behavior. If determinism did not hold, none of the research findings described in this text would be possible. The predictive and control learning principles described have been found to apply throughout the animal kingdom. Chapters 5 and 8 provide examples from the sizable research literature documenting the effectiveness of predictive and control learning procedures in addressing important human concerns. In this chapter, we have reviewed lawful relationships regarding the choices animals, including humans, make. Clearly, the research findings support the applicability of the assumption of determinism to the study of psychology.

In Chapter 13, we contrasted the very different human conditions experienced by the Nukak and by us. There is no reason to suspect that the Nukak feel less "free" than we do in striving to reach their goals and realize their potential. From our perspective, however, we might question whether this is true. Do the constraints of the Nukak's physical environment as well as the limitations of their educational experiences result in our being able to think about things, feel things, and act in ways that they cannot? And, is not the reverse also true because we have such limited experience in the rainforest in comparison to them? Is it not true that none of us is "free" to do whatever we wish, live however we want, or become whomever we choose?

> ■ Describe the implications of predictive learning and control learning research findings with respect to the assumption of determinism and human behavior.

## LIGHTNING, SHARKS, AND HUMAN PREDATORS

Accepting the assumption of determinism has important implications for how we understand and address natural problems. For example, if someone is struck by lightning, we ordinarily do not blame or hate or seek vengeance against the lightning bolt. We recognize that lightning is dangerous and do all we can to protect ourselves from being struck. We construct lightning rods and remain inside during thunderstorms.

In *Moby Dick*, Melville (1851) created Ahab, a vivid character obsessed with seeking vengeance against a whale. Many people might not feel as Ahab did about an injury or death caused by an animal such as a shark or pit bull as they might to such an event caused by lightning. It is possible, however, to reason along the same lines. Just as lightning is considered a physical force of nature, an animal may be considered a biological force of nature. Sharks have not undergone any evolutionary changes for the past 350 million years! This indicates that none of the mutations occurring over this enormous span of time resulted in a creature more adapted to survive in its environmental niche. In a sense, the shark is an example of a "perfect" animal. If a human being enters into a shark's niche and is mistaken for food, the result is as inevitable as being hit by a bolt of lightning. In the same way that we try to prevent being hit by lightning, we can do our best to avoid coming into contact with sharks in the ocean (as opposed to aquariums).

Almost everyone will blame and possibly feel hate for and seek vengeance against someone who committed an act leading to the severe injury or death of an innocent person. Although we can probably describe how such feelings could have been adaptive for StoneAge individuals, the same may not be true for those living in technologically enhanced environments. Hate is an unpleasant and potentially self-destructive emotion. Acting upon it in a violent way in a contemporary society is usually illegal and failing to act upon it can be enormously frustrating. Thus, hate is a lose-lose emotional experience. Is there an alternative? One possibility is to apply the same reasoning to a human perpetrator as previously applied to a shark. A dangerous individual is a psychological force of nature. That is, individuals having genetic predispositions and specific environmental experiences are likely to develop violent tendencies. As with sharks, we should do everything within our power to avoid coming into contact with human predators. This means staying away from certain places at certain times and relying upon our police and laws to protect us from such individuals. It also means doing our best to eliminate the environmental circumstances that cause these situations.

In the United States, we live in a culture that prizes freedom and individual responsibility. As we have seen, these seeming ideals are misleading and could prove counterproductive. In reality, our genes, learning history, and environmental circumstances place limitations upon our freedom and our ability to behave responsibly. It is interesting to note that when the concept of choice is activated (e.g., by asking subjects to describe how often people make a choice during a video rather than asking them how often they point to objects), college students are more likely to blame individuals for their circumstances (Savani, Stephens, & Markus, 2011). They become less likely to support policies designed to address prior discrimination (e.g., affirmative action) or the public good (e.g., reducing environmental pollution). Ultimately, we must reconcile our values and ideals with the empirical findings regarding human behavior.

# WILL POWER AND SELF-CONTROL

> Not being able to govern events, I govern myself, and apply myself to them, if they will not apply themselves to me.
>
> **Michel de Montaigne**

We have repeatedly observed lawful relationships between specific experiences and specific behaviors in individual animals, including human beings. Such lawfulness indicates that the assumption of determinism applies to the study of psychology. Basic principles of predictive and control learning could not be established in a nondeterministic (i.e., nonlawful) world. In the previous section, we considered the implications of determinism with respect to understanding the behavior of others. Now we consider the implications with respect to ourselves.

I assign "Self-Understanding" and "Self-Control" projects in courses I teach. Neither assignment would make any sense if human behavior were not lawful. In the Self-Understanding project, I ask students how their genetics, health, socioeconomic status, parents, siblings, friends, schools, and jobs influenced the person they have become. Students actually thank me for requiring them to think about these questions. By the end of the course, they do not consider it at all controversial or problematic to agree that all those factors impacted them.

In the previous chapter, we used Maslow's hierarchy of human needs to contrast the adaptive learning requirements of cultures living under Stone Age and technologically enhanced conditions. We saw how, without the benefits of technology, it is necessary for humans to dedicate practically all their time and effort to basic survival needs and the raising of children. Humans can be very much like the other animals portrayed in Hardin's cartoon (see Chapter 1), struggling to eat, survive, and reproduce. Yet, even under the challenging environmental conditions posed by the Amazonian rainforest, the Nukak exhibit distinctly human examples of self-consciousness. They create jewelry and paint their bodies to signify who they are. They transmit a creation story and other myths to try to answer Hardin's existential question: "What's it all about?" Hardin, in apparent agreement with Maslow, believes humans strive to achieve more than personal and species survival.

What should I do, how should I live, and whom should I become? These are the questions Haidt (2006) considered fundamental to human happiness. In Chapter 11, I described Goldfried and Davison's (1976, pp. 186–207) general problem-solving process can be used to apply a self-control assignment to yourself (i.e., a "do it to yourself project"). If you still find it unsettling to admit that you are not free in the sense of being able to behave in any way imaginable, perhaps it will help to recognize one very significant benefit. In a sense, you become freer by accepting that you are a lawful part of nature. It means that you can apply the principles of adaptive learning to yourself in order to accomplish your own objectives. This places you in more control of your life. Is that not what we mean by freedom? Montaigne (1588/1993) seems to imply so in the quote at the beginning of this section.

---

■ Relate the possibility of self-control to the issue of freedom of the will.

## SELF-CONTROL AS PROBLEM SOLVING

A substantial research literature attests to the importance of self-control skills. It has been demonstrated that eighth-graders' self-discipline scores were more predictive than IQ for school attendance, homework time, and final grades (Duckworth & Seligman, 2005, 2006). Wills and his coworkers have documented that self-control skills reduce the risk of tobacco, alcohol, and marijuana abuse in 9-year-olds and middle and high-school students (Wills, Ainette, Mendoza, Gibbons, & Brody, 2007; Wills, Ainette, Stoolmiller, Gibbons, & Shinar, 2008; Wills & Stoolmiller, 2002; Wills, Walker, Mendoza, & Ainette, 2006). College students who avoid and seek alternatives to situations associated with heavy drinking have been shown to consume less alcohol (Sugarman & Carey, 2007). Thus, to a large extent, success in life appears related to the ability to resist short-term temptations in order to achieve long-term goals.

Parenting styles have been shown to relate to the development of self-control skills in children. Mothers' manner of instruction and level of emotional support for their preschoolers were shown to relate to their children's behavioral control and task persistence later in school (Neitzel & Stright, 2003). Religiosity as well as the quality of parent-adolescent communication has been shown to relate to substance abuse and sexual behaviors in African American adolescents (Wills, Gibbons, Gerrard, Murry, & Brody, 2003). A major review article addressed the relationship of religiosity to self-control. It was suggested that religion promotes self-control by encouraging self-monitoring and attainment of behavioral goals (McCullough & Willoughby, 2009).

You have the ability to apply self-control techniques to yourself in what is essentially an exercise in problem solving. Individuals often fail to identify circumstances as requiring self-control and thereby fail to act in their long-term self-interest (Myrseth & Fishbach, 2009). A problem exists when there is a discrepancy between the way things are and the way you would like them to be. Within the context of self-control, this means you would like to change the way you behave, feel, or think under specific circumstances. Note the advantage you have when you are both "client" and "practitioner." It is logistically problematic, if not impossible, for someone else to monitor your overt behavior every waking moment. It is absolutely impossible for someone else to monitor your covert behavior at all. Despite your friend's belief that she/he "feels your pain" or can "read your mind," only you have direct access to your feelings and thoughts. The best your friend can do is make inferences about your feelings and thoughts based upon how you overtly behave. You have a distinct advantage over anyone else in solving your own overt and covert behavioral problems.

### Defining and Measuring the Problem

The first step in problem solving is to objectively describe the current and desired states. Vague descriptions such as I want to be in better shape, be neater, or control my anger are not sufficient. As described in Chapter 1, psychology relies upon observable and measurable observations of behavior. Response measures typically consist of the frequency, amount, or duration of the target behavior. Following is an alphabetical listing of self-modification project response measures submitted by my students:

| Behavior | Response Measure(s) | Type |
|---|---|---|
| Anger | instances/week | Frequency |
| Chewing tobacco | times/day | Frequency |
| Cigarette smoking | number/day | Frequency |
| Cleaning room | minutes/week | Duration |
| Clutter reduction | items on desk | Amount |
| Coffee consumption | ounces/day | Amount |
| Conversations with child | number/week | Frequency |
| Excess credit card spending | dollars/week | Amount |
| Exercise | minutes/day | Duration |
| Exercise | repetitions | Frequency |
| Guitar practice | minutes/day | Duration |
| Knuckle cracking | times/day | Frequency |
| Measurements | inches | Amount |
| Meditation time | minutes/day | Duration |
| Nail and cuticle biting | length of nails | Amount |
| Public speaking anxiety | subjective units of distress | Amount |
| Punctuality | minutes late/instance | Duration |
| Reading | pages/week | Amount |
| Sleep | hours/night | Duration |
| Soda consumption | ounces/day | Amount |
| Stress | subjective units of distress | Amount |
| Studying | minutes/day | Duration |
| Task completion | number/day | Frequency |
| Television viewing | hours/day | Duration |
| Weight | pounds | Amount |
| Worrying | instances/week | Frequency |
| Writing | pages/day | Amount |

## Collecting Baseline and Intervention Data

Once response measures have been decided, data collection can start. Fulfilling the objective of a self-control project requires being able to determine whether an intervention is working. One must therefore collect baseline and intervention data. Unlike the small-*N* designs described in Chapter 2, there is no need to determine cause and effect. It is not necessary to include a reversal phase or a multiple baseline. It is only necessary to demonstrate an improvement in the target behavior. The only instance when a baseline is unnecessary is if the behavior does not occur at all. For example, some students report never exercising before starting their self-control project. Recall that a good baseline is either stable or moving in the wrong direction. Once that is attained, improvement (or lack thereof) will become apparent when graphing the intervention data.

When working on a behavioral deficit such as cleaning one's room, exercising, studying, completing a task, or writing, it is usually unnecessary to collect information on antecedents or consequences of the target behavior. This information can be invaluable, however, in addressing behavioral excesses such as smoking, overspending, nail chewing, TV viewing, and worrying. Knowing the conditions under which one is more or less likely to display the target behavior (i.e., antecedents) and knowing what the likely consequences are in the different circumstances can provide helpful tips as to what situations to avoid or what consequences to modify. Just the act of assessing and graphing baseline data for behavioral excesses sometimes leads to improvement (Maletsky, 1974). My students often report that the requirement to record instances of their problem behavior focused their attention in such a manner that they were able to suppress it.

## Manipulating As and Cs to Affect Bs

We have discussed the control learning ABCs at length. Now we see how it is possible to manipulate the antecedents and consequences of one's own behaviors in order to change in a desired way. In Chapter 6, we saw how prompting may be used to speed the acquisition process. A **prompt** is any stimulus that increases the likelihood of a behavior. People have been shopping from lists and pasting signs to their refrigerators for years. My students believe it rains "Post-it" notes in my office! Sometimes, it may be sufficient to address a behavioral deficit by placing prompts in appropriate locations. For example, you could put up signs or pictures as reminders to clean your room, organize clutter, converse with your children, exercise, and so on. Place healthy foods in the front of the refrigerator and pantry so that you see them first. In the instance of behavioral excesses, your objective is to reduce or eliminate prompts (i.e., "triggers") for your target behavior. Examples would include restricting eating to one location in your home and avoiding situations in which you are likely to smoke, eat, or drink to excess. Reduce the effectiveness of powerful negative prompts by keeping them out of sight and/or creating delays in the amount of time required to consume them. For example, fattening foods could be kept in the back of the refrigerator wrapped in several bags.

**Prompt**

Any stimulus that increases the likelihood of a behavior. The most common forms of prompts are physical, gestural, and verbal.

Throughout this book, we have stressed the human ability to transform the environment. You have the power to structure your own environment to encourage desirable behaviors and discourage undesirable acts. Sometimes adding prompts and eliminating triggers is sufficient to achieve your personal objectives. If this is the case, it will become apparent as you graph your intervention phase data. If manipulating antecedents is insufficient, you can manipulate the consequences of your thoughts, feelings, or overt acts.

If you are addressing a behavioral deficit (e.g., you would like to exercise or study more), you need to identify a convenient and effective reinforcer (i.e., reward or appetitive stimulus). Straightforward possibilities include money (a powerful generalized reinforcer that can be earned immediately) and favored activities that can be engaged in daily (e.g., pleasure reading, watching TV, listening to music, engaging in online activities, playing video games, texting). Maximize the likelihood of success by starting with minimal requirements and gradually increasing the performance levels required to earn rewards (i.e., use the shaping procedure). For example, you might start out by walking slowly on a treadmill for brief periods of time, gradually increasing the speed and duration of sessions.

Even if you are addressing a behavioral excess (e.g., fingernail biting or smoking), you should "think positive." That is, manipulate rewards rather than punishers. This can be done in two ways. You can examine your baseline data to determine the consequences of smoking and eliminate reinforcers when possible. The other approach is to use one of the differential reinforcement procedures described in Chapter 9 (DRL, DRO, DRA, or DRI) to reduce the frequency of the target behavior. For example, if you are trying to reduce caffeine but enjoy the morning coffee breaks with colleagues, you can use differential reinforcement of alternative responding (DRA) by substituting decaffeinated coffee or a non-caffeinated drink for coffee.

After implementing self-control manipulations of antecedents and consequences, it is important to continue to accurately record the target behavior during the intervention phase. If the results are less than satisfactory, it should be determined whether there is an implementation problem (e.g., the reinforcer is too delayed or not powerful enough), or whether it is necessary to change the procedure. The current research literature is the best source for problem-solving strategies. The great majority of my students are quite successful in attaining their self-control project goals. Some have taken advantage of developing technologies in their projects. The smart phone is gradually becoming an all-purpose "ABC" device. As antecedents, students are using "to do" lists and alarm settings as prompts. They use the note pad to record behavioral observations. One student attempting to go to bed earlier discovered an application to convert her phone into a "dead man's switch." She held onto a button on the phone when she got into bed and would naturally let it go upon falling asleep. The phone recorded how long her finger was on the button, permitting her to accurately determine the time she fell asleep. Some have used applications to quickly determine the number of calories they are consuming at meals. As a consequence (reinforcer), one can use access to games or music on the phone (or to the phone itself).

---

■ Give an example of an application of the stages of the self-control process.

---

## IMPROVING THE HUMAN CONDITION THROUGH HUMANISTIC ECOLOGY

The Golden Rule: Do unto others as you would have others do unto you.

I chaired the Department of Psychology at Seton Hall University for 24 years, an unusually long stretch. Often, less-experienced chairs from other departments would ask me about my "administrative style." Eventually I arrived at the term humanistic ecologist to describe my interpretation of the chair's role. The same term could be applied to the roles of parent, friend, teacher, mentor, administrator, clergy member, coach, or helping professional. One is even being a humanistic ecologist when engaged in a self-control project. From Abraham Maslow's perspective, humanism requires supporting others in their quests to self-actualize. An ecologist studies the relationships between organisms

**Humanistic Ecology**

This term, coined by the author, describes the attempt to identify and create niches in which individuals are able to achieve their self-defined goals while serving the needs of a social group (e.g., family, workplace, team, community, nation).

and their environments. **Humanistic ecology** involves the attempt to identify and create niches in which individuals are able to achieve their self-defined goals while serving the needs of a social group (e.g., family, work colleagues, team, community, nation). Essentially, humanistic ecology is an application of the Golden Rule.

As chair, I did my best to assess the interests, priorities, and long-term goals of faculty and take these into consideration in assigning teaching schedules, research space, and committee assignments. I frequently served as an advocate for my colleagues in obtaining resources from the higher administration. While attempting to define and provide support for each faculty member's niche, it was understood that everyone had a particular departmental role and set of responsibilities. We can assume the role of humanistic ecologist in many of our interpersonal interactions by attempting to understand the goals and dreams of the people we meet and doing our best to assist them in their realization.

In this text, I have tried to demonstrate the effectiveness and practicality of adaptive learning principles in understanding and improving the human condition. This is true for individuals living in prehistoric or technologically enhanced environments. Where one is born is arbitrary, but all humans are genetically prepared to adapt to and alter their circumstances. Ideally, a humanistic ecology will emerge for every person on the planet as we continue to self-actualize as a species.

## Summary

The study of individuals adapting to concurrent schedules of reinforcement enables analysis of the variables influencing choice. The matching law, in which response frequency to different alternatives mirrors (matches) reinforcement frequency to those alternatives, has been found to apply in humans and other species. The lawfulness of behavior exemplified throughout this text supports the assumption of determinism with respect to adaptive learning.

Individuals are much more influenced by immediate than delayed consequences. Many human problems (e.g., addictive disorders, procrastination, interpersonal aggression) stem from this heightened influence. Application of self-control procedures enables one to apply and assess principles of adaptive learning in a systematic manner in order to attain personal objectives. This maximizes the degree of freedom (i.e., selection of behavioral options) within a deterministic world.

## References

Alferink, L. A., Critchfield, T. S., & Hitt, J. L. (2009). Generality of the matching law as a descriptor of shot selection in basketball. *Journal of Applied Behavior Analysis, 42,* 595–608.

Bickel, W. K., Green, L., & Vuchinich, R. E. (1995). Behavioral economics. *Journal of the Experimental Analysis of Behavior, 64,* 257–262.

Billington, E. J., & DiTommaso, N. M. (2003). Demonstrations and applications of the matching law in education. *Journal of Behavioral Education, 12,* 91–104.

Catania, A. C. (1963). Concurrent performances: Reinforcement interaction and response independence. *Journal of the Experimental Analysis of Behavior, 6,* 253–263.

Chung, S. H., & Herrnstein, R. J. (1967). Choice and delay of reinforcement. *Journal of the Experimental Analysis of Behavior, 10,* 67–74.

Duckworth, A. L., & Seligman, M. E. (2005). Self-discipline outdoes IQ in predicting academic performance of adolescents. *Psychological Science, 16*, 939–944.

Duckworth, A. L., & Seligman, M. E. (2006). Self-discipline gives girls the edge: Gender in self-discipline, grades, and achievement test scores. *Journal of Educational Psychology, 98*, 198–208.

Estes, W. K. (1964). Probability learning. In A.W. Melton (Ed.), *Categories of human learning* (pp. 89–128). New York: Academic Press.

Francisco, M. T., Madden, G. J., & Borrero, J. (2009). Behavioral economics: Principles, procedures, and utility for applied behavior analysis. *The Behavior Analyst Today, 10*, 277–295.

Gharib, A., Gade, C., & Roberts, S. (2004). Control of variation by reward probability. *Journal of Experimental Psychology: Animal Behavior Processes, 30*, 271–282.

Goldfried, M. R., & Davison, G. C. (1976). *Clinical behavior therapy*. New York: Holt, Rinehart and Winston.

Haidt, J. (2006). *The happiness hypothesis*. New York: Basic Books.

Herrnstein, R. J. (1961). Relative and absolute strength of response as a function of frequency of reinforcement. *Journal of the Experimental Analysis of Behavior, 4*, 267–272.

Herrnstein, R. J. (1970). On the law of effect. *Journal of the Experimental Analysis of Behavior, 13*, 243–266.

Herrnstein, R. J. (1974). Formal properties of the matching law. *Journal of the Experimental Analysis of Behavior, 21*, 159–164.

Hoch, H., McComas, J. J., Johnson, L., Faranda, N., & Guenther, S. L. (2002). The effects of magnitude and quality of reinforcement on choice responding during play activities. *Journal of Applied Behavior Analysis, 35*, 171–181.

Kagel, J. H., Green, L., & Caraco, T. (1986). When foragers discount the future: Constraint or adaptation? *Animal Behaviour, 36*, 271–283.

Keller, J. V., & Gollub, L. R. (1977). Duration and rate of reinforcement as determinants of concurrent responding. *Journal of the Experimental Analysis of Behavior, 28*, 145–153.

Koehler, D. J., & James, G. (2010). Probability matching and strategy availability.*Memory and Cognition, 38*, 667–676.

Logue, A. W. (1995). *Self-control*. Englewood Cliffs, NJ: Prentice Hall.

Logue, A. W., & Mazur, J. E. (1981). Maintenance of self-control acquired through a fading procedure: Follow-up on Mazur and Logue (1978). *Behavior Analysis Letters, 1*, 131–137.

Mace, F. C., Neef, N. A., Shade, D., & Mauro, B. C. (1996). Effects of problem difficulty and reinforcer quality on time allocated to concurrent arithmetic problems. *Journal of Applied Behavior Analysis, 29*, 11–24.

Madden, G. J., & Bickel, W. K. (1999). Abstinence and price effects on demand for cigarettes: A behavioral-economic analysis. *Addiction, 94*, 577–588.

Maletsky, B. M. (1974). Behavior recording as treatment: A brief note. *Behavior Therapy, 5*, 107–111.

Mazur, J. E. (1987). An adjusting procedure for studying delayed reinforcement. In M. L. Commons, J. E. Mazur, J. A. Nevin, & H. Rachlin (Eds.), *Quantitative analysis of behavior: The effects of delay and of intervening events on reinforcement value* (Vol. 5, pp. 55–73). Hillsdale, NJ: Lawrence Erlbaum.

Mazur, J. E., & Logue, A. W. (1978). Choice in a "self-control" paradigm: Effects of a fading procedure. *Journal of the Experimental Analysis of Behavior, 1*, 11–17.

McCullough, M. E., & Willoughby, B. L. (2009). Religion, self-regulation, and self-control: Associations, explanations, and implications. *Psychological Bulletin, 135*, 69–93.

Melville, H. (1851). *Moby-Dick*. New York: Harper and Brothers.

Miller, H. L., & Loveland, D. H. (1974). Matching when the number of response alternatives is large. *Animal Learning and Behavior, 2*, 106–110.

Mischel, W., & Ebbesen, E. B. (1970). Attention in delay of gratification. *Journal of Personality and Social Psychology, 16*, 329–337.

Mischel, W., Ebbesen, E. B., & Raskoff Zeiss, A. (1972). Cognitive and attentional mechanisms in delay of gratification. *Journal of Personality and Social Psychology, 21*, 204–218.

Mischel, W., Shoda, Y., & Peake, P. K. (1988). The nature of adolescent competencies predicted by preschool delay of gratification. *Journal of Personality and Social Psychology, 54*, 687–696.

Mischel, W., Shoda, Y., & Rodriguez, M. L. (1989). Delay of gratification in children. *Science, 244*, 933–938.

Mischel, W., & Yates, B. (1979).Young children's preferred attentional strategiesfor delaying gratification. *Journal of Personality and Social Psychology, 37*, 286–300.

Montaigne, M. (1993). *The complete essays* (M. A. Screech, Trans.). London/New York: Penguin (originally published 1588).

Murphy, J. G., Barnett, N. P., & Colby, S. M. (2006). Alcohol-related and alcohol-free activity participation and enjoyment among college students: Behavioral theories of choice analysis. *Experimental and Clinical Psychopharmacology, 14*, 339–349.

Murphy, J. G., Correia, J. C., & Barnett, N. P. (2007). Behavioral economic approaches to reduce college student drinking. *Addictive Behaviors, 32*, 2573–2585.

Murphy, J. G., Correia, J. C., Colby, S. M., & Vuchinich, R. E. (2005). Using behavioral theories of choice to predict drinking outcomes following a brief intervention. *Experimental and Clinical Psychopharmacology, 13*, 93–101.

Myrseth, K. R., & Fishbach, A. (2009). Self-control: A function of knowing when and how to exercise restraint. *Current Direction in Psychological Science, 18*, 247–252.

Neef, N. A., Mace, D. F., Shea, M. C., & Shade, D. (1992). Effects of reinforcement rate and reinforcement quality on time allocation: Extensions of matching theory to educational settings. *Journal of Applied Behavior Analysis, 25*, 691–699.

Neitzel, C., & Stright, A. D. (2003). Mother's scaffolding of children's problem-solving: Establishing a foundation of academic self-regulatory competence. *Journal of Family Psychology, 17*, 147–159.

Politis, G. G. (2007). *Nukak.* Walnut Creek: University College, London Institute of Archeology Publications.

Rachlin, H. (1989). *Judgment, decision, and choice.* New York: W. H. Freeman.

Rachlin, H., & Green, L. (1972). Commitment, choice, and self-control. *Journal of Experimental Analysis of Behavior, 17*, 15–22.

Reed, D. D., Critchfield, T. S., & Martens, B. K. (2006). The generalized matching law in elite sport competition: Football play calling as operant choice. *Journal of Applied Behavior Analysis, 39*, 281–297.

Richards, J. B., Mitchell, S. H., de Wit, H., & Seiden, L. S. (1997). Determination of discount functions in rats with an adjusting-amount procedure. *Journal of the Experimental Analysis of Behavior, 67*, 353–366.

Savani, K., Stephens, N. M., & Markus, H. R. (2011). The unanticipated interpersonal and societal consequences of choice: Victim blaming and reduced support for the public good. *Psychological Science, 22*, 795–802.

Schweitzer, J. B., &Sulzer-Azaroff, B. (1988). Self control: Teaching tolerance for delay in impulsive children.

*Journal of the Experimental Analysis of Behavior, 50*, 173–186.

Shoda, Y., Mischel, W., & Peake, P. K. (1990). Predicting adolescent cognitive and self-regulatory competencies from preschool delay of gratification: Identifying diagnostic conditions. *Developmental Psychology, 26*, 978–986.

Stahlman, W. D., & Blaisdell, A. P. (2011). Reward probability and the variability of foraging behavior in rats. *International Journal of Comparative Psychology, 24*, 168–176.

Sugarman, D. E., & Carey, K. B. (2007). The relationship between drinking control strategies and college student alcohol use. *Psychology of Addictive Behaviors, 21*, 338–345.

West, R. F., & Stanovich, K. E. (2003). Is probability matching smart? Associations between probabilistic choices and cognitive ability. *Memory & Cognition, 31*, 243–251.

Wills, T. A., Ainette, M. G., Mendoza, D., Gibbons, F. X., & Brody, G. H. (2007). Self-control, symptomatology, and substance use precursors: Test of a theoretical model in a community sample of 9-year-old children. *Psychology of Addictive Behaviors, 21*, 205–215.

Wills, T. A., Ainette, M. G., Stoolmiller, M., Gibbons, F. X., & Shinar, O. (2008). Good self-control as a buffering agent for adolescent substance use: An investigation in early adolescencewith time-varying covariates. *Psychology of Addictive Behaviors, 22*, 459–471.

Wills, T. A., Gibbons, F. X., Gerrard, M., Murry, V. M., & Brody, G. H. (2003). Family communication and religiosity related to substance use and sexual behavior in early adolescence: A test for pathways through self-control and prototype perceptions. *Psychology of Addictive Behaviors, 17*, 312–323.

Wills, T. A., & Stoolmiller, M. (2002). The role of self-control in early escalation of substance use: A time-varying analysis. *Journal of Consulting and Clinical Psychology, 70*, 986–997.

Wills, T. A., Walker, C., Mendoza, D., & Ainette, M. G. (2006). Behavioral and emotional self-control: Relations to substance abuse in samples of middle and high school students. *Psychology of Addictive Behaviors, 20*, 265–278.

# GLOSSARY

**ABCs** Applied behavior analysis acronym for antecedents, behaviors, and consequences.

**Abstinence violation effect** A minor lapse followed by a full-blown binge. For example, if an individual overeats at one meal and then completely goes off a diet.

**Acquired taste aversion** A classical conditioning procedure in which the CS is food and the US is a stimulus resulting in sickness.

**Acquisition (of a conditioned response)** A procedure or process whereby one stimulus (the CS) is presented in a predictive relationship with another stimulus (the US). Eventually the subject will acquire a response (CR) to the CS in anticipation of the US.

**Adaptive learning** Acquiring the ability to predict and control the environment.

**Adolescence** Demarcated by the onset of puberty as males and females become physically capable of reproduction. Adolescence ends with the assumption of adult responsibilities (e.g., financial independence, having a family).

**Ages (Stone, Iron, Bronze)** Many archeologists divide the time period prior to recorded history into three ages. The Stone Age lasted for approximately 2.5 million years. During this period, humans and their ancestors fashioned tools made with hard edges and points from items found in nature. It took until the Bronze Age (3300–1200 B.C.) and Iron Age (1200–900 B.C.) for tools to be manufactured.

**Antecedents** Events taking place prior to a behavior (e.g., discriminative stimuli and warning stimuli).

**Anthropomorphizing** Attributing human thought processes to other animals.

**Anticipation method** A procedure demonstrating classical conditioning by presenting a CS and observing whether the CR occurs prior to presentation of the US.

**Appetitive event** A stimulus that an individual approaches (e.g., food when hungry, water when thirsty).

**Applied Behavior Analysis (ABA)** A treatment approach based upon the Skinnerian operant conditioning literature.

**Approach/avoidance conflict** A situation in which a behavior is followed by both an appetitive and an aversive stimulus. For example, a rat may receive both food and shock at the end of a runway.

**Arabic numbering system** System of written representation of any quantity, real or imagined, that is fundamental to mathematics and the scientific method, which rely on quantification and measurement.

**Assimilation, leveling, sharpening** Bartlett found that in retelling stories, people tended to alter them in systematic ways. He concluded that memory is a reconstructive, rather than a reproductive, process that involves leveling (simplification), sharpening (exaggeration of specific details), and assimilation (incorporation into existing schemas).

**Attention theory** A description of discrimination learning as first identifying the relevant dimension and then determining the value that leads to reinforcement. The first task is considered more difficult. For example, once it is determined that shape is the relevant dimension, it is easy to select a circle or a square.

**Attributions** The assumed causes of events. For example, one may attribute loss of a job to internal factors such as lack of aptitude and skills or to external factors such as a downturn in the economy.

**Autism** A severe developmental disorder characterized by extreme behavioral deficits (e.g., an apparent lack of interest in other people, lack of speech) and excesses (e.g., tantrums, self-stimulatory behavior such as rocking back and forth or flapping hands, and self-destructive behaviors such as head banging).

**Autoshaping (sign tracking)** Animals will track stimuli that have been paired with appetitive substances. For examples, pigeons will peck a key that has been followed in time by food.

**Aversive control** The effects of punishment and negative reinforcement.

**Aversive cue learning** The person administering punishment is associated with the aversive event and will become a warning stimulus (cue) as well as a conditioned punisher.

**Aversive event** A stimulus that an individual avoids (e.g., electric shock, extreme heat or cold).

**Avoidance** A response that postpones or eliminates contact with an aversive event; for example, if bar pressing results in not being shocked.

**Avoidance paradox** The apparent violation of the law of temporal contiguity whereby a response is maintained by the absence of an event.

**Backward chaining** Establishing the components of a stimulus-response chain in reverse order; for example, first teaching a rat to press a bar for food in the presence of a light, then to push a rod to turn on the light.

**Backward conditioning** A classical conditioning procedure in which the US precedes the CS.

**Baseline** The first phase of a small-$N$ design in which performance is assessed prior to the manipulation of an independent variable.

**Behavioral deficits** Problems resulting from the absence of performance (e.g., lack of assertiveness, illiteracy, failure to wear seat belts).

**Behavioral economics** A developing research area empirically investigating economic concepts (e.g., the extent to which an individual's income, the price of an object, deprivation of the object, or availability of a suitable substitute affects the likelihood of its purchase).

**Behavioral excesses** Problems resulting from the presence of behavior (e.g., aggressive acts, excessive drinking, tics).

**Behavioral neuroscientist** A scientist who makes inferences regarding neurological mechanisms based upon behavioral observations.

**Behavioral trapping** A phenomenon whereby naturally existing reinforcers are sufficient to maintain a behavior. For example, even after a child no longer receives stars for reading, the child continues to read just for the pleasure.

**Behaviorism** An early school of psychology reacting to structuralism and advocating psychology as a natural science with the goal of predicting and controlling observable behavior.

**Bibliotherapy** Treatment for a behavioral problem in the form of textual material.

**Blank trials procedure** A procedure demonstrating classical conditioning by the CR occurring on test trials on which the CS is presented without the US.

**Blocking** The interfering effect of prior experience on learning an association between a CS and a US.

**Blowpipe** This object, fashioned from cane, is the primary hunting tool for many Stone Age tribes living in the Amazonian rain forest. Pointed darts are fired at prey from long distances.

**Body painting** Some Amazonian tribes use plant dyes to serve as a means of indicating gender and band identity. The painting may be more extensive and elaborate in preparation for meetings and ceremonies.

**Classical conditioning** Procedures developed by Pavlov to study learning when a stimulus event may be predicted but not controlled. In the original procedure, meat powder (the US) was presented after a tone (an initially neutral stimulus that becomes a CS) resulting in salivation (CR) to the tone. Pavlov's dogs could predict food but not control when it occurred.

**Cognitive-behavioral treatment of depression** A treatment approach based on the assumption that feelings and behavior are influenced by one's thoughts (see attributions). Individuals are encouraged to change the attributions for their problems from being internal, global, and permanent to being external, specific, and temporary.

**Cognitive theory of avoidance** A theory explaining avoidance learning as the result of acquisition of two expectancies: A specific response results in nonoccurrence of an aversive event, and failure to make the response results in occurrence of the aversive event. Avoidance responding continues as long as the first expectancy is confirmed (see avoidance paradox).

**Commitment response** In a self-control context, the act of making a response in advance that increases the likelihood of choosing a larger delayed reward over a smaller immediate reward.

**Comparative psychologist** A scientist who studies the behavior of different species of animals.

**Compensatory response** A CR that counteracts the biological effect of a US.

**Compound stimulus** Two or more stimuli overlapping in time (e.g., a light and tone going on and off together).

**Concept learning** The acquisition of the ability to respond in the same way to all instances of a stimulus class (i.e., a collection of stimuli sharing at least one common property such as circle or red).

**Concurrent schedule of reinforcement** A procedure in which different response options are associated with different types, magnitudes, delays, or schedules of reinforcement. This enables the study of how different variables influence preference, choice, and decision making.

**Conditioned masochism** A procedure in which a behavior is reinforced in the presence of an aversive stimulus that gradually increases in intensity. This can result in the maintenance of responding despite being severely punished. This process is similar to the desensitization procedure effective in reducing fear and anxiety.

**Conditioned reinforcers** Reinforcers that acquire their effectiveness through experience, either being paired with or exchangeable for other reinforcers; for example, a coupon exchangeable for a particular item, a star provided for a correct answer.

**Conditioned response (CR)** The learned response to a previously neutral stimulus (eventually a CS) resulting from its being presented immediately prior to another stimulus (the US).

**Conditioned stimulus (CS)** A novel stimulus that acquires the capacity to elicit a response (the CR) as the result of occurring prior to another stimulus (the US).

**Conditioned suppression** This procedure determines the strength of a conditioned stimulus predictive of shock from the extent to which the stimulus disrupts ongoing instrumental behavior.

**Confounding variables** Noncontrolled variables in an experiment that could impact the dependent variable. For example, wind could affect the time it takes for objects to fall.

**Contingencies (i.e., consequences)** The relationship between one's behavior and subsequent events (e.g., reinforcement and punishment).

**Contingency management** The manipulation of consequences to promote desirable changes in behavior.

**Control group** An experimental condition either not exposed to or exposed to a different level of an independent variable than the experimental group.

**Control learning** Acquiring the ability to change the environment (see also operant conditioning; instrumental conditioning).

**Conventional morality** When right and wrong are based on appeals to an authority figure (e.g., parent, teacher, clergy member) or written source (e.g., the Constitution, Bible) This is the second major stage of Lawrence Kohlberg's (1976) influential model of moral development.

**Correlation** A measure of the degree of relationship between two variables. For example, one could ask subjects how much coffee they drink and how many hours they sleep. There is no manipulation of an independent variable and subjects are not randomly assigned to conditions.

**Counterconditioning** A procedure designed to substitute a desirable for an undesirable behavior (i.e., substituting relaxation for anxiety).

**Culture** An adaptive learning perspective would describe culture as consensually agreed-upon rules relating antecedents, behaviors, and consequences.

**Cumulative recorder** An automated graphing device developed by B. F. Skinner. It plots an animal's rate of responding during a session in an operant chamber.

**Delay conditioning** A classical conditioning procedure in which a novel stimulus (eventually a CS) precedes and stays on until an unconditioned stimulus (US) is presented.

**Delay discounting** The preference for choosing smaller immediate rewards over larger, delayed ones.

**Dependent variable** The variable potentially affected by the independent variable in an experiment. In psychology, the dependent variable is always a type of behavior.

**Deprivation** Manipulating the amount of time until an individual can consume a stimulus (e.g., food, water).

**Desensitization** The process of exposing an individual to gradually increasing levels of anxiety-provoking situations in order to reduce the anxiety. For example, one may be exposed to larger and larger dogs, higher and higher rungs on a ladder, and so on.

**Determinism** The assumption by all sciences that nature is lawful and may be understood through systematic study.

**Differential reinforcement of alternative responding (DRA)** Reinforcing a specific behavior other than the one you wish to reduce (e.g., rewarding a child for playing with a sibling rather than fighting).

**Differential reinforcement of incompatible responding (DRI)** Reinforcing a specific behavior that cannot occur at the same time as the one you wish to reduce (e.g., reinforcing a child who hits himself in the head for holding a soft toy).

**Differential reinforcement of low rates of responding (DRL)** Reinforcing a specific behavior once a specified amount of time passes without an instance (e.g., a reward is provided for waiting an hour between cigarettes).

**Differential reinforcement of other (or zero) responding (DRO)** Providing reinforcement if a time interval lapses without a behavior occurring (e.g., if a child has gone a certain amount of time without teasing a sibling).

**Differential reinforcement schedules** These are alternatives to punishment procedures as treatment of behavioral excesses. They involve the positive reinforcement of behaviors other than the behavioral excess (see DRA, DRI, DRL, and DRO for examples).

**Direct learning** A change in behavior resulting from personal interaction with the environment.

**Discrete-trial apparatus** By placing the animal in the apparatus, the researcher determines the opportunity to make a single response. After the response occurs, it cannot be made again until the animal is returned to the starting point of the apparatus. The maze, runway, and shuttle box are examples.

**Discriminative stimulus** A stimulus that signals that a particular behavior will be reinforced (i.e., followed by an appetitive stimulus). For example, a light might signal the availability of food.

**Disinhibition** If during extinction, a novel stimulus is presented simultaneously with a previously established CS, the likelihood of the CR is increased on that trial.

**Displaced aggression** A Freudian term indicating that individuals experiencing frustration or pain are likely to become aggressive toward innocent others.

**Easy-to-hard discrimination effect** The finding that training on an easy discrimination (e.g., black vs. white) facilitates learning a difficult discrimination (e.g., between two shades of gray).

**Elasticity of demand** The extent to which an individual's income, the price of an object, deprivation of the object, or availability of a suitable substitute affects the likelihood of its purchase.

**Emerging adulthood** Arnett's (2000) suggested developmental phase between what we ordinarily consider the end of adolescence (graduation from high school at about the age of 18) and the assumption of adult responsibilities (being financially independent, living apart from one's parents, starting a family, etc.).

**Emerging adulthood** A developmental period for individuals perceiving themselves as no longer adolescents, but not quite adults, because they may continue to live at home or be financially dependent upon their parents. Most college and graduate students regard themselves as being in this stage, which may last into the mid-to-late 20s.

**Empirical** Observable and measurable.

**Empirically validated therapeutic techniques** Approaches to intervention supported by multiple experimental research findings.

**Escape** A response that removes an aversive event; for example, a bar press might terminate shock.

**Evaluative conditioning** Using classical conditioning procedures to establish likes and dislikes by pairing neutral objects with positive and negative stimuli.

**Excitatory learning** Learning that one event will be followed by another. For example, lightning is followed by thunder.

**Experimental group** A research condition exposed to an independent variable.

**Experimentation** A research method in which an independent variable is manipulated in order to determine an effect on a specific dependent variable.

**External inhibition** If during acquisition, a novel stimulus is presented simultaneously with the CS on an individual trial, a decrease in the strength of the CR occurs on that trial.

**External validity** The ability to apply cause-and-effect conclusions under naturalistic conditions.

**Extinction** A procedure in which a previously established predictive stimulus (CS) is no longer followed by the second stimulus (US) or an instrumental response is no longer followed by a consequence. This usually results in a reduction in strength of the CR or a reduction in the frequency of an instrumental response.

**Extradimensional shift** Learning a discrimination on a dimension (e.g., red vs. green) followed by learning a discrimination on another dimension (e.g., circle vs. square). Consistent with the assumptions of attention theory, this is more difficult than a transfer task on the same dimension (see attention theory; intradimensional shift).

**Fading procedure** A procedure involving gradual elimination of one stimulus in order to establish control by another. For example, one might prompt a dog to roll over by physically producing the response and then gradually reducing the amount of pressure.

**Feedback** An environmental change occurring after a behavior.

**Fixed interval (FI) schedule** The opportunity for reinforcement is available after the passage of a constant amount of time since the previous reinforced response (e.g., an individual on a FI 5-minute schedule is reinforced for the first response occurring after 5 minutes lapse since the previous reinforcement).

**Fixed ratio (FR) schedule** Reinforcement occurs after a constant number of responses (e.g., an individual on an FR 3 schedule is reinforced after every third response).

**Flooding** The process of requiring an individual to remain in an anxiety-provoking situation in order to reduce the anxiety.

**Free-feeding body-weight** The weight an animal attains after being allowed constant access to food.

**Free-operant** In comparison to discrete-trial apparatuses, animals may repeatedly make a response. The operant chamber (Skinner box) is an example.

**Frustration theory** Explains the partial reinforcement extinction effect (PREE) as resulting from the acquisition of frustration tolerance.

**Frustration tolerance** The continuation of responding in the absence of reinforcement. It is developed by experiencing reinforcement while feeling frustrated (see PREE).

**Functional analysis** Behavior is monitored while potential consequences are systematically removed and reinstated. This is implemented to determine what is maintaining a (usually problematic) behavior.

**Functional fixedness** A special case of the phenomenon of "set" in which prior experience interferes with problem solving. In this instance, previous experience with the use of an object (e.g., a brick) interferes with its being used in another way (e.g., as a door stop).

**Functionalism** An early school of psychology interested in how conscious experience enabled individual adaptation to environmental demands.

**General problem-solving process** A five-stage strategy consisting of (1) general orientation, (2) problem definition and formulation, (3) generation of alternatives, (4) decision making, and (5) verification.

**Generalized reinforcers** Conditioned reinforcers paired with or exchangeable for a variety of other reinforcers (e.g., tokens and money).

**Generalized suppression** When individuals experience aversive stimuli within an environmental context, they will become afraid to respond at all unless they can discriminate the circumstances under which a specific behavior will be punished.

**Gestalt psychology** An early school of psychology rejecting structuralism's goal of analyzing conscious experience and arguing that conscious experience consists of organized meaningful units. Its perspective is summarized by the statement "the whole is greater than the sum of its parts."

**Good Behavior Game (GBG)** A comprehensive program to address classroom management challenges for the teacher recommended by the Coalition for Evidence-Based Policy, a member of the Council for Excellence in Government. The experimental findings for the effectiveness of the GBG have been so consistent and powerful that it has been recommended as an extremely cost-efficient "universal behavioral vaccine" (Embry, 2002).

**Group design** An experimental method in which subjects are randomly assigned to conditions and the results are analyzed statistically (e.g., $t$ test, analysis of variance).

**Habituation** A behavioral response decrement that results from repeated stimulation and that does not involve sensory adaptation/sensory fatigue or motor fatigue. For example, one usually does not "hear" the constant background noises in a room (e.g., a fan).

**Health psychology** An emerging subdiscipline of psychology dedicated to the prevention and treatment of illness through behavior change methods.

**Hierarchy of human needs** Abraham Maslow's proposed schema for organizing and prioritizing aspects of the human condition. The hierarchy is often portrayed as a pyramid with survival needs forming the base, followed by safety and security, interpersonal relationships, accomplishment (see self-esteem), and fulfilling one's personal goals and potential (see self-actualization) at the peak.

**Higher-order conditioning** A procedure or process whereby a previously neutral stimulus (CS 2, e.g., a light) is presented in a predictive relationship with a second, previously established CS 1 (e.g., a tone that had already been paired with a US of shock). This usually results in a CR occurring to CS 2 (the light) despite never having been paired with the shock.

**Homeostasis** The maintenance of an optimum level of a biological state (e.g., blood sugar level, temperature).

**Human homunculus** (little person) A visual representation of the amount of "brain space" allotted to different parts of the body.

**Humanistic ecology** This term, coined by the author, describes the attempt to identify and create niches in which individuals are able to achieve their self-defined goals while serving the needs of a social group (e.g., family, workplace, team, community, nation).

**Impulsive** A behavioral pattern of choosing a smaller, immediate reward over a larger, delayed one (see self-control).

**Independent variable** The potential causal variable manipulated in an experiment.

**Indirect learning** A change in behavior resulting from observation of others or symbolic communication (i.e., language).

**Inhibitory learning** Learning that one event will not be followed by another. For example, sunshine is not followed by thunder.

**Insight** Kohler created a number of naturalistic problems for his subjects, primarily chimpanzees, and characterized the problem-solving process as the attainment of insight. He considered insight to be a process requiring perceptual reorganization of the field in order to attain closure. For example, a chimpanzee may appear to suddenly recognize the need to join two sticks together to reach a banana.

**Instrumental conditioning** A research paradigm studying the effect of consequences (response-event learning) when control is possible. For example, Skinner's rats could influence the delivery of food by pressing a bar. The term was introduced by Thorndike to describe acquisition of a behavior that affects the environment (see also control learning; operant conditioning).

**Inter stimulus interval (ISI)** The time between the onset of the CS and onset of the US.

**Intermittent schedules of reinforcement** When some but not all responses are reinforced.

**Internal validity** The ability to draw cause-and-effect conclusions from research findings.

**Intradimensional discrimination training** Reinforcing responding to one value of a stimulus on a dimension and not reinforcing responding to another value on the same dimension during acquisition. For example, subjects could be reinforced for responding to 580 nm and not reinforced for responding to 620 nm on the visual wavelength dimension or reinforced for responding to 1000 Hz and not 800 Hz on the auditory frequency dimension.

**Intradimensional shift** Learning a discrimination on a dimension (e.g., red vs. green) followed by learning another discrimination on the same dimension (e.g., blue vs. yellow). Consistent with the assumptions of attention theory, this is easier than a transfer task on a different dimension (see attention theory; extradimensional shift).

**Introspection** A methodology in which individuals are asked to describe their conscious experience.

**Language** A consensually agreed-upon collection of arbitrary symbols used to represent objects, actions, relationships, thoughts, and feelings. Language enables humans to learn indirectly, resulting in similar adaptive responding as occurs after direct experience.

**Language acquisition device** According to Chomsky, the mechanism responsible for humans' learning to speak.

**Latent extinction (CS pre-exposure)** A phenomenon whereby prior exposure to a neutral stimulus slows down the process of the stimulus becoming a CS when followed by a US.

**Latent learning** Learning is not necessarily reflected in overt behavior. Performance may be influenced by motivational and other factors as well as learning.

**Law of accelerating returns** Raymond Kurzweil's description of the speeding up of the pace of technological change. For example, there were far more inventions in the 20th century than the 19th, and so on.

**Learned helplessness** When individuals do not have control over significant events in one situation, they may not assert control in other situations in which control is possible. This experience can also result in depressive symptoms (e.g., crying, loss of weight).

**Learned industriousness** Persistence (i.e., frustration tolerance), the willingness to expend maximum effort, and self-control (i.e., choosing large delayed reinforcers rather than small immediate ones) appear to be related. Improvement on one results in improvement on the other two.

**Learning (operational definition)** A relatively permanent change in behavior potential resulting from experience.

**Learning curve** A graph showing a change in performance as the result of experience plotted on the y-axis and time or trials plotted on the x-axis.

**Learning sets** The provision of a series of experiences having something in common. It can result in acquisition of a strategy useful for all related experiences. The term is sometimes used to refer to the experiences (i.e., the independent variable) and sometimes to the effect (i.e., dependent variable) of those experiences. For example, Harlow demonstrated that with experience, chimps became more and more proficient at solving examples of two-choice discrimination problems.

**Long-delay conditioning** A procedure combining the elements of delay and temporal conditioning in which the CS comes on and stays on for a constant extended period of time until the US occurs (e.g., a light comes on and stays on for 1 minute followed by food). Usually, with training the individual increasingly delays making a response (e.g., salivation) until the time is almost up.

**Magazine training** A process designed to facilitate an animal's learning the location of food as well as the sound of the food delivery mechanism in a Skinner box.

**Marshmallow test** Walter Mischel developed this procedure to study impulsiveness and self-control. Children are given the choice of eating a marshmallow immediately or waiting a period of time for the opportunity to eat two marshmallows.

**Matching law** A straightforward relationship that holds under certain conditions with concurrent schedules of reinforcement. With variable interval (VI) schedules, the frequency of responding to each of the alternatives mirrors (matches) the frequency of reinforcement to that alternative. The matching law has also been found to apply to the magnitude of reinforcement, duration of reinforcement, and delay of reinforcement. It has been shown to apply to humans in the form of probability matching.

**Maturation** A change in behavior resulting from aging.

**Migratory agriculture** The practice by some Amazonian nomadic tribes of planting seeds when abandoning campsites, resulting in the creation of future sources of edible plants. The seeds left from previous occupancy result in larger and denser patches of fruit than typically occur in the rain forest.

**Moore's law** Gordon Moore (1965) calculated that since the invention of the integrated circuit in 1958, the number of transistors that could be contained on a computer chip doubled approximately every year. Now known as Moore's law, this geometric relationship has been shown to hold with regard to computing speed as well as memory.

**Multiple baseline design** A small-*N* design consisting of a baseline followed by an intervention phase repeated at different times across different subjects, situations, or behaviors.

**Multiple schedule** The occurrence of different reinforcement contingencies reliably associated with distinct antecedent stimuli. For example, one may be smiled at when screaming at a football game but not when screaming in the library.

***N*-length** The number of nonreinforced responses followed by a reinforcer. For example, if reinforcement occurs after the 5th and 15th responses, this would constitute *N*-lengths of 5 and 10.

**Natural selection** A process whereby inherited traits increasing the likelihood of survival and reproduction are more likely to be transmitted to future generations.

**Nature-nurture controversies** Debates regarding the importance of genetic as opposed to experiential factors with respect to various behaviors.

**Negative correlation** A stimulus predicts that another will not happen or has already occurred.

**Negative modeling** When administering punishment results in an individual demonstrating the same behavior she/he is attempting to suppress.

**Negative occasion setter** A signal that a stimulus is inhibitory (i.e., predicts the absence of an event). For example, a leash indicates that a large dog will not jump on you.

**Negative punishment** A consequence in which removing (response cost) or preventing (time out) an appetitive stimulus results in a decrease in the frequency of behavior.

**Negative reinforcement** A consequence in which removing (escape) or postponing (avoidance) an aversive stimulus results in an increase in the frequency of behavior.

**Neutral stimulus (novel stimulus)** A stimulus that does not initially elicit any behavior related to a potential CS. For example, Pavlov's tone was a neutral stimulus until it acquired the capacity to elicit salivation (a CR).

**No (zero) correlations** Two stimulus events are unrelated.

**Nonsignaled avoidance** The study of avoidance conditioning in a Skinner box without an external warning stimulus. Avoidance might require making a response within a particular time period.

**Nukak** One of the few remaining cultures continuing to practice the nomadic hunter/gatherer lifestyle characteristic of the earliest members of our species. This tribe lives in the Colombian Amazon rainforest.

**Observational learning** The process through which an individual acquires the ability to make a response based upon observation of the response. Bandura proposed that in order for an observer to imitate a model, it is essential that the observer attend to the model's behavior, retain information regarding the important components, have the ability to perform the same actions, and be motivated to do so.

**Occasion setter** A stimulus signaling whether a CS is predictive.

**Operant chamber (Skinner box)** An apparatus permitting the manipulation of contingencies of reinforcement and punishment and continuous study of ongoing behavior.

**Operant conditioning** A term introduced by Skinner to describe acquisition of a behavior that operates on the environment (see also instrumental conditioning; control learning).

**Operational definition** Describes the procedures used to measure the particular term; for example, "intelligence" is defined by the score on a paper-and-pencil test.

**Overexpectation effect** A phenomenon that occurs when two CSs are separately conditioned to the point that the individual is no longer surprised by either. If the elements are then presented in compound with the same US, the CR is reduced to each of the elements presented separately.

**Overshadowing** Only the more intense element of a compound CS is associated with the US and elicits a CR.

**Overtraining reversal effect** Subjects receiving additional training on a two-choice discrimination task will switch to the other stimulus more rapidly after a change in the contingencies (i.e., S+ becoming S– and S– becoming S+) than subjects receiving less training.

**Paradigm shifts** Life-transforming events: for example, during the Stone Age, it took tens of thousands of years to discover the use of stone tools, the control of fire, and the invention of the wheel. The pace of change has increased geometrically leading to Kurzweil's proposal of the law of accelerating returns.

**Parametric study** An experimental procedure in which different values of an independent variable are presented. For example, one could present different magnitudes of a reward or present it after different delays.

**Partial reinforcement extinction effect (PREE)** Intermittently reinforced responses are more resistant to extinction than continuously reinforced responses (see frustration tolerance).

**Peak shift** This occurs when intradimensional discrimination training is provided with stimuli close in value on a dimension. The peak of the stimulus control gradient is shifted in the direction opposite the S–. For example, if pigeons are taught to respond to a 1000 Hz tone and not a 950 Hz tone, the peak of the stimulus control gradient will be to a value higher than 1000.

**Phi phenomenon** The perceptual experience of apparent movement studied by Gestalt psychologists. For example, individual lights going on and off in sequence are perceived as a single light in motion.

**Phonetic alphabet** Visual symbols representing sounds, permitting written representation of any pronounceable word in a language.

**Positive correlation** One stimulus predicts that another will occur.

**Positive occasion setter** A signal that a stimulus is excitatory (i.e., predicts the occurrence of an event). For example, a hotdog signals that mustard will taste good.

**Positive punishment** A consequence in which adding an aversive stimulus results in a decrease in the frequency of behavior.

**Positive reinforcement** A consequence in which adding an appetitive stimulus results in an increase in the frequency of behavior.

**Post hoc** Explanations for events provided after they have already taken place.

**Post-conventional morality** When right and wrong are based on the application of universal principles such as the Golden Rule (Do unto others as you would have others do unto you). This is the third major stage of Lawrence Kohlberg's (1976) influential model of moral development.

**Pre-conventional morality** When right and wrong are based on extrinsic rewards and punishers. This is the first major stage of Lawrence Kohlberg's (1976) influential model of moral development.

**Precision grip** The ability to move our fingers and opposable thumbs in order to grasp and manipulate objects of different sizes and shapes. This ability enabled humans to create and use tools.

**Predictive learning** Acquiring the ability to anticipate an event.

**Preparatory response** A conditioned response that enables an individual to respond appropriately to the occurrence of a subsequent event (US). For example, salivation is an appropriate response in preparation for food, an eyeblink is an appropriate response in preparation for a puff of air, an increase in blood sugar level is an appropriate response in preparation for a lowering of blood sugar level, and so on.

**Presence/absence discrimination training procedure** A discrimination training procedure in which reinforcement is provided when a stimulus is there (e.g., a lit key) but not when it is not there.

**Proactive interference** The reduction of memory of new information resulting from prior learning. For example, first learning to drive in the United States will slow down learning to drive in England where the steering wheel is to the right of the car and people drive in the left lane.

**Probability matching** An application of the matching law to humans in situations when events occur with different probabilities. For example, subjects might win money for choosing which of an array of lights will go on. Over a series of trials, the subject's choices tend to match the actual probabilities for each light.

**Prompt** Any stimulus that increases the likelihood of a behavior. The most common forms of prompts are physical, gestural, and verbal.

**Prompting** The use of a stimulus to increase the likelihood of a desired response. For example, one might physically roll a dog over (physical prompt), move one's arm to signal "roll over" (gestural prompt), or say "roll over" (verbal prompt).

**Pseudo-explanation** Use of a descriptive label for a behavior as its explanation (e.g., saying someone hits another person because he/she is aggressive). Explanation requires specification of an independent variable (cause).

**Psychological explanation** Description of how hereditary (nature) and experiential (nurture) variables affect behavior.

**R-S (response shock) clock** After successfully avoiding shock, the amount of time within which a response must occur to avoid the next shock (see nonsignaled avoidance).

**Random assignment** A procedure whereby an individual subject is equally likely to be exposed to any of the experimental conditions.

**Reactive procedure** One in which observing a phenomenon influences the results. For example, watching someone perform could affect the performance.

**Relapse prevention** A strategy designed to sustain the benefits of effective intervention. The methods include identifying personal high-risk situations and acquiring coping skills.

**Renewal effect** The finding that a behavior extinguished in one context is likely to occur if the CS is presented in a different context.

**Rescorla–Wagner model** An influential mathematical model of the classical conditioning process. It assumes that the amount of learning on an individual trial is related to the degree an individual is surprised by the occurrence of an unexpected event (see surprise factor).

**Respondent conditioning** A term introduced by Skinner to describe acquisition of a behavior elicited by a specific stimulus (see also classical conditioning).

**Response cost** Removal of an appetitive stimulus (e.g., a fine for speeding).

**Response expectancies** Anticipating the effects of one's behavior on the environment (i.e., response-event learning). For example, "If I do this, then that happens."

**Retardation-of-acquisition procedure** A procedure used to measure inhibitory learning by demonstrating that the acquisition process is slowed down for a potential CS.

**Retroactive interference** The reduction of memory of old information resulting from subsequent learning. For example, learning to drive in England will slow down the return to driving in the United States.

**Reversal design (ABA)** A small-$N$ design in which a baseline phase is followed by an intervention and then a return to the baseline procedures.

**Rule** A verbal statement including each of the control learning ABCs specifying the circumstances (antecedents) under which a particular act (behavior) is rewarded or punished (consequence).

**Runway** A long alley way with infrared sensors enabling precise timing of when a subject leaves the start area and arrives at the goal area.

**S-S (shock-shock) clock** After failing to avoid shock, the amount of time within which a response must occur to avoid the next shock. If the animal did not press the bar at all, it would be shocked according to the S-S (shock-shock) clock (see nonsignaled avoidance).

**Salient** A stimulus stands out from its background.

**Sample size** The total number of subjects in a research study.

**Scaffolding** Vygotsky introduced this term to describe the process of supporting the development of a child's behavior.

**Schema learning** The acquisition of a coherent structure capable of incorporating separate entities having definable characteristics. For example, children acquire a schema that enables them to differentiate grammatical from nongrammatical groups of words.

**Scientific explanation** A statement of cause and effect involving specification of the relationship between separately observable independent and dependent variables.

**Scientific method** A reliable, powerful strategy for determining cause and effect in nature when the limitations of observability, testability, and replicability are met.

**Scientific schema** A format for research articles consisting of an introduction placing the study within the context of prior research; a methods sections providing sufficient detail to replicate the procedures used in the study; reporting of results and statistical analyses; and discussion of the conclusions, implications, and limitations of the research.

**Second signal system** Through classical conditioning, words acquire the capacity to serve as indirect CSs and USs, functioning much as direct experience. For example, one can be told that eating mushrooms can make you sick resulting in feeling nauseous (a CR) to the thought or presence of mushrooms.

**Self-actualization** The highest of human needs in Maslow's hierarchy, at the peak of his pyramid. Self-actualization occurs with attainment of one's personal goals and fulfillment of one's potential.

**Self-control** A behavioral pattern of choosing a larger, delayed reward over a smaller, immediate one (see impulsive).

**Self-esteem** An individual's personal assessment of worth.

**Self-fulfilling prophecy** When the belief about a natural phenomenon influences the result in the described direction. For example, being told that a child is "difficult" might influence how the child is treated resulting in the continuation/intensification of the problem behavior.

**Self-injurious behavior inhibiting system (SIBIS)** A device developed by collaboration among psychological researchers, engineers, autism advocates, and medical manufacturers. A sensor module that straps onto the head is attached to a radio transmitter. The sensor can be adjusted for different intensities of impact and contingent shock can immediately be delivered to the arm or leg.

**Semantic generalization** Stimulus generalization based on similarity in meaning rather than similarity on a physical dimension (i.e., a conditioned response acquired to a blue light occurs to the word *blue* and vice versa).

**Sensitization/aversion therapy** A counterconditioning procedure designed to change an appetitive stimulus into an aversive stimulus. For example, emetics (drugs causing one to feel sick) have been paired with alcohol in order to reduce excessive consumption.

**Sensory preconditioning** A procedure or process whereby one neutral stimulus (CS 2, e.g., a light) is presented in a predictive relationship with a second neutral stimulus (CS 1, e.g., a tone). When CS 1 is followed by a US (e.g., shock), this usually results in CRs to CS 2 as well as CS 1 even though CS 2 was never followed by shock.

**Sequential theory** Explains the PREE as resulting from memory of patterns of reinforcement and nonreinforcement occurring during acquisition (see *N*-length, PREE).

**Serial learning** Recalling items in a specific order (e.g., the letters of the alphabet, numbers).

**Serial-position effect** People usually learn the items at the beginnings and ends of serial lists before learning the items in the middle.

**Shaping** Reinforcing successive approximations to a desired response. For example, first reinforcing a rat for approaching a bar, then staying in front of the bar, then touching the bar, and so on.

**Shuttle box** An apparatus consisting of separate compartments that permit a subject to move from one to the other.

**Sign tracking** Following or responding to stimuli paired with appetitive stimuli. For example, pigeons will peck a lit key if it had previously been paired with food.

**Simultaneous conditioning** A classical conditioning procedure in which a CS and a US overlap in time.

**Small-N design** An experimental design involving systematic manipulation of an independent variable and ongoing measurement of the dependent variable.

**Socialization** The implementation of rules regarding antecedents, behaviors, and consequences in parenting, schooling, and other interpersonal relations (i.e., consensually agreed-upon rules).

**Species-specific characteristics** Inherited behaviors characteristic of all the members of a species.

**Species-specific defense reactions (SSDR)** Inherited behaviors likely to result under dangerous conditions. For example, when in danger of being shocked, many animals will run or freeze.

**Spence's discrimination learning model** An explanation of discrimination learning based on the Pavlovian concepts of excitation and inhibition. It is assumed that these opposing processes may apply to an individual stimulus with the likelihood of responding to that stimulus being based on the net (i.e., excitatory minus inhibitory) excitatory strength.

**Spoiling effect** Prior exposure to noncontingent food presentations produces similar detrimental effects to noncontingent shock presentations on the acquisition of an escape response (see learned helplessness).

**Spontaneous recovery** An increase in the strength of a prior learned response after an extended time period lapses between extinction trials.

**Stimulus control** This term subsumes the phenomena of generalization and discrimination into one unifying dimension. It measures the extent to which the value of a stimulus affects responding. This is usually assessed with a stimulus control graph plotting the number of responses as a function of value on a continuum (e.g., wavelength of light, frequency of a tone).

**Stimulus discrimination** Occurs during acquisition when one stimulus (the CS+, e.g., a light) is predictive of a second stimulus (US, e.g., food), but a different stimulus (CS–, e.g., a tone) is never followed by the US. A CR (e.g., salivation) will occur to the CS+ (light) and not to the CS– (tone).

**Stimulus expectancies** Anticipating events based upon patterns of stimuli in the environment (i.e., event-event learning). For example, "If this happens, then that happens."

**Stimulus generalization** When a previously acquired learned response occurs in the presence of stimuli other than the original one, the likelihood being a function of the degree of similarity. For example, if food has been paired with a 1000 Hz tone, salivation will occur most to 1000 Hz, less to 900 Hz and 1100 Hz and so on.

**Stimulus substitution model** Pavlov's model of classical conditioning describing the CS as becoming a substitute for the US.

**Stimulus-response chain** A sequence of behaviors in which each response alters the environment producing the discriminative stimulus for the next response. For example, an animal could learn to push a rod to turn on a light and then press a bar to obtain food.

**Structural/functional definition of learning** Defining learning as involving the acquisition of stimulus and response expectancies resulting in adaptive responding. The definition is structural in the sense that expectancies are considered the elements of conscious experience forming the basis of learning. It is functional in that it describes the purpose of learning as adaptive responding.

**Structuralism** Wundt's initial approach to psychology having the goal of analyzing conscious experience.

**Summation (compound stimulus) procedure** A procedure used to measure inhibitory learning by demonstrating that responding to a compound stimulus including a presumed inhibitory element is different from responding to the other element by itself. For example, if a light is presumed to be inhibitory, it could be combined with a tone that had previously been paired with shock. If the conditioned response to the light/tone compound was less than to the tone alone, one could conclude the light is inhibitory.

**Suppression (CER) ratio** An indirect procedure used to measure the strength of classical conditioning. The formula for suppression (CER) ratios divides the number of responses occurring when a CS is present by the number of responses occurring when it is present and absent.

**Surprise factor (λ–V)** This part of the Rescorla–Wagner equation determines the degree of surprise on an individual trial by subtracting the amount of predictive value accumulated on previous trials from the maximum degree of surprise possible with a particular US.

**Systematic desensitization** A counterconditioning procedure designed to reduce anxiety by teaching an individual to relax while being exposed to a hierarchy (ordered list) of anxiety-eliciting events, starting with the least anxiety provoking event. The procedure may be administered in vivo (under the actual circumstances) or through one's imagination.

**Tapir** A relatively large (about 3 feet tall and 6.5 feet long) four-legged animal resembling a swine with a long snout. It, along with the deer and jaguar, are the largest animals indigenous to the Amazon. The Nukak are prohibited from killing or eating these animals because they are thought to be like people and to embody spirit-ancestors. The tapir is given special spiritual status among these and killing one is believed to cause thunder, the spirit-ancestor of a powerful enemy.

**Temporal conditioning** A classical conditioning procedure in which there is no external novel stimulus (e.g., a light or a tone). Instead, the US comes on after passage of a constant amount of time (e.g., every minute).

**The World Is Flat** The title of Thomas Friedman's book describing how advances in computer hardware and software and installation of optical fiber networks connecting the continents enabled the social and vocational networking of millions of people, globalization, and the transformation of the human condition for most of the planet.

**Time out** Removal from circumstances in which an appetitive stimulus is available (e.g., being sent to one's room without dessert for teasing a sibling).

**TOTE (test-operate-test-exit)** An acronym for a problem-solving process in which one assesses the environment (test) to determine whether to implement a procedure (operate), and assesses (test) again to determine whether to continue the operation or terminate implementation upon solution (exit). A thermostat is a useful metaphor for the process.

**Trace conditioning** A procedure similar to delay conditioning except that the CS comes on and goes off a consistent amount of time prior to the onset of the US. For example, a tone comes on for 5 seconds and goes off followed by food 10 seconds later. The gap between the offset of the tone and onset of the food is the trace interval.

**Trace interval** Refers to the time gap between offset of the CS and onset of the US in trace conditioning.

**Transposition** The transfer of responding from one circumstance to another on the basis of stimulus relationships (e.g., picking out the middle-sized object from different arrays).

**Two-factor theory** A theory involving classical and instrumental conditioning to address the avoidance paradox. This theory converted avoidance into escape by assuming that after the warning stimulus was paired with shock, avoidance was followed by a reduction in fear (Mowrer) or termination of the warning stimulus (Schoenfeld).

**Unconditioned reinforcers** Reinforcers that acquire their effectiveness through genetic mechanisms (e.g., food, water).

**Unconditioned response (UR)** A response elicited by a stimulus (US) as the result of heredity (e.g. food reflexively elicits salivation, a puff of air elicits an eye blink, etc.). See also reflexive behavior.

**Unconditioned stimulus (US)** A stimulus that elicits a response (UR) as the result of heredity (e.g., food reflexively elicits salivation, a puff of air elicits an eyeblink).

**Unusual uses test** A popular assessment of creativity based upon the concept of functional fixedness. One is asked to list as many uses as possible for different objects (e.g., "What can you do with a brick?").

**US pre-exposure effect** This refers to the finding that prior exposure to a US makes it more difficult for an individual to later associate it with a CS. The Rescorla–Wagner model explains this as a form of blocking in which pre-exposure results in predictive value accruing to the context in which the US was presented.

**Variable interval (VI) schedule** The opportunity for reinforcement is available after the passage of an average amount of time since the previous reinforced response (e.g., an individual on a VI 5-minute schedule is reinforced for the first response occurring after different intervals averaging 5 minutes since the previous reinforcement).

**Variable ratio (VR) schedule** Reinforcement occurs after an average number of responses. For example, an individual on a VR 3 schedule would be reinforced on the average every third response.

**Vicarious** Experiencing an event indirectly through observation of another individual's behavior.

**Warning stimulus** A signal that a particular behavior will be punished (followed by an aversive event).

**Win-stay lose-shift strategy** The ideal performance pattern with two-choice discrimination problems. If correct, one would continue to choose the same stimulus; if incorrect, one would switch to the other possibility.

**Yoked-control** An experimental procedure in which what happens to one subject is determined by the behavior of another. For example, one animal might receive food when another completes a ratio requirement.

**Zone of proximal development** Vygotsky proposed that during instruction, adults must take a child's readiness into consideration.

# REFERENCES

Aarts, H., & Dijksterhuis, A. (2000). Habits as knowledge structures: Automaticity in goal-directed behavior. *Journal of Personality and Social Psychology, 78*, 53–63.

Abramson, L. Y., Seligman, M. E., & Teasdale, J. (1978). Learned helplessness in humans: Critique and reformulation. *Journal of Abnormal Psychology, 87*, 49–74.

Adelman J. S., Marquis, S. J., & Sabatos-DeVito, M. G. (2010). Letters in words are read simultaneously, not in left-to-right sequence. *Psychological Science, 21*, 1799–1801.

Alferink, L. A., Critchfield, T. S., & Hitt, J. L. (2009). Generality of the matching law as a descriptor of shot selection in basketball. *Journal of Applied Behavior Analysis, 42*, 595–608.

Allen, K. E., & Harris, F. R. (1966). Elimination of a child's excessive scratching by training the mother in reinforcement procedures. *Behaviour Research and Therapy, 4*, 79–84.

American Psychological Association. (1995). Training in and dissemination of empirically-validated psychological treatments: Report and recommendations. *The Clinical Psychologist, 48*, 2–24.

Amsel, A. (1958). The role of frustrative nonreward on noncontinuous reward situations. *Psychological Bulletin, 55*, 102–118.

Amsel, A. (1992). *Frustration theory*. Cambridge, Eng.: Cambridge University Press.

Amsel, A., & Roussel, J. (1952). Motivational properties of frustration. *Journal of Experimental Psychology, 43*, 363–368.

Anderson, R. C., & Freebody, P. (1981). Vocabulary knowledge. In J. Guthrie (Ed.), *Comprehension and teaching: Research reviews* (pp. 77–117). Newark, DE: International Reading Association.

Angell, J. R. (1903). The relation of structural and functional psychology to philosophy. *Philosophical Review, 12*, 243–271.

Angell J. R. (1907). The province of functional psychology. *Psychological Review, 14*, 61–91.

Anger, D. (1963). The role of temporal discrimination in the reinforcement of Sidman avoidance behavior. *Journal of the Experimental Analysis of Behavior, 6*, 477–506.

Arcediano, F., Matute, H., & Miller, R. R. (1997). Blocking of Pavlovian conditioning in humans. *Learning and Motivation, 28*, 188–199.

Arnett, J. J. (2000). Emerging adulthood: A theory of development from the late teens through the twenties. *American Psychologist, 55*, 469–480.

Arnett, J. J. (2001). *Adolescence and emerging adulthood: A cultural approach*. Upper Saddle River, NJ: Prentice Hall.

Arnett, J. J., & Taber, S. (1994). Adolescence terminable and interminable: When does adolescence end? *Journal of Youth and Adolescence, 23*, 517–537.

Arriaga, P., Benedicta, M., & Esteves, F. (2011). Effects of playing computer games on emotional desensitization and aggressive behavior. *Journal of Applied Social Psychology, 41*, 1900–1925.

Austin, J., Alvero, A. M., & Olson, R. (1998). Prompting patron safety belt use at a restaurant. *Journal of Applied Behavior Analysis, 31*, 655–657.

Austin, J., & Bevan, D. (2011). Using differential reinforcement for low rates to reduce children's requests for teacher attention. *Journal of Applied Behavior Analysis, 44*, 451–461.

Austin, J., Hackett, S., Gravina, N., & Lebbon, A. (2006). The effects of prompting and feedback on drivers' stopping at stop signs. *Journal of Applied Behavior Analysis, 39*, 117–121.

Azrin, N. H., & Holz, W. C. (1966). Punishment. In W. K. Honig (Ed.), *Operant behavior: Areas of research and application*. Englewood Cliffs, NJ: Prentice Hall.

Azrin, N. H., Holz, W. C., & Hake, D. F. (1963). Fixed-ratio punishment. *Journal of the Experimental Analysis of Behavior, 6*, 141–148.

Azrin, N. H., Hutchinson, R. R., & Hake, D. F. (1963). Pain-induced fighting in the squirrel monkey. *Journal of the Experimental Analysis of Behavior, 6*, 620.

Azrin, N. H., Hutchinson, R. R., & Hake, D. F. (1966). Extinction-induced aggression. *Journal of the Experimental Analysis of Behavior, 9*, 191–204.

Azrin, N. H., Hutchinson, R. R., & Sallery, R. D. (1964). Pain-aggression toward inanimate objects. *Journal of the Experimental Analysis of Behavior, 7*, 223–228.

Azzi, R., Fix, D. S. R., Keller, F. S., & Rocha E Silva, M. I. (1964). Exteroceptive control of response under delayed reinforcement. *Journal of the Experimental Analysis of Behavior, 7*, 159–162.

Bandura, A. (1962). Social learning through imitation. In M. R. Jones (Ed.), *Nebraska Symposium on Motivation, 10*, 211–274.

Bandura, A. (1965). Influence of model's reinforcement contingencies on the acquisition of imitative responses. *Journal of Personality and Social Psychology, 1*, 589–595.

Bandura, A. (1969). *Principles of behavior modification*. New York: Holt, Rinehart, and Winston.

Bandura, A. (1971). Vicarious and self-reinforcement processes. In R. Glaser (Ed.), *The nature of reinforcement* (pp. 228–278). New York: Academic Press.

Bandura, A. (1973). *Aggression: A social learning analysis.* Englewood Cliffs, NJ: Prentice Hall.

Bandura, A. (1977a). *Social learning theory.* Englewood Cliffs, NJ: Prentice Hall.

Bandura, A. (1977b). Self-efficacy: Toward a unifying theory of behavioral change. *Psychological Review, 84,* 191–215.

Bandura, A. (1978). The self system in reciprocal determinism. *American Psychologist, 33,* 344–358.

Bandura, A. (1986). *Social foundations of thought and action.* Englewood Cliffs, NJ: Prentice Hall.

Bandura, A., Grusec, J. E., & Menlove, F. L. (1967). Vicarious extinction of avoidance behavior. *Journal of Personality and Social Psychology, 5,* 16–23.

Bandura, A., & Jeffrey, R. W. (1973). Role of symbolic coding and rehearsal processes in observational learning. *Journal of Personality and Social Psychology, 26,* 122–130.

Bandura, A., & Menlove, F. L. (1968). Factors determining vicarious extinction of avoidance behavior through symbolic modeling. *Journal of Personality and Social Psychology, 8,* 99–108.

Bandura, A., Ross, D., & Ross, S. (1961). Transmission of aggressions through imitation of aggressive models. *Journal of Abnormal and Social Psychology, 63,* 575–582.

Bandura, A., Ross, D., & Ross, S. (1963a). Imitation of film-mediated aggressive models. *Journal of Abnormal and Social Psychology, 66,* 3–11.

Bandura, A., Ross, D., & Ross, S. (1963b). Vicarious reinforcement and imitative learning. *Journal of Abnormal and Social Psychology, 67,* 601–607.

Bandura, A., & Walters, R. H. (1963). *Social learning and personality development.* New York: Holt, Rinehart & Winston.

Banks, R. K. (1966). Persistence to continuous punishment following intermittent punishment training. *Journal of Experimental Psychology, 71,* 373–377.

Barlow, D. H., Craske, M. G., Cerny, J. A., & Klosko, J. S. (1989). Behavioral treatment of panic disorder. *Behavior Therapy, 20,* 261–282.

Barrish, H. H., Saunders, M., & Wolf, M. M. (1969). Good behavior game: Effects of individual contingencies for group consequences on disruptive behavior in a classroom. *Journal of Applied Behavior Analysis, 2,* 119–124.

Barsky, A. J., & Ahern, D. K. (2004). Cognitive behavior therapy for hypochondriasis: A randomized controlled trial. *Journal of the American Medical Association, 291,* 1464–1470.

Bartlett, F. C. (1932). *Remembering: A study in experimental and social psychology.* New York: Macmillan.

Baum, W. M. (1973). The correlation-based law of effect. *Journal of the Experimental Analysis of Behavior, 20,* 137–153.

Baumrind, D. (1968). Authoritative vs. authoritarian parental control. *Adolescence, 3,* 255–272.

Baumrind, D. (1971). Current patterns of parental authority. *Developmental Psychology Monographs, 4*(1, Pt. 2).

Bednar R., Wells, M., & Peterson, S. (1995). *Self-esteem* (2nd ed.). Washington, DC: American Psychological Association.

Berger, S. (1962). Conditioning through vicarious instigation. *Psychological Review, 69,* 450–466.

Bettelheim, B. (1985, November). Punishment versus discipline. *Atlantic Magazine.* Available at http://www.theatlantic.com/magazine/archive/1985/11/punishment-versus-discipline/4097/

Bickel, W. K., Green, L., & Vuchinich, R. E. (1995). Behavioral economics. *Journal of the Experimental Analysis of Behavior, 64,* 257–262.

Billington, E. J., & DiTommaso, N. M. (2003). Demonstrations and applications of the matching law in education. *Journal of Behavioral Education, 12,* 91–104.

Birch, H. G. (1945). The role of motivational factors in insightful problem-solving. *Journal of Comparative Psychology, 38,* 295–317.

Birch, H. G., & Rabinowitz, H. S. (1951). The negative effect of previous experience on productive thinking. *Journal of Experimental Psychology, 41,* 121–125.

Black, A. H. (1959). Heart rate changes during avoidance learning in dogs. *Canadian Journal of Psychology, 13,* 229–242.

Black, A. H., Carlson, N. J., & Solomon, R. C. (1962). Exploratory studies of the conditioning of automatic responses in curarized dogs. *Psychological Monographs, 76* (1, Whole No. 29).

Blake, C. S., & Hamrin, V. (2007). Current approaches to the assessment and management of anger and aggression in youth: A review. *Journal of Child and Adolescent Psychiatric Nursing, 20,* 209–221.

Blough, D. S. (1982). Pigeon perception of letters of the alphabet. *Science, 218,* 397–398.

Bolles, R. C. (1970). Species-specific defense reactions and avoidance learning. *Psychological Review, 77,* 32–46.

Borkovec, T. D., Newman, M. G., Pincus, A. L., & Lytle, R. (2002). A component analysis of cognitive-behavioral therapy for generalized anxiety disorder and the role of interpersonal problems. *Journal of Consulting and Clinical Psychology, 70,* 288-298.

Bouchard, S., Paquin, B., Payeur, R., Allard, M., Rivard, V., Fournier, T., Renaud, P., & Lapierre, J. (2004). Delivering cognitive-behavior therapy for panic disorder with agoraphobia in videoconference. *Telemedicine Journal and e-Health, 10,* 13–24.

Bouton, M. E. (1984). Differential control by context in the inflation and reinstatement paradigms. *Journal of Experimental Psychology: Animal Behavior Processes, 10,* 56–74.

Bouton, M. E. (2000). A learning theory perspective on lapse, relapse, and the maintenance of behavior change. *Health Psychology, 19*(Supplement), 57–63.

Bouton, M. E. (2004). Context and behavioral processes in extinction. *Learning and Memory, 11,* 485–494.

Bouton, M. E., & King, D. A. (1983). Contextual control of the extinction of conditioned fear: Tests for the associative value of the context. *Journal of Experimental Psychology: Animal Behavior Processes, 9,* 248–265.

Bouton, M. E., & Nelson, J. B. (1998). The role of context in classical conditioning: Some implications for cognitive behavior therapy. In W. T. O'Donohue (Ed.), *Learning and behavior therapy* (pp. 59–84). Needham Heights, MA: Allyn & Bacon.

Bower, G. H., Starr, R., & Lazarovitz, L. (1965). Amount of response-produced change in the CS and avoidance training. *Journal of Comparative and Physiological Psychology, 59,* 13–17.

Britton, L. N., Carr, J. E., Landaburu, H. J., & Romick, K. S. (2002). The efficacy of non-contingent reinforcement as treatment for automatically reinforced stereotypy. *Behavioral Interventions, 17,* 93–103.

Brown, C. H. (1993). Statistical methods for preventive trials in mental health. *Statistics in Medicine, 12,* 289–300.

Brown, P. L. & Jenkins, H. M. (1968). Autoshaping of the pigeon's key peck. *Journal of the Experimental Analysis of Behavior, 11,* 1–8.

Brownell, K. D., Marlatt, G. A., Lichtenstein, E., & Wilson, G. T. (1986). Understanding and preventing relapse. *American Psychologist, 41,* 765–782.

Burroughs, E. R. (1914). *Tarzan of the apes.* New York: A. L. Burt Company.

Buss, D. (1989). Sex differences in human mate preferences: Evolutionary hypothesis tested in 37 cultures. *Behavior and Brain Sciences, 12,* 1–49.

Butler, R. A. (1953). Discrimination learning by rhesus-monkeys to visual-exploration motivation. *Journal of Comparative and Physiological Psychology, 46,* 95–98.

Cameron, W. B. (1963). *Informal sociology: A casual introduction to sociological thinking.* New York: Random House.

Camp, D. C., Raymond, G. A., & Church, R. M. (1967). Temporal relationship between response and punishment. *Journal of Experimental Psychology, 74,* 114–123.

Capaldi, E. J. (1964). Effect of N-length, number of different N-lengths, and number of reinforcements on resistance to extinction. *Journal of Experimental Psychology, 68,* 230–239.

Capaldi, E. J. (1966). Partial reinforcement: A hypothesis of sequential effects. *Psychological Review, 73,* 459–479.

Capaldi, E. J. (1967). A sequential hypothesis of instrumental learning. In K. W. Spence & J. T. Spence (Eds.), *The psychology of learning and motivation* (Vol. 1, pp. 67–156). New York: Academic Press.

Carr, E. G., & Durand, V. M. (1985). Reducing behavior problems through functional communication training. *Journal of Applied Behavior Analysis, 18,* 111–126.

Carr, J. E., Severtson, J. M. & Lepper, T. L. (2009). Non-contingent reinforcement is an empirically-supported treatment for problem behavior exhibited by individuals with developmental disabilities. *Research in Developmental Disabilities, 30,* 44–57.

Carroll, J., & Wolpe, P. (1996). *Sexuality and gender in society.* New York: HarperCollins.

Carroll, K. M., Ball, S. A., Martino, S., Nich, C., Babuscio, T. A., & Rounsaville, B. J. (2009). Enduring effects of a computer-assisted training program for cognitive behavior therapy: A 6-month follow-up of CBT4CBT. *Drug and Alcohol Dependence, 100,* 178–181.

Carroll, K. M., Ball, S. A., Martino, S., Nich, C., Gordon, M. A., Portnoy, G. A. & Rounsaville, B. J. (2008). Computer-assisted delivery of cognitive behavioral therapy for addiction: A randomized trial of CBT4CBT. *The American Journal of Psychiatry, 165,* 881–889.

Catania, A. C. (1963). Concurrent performances: Reinforcement interaction and response independence. *Journal of the Experimental Analysis of Behavior, 6,* 253–263.

Cautela, J. (1966). Treatment of compulsive behavior by covert sensitization. *Psychological Record, 16,* 33–41.

Chomsky, N. (1959). Review of Skinner's Verbal behavior. *Language, 35,* 26–58.

Chronis, A. M., & Jones, H. A. (2006). Evidence-based psychosocial treatments for children and adolescents with attention-deficit/hyperactivity disorder. *Clinical Psychology Review, 26,* 486–502.

Chung, S. H., & Herrnstein, R. J. (1967). Choice and delay of reinforcement. *Journal of the Experimental Analysis of Behavior, 10,* 67–74.

Church, R. M. (1969). Response suppression. In B. A. Campbell & R. M. Church (Eds.), *Punishment and aversive behavior* (pp. 111–156). New York: Appleton-Century-Crofts.

Clark, F. C. (1958). The effect of deprivation and frequency of reinforcement on variable-interval responding. *Journal of Experimental Analysis of Behavior, 1,* 221–227.

Clayton, M., Helms, B., & Simpson, C. (2006). Active prompting to decrease cell phone use and increase seat belt use while driving. *Journal of Applied Behavior Analysis, 39,* 341–349.

Clingman, J., & Fowler, R. (1975). The effects of contingent and noncontingent reinforcement on the I.Q. scores of children of above-average intelligence. *Journal of Applied Behavior Analysis, 8*, 90.

Clingman, J., & Fowler, R. (1976). The effects of primary reward on the I.Q. performance of grade-school children as a function of initial I.Q. level. *Journal of Applied Behavior Analysis, 9*, 19–23.

Clum, G. A., Clum, G. A., & Surls, R. (1993). A meta-analysis of treatment for panic disorder. *Journal of Consulting and Clinical Psychology, 61*, 317–326.

Collier, G. (1969). Body weight loss as a measure of motivation in hunger and thirst. *Annals of the New York Academy of Science, 157*, 594–609.

Confer, J. C., Easton, J. A., Fleischman, C. D., Goetz, D. M., Lewis, C. P., & Buss, D. M. (2010). Evolutionary psychology: Controversies, questions, prospects, and limitations. *American Psychologist, 65*, 110–126.

Cook, M., & Mineka, S. (1990). Selective associations in the observational learning of fear in monkeys. *Journal of Experimental Psychology: Animal Behavior Processes, 16*, 372–389.

Cowdery, G. E., Iwata, B. A., & Pace, G. M. (1990). Effects and side-effects of DRO as treatment for self-injurious behavior. *Journal of Applied Behavior Analysis, 23*, 497–506.

Crichton, M. (1990). *Jurassic park*. New York: Alfred A. Knopf.

Crowley-Koch, B. J., Van Houten, R., & Lim, E. (2011). Effects of pedestrian prompts on motorist yielding at crosswalks. *Journal of Applied Behavior Analysis, 44*, 121–126.

Cox, B. S., Cox, A. B., & Cox, D. J. (2000). Motivating signage prompts safety belt use among drivers exiting senior communities. *Journal of Applied Behavior Analysis, 33*, 635–638.

Cukrowicz, K. C., White, B., Reitzel, L. R., Burns, A. B., Driscoll, K. A., Kemper, T. S., & Joiner, T. E. (2005). Improved treatment outcome associated with the shift to empirically supported treatments in a graduate training clinic. *Professional Psychology: Research and Practice, 36*, 330–337.

Darwin, C. (1859). *On the origin of species by means of natural selection*. London: Murray.

DeGrandpre, R. (2000). A science of meaning. *American Psychologist, 55*, 721–739.

De Houwer, J. D. (2007). A conceptual and theoretical analysis of evaluative conditioning. *The Spanish Journal of Psychology, 10*, 230–241.

De Houwer, J. D., Thomas, S., & Baeyens, F. (2001). Associative learning of likes and dislikes: A review of 25 years of research on human evaluative conditioning. *Psychological Bulletin, 127*, 853–869.

Deitz, S. M., & Repp, A. C. (1973). Decreasing classroom misbehavior through the use of DRL schedules of reinforcement. *Journal of Applied Behavior Analysis, 6*, 457–463.

De Montpellier, G. (1933). An experiment on the order of elimination of blind alleys in maze learning. *Journal of Genetic Psychology, 43*, 123–139.

Dempsey, M. A., & Mitchell, A. A. (2010). The influence of implicit attitudes on choice when consumers are confronted with conflicting attribute information. *Journal of Consumer Research, 37*, 614–625.

de Silva, P., Rachman, S., & Seligman, M. (1977). Prepared phobias and obsessions: Therapeutic outcomes. *Behavior Research and Therapy, 15*, 65–78.

Dewey, J. (1896). The reflex-arc concept in psychology. *Psychological Review, 3*, 357–370.

Dewey, J. (1900). Psychology and social practice. *Psychological Review, 7*, 105–124.

Diamond, J. (2005). *Guns, germs, and steel*. New York: W. W. Norton & Company.

Dickens, C. (2003/1859). *A tale of two cities*. Edited and with an introduction and notes by Richard Maxwell. London: Penguin Classics (originally published 1859).

Dickinson, A., Hall, G., & Mackintosh, N. J. (1976). Surprise and the attenuation of blocking. *Journal of Experimental Psychology: Animal Behavior Processes, 2*(4), 313–322.

Dijksterhuis, A. (2004). I like myself but I don't know why: Enhancing implicit self-esteem by subliminal evaluative conditioning. *Journal of Personality and Social Psychology, 86*, 345–355.

Dobzhansky, T. (1960). The present evolution of man. *Scientific American, 203*, 206–217.

Dolan, L., Kellam, S. G., Brown, C. H., Werthamer-Larsson, L., Rebok, G. W., & Mayor, L. S. (1993). The short-term impact of two classroom-based preventive intervention trials on aggressive and shy behaviors and poor achievement. *Journal of Applied Developmental Psychology, 14*, 317–345.

Domjan, M. (2005a). Pavlovian conditioning: A functional perspective. *Annual Review of Psychology, 56*, 179–206.

Domjan, M. (2005b). *The essentials of conditioning and learning* (3rd ed.). Belmont: CA: Wadsworth.

Domjan, M. (2009). The *principles of learning and behavior: Active learning edition*, Belmont, CA: Wadsworth.

Donaldson, J. M., Vollmer, T. R., Krous, T., Downs, S., & Beard, K. P. (2011). An evaluation of the Good behavior game in kindergarten classrooms. *Journal of Applied Behavior Analysis, 44*, 605–609.

Donohue, B., van Hasselt, V. B., & Hersen, M. (1994). Behavioral assessment and treatment of social phobia: An evaluative review. *Behavior Modification, 18*, 262–288.

DuBois, D., Bull, C., Sherman, M., & Roberts, M. (1998). Self-esteem and adjustment in early adolescence: A social-contextual perspective. *Journal of Youth & Adolescence, 27*, 557–584.

DuBois, D., & Tevendale, H. (1999). Self-esteem in childhood and adolescence: Vaccine or epiphenomenon? *Applied & Preventive Psychology, 8*, 103–117.

Duckworth, A. L., & Seligman, M. E. (2005). Self-discipline outdoes IQ in predicting academic performance of adolescents. *Psychological Science, 16*, 939–944.

Duckworth, A. L., & Seligman, M. E. (2006). Self-discipline gives girls the edge: Gender in self-discipline, grades, and achievement test scores. *Journal of Educational Psychology, 98*, 198–208.

Duncker, K. (1945). On problem solving. *Psychological Monographs, 58*(5).

Dunleavy, M., Dexter, S., & Heinecke, W. F. (2007). What added value does a 1:1 student to laptop ratio bring to technology-supported teaching and learning? *Journal of Computer Assisted Learning, 23*, 440–452.

Durand, V. M., & Carr, E. G. (1987). Social influences on "self-stimulatory behavior": Analysis and treatment application. *Journal of Applied Behavior Analysis, 20*, 119–132.

Durand, V. M., & Carr, E. G. (1991). Functional communication training to reduce challenging behavior: Maintenance and application in new settings. *Journal of Applied Behavior Analysis, 24*(2), 251–264.

D'Zurilla, T. J., & Goldfried, M. R. (1971). Problem solving and behavior modification. *Journal of Abnormal Psychology, 78*, 107–126.

Ebbinghaus, H. (1885, translated 1913). *Memory: A contribution to experimental psychology* (H. A. Ruger & C. E. Bussenius, Trans.). New York: Teachers College, Columbia University, Bureau of Publications.

Edlund, C. (1972). The effect on the test behavior of children, as reflected in the I.Q. scores, when reinforced after each correct response. *Journal of Applied Behavior Analysis, 5*, 317–320.

Eisenberger, R. (1992). Learned industriousness. *Psychological Review, 99*, 248–267.

Elkin, I., Shea, M. T., Watkins, J. T., Imber, S. D., Sotsky, S. M., & Collins, J. F. (1989). National Institute of Mental Health Treatment of Depression Collaborative Research Program: General effectiveness treatments. *Archives of General Psychiatry, 46*, 971–982.

Elkins, R. (1980). Covert sensitization and alcoholism: Contributions of successful conditioning to subsequent abstinence maintenance. *Addictive Behaviors, 5*, 67–89.

Embry, D. D. (2002). The good behavior game: A best practice candidate as a universal behavioral vaccine. *Clinical Child and Family Psychology Review, 5*, 273–297.

Engelhardt, C. R., Bartholow, B. D., Kerr, G. T., & Bushman, B. J. (2011). This is your brain on violent video games: Neural desensitization to violence predicts increased aggression following violent video game exposure. *Journal of Experimental Social Psychology, 47*, 1033–1036.

Engerman, J. A., Austin, J., & Bailey, J. S. (1997). Prompting patron safety belt use at a supermarket. *Journal of Applied Behavior Analysis, 30*, 577–579.

Epstein, R., Kirshnit, C. E., Lanza, R. P., & Rubin, L. C. (1984). "Insight" in the pigeon: Antecedents and determinants of intelligent performance. *Nature, 308*, 61–62.

Estes, W. K. (1944). An experimental study of punishment. *Physiological Monographs, 57*, (3, Whole No. 263).

Estes, W. K. (1964). Probability learning. In A. W. Melton (Ed.), *Categories of human learning* (pp. 89–128). New York: Academic Press.

Estes, W. K., & Skinner, B. F. (1941). Some quantitative properties of anxiety. *Journal of Experimental Psychology, 29*, 390–400.

Fechner, G. (1860/1966). *Elements of psychophysics* (H. Adler, Trans.). Leipzig: Briet Kopf & Hartel. New York: Holt, Rinehart & Winston.

Ferster, C. B., & Skinner, B. F. (1957). *Schedules of reinforcement.* New York: Appleton-Century-Crofts.

Fischer, S. M., Iwata, B. A., & Mazaleski, J. L. (1997). Noncontingent delivery of arbitrary reinforcers as treatment for self-injurious behavior. *Journal of Applied Behavior Analysis, 30*, 239–249.

Foa, E. B., Kozak, M. J., Goodman, W. K., Hollander, E., Jenike, M. A., & Rasmussen, M. D. (1995). DSM-IV field trial: Obsessive-compulsive disorder. *American Journal of Psychiatry, 152*, 90–96.

Foley, J. P., & Cofer, C. N. (1943). Mediated generalization and the interpretation of verbal behavior: II. Experimental study of certain homophone and synonym gradients. *Journal of Experimental Psychology, 32*, 168–175.

Fouts, R. (1997). *Next of kin.* New York: Avon Books.

Fowler H., & Trapold, M. A. (1962). Instrumental escape performance as a function of the intensity of noxious stimulation. *Journal of Experimental Psychology, 60*, 323–326.

Francisco, M. T., Madden, G. J., & Borrero, J. (2009). Behavioral economics: Principles, procedures, and utility for applied behavior analysis. *The Behavior Analyst Today, 10*, 277–295.

Freud, S. (1913). *The interpretation of dreams* (3rd ed. A. A. Brill, Trans.). New York: Macmillan.

Freud, S. (1955). The analysis of a phobia in a five-year-old boy. In J. Strachey (Ed., trans.), *The standard edition of the complete psychological works of sigmund freud (Vol. 10)*. London: Hogarth (originally published 1909).

Freud, S. (2002). *Civilization and its discontents*. London: Penguin.

Friedman, T. L. (2006). *The world is flat*. New York: Farrar, Straus and Giroux.

Garcia, J., Ervin, F. R., & Koelling, R. A. (1966). Learning with prolonged delay of reinforcement. *Psychonomic Science, 5*, 121–122.

Garcia, J., & Koelling, R. (1966). Relation of cue to consequence in avoidance learning. *Psychonomic Science, 4*, 123–124.

Geller, E. S., Bruff, C. D., & Nimmer, J. G. (1985). Flash for life: Community-based prompting for safety belt promotion. *Journal of Applied Behavior Analysis, 18*, 309–314.

Geller, E. S., Casali, J. G., & Johnson, R. P. (1980). Seat belt usage: A potential target for applied behavior analysis. *Journal of Applied Behavior Analysis, 13*, 669–675.

Gharib, A., Gade, C., & Roberts, S. (2004). Control of variation by reward probability. *Journal of Experimental Psychology: Animal Behavior Processes, 30*, 271–282.

Goldfried, M. R., & Davison, G. C. (1976). *Clinical behavior therapy*. New York: Holt, Rinehart, and Winston.

Goodkin, F. (1976). Rats learn the relationship between responding and environmental events: An expansion of the learned helplessness hypothesis. *Learning and Memory, 7*, 382–393.

Gormezano, I. (1966). Classical Conditioning. In J. B. Sidowski (Ed.), *Experimental methods and instrumentation in psychology* (pp. 385–420). New York, NY: McGraw-Hill.

Grant, D. A., & Schipper, L. M. (1952). The acquisition and extinction of conditioned eyelid responses as a function of the percentage of fixed ratio random reinforcement. *Journal of Experimental Psychology, 43*, 313–320.

Green, G., & Osborne, J. (1985). Does vicarious instigation provide support for observational learning theories? A critical review. *Psychological Bulletin, 97*, 3–17.

Grice, G. R. (1948). The relation of secondary reinforcement to delayed reward in visual discrimination learning. *Journal of Experimental Psychology, 38*, 1–16.

Guilford, J. P., & Guilford, J. (1980). *Alternative uses manual*. Orange, CA: Sheridan Psychological Services.

Guilford, J. P., Merrifield, P. R., & Wilson, R. C. (1958). *Unusual uses test*. Orange, CA: Sheridan Psychological Services.

Guttman, N. (1954). Equal reinforcing values for sucrose and glucose solutions compared with sweetness values. *Journal of Comparative and Physiological Psychology, 47*, 358–361.

Guttman, N., & Kalish, H. I. (1956). Discriminability and stimulus generalization. *Journal of Experimental Psychology, 51*, 79–88.

Haidt, J. (2006). *The happiness hypothesis*. New York: Basic Books.

Hall, G. S. (1904). *Adolescence: Its psychology and its relation to physiology, anthropology, sociology, sex, crime, religion, and education* (Vols. 1 and 2). Englewood Cliffs, NJ: Prentice Hall.

Hamilton, J., Stephens, L., & Allen, P. (1967). Controlling aggressive and destructive behavior in severely retarded institutionalized residents. *American Journal of Mental Deficiency, 71*, 852–856.

Hanley, G. P., Iwata, B. A., & McCord, B. E. (2003). Functional analysis of problem behavior: A review. *Journal of Applied Behavior Analysis, 36*, 147–185.

Harlow, H. F. (1949). The formation of learning sets. *Psychological Review, 56*, 51–65.

Harris, B. (1979). Whatever happened to Little Albert? *American Psychologist, 34*, 151–160.

Harris, J. (2011). The acquisition of conditioned responding. *Journal of Experimental Psychology: Animal Behavior Processes, 37*, 151–164.

Hart, B., & Risley, R. T. (1995). *Meaningful differences in the everyday experience of young American children*. Baltimore, MD: Paul H. Brookes.

Harter, S. (1990). Self and identity development. In S. Feldman & G. Elliott (Eds.), *At the threshold: The developing adolescent* (pp. 352–387). Cambridge, MA: Harvard University Press.

Hastings, S. E., & Obrist, P. A. (1967). Heart rate during conditioning in humans: Effect of varying interstimulus (CS-UCS) interval. *Journal of Experimental Psychology, 74*, 431–442.

Haukebo, K., Skaret, E., Öst, L., Raadal, M., Berg, E., Sundberg, H., & Kvale, G. (2008). One- vs. five-session treatment of dental phobia: A randomized controlled study. *Journal of Behavior Therapy and Experimental Psychiatry, 39*, 381–390.

Hayes, K. J., & Hayes, C. (1951). The intellectual development of a home-raised chimpanzee. *Proceedings of the American Philosophical Society, 95*, 105–109.

Hayes, S. C. (1989). *Rule-governed behavior: Cognition, contingencies, and instructional control*. New York: Plenum Press.

Helmholtz, H. V. (1924). *Physiological optics* (J. P. Southall, Trans. from the 3rd German edition). Washington, DC: Optical Society of America.

Herman, R. L., & Azrin, N. H. (1964). Punishment by noise in an alternative response situation. *Journal of the Experimental Analysis of Behavior, 7*, 185–188.

Herrnstein, R. J. (1961). Relative and absolute strength of response as a function of frequency of reinforcement. *Journal of the Experimental Analysis of Behavior, 4*, 267–272.

Herrnstein, R. J. (1966). Superstition: A corollary of the principles of operant conditioning. In W. K. Honig (Ed.), *Operant behavior: Areas of research and applications* (pp. 33–51). New York: Appleton-Century-Crofts.

Herrnstein, R. J. (1970). On the law of effect. *Journal of the Experimental Analysis of Behavior, 13*, 243–266.

Herrnstein, R. J. (1974). Formal properties of the matching law. *Journal of the Experimental Analysis of Behavior, 21*, 159–164.

Herrnstein, R. J., & Loveland, D. H. (1964). Complex visual concept in the pigeon. *Science, 146*, 549–551.

Hernstein, R. J., Loveland, D. H., & Cable, C. (1976). Natural concepts in pigeons. *Journal of Experimental Psychology: Animal Behavior Processes, 2*, 285–302.

Higgins, S. T., Delaney, D. D., Budney, A. J., Bickel, W. K., Hughes, J. R., Foerg, F., & Fenwick, J. W. (1991). A behavioral approach to achieving initial cocaine abstinence. *American Journal of Psychiatry, 148*, 1218–1224.

Hilgard, E. R., & Bower, G. H. (1975). *Theories of learning.* Englewood Cliffs, NJ: Prentice Hall.

Hilgard, E. R., & Marquis, D. G. (1940). *Conditioning and learning.* New York: Appleton-Century-Crofts.

Hoch, H., McComas, J. J., Johnson, L., Faranda, N., & Guenther, S. L. (2002). The effects of magnitude and quality of reinforcement on choice responding during play activities. *Journal of Applied Behavior Analysis, 35*, 171–181.

Hockett, C. F. (1960). The origin of speech. *Scientific American, 203*, 88–111.

Hofmann, W., De Houwer, J., Perugini, M., Baeyens, F., & Crombez, G. (2010). Evaluative conditioning in humans: A meta-analysis. *Psychological Bulletin, 136*, 390–421.

Hokoda, A., & Fincham, F. D. (1995). Origins of children's helpless and mastery achievement patterns in the family. *Journal of Educational Psychology, 87*, 375–385.

Holden, B. (2005). Non-contingent reinforcement: An introduction. *European Journal of Behavior Analysis, 6*, 1–8.

Holland, P. C. (1984). Differential effects of reinforcement of an inhibitory feature after serial and simultaneous feature negative discrimination training. *Journal of Experimental Psychology: Animal Behavior Processes, 10*, 461–475.

Hollands, G. J., Prestwich, A., & Marteau, T. M. (2011). Using aversive images to enhance healthy food choices and implicit attitudes: An experimental test of evaluative conditioning. *Health Psychology, 30*, 195–203.

Hollis, K. L. (1997). Contemporary research on Pavlovian conditioning: A "new" functional analysis. *American Psychologist, 52*, 956–965.

Houben, K., Havermans, R. C., & Wiers, R. W. (2010). Learning to dislike alcohol: Conditioning negative implicit attitudes toward alcohol and its effect on drinking behavior. *Psychopharmacology, 211*, 79–86.

Hovland, C. I. (1938). Experimental studies in rote learning theory: III. Distribution of practice with varying speeds of syllable presentation. *Journal of Experimental Psychology, 25*, 622–633.

Huey, W. C., & Rank, R. C. (1984). Effects of counselor and peer-led group assertive training on Black adolescent aggression. *Journal of Counseling Psychology, 31*, 95–98.

Hull, C. L. (1943). *Principles of behavior.* New York: Appleton-Century-Crofts.

Hunt, W. A., Barnett, L. W., & Branch, L. G. (1971). Relapse rates in addiction programs. *Journal of Clinical Psychology, 27*, 455–456.

Imada, H., & Imada, S. (1983). Thorndike's (1898) puzzle-box experiments revisited. *Kwansei Gakuin University Annual Studies, 32*, 167–184.

Irvin, J. E., Bowers, C. A., Dunn, M., & Wang, M. C. (1999). Efficacy of relapse prevention: A meta-analytic review. *Journal of Consulting and Clinical Psychology, 67*, 563–570.

Jacobson, N. S., Dobson, K. S., Truax, P. A., Addis, M. E., Koerner, K., Gollan, J. K., … Prince, S. E. (1996). A component analysis of cognitive behavioral treatment for depression. *Journal of Consulting and Clinical Psychology, 64*, 295–304.

James, W. (1890). *The principles of psychology.* New York. Holt, Rinehart & Winston.

Jenkins, H. M. (1962). Resistance to extinction when partial reinforcement is followed by regular reinforcement. *Journal of Experimental Psychology, 64*, 441–450.

Jenkins, H. M., & Harrison, R. H. (1960). Effects of discrimination training on auditory generalization. *Journal of Experimental Psychology, 59*, 246–253.

Jenkins, H. M., & Harrison, R. H. (1962). Generalization gradients of inhibition following auditory discrimination learning. *Journal of the Experimental Analysis of Behavior, 5*, 435–441.

Jenkins, W. O., McFann, H., & Clayton, F. L. (1950). A methodological study of extinction following aperiodic and continuous reinforcement. *Journal of Comparative and Physiological Psychology, 43*, 155–167.

Jones, M. C. (1924). The elimination of children's fears. *Journal of Experimental Psychology, 7*, 382–390.

Kagel, J. H., Green, L., & Caraco, T. (1986). When foragers discount the future: Constraint or adaptation? *Animal Behaviour, 36*, 271–283.

Kamin, L. J. (1957). The gradient of delay of secondary reward in avoidance learning. *Journal of Comparative and Physiological Psychology, 50,* 445–449.

Kamin, L. J. (1969). Predictability, surprise, attention, and conditioning. In B. A. Campbell & R. M. Church (Eds.), *Punishment and aversive behavior* (pp. 279–296). New York: Appleton-Century-Crofts.

Kamin, L. J., Brimer, C. J., & Black, A. H. (1963). Conditioned suppression as a monitor of fear of the CS in the course of avoidance training. *Journal of Comparative and Physiological Psychology, 56,* 497–501.

Kellam, S. G., & Anthony, J. C. (1998). Targeting early antecedents to prevent tobacco smoking: Findings from an epidemiologically-based randomized field trial. *American Journal of Public Health, 88,* 1490–1495.

Kellam, S. G., Brown, C. H., Poduska, J. M., Ialongo, N. S., Wang, W., Toyinbo, P., & Wilcox, H. C. (2008). Effects of a universal classroom behavior management program in first and second grades on young adult behavioral, psychiatric, and social outcomes. *Drug and Alcohol Dependence, 95,* 5–28.

Kellam, S. G., Rebok, G. W., Ialongo, N., & Mayer, L. S. (1994). The course and malleability of aggressive behavior from early first-grade into middle-school: Result of a developmental epidemiologically-based preventive trial. *Journal of Child Psychology and Psychiatry, 35,* 359–382.

Keller, J. V., & Gollub, L. R. (1977). Duration and rate of reinforcement as determinants of concurrent responding. *Journal of the Experimental Analysis of Behavior, 28,* 145–153.

Kendler, H. H. (1987). *Historical foundations of modern psychology.* Pacific Grove, CA: Brooks/Cole.

Killeen, P. (1969). Reinforcement frequency and contingency as factors in fixed-ratio behavior. *Journal of the Experimental Analysis of Behavior, 12,* 391–395.

Kimble, G. A. (1961). *Hilgard and Marquis' conditioning and learning* (2nd ed.). New York: Appleton-Century-Crofts.

Kimble, G. A., & Reynolds, B. (1967). Eyelid conditioning as a function of the interval between conditioned and unconditioned stimuli. In G. A. Kimble (Ed.), *Foundations of conditioning and learning.* New York: Appleton-Century-Crofts.

Kirsch, I., Lynn, S. J., Vigorito, M., & Miller, R. R. (2004). The role of cognition in classical and operant conditioning. *Journal of Clinical Psychology, 60,* 369–392.

Knight, M. F., & McKenzie, H. S. (1974). Elimination of bedtime thumb-sucking in home settings through contingent reading. *Journal of Applied Behavior Analysis, 7,* 33–38.

Koehler, D. J., & James, G. (2010). Probability matching and strategy availability. *Memory and Cognition, 38,* 667–676.

Koffka, K. (1935). *Principles of gestalt psychology.* New York: Harcourt Brace.

Kohlberg, L. (1976). Moral stages and moralization: The cognitive-development approach. In T. Lickona (Ed.), *Moral development and behavior* (pp. 31–53). New York: Holt, Rinehart, and Winston.

Kohler, W. (1925). *The mentality of apes* (E. Winter, Trans.). New York: Harcourt Brace.

Kohler, W. (1929). *Gestalt psychology.* New York: Liveright Publishing Corporation.

Kohler, W. (1959). Gestalt psychology today. *American Psychologist, 14,* 727–734.

Krahé, B. M., Moller, I., Huesmann, L. R., Kirwil, L., Felber, J., & Berger, A. (2011). Desensitization to media violence: Links with habitual media violence exposure, aggressive cognitions, and aggressive behavior. *Journal of Personality and Social Psychology, 100,* 630–646.

Krechevsky, I. (1932). "Hypotheses" in rats. *Psychological Review, 39,* 516–532.

Kremer, E. F. (1978). The Rescorla-Wagner model: Losses in associative strength in compound conditioned stimuli. *Journal of Experimental Psychology: Animal Behavior Processes, 4,* 22–36.

Kurzweil, R. (2001). *The law of accelerating returns.* Available at *KurzweilAI.net,* http://www.kurzweilai.net/the-law-of-accelerating-returns

Lashley, K. S. (1929). *Brain mechanisms and intelligence.* Chicago: University of Chicago Press.

Lashley, K. S., & Wade, M. (1946). The Pavlovian theory of generalization. *Psychological Review, 53,* 72–84.

Lattal, K. M., & Nakajima, S. (1998). Overexpectation in appetitive Pavlovian and instrumental conditioning. *Animal Learning and Behavior, 26,* 351–360.

Lawrence, D. H. (1952). The transfer of a discrimination along a continuum. *Journal of Comparative and Physiological Psychology, 45,* 511–516.

Leitenberg, H., Burchard, J. D., Burchard, S. N., Fuller, E. J., & Lysaght, T. V. (1977). Using positive reinforcement to suppress behavior: Some experimental comparisons with sibling conflict. *Behavior Therapy, 8,* 168–182.

Lemere, F., & Voegtlin, W. (1950). An evaluation of the aversion treatment of alcoholism. *Quarterly Journal of Studies on Alcohol, 11,* 199–204.

Lennox, D. E., Miltenberger, R. G., & Donnelly, D. (1987). Response interruption and DRL for the reduction of rapid eating. *Journal of Applied Behavior Analysis, 20,* 279–284.

Levy, J. C. (1975). The effects of sequential ordering training on middle-size transposition in preschool children. *Child Development, 46*, 416–423.

Levy, J. C. (1978). Effects of contingencies of reinforcement on same-sexed and cross-sexed interpersonal interactions, *Psychological Reports, 43*, 1063–1069.

Levy, J. C. (1991). Maps, guides, and making it through a course. *The Teaching Professor, 5*, 5.

Linden, E. (1974). *Apes, men, and language*. New York: Penguin Books.

Linehan, M. M. (1993). *Cognitive-behavioral treatment of border-line personality disorder*. New York: Guilford.

Linscheid, T. R., Iwata, B. A., Ricketts, R. W., Williams, D. E., & Griffin, J. C. (1990). Clinical evaluation of the self-injurious behavior inhibiting system (SIBIS). *Journal of Applied Behavior Analysis, 23*, 53–78.

Liu, E. H., Mercado, E., Church, B. A., & Orduna, I. (2008). The easy-to-hard effect in human (Homo sapiens) and rat (Rattus norvegicus) auditory identification. *Journal of Comparative Psychology, 122*, 132–45.

Logue, A. W. (1995). *Self-control*. Englewood Cliffs, NJ: Prentice Hall.

Logue, A. W., & Mazur, J. E. (1981). Maintenance of self-control acquired through a fading procedure: Follow-up on Mazur and Logue (1978). *Behavior Analysis Letters, 1*, 131–137.

Lovaas, O. I. (1967). A behavior therapy approach to the treatment of childhood schizophrenia. In J. P. Hill (Ed.), *Minnesota symposia on child psychology* (Vol. I, pp. 108–159). Minneapolis, MN: University of Minnesota Press.

Lovaas, O. I. (1969). *Behavior modification: Teaching language to psychotic children*. New York: Appleton-Century-Crofts (Film).

Lovaas O. I. (1987). Behavioral treatment and normal educational and intellectual functioning in young autistic children. *Journal of Consulting and Clinical Psychology, 55*, 3–9.

Lovaas, O. I., Koegel, R. L., Simmons, J. Q., & Long, J. S. (1973). Some generalization and follow-up measures on autistic children in behavior therapy. *Journal of Applied Behavior Analysis, 6*, 131–165.

Lovaas, O. I., & Newsom, C. D. (1976). Behavior modification with psychotic children. In H. Leitenberg (Ed.), *Handbook of behavior modification and behavior therapy* (pp. 303–360). Englewood Cliffs, NJ: Prentice Hall.

Lovaas, O. I., Schaeffer, B., & Simmons, J. Q. (1965). Experimental studies in childhood schizophrenia: Building social behavior in autistic children by use of electric shock. *Journal of Experimental Research in Personality, 1*, 99–109.

Lubow, R. E. (1965). Latent inhibition. *Journal of Comparative and Physiological Psychology, 60*, 454–457.

Luchins, A. S. (1942). Mechanization in problem solving. *Psychological Monographs, 54*, Whole 24B.

Lynch, J. J. (1973). Pavlovian inhibition of delay in cardiac and somatic responses in dogs: Schizokenesis. *Psychological Review, 32*, 1339–1346.

Maccoby, E., & Martin, J. (1983). Socialization in the context of the family: Parent-child interaction. In E. M. Hetherington (Ed.), *Handbook of child psychology: Socialization, personality, and social development* (Vol. 4, pp. 1–101). New York: Wiley.

MacCorquodale, K. (1969). B. F. Skinner's *Verbal behavior*: A retrospective appreciation. *Journal of the Experimental Analysis of Behavior, 12*, 831–841.

MacCorquodale, K. (1970). On Chomsky's review of Skinner's *Verbal behavior. Journal of the Experimental Analysis of Behavior, 13*, 83–99.

Mace, F. C., Neef, N. A., Shade, D., & Mauro, B. C. (1996). Effects of problem difficulty and reinforcer quality on time allocated to concurrent arithmetic problems. *Journal of Applied Behavior Analysis, 29*, 11–24.

Mackintosh, N. J. (1964). Overtraining and transfer within and between dimensions in the rat. *Quarterly Journal of Experimental Psychology, 16*, 250–256.

Mackintosh, N. J. (1965). Selective attention in animal discriminative learning. *Psychological Bulletin, 64*, 124–150.

Mackintosh, N. J. (1975). A theory of attention: Variations in the associability of stimuli with reinforcement. *Psychological Review, 82*, 276–298.

Mackintosh, N. J., & Little, L. (1969). Intradimensional and extradimensional shift learning by pigeons. *Psychonomic Science, 14*, 5–6.

MacPhail, E. M. (1968). Avoidance conditioning in pigeons. *Journal of the Experimental Analysis of Behavior, 11*, 625–632.

Madden, G. J., & Bickel, W. K. (1999). Abstinence and price effects on demand for cigarettes: A behavioral-economic analysis. *Addiction, 94*, 577–588.

Madsen, C. H., Becker, W. C., Thomas, D. R., Koser, L., & Plager, E. (1970). An analysis of the reinforcing function of "sit down" commands. In R. K. Parker (Ed.), *Readings in educational psychology* (pp. 265–278). Boston, MA: Allyn & Bacon.

Maier, N. R. F. (1930). Reasoning in humans I: On direction. *Journal of Comparative Psychology, 10*, 115–143.

Maier, N. R. F. (1931). Reasoning in humans II: The solution of a problem and its appearance in consciousness. *Journal of Comparative Psychology, 12*, 181–194.

Maier, N. R. F., & Janzen, J. C. (1968). Functional values as aids and distractors in problem solving, *Psychological Reports, 22*, 1021–1034.

Maletsky, B. M. (1974). Behavior recording as treatment: A brief note. *Behavior Therapy, 5*, 107–111.

Marlatt, G. A. (1978). Craving for alcohol, loss of control, and relapse: A cognitive-behavioral analysis. In P. E. Nathan, G. A. Madatt, & T. Loberg (Eds.), *Alcoholism: New directions in behavioral research and treatment* (pp. 71–117). New York: Plenum.

Marlatt, G. A., & Donovan, D. M. (2005). Relapse prevention: Maintenance strategies in the treatment of addictive behaviors (2nd ed.). New York: Guilford

Marlatt, G. A., & Gordon, J. R. (1980). Determinants of relapse: Implications for the maintenance of behavior change. In P. O. Davidson & S. M. Davidson (Eds.), *Behavioral medicine: Changing health lifestyles* (pp. 410–452). New York: Brunner/Mazel.

Marlatt, G. A., & Gordon, J. R. (Eds.). (1985). *Relapse prevention: Maintenance strategies in the treatment of addictive behaviors.* New York: Guilford.

Maslow, A. H. (1943). A theory of human motivation. *Psychological Review, 50*, 370–396.

Matarazzo, J. D. (1980). Behavioral health and behavioral medicine: Frontiers for a new health psychology. *American Psychologist, 35*, 807–817.

Mattick, R. P., Peters, L., & Clarke, J. C. (1989). Exposure and cognitive restructuring for social phobia: A controlled study. *Behavior Therapy, 20*, 3–23.

Mazaleski, J. L., Iwata, B. A., Vollmer, T. R., Zarcone, J. R., & Smith, R. G. (1993). Analysis of the reinforcement and extinction components in DRO contingencies with self injury. *Journal of Applied Behavior Analysis, 26*, 143–156.

Mazur, J. E. (1987). An adjusting procedure for studying delayed reinforcement. In M. L. Commons, J. E. Mazur, J. A. Nevin, & H. Rachlin (Eds.), *Quantitative analysis of behavior: The effects of delay and of intervening events on reinforcement value* (Vol. 5, pp. 55–73). Hillsdale, NJ: Lawrence Erlbauum.

Mazur, J. E. (2006). *Learning and behavior* (6th ed.). Upper Saddle River, NJ: Pearson/Prentice Hall.

Mazur, J. E., & Logue, A. W. (1978). Choice in a "self-control" paradigm: Effects of a fading procedure. *Journal of the Experimental Analysis of Behavior, 1*, 11–17.

McCaffrey, T. (2012). Innovation relies on the obscure: A key to overcoming the classic problem of functional fixedness. *Psychological Science, 23*, 215–218.

McCullough, D. (2001). *John Adams.* New York: Simon & Schuster.

McCullough, J. P. (2000). The case of Katrina: Skating on thin ice. *Cognitive and Behavioral Practice, 7*, 510–514.

McCullough, M. E., & Willoughby, B. L. (2009). Religion, self-regulation, and self-control: Associations, explanations, and implications. *Psychological Bulletin, 135*, 69–93.

McDonell, M. G., Howell, D. N., McPherson, S., Cameron, J. M., Srebnik, D., Roll, J. M., & Ries, R. K. (2012). Voucher-based reinforcement for alcohol abstinence using the ethyl-glucuronide alcohol biomarker. *Journal of Applied Behavior Analysis, 45*, 161–165.

Meltzoff, A. N., & Moore, M. K. (1977). Imitation of facial and manual gestures by human neonates. *Science, 198*, 75–78.

Meltzoff, A. N., & Moore, M. K. (1983). Newborn infants imitate adult facial gestures. *Child Development, 54*, 702–709.

Melville, H. (1851). *Moby-Dick.* New York: Harper and Brothers.

Meyerson, L., & Michael, J. (1964). Hearing by operant conditioning procedures. *Proceedings of the International Congress on Education of the Deaf, 1964*, 238–242.

Miller, G. A., Galanter, E., & Pribram, K. H. (1960). *Plans and the structure of behavior.* New York: Holt.

Miller, H. L., & Loveland, D. H. (1974). Matching when the number of response alternatives is large. *Animal Learning and Behavior, 2*, 106–110.

Miller, N. E. (1948). Studies of fear as an acquirable drive: I. Fear as motivation and fear reduction as reinforcement in the learning of responses. *Journal of Experimental Psychology, 38*, 89–101.

Miller, N. E. (1960). Learning resistance to pain and fear: Effects of overlearning, exposure, and rewarded exposure in context. *Journal of Experimental Psychology, 60*, 137–145.

Miller, N. U., Pedersen, W. C., Earleywine, M., & Pollock, V. E. (2003). A theoretical model of triggered displaced aggression. *Personality and Social Psychology Review, 7*, 75–97.

Miller, R. R., Barnet, R. C., & Grahame, N. J. (1995). Assessment of the Rescorla-Wagner model. *Psychological Bulletin, 117*, 363–386.

Mineka, S. (2008). The relevance of recent developments in classical conditioning to understanding the etiology and maintenance of anxiety disorders. *Acta Psychologica, 127*, 567–580.

Mineka, S., & Cook, M. (1986). Immunization against the observational learning of snake fears in rhesus monkeys. *Journal of Abnormal Psychology, 95*, 307–318.

Mineka, S., Davidson, M., Cook, M., & Keir, R. (1984). Observational conditioning of snake fear in rhesus monkeys. *Journal of Abnormal Psychology, 93*, 355–372.

Mineka, S., Keir, R., & Price, V. (1980). Fear of snakes in wild- and lab-reared rhesus monkeys. *Animal Learning and Behavior, 8*, 653–663.

Mischel, W., & Ebbesen, E. B. (1970). Attention in delay of gratification. *Journal of Personality and Social Psychology, 16*, 329–337.

Mischel, W., Ebbesen, E. B., & Raskoff Zeiss, A. (1972). Cognitive and attentional mechanisms in delay of gratification. *Journal of Personality and Social Psychology, 21*, 204–218.

Mischel, W., Shoda, Y., & Peake, P. K. (1988). The nature of adolescent competencies predicted by preschool delay of gratification. *Journal of Personality and Social Psychology, 54*, 687–696.

Mischel, W., Shoda, Y., & Rodriguez, M. L. (1989). Delay of gratification in children. *Science, 244*, 933–938.

Mischel, W., & Yates, B. (1979). Young children's preferred attentional strategies for delaying gratification. *Journal of Personality and Social Psychology, 37*, 286–300.

Montaigne, M. (1993). *The complete essays* (M. A. Screech, Trans.). London/New York: Penguin (originally published 1588).

Moore, G. E. (1965). Cramming more components onto integrated circuits. *Electronics, 38*, 1–4.

Moore, J. W. (1972). Stimulus control: Studies of auditory generalization in rabbits. In A. H. Black & W. F. Prokasy (Eds.), *Classical conditioning II: Current research and theory* (pp. 206–230). New York: Appleton-Century-Crofts

Morokuma, S., Fukushima, K., Kawai, N., Tomonaga, M., Satoh, S., & Nakano, H. (2004). Fetal habituation correlates with functional brain development. *Behavioral Brain Research, 153*, 459–463.

Mowrer, O. H. (1947). On the dual nature of learning: A reinterpretation of "conditioning" and "problem-solving." *Harvard Educational Review, 17*, 102–148.

Murphy, J. G., Barnett, N. P., & Colby S. M. (2006). Alcohol-related and alcohol-free activity participation and enjoyment among college students: Behavioral theories of choice analysis. *Experimental and Clinical Psychopharmacology, 14*, 339–349.

Murphy, J. G., Correia, J. C., & Barnett, N. P. (2007). Behavioral economic approaches to reduce college student drinking. *Addictive Behaviors, 32*, 2573–2585.

Murphy, J. G., Correia, J. C., Colby, S. M., & Vuchinich, R. E. (2005). Using behavioral theories of choice to predict drinking outcomes following a brief intervention. *Experimental and Clinical Psychopharmacology, 13*, 93–101.

Myrseth, K. R., & Fishbach, A. (2009). Self-control: A function of knowing when and how to exercise restraint. *Current Direction in Psychological Science, 18*, 247–252.

Nathan, P. E., & Gorman, J. M. (2002). *Treatments that work* (2nd ed.). New York: Oxford University Press.

Neef, N. A., Mace, D. F., Shea, M. C., & Shade, D. (1992). Effects of reinforcement rate and reinforcement quality on time allocation: Extensions of matching theory to educational settings. *Journal of Applied Behavior Analysis, 25*, 691–699.

Neitzel, C., & Stright, A. D. (2003). Mother's scaffolding of children's problem-solving: Establishing a foundation of academic self-regulatory competence. *Journal of Family Psychology, 17*, 147–159.

Newman, M. G., Hoffman, S. G., Trabert, W., Roth, W. T., & Taylor, C. B. (1994). Does behavioral treatment of social phobia lead to cognitive changes? *Behavior Therapy, 25*, 503–517.

Nyp, S. S., Barone, V. J., Kruger, T., Garrison, C. B., Robertsen, C., & Christopherson, E. R. (2011). Evaluation of developmental surveillance by physicians at the two-month preventive care visit. *Journal of Applied Behavior Analysis, 44*, 181–185.

O'Brien, S., & Repp, A. C. (1990). Reinforcement-based reductive procedures: A review of 20 years of their use with severe or profound retardation. *Journal of the Association of Persons with Severe Handicaps, 15*, 148–159.

O'Donnell, J., Crosbie, J., Williams, D. C., & Saunders, K. J. (2000). Stimulus control and generalization of point-loss punishment with humans. *Journal of the Experimental Analysis of Behavior, 73*, 261–274.

Okinaka, T., & Shimazaki, T. (2011). The effects of prompting and reinforcement on safe behavior of bicycle and motorcycle riders. *Journal of Applied Behavior Analysis, 44*, 671–674.

Olsson, A., & Phelps, E. (2004). Learned fear of "unseen" faces after Pavlovian, observational, and instructed fear. *Psychological Science, 15*, 822–828.

Orwell, G. (1949). *Nineteen eighty-four.* New York: Harcourt, Brace & Company.

Osgood, C. E. (1957). A behavioristic analysis of perception and language as cognitive phenomena. In J. Bruner (Ed.), *Contemporary approaches to cognition* (pp. 75–118). Cambridge, MA: Harvard University Press.

Ouimette, P. C., Finney, J. W., & Moos, R. H. (1997). Twelve step and cognitive-behavioral treatment for substance abuse: A comparison of treatment effectiveness. *Journal of Consulting and Clinical Psychology, 65*, 230–240.

Paul, G. L. (1969). Outcome of systematic desensitization: II. Controlled investigations of individual treatment, technique variations, and current status. In C. M. Franks (Ed.), *Behavior therapy: Appraisal and status* (pp. 105–159). New York: McGraw-Hill.

Pavlov, I. P. (1927). *Conditioned reflexes: An investigation of the physiological activity of the cerebral cortex.* Oxford, Eng.: Oxford University Press.

Pavlov, I. P. (1928). *Lectures on conditioned reflexes*. New York: International Publishers.

Pearce, J. M., & Hall, G. (1980) A model for Pavlovian learning: Variations in the effectiveness of conditioned but not of unconditioned stimuli. *Psychological Review, 87*, 532–552.

Pelaez, M., Virues-Ortega, J., & Gewirtz, J. L. (2011). Reinforcement of vocalizations through contingent vocal imitation. *Journal of Applied Behavior Analysis, 44*, 33–40.

Perri, M. G., & Richards, C. S. (1977). An investigation of naturally-occurring episodes of self-controlled behavior. *Journal of Counseling Psychology, 25*, 178–183.

Politis, G. G. (2007). *Nukak*. Walnut Creek: University College, London Institute of Archeology Publications.

Pollard, K. S. (2009). What makes us human? *Scientific American, 300*, 44–49.

Porter, J. J., Madison, H. L., & Senkowski, P. C. (1968). Runway performance and competing responses as a function of drive level and method of drive measurement. *Journal of Experimental Psychology, 78*, 281–284.

Powell, R. A., Symbaluk, D. G., & MacDonald, S. E. (2009). *Introduction to Learning and Behavior* (3rd edition), Belmont, CA: Wadsworth.

Powers, R. (1999, April 18). Best idea: Eyes wide open. *New York Times Magazine*. Available at http://www.nytimes.com/1999/04/18/magazine/best-idea-eyes-wide-open.html?pagewanted=all&src=pm

Pratt, M. W., Green, D., MacVicar, J., & Bountrogianni, M. (1992). The mathematical parent: Parental scaffolding, parenting style and learning outcomes in long-division mathematics homework. *Journal of Applied Developmental Psychology, 13*, 17–34.

Probst, B. (2008). Issues in portability of evidence-based treatment for adolescent depression. *Child & Adolescent Social Work Journal, 25*, 111–123.

Rachlin, H. (1989). *Judgment, decision, and choice*. New York: W. H. Freeman.

Rachlin, H., & Green, L. (1972). Commitment, choice, and self-control. *Journal of Experimental Analysis of Behavior, 17*, 15–22.

Rankin, C. H., Abrams, T., Barry, R., Bhatnagar, S., Clayton, D. F., Colombo, J. ... Thompson, R. F. (2009). Habituation revisited: An updated and revised description of the behavioral characteristics of habituation. *Neurobiology of Learning and Memory, 92*, 135–138.

Rapee, R. M., Abbott, M. J., & Lyneham, H. J. (2006). Bibliotherapy for children with anxiety disorders using written materials for parents: A randomized controlled trial. *Journal of Consulting and Clinical Psychology, 74*, 436–444.

Raymond, M. J. (1964). The treatment of addiction by aversion conditioning with apomorphine. *Behavior Research and Therapy. 1*, 287–291.

Rayner, K. (1998). Eye movements in reading and information processing: 20 years of research. *Psychological Bulletin, 124*, 372–422.

Razran, G. H. (1938). Conditioning away social bias by the luncheon technique. *Psychological Bulletin, 36*, 693. (Abstract)

Razran, G. H. (1939). A quantitative study of meaning by a conditioned salivary technique (semantic conditioning). *Science, 90*, 89–90.

Razran, G. H. (1940). Conditioned response changes in rating and appraising sociopolitical slogans. *Psychological Bulletin, 37*, 481. (Abstract)

Reberg, D., & Black, A. H. (1969). Compound testing of individually conditioned stimuli as an index of excitatory and inhibitory properties. *Psychonomic Science, 17*, 30–31.

Reed, D. D., Critchfield, T. S., & Martens, B. K. (2006). The generalized matching law in elite sport competition: Football play calling as operant choice. *Journal of Applied Behavior Analysis, 39*, 281–297.

Reese, H. W. (1968). *The perception of stimulus relations*. New York: Academic Press.

Reid, G. S. (1953). The development of noncontinuity behavior through continuity learning. *Journal of Experimental Psychology, 46*, 107–112.

Rescorla, R. A. (1966). Predictability and number of pairings in Pavlovian fear conditioning. *Psychonomic Science, 4*, 383–384.

Rescorla, R. A. (1968). Probability of shock in the presence and absence of CS in fear conditioning. *Journal of Comparative and Physiological Psychology, 66*, 1–5.

Rescorla, R. A. (1970). Reduction in the effectiveness of reinforcement after prior excitatory conditioning. *Learning and Motivation, 1*, 372–381.

Rescorla, R. A. (1988). Classical conditioning: It's not what you think it is. *American Psychologist, 43*, 151–160.

Rescorla, R. A., & Wagner, A. R. (1972). A theory of Pavlovian conditioning: Variations in the effectiveness of reinforcement and nonreinforcement. In A. H. Black & W. E Prokasy (Eds.), *Classical conditioning II: Current research and theory* (pp. 64–99). New York: Appleton-Century-Crofts.

Reynolds, G. S. (1961). Relativity of response rate and reinforcement frequency in a multiple schedule. *Journal of Experimental Analysis of Behavior, 4*, 179–183.

Reynolds, G. S. (1968). *A primer of operant conditioning*. Glendale, IL: Scott, Foresman.

Richards, J. B., Mitchell, S. H., de Wit, H., & Seiden, L. S. (1997). Determination of discount functions in rats with an adjusting-amount procedure. *Journal of the Experimental Analysis of Behavior, 67*, 353–366.

Rindermann, H., & Thompson, J. (2011). Cognitive capitalism: The effect of cognitive ability on wealth, as mediated through scientific achievement and economic freedom. *Psychological Science, 22*, 754–763.

Rogers, C. (1957). The necessary and sufficient conditions of therapeutic personality change. *Journal of Consulting Psychology, 21*, 95–103.

Ross, R. T., & Holland, P. C. (1981). Conditioning of simultaneous and serial feature-positive discriminations. *Animal Learning and Behavior, 9*, 293–303.

Routh, D. (1969). Conditioning of vocal response differentiation in infants. *Developmental Psychology, 1*, 219–225.

Rudd, M. D., Joiner, T., & Rajab, M. H. (2001). *Treating suicidal behavior: An effective time-limited approach.* New York: Guilford Press.

Sanderson, E. W., & Boyer, M. (2009). *Mannahatta: A natural history of New York City.* New York: Abrams.

Savani, K., Stephens, N. M., & Markus, H. R. (2011). The unanticipated interpersonal and societal consequences of choice: Victim blaming and reduced support for the public good. *Psychological Science, 22*, 795–802.

Schneiderman, N., Fuentes, I., & Gormezano, I. (1962). Acquisition and extinction of the classically conditioned eyelid response in the albino rabbit. *Science, 136*, 650–652.

Schneiderman, N., & Gormezano, I. (1964). Conditioning of the nictitating membrane of the rabbit as a function of CS-US interval. *Journal of Comparative and Physiological Psychology, 57*, 188–195.

Schoenfeld, W. N. (1950). An experimental approach to anxiety, escape, and avoidance behavior. In P. H. Hock & J. Zubin (Eds.), *Anxiety* (pp. 70–99). New York: Grune & Stratton.

Schwartz, B. (1973). Maintenance of keypecking in pigeons by a food avoidance but not a shock avoidance contingency. *Animal Learning and Behavior, 1*, 164–166.

Schwartz, B., Wasserman, E. A., & Robbins, S. J. (2002). *Psychology of learning and behavior* (5th edition), New York: W. W. Norton.

Schweitzer, J. B., & Sulzer-Azaroff, B. (1988). Self control: Teaching tolerance for delay in impulsive children. *Journal of the Experimental Analysis of Behavior, 50*, 173–186.

Seligman, M. E. P. (1971). Phobias and preparedness. *Behavior Therapy, 2*, 307–320.

Seligman, M. E. P. (1975). *Helplessness: On depression, development, and death.* San Francisco, CA: Freeman.

Seligman, M. E. P. (1990). *Learned optimism.* New York: Knopf.

Seligman, M. E. P., & Johnston, J. C. (1973). A cognitive theory of avoidance learning In F. J. McGuigan & D. B. Lumsden (Eds.), *Contemporary approaches to conditioning and learning* (pp. 69–110). Washington, DC: Winston-Wiley.

Seligman, M. E. P., & Maier, S. F. (1967). Failure to escape traumatic shock. *Journal of Experimental Psychology, 74*, 1–9.

Seligman, M. E. P., Maier, S., & Geer, J. (1968). The alleviation of learned helplessness in the dog. *Journal of Abnormal and Social Psychology, 73*, 256–262.

Serran, G., Fernandez, Y., Marshall, W. L., & Mann, R. E. (2003). Process issues in treatment: Application to sexual offender programs. *Professional Psychology: Research and Practice, 34*, 368–374.

Seyfarth, R., Cheney, D., & Marler, P. (1980). Monkey responses to three different alarm calls: Evidence of predator classification and semantic communication. *Science, 210*, 801–803.

Shoda, Y., Mischel, W., & Peake, P. K. (1990). Predicting adolescent cognitive and self-regulatory competencies from preschool delay of gratification: Identifying diagnostic conditions. *Developmental Psychology, 26*, 978–986.

Sidman, M. (1953). Two temporal parameters of the maintenance of avoidance behavior in the white rat. *Journal of Comparative and Physiological Psychology, 46*, 253–261.

Sidman, M. (1955). Some properties of the warning stimulus and avoidance behavior. *Journal of Comparative and Physiological Psychology, 48*, 444–450.

Siegel, S. (1975). Conditioning insulin effects. *Journal of Comparative and Physiological Psychology, 89*, 189–199.

Siegel, S. (1977). Morphine tolerance acquisition as an associative process. *Journal of Experimental Psychology: Animal Behavior Processes, 3*, 1–13.

Siegel, S. (1983). Classical conditioning, drug tolerance, and drug dependence. In Y. Israel, F. B. Glaser, H. Kalant, R. E. Popham, W. Schmidt, & R. G. Smart (Eds.), *Research advances in alcohol and drug problems* (Vol. 7, pp. 207–246). New York: Plenum Press.

Siegel, S. (1984). Pavlovian conditioning and heroin overdose: Reports by overdose victims. *Bulletin of the Psychonomic Society, 22*, 428–430.

Siegel, S. (2005). Drug tolerance, drug addiction, and drug anticipation. *Current Directions in Psychological Science, 14*, 296–300.

Siegel, S. (2008). Learning and the wisdom of the body. *Learning and Behavior, 36*, 242–252.

Siegel, S., Hinson, R. E., Krank, M. D., & McCully, J. (1982). Heroin "overdose" death: The contribution of drug-associated environmental cues. *Science, 216*, 436–437.

Siegelbaum, S. A., Camardo, J. S., & Kandel, E. R. (1982). Serotonin and cyclic AMP close single K+ channels in Aplysia sensory neurons. *Nature, 299*, 413–417.

Skinner, B. F. (1938). *The behavior of organisms.* Englewood Cliffs, NJ: Prentice Hall.

Skinner, B. F. (1948). *Walden two.* New York: Macmillan.

Skinner, B. F. (1953). *Science and human behavior.* New York: Macmillan.

Skinner, B. F. (1956). A case history in scientific method. *American Psychologist, 11*, 221–233.

Skinner, B. F. (1957). *Verbal behavior.* Englewood Cliffs, NJ: Prentice-Hall

Skinner, B. F. (1960). Pigeons in a pelican. *American Psychologist, 15*, 574–591.

Skinner, B. F. (1986). The evolution of verbal behavior. *Journal of the Experimental Analysis of Behavior, 45*, 115–122.

Skinner, B. F. (1990). Can psychology be a science of mind? *American Psychologist, 45*, 1206–1210.

Slamecka, N. J., & Ceraso, J. (1960). Retroactive and proactive inhibition of verbal learning. *Psychological Bulletin, 57*, 449–475.

Smith, J. C., & Roll, D. L. (1967). Trace conditioning with X-rays as an aversive stimulus. *Psychonomic Science, 9*, 11–12.

Smith, M. C., Coleman, S. R., & Gormezano, I. (1969). Classical conditioning of the rabbits' nictitating membrane response. *Journal of Comparative and Physiological Psychology, 69*, 226–231.

Smith, R. E. (1973). The use of humor in the counterconditioning of anger responses: A case study. *Behavior Therapy, 4*, 576–580.

Solomon, R. L., & Wynne, L. C. (1953). Traumatic avoidance learning: Acquisition in normal dogs. *Psychological Monographs, 67*(354), 19.

Spence, K. W. (1936). The nature of discrimination learning in animals. *Psychological Review, 43*, 427–449.

Spence, K. W. (1937). The differential response in animals to stimuli varying within a single dimension. *Psychological Review, 44*, 430–444.

Staats, A. W. (1968). *Learning, language, and cognition.* New York: Holt, Rinehart & Winston.

Staats, A. W., & Staats, C. K. (1958). Attitudes established by classical conditioning. *Journal of Abnormal and Social Psychology, 57*, 37–40.

Staats, A. W., & Staats, C. K. (1959). Effect of number of trials on the language conditioning of meaning. *Journal of General Psychology, 61*, 211–223.

Staats, A. W., Staats, C. K., & Crawford, H. L. (1962). First-order conditioning of meaning and the paralleled conditioning of a GSR. *Journal of General Psychology, 67*, 159–167.

Staats, A. W., Staats, C. K., & Heard, W. G. (1959). Language conditioning of meaning to meaning using a semantic generalization paradigm. *Journal of Experimental Psychology, 57*, 187–192.

Staats, A. W., Staats, C. K., & Heard, W. G. (1961). Denotative meaning established by classical conditioning. *Journal of Experimental Psychology, 61*, 300–303.

Staats, A. W., Staats, C. K., Heard, W. G., & Nims, L. P. (1959). Replication report: Meaning established by classical conditioning. *Journal of Experimental Psychology, 57*, 64.

Staats, C. K., & Staats, A. W. (1957). Meaning established by classical conditioning. *Journal of Experimental Psychology, 54*, 74–80.

Stahlman, W. D., & Blaisdell, A. P. (2011). Reward probability and the variability of foraging behavior in rats. *International Journal of Comparative Psychology, 24*, 168–176.

Stanovich, K. E., & Cunningham, A. E. (1993). Where does knowledge come from? Specific associations between print exposure and information acquisition. *Journal of Educational Psychology, 85*, 211–229.

Strushaker, T. (1967). Auditory communication among vervet monkeys (Cercopithecus aethiops). In S. A. Altmann (Ed.), *Social communication among primates* (pp. 281–324). Chicago: University of Chicago Press.

Sugarman, D. E., & Carey, K. B. (2007). The relationship between drinking control strategies and college student alcohol use. *Psychology of Addictive Behaviors, 21*, 338–345.

Sutherland, N. S., & Mackintosh, N. J. (1971). *Mechanisms of animal discrimination learning.* New York: Academic Press.

Tanner, D. (1972). *Secondary education.* New York: Macmillan.

Tarpy, R. M. (1982). *Principles of animal learning and motivation.* Glenview, IL: Scott Foresman and Company.

Terrace, H. S. (1963a). Discrimination learning with and without "errors." *Journal of the Experimental Analysis of Behavior, 6*, 1–27.

Terrace, H. S. (1963b). Errorless transfer of a discrimination across two continua. *Journal of the Experimental Analysis of Behavior, 6*, 223–232.

Thein, T., Westbrook, R. F., & Harris, J. (2008). How the associative strengths of stimuli combine in compound: Summation and overshadowing. *Journal of Experimental Psychology: Animal Behavior Processes, 34*, 155–166.

Thorndike, E. L. (1898). Animal intelligence. An experimental study of the associative processes in animals. *Psychological Review Monographs, 2*(8).

Thorndike, E. L. (1911). *Animal intelligence*. New York: Macmillan.

Thyer, B. A., Geller, E. S., Williams, M., & Purcell, E. (1987). Community-based "flashing" to increase safety belt use. *Journal of Experimental Education, 55*, 155–159.

Till, B. D., Stanley, S. M., & Priluck, R. (2008). Classical conditioning and celebrity endorsers: An examination of belongingness and resistance to extinction. *Psychology and Marketing, 25*, 179–196.

Tingstrom, D. H., Sterling-Turner, H. E., & Wilczynski, S. M. (2006). The good behavior game: 1969–2002. *Behavior Modification, 30*, 225–253.

Titchener, E. B. (1898). The postulates of a structural psychology. *Philosophical Review, 7*, 449–465.

Titchener, E. B. (1899). Structural and functional psychology. *Philosophical Review, 8*, 290–299. [Reply to Caldwell, 1899.]

Toffler, A. (1970). *Future shock*. New York: Random House.

Tolman, E. C. (1932). *Purposive behavior in animals and men*. New York: Appleton-Century.

Tolman, E. C., & Honzik, C. H. (1930). Introduction and removal of reward, and maze performance in rats. *University of California Publications in Psychology, 4*, 257–275.

Touchette, P. E. (1970). Transfer of stimulus control: Measuring the moment of transfer. *Journal of the Experimental Analysis of Behavior, 15*, 347–354.

Towe, A. L. (1954). A study of figural equivalence in the pigeon. *Journal of Comparative and Physiological Psychology, 47*, 283–287.

Ulrich, R. E., & Azrin, N. H. (1962). Reflexive fighting in response to aversive stimulation. *Journal of the Experimental Analysis of Behavior, 5*, 511–520.

Ventis, W. L. (1973). Case history: The use of laughter as an alternative response in systematic desensitization. *Behavior Therapy, 4*, 120–122.

Voegtlin, W. L., Lemere, F., Broz, W. R., & O'Hollaren, P. (1941). Conditioned reflex therapy of chronic alcoholism. *Quarterly Journal of Studies on Alcohol, 2*, 505–511.

Vygotsky, L. S. (1962). *Thought and language*. Cambridge, MA: MIT Press. (Original work published 1934.)

Vygotsky, L. S. (1978). *Mind in society: The development of higher psychological processes* (M. Cole, V. John-Steiner, S. Scribner, & E. Souberman, Eds.). Cambridge, MA: Harvard University Press.

Walker, J. M. T. (2008). Looking at teacher practices through the lens of parenting style. *The Journal of Experimental Education, 76*, 218–240.

Walther, E., Weil, R., & Dusing, J. (2011). The role of evaluative conditioning in attitude formation. *Current Directions in Psychological Science, 20*, 192–196.

Warren, J. M. (1965). Primate learning in comparative perspective. In A. M. Schrier, H. F. Harlow, & F. Stollnitz (Eds.), *Behavior of nonhuman primates* (Vol. 1). New York: Academic Press.

Wasserman, E. A., & Molina, E. J. (1975). Explicitly unpaired key light and food presentations: Interference with subsequent autoshaped key pecking in pigeons. *Journal of Experimental Psychology: Animal Behavior Processes, 1*, 30–38.

Watson, J. B. (1913). Psychology as the behaviorist views it. *Psychological Review, 20*, 158–177.

Watson, J. B. (1917). The effect of delayed feeding upon learning. *Psychobiology, 1*, 51–60.

Watson, J. B. (1930). *Behaviorism*. New York: Norton.

Watson, J. B., & Raynor, R. (1920). Conditioned emotional reactions. *Journal of Experimental Psychology, 3*, 1–14.

Waxler, C. Z., & Yarrow, M. R. (1975). An observational study of maternal models. *Developmental Psychology, 11*, 485–494.

Weiss, R. F. (1960). Deprivation and reward magnitude effects on speed throughout the goal gradients. *Journal of Experimental Psychology, 60*, 384–390.

Wertheimer, M. (1945). *Productive thinking*. New York: Harper.

West, R. F., & Stanovich, K. E. (2003). Is probability matching smart? Associations between probabilistic choices and cognitive ability. *Memory & Cognition, 31*, 243–251.

Whaley, D. L., & Malott, R. W. (1971). *Elementary principles of behavior*. New York: Appleton-Century-Crofts.

Wiens, A. N., & Menustik, C. E. (1983). Treatment outcome and patient characteristics in an aversion therapy program for alcoholism. *American Psychologist, 38*, 1089–1096.

Wilcoxin, H. D., Dragoin, W. B., & Kral, P. A. (1971). Illness-induced aversions in rat and quail: Relative salience of visual and gustatory cues. *Science, 171*, 826–828.

Williams, C. D. (1959). The elimination of tantrum behavior by extinction procedures. *Journal of Abnormal and Social Psychology, 59*, 269.

Wills, T. A., Ainette, M. G., Mendoza, D., Gibbons, F. X., & Brody, G. H. (2007). Self-control, symptomatology, and substance use precursors: Test of a theoretical model in a community sample of 9-year-old children. *Psychology of Addictive Behaviors, 21*, 205–215.

Wills, T. A., Ainette, M. G., Stoolmiller, M., Gibbons, F. X., & Shinar, O. (2008). Good self-control as a buffering agent for adolescent substance use: An investigation in early adolescence with time-varying covariates. *Psychology of Addictive Behaviors, 22*, 459–471.

Wills, T. A., Gibbons, F. X., Gerrard, M., Murry, V. M., & Brody, G. H. (2003). Family communication and religiosity related to substance use and sexual behavior in early adolescence: A test for pathways through self-control and prototype perceptions. *Psychology of Addictive Behaviors, 17,* 312–323.

Wills, T. A., & Stoolmiller, M. (2002). The role of self-control in early escalation of substance use: A time-varying analysis. *Journal of Consulting and Clinical Psychology, 70,* 986–997.

Wills, T. A., Walker, C., Mendoza, D., & Ainette, M. G. (2006). Behavioral and emotional self-control: Relations to substance use. *Psychology of Addictive Behaviors, 20,* 265–278.

Wilson, G. T., & Tracey, D. A. (1976). An experimental analysis of aversive imagery versus electrical aversive conditioning in the treatment of chronic alcoholics. *Behaviour Research and Therapy, 14,* 41–51.

Wolf, M. M., Risley, T., & Mees, H. (1964). Application of operant conditioning procedures to the behavior problems of an autistic child. *Behavior Research and Therapy, 1,* 305–312.

Wolfe, J. B. (1934). The effect of delayed reward upon learning in the white rat. *Journal of Comparative and Physiological Psychology, 17,* 1–21.

Wolpe, J. (1958). *Psychotherapy by reciprocal inhibition.* Stanford, CA: Stanford University Press.

Wolpe, J., & Lazarus, A. A. (1966). *Behavior therapy techniques: A guide to the treatment of neurosis.* New York: Pergamon.

World changing ideas: Ten thoughts, trends and technologies that have the power to transform our lives. (2010). *Scientific American, 303*(6), 42–53.

Wundt, W. M. (1873). *Principles of physiological psychology.* Leipzig: Engelmann.

Wundt, W. M. (1896). *Lectures on human and animal psychology.* New York: Macmillan.

Yeo, A. G. (1974). The acquisition of conditioned suppression as a function of interstimulus interval duration. *Quarterly Journal of Experimental Psychology, 26,* 405–416.

Zener, K. (1937). The significance of behavior accompanying conditioned salivary secretion for theories of the conditioned response. *American Journal of Psychology, 50,* 384–403.

Zentall, T. T. (2004). Action imitation in birds. *Learning and Behavior, 32,* 15–23.

# CREDITS

## PHOTO CREDITS

**Chapter 1:** p. 2 (top), Funny Times www.cartoonstock.com, Patrick Hardin, February 3, 1999; p. 2 (bottom), JOBARD/SIPA/Newscom; p. 3, Markley Boyer/Mannahatta Project/Wildlife Conservation Society; p.3, Yann Arthus-Bertrand/Corbis.

**Chapter 3:** p. 33, McGraw-Hill.

**Chapter 5:** p. 71, Benjamin Harris; p. 77, Bill Aron/ PhotoEdit.

**Chapter 6:** p. 84, Omikron/Photo Researchers, Inc.

**Chapter 10:** p. 161, Science Source/Photo Researchers, Inc.

**Chapter 11:** p. 173, Ancient Art & Architecture Collection Ltd/Alamy (Left); Robert Harding Picture Library Ltd/ Alamy (Right); p. 176, SuperStock/SuperStock (a, b & c); p. 181, Arkady/Shutterstock (Top); picture History/ Newscom (Bottom left); Everett Collection Inc/Alamy (Bottom right); p. 182, GL Archive/Alamy; p. 183, Adrian Sherratt/Alamy (Top left); Alfonso Vicente/Alamy (Top right); MARKA/Alamy (Mid right); Juice Images/Alamy (Mid left); Mary Evans Picture Library/Alamy (Bottom left); Jose Luis Pelaez, Inc./CORBIS/Glow Images (Bottom right); p. 184, akg-images/Newscom (Top left); David J. Green - technology/Alamy (Top right); p. 186, crixtina/Shutterstock; p. 187, Mary Evans Picture Library/ Alamy (Top left); Hand-out/THE SOURCE/Newscom (Top right).

**Chapter 12:** p. 192, Albert Bandura.

**Chapter 13:** p. 202, © Elenarts/Shutterstock; pp. 203– 204, Left Coast Press, Inc.; p. 207, Left Coast Press, p. 209, JOBARD/SIPA/Newscom (Top); Left Coast Press, Inc. (Bottom); p. 210, Left Coast Press, Inc.; p. 216, Left Coast Press, Inc.

**Chapter 14:** p. 222, Bill Aron/PhotoEdit, Inc.

## TEXT CREDITS

**Chapter 3:** p. 35, Adapted from CONDITIONING AND LEARNING by E.R. Hilgard and D.G. Marquis. Copyright © 1940 by Appleton-Century-Crofts. Reprinted and Electronically reproduced by permission of Pearson Education, Inc., Upper Saddle River, New Jersey.

**Chapter 8:** p. 131, LEITENBERG, II., HANDBOOK OF BEHAVIOR MODIFICATION AND BEHAVIOR THERAPY, 1st Ed., © 1976. Reprinted and Electronically reproduced by permission of Pearson Education, Inc., Upper Saddle River, New Jersey.

**Chapter 11:** p. 184, Figure from "The Law of Accelerating Returns" published by KurzweilAI.net, March 7, 2001. Courtesy of Kurzweil Technology Inc.

**Chapter 12:** pp. 189–190, Excerpted from the book CHILDREN LEARN WHAT THEY LIVE. Copyright © 1998 by Dorothy Law Nolte and Rachel Harris. The poem "Children Learn What They Live" Copyright © 1972 by Dorothy Law Nolte. Used by permission of Workman Publishing Co., Inc., New York. All rights reserved.

**Chapter 13:** pp. 205–206, Nukak: Ethnoarchaeology of an Amazonian People by Gustavo G. Politis. Reprinted with permissions from Left Coast Press, Inc. © 2007 Gustave Politis. All rights reserved.

# INDEX

CPSIA information can be obtained at www.ICGtesting.com
Printed in the USA
LVOW09*0842130916

504386LV00010B/60/P